Boiotia in Ancient Times

Boiotia in Ancient Times

Some Studies of Its Topography, History, Cults and Myths

By

John M. Fossey
D ès L, FRSC, FSA, RPA
McGill University &
Montréal Museum of Fine Arts

With a Contribution by

S.M.L. Stringer M.A.
Concordia University, Montréal

BRILL

LEIDEN | BOSTON

Cover illustrations: (front) Kakósi/Thisbe, plateau site, South West Tower, photo John M. Fossey; (back) Boiotian shields in use, detail from an Attic Black-figure Siana Cup by the "C" Painter, 575–550 BCE. Montreal Museum of Fine Arts inv. 1959.Cb.2. Photo Christine Guest.

Library of Congress Cataloging-in-Publication Data

Names: Fossey, John M., author.
Title: Boiotia in ancient times : some studies of its topography, history, cults and and myths / by John M. Fossey.
Description: Leiden ; Boston : Brill, [2019] | Includes bibliographical references and index. | Summary: "This is the concluding volume presenting results of the author's fieldwork spread over more than fifty years concerning the Archaeology and Topography of Ancient Boiotia that includes also discussions of the distribution within the topography of certain ancient cults, especially those of Artemis, Herakles and the Horseman Hero. Within the more purely topographic section there is much discussion of regional defense systems, all set against the history of the Boiotian League, especially its early coinage, its origins and its confrontation with Sparta and the pivotal battle of Leuktra"—Provided by publisher.
Identifiers: LCCN 2019024714 (print) | LCCN 2019024715 (ebook) | ISBN 9789004382831 (hardback) | ISBN 9789004382855 (ebook)
Subjects: LCSH: Voiōtia (Greece)—Civilization. | Voiōtia (Greece)—History. | Voiōtia (Greece)—Antiquites. | Excavations (Archaeology)—Greece—Voiōtia. | Geography—Greece—Voiōtia. | Coins, Greek—Greece—Voiōtia.
Classification: LCC DF261.B5 F668 2019 (print) | LCC DF261.B5 (ebook) | DDC 938/.4—dc23
LC record available at https://lccn.loc.gov/2019024714
LC ebook record available at https://lccn.loc.gov/2019024715

Typeface for the Latin, Greek, and Cyrillic scripts: "Brill". See and download: brill.com/brill-typeface.

ISBN 978-90-04-38283-1 (hardback)
ISBN 978-90-04-38285-5 (e-book)

Copyright 2019 by Koninklijke Brill NV, Leiden, The Netherlands.
Koninklijke Brill NV incorporates the imprints Brill, Brill Hes & De Graaf, Brill Nijhoff, Brill Rodopi, Brill Sense, Hotei Publishing, mentis Verlag, Verlag Ferdinand Schöningh and Wilhelm Fink Verlag.
All rights reserved. No part of this publication may be reproduced, translated, stored in a retrieval system, or transmitted in any form or by any means, electronic, mechanical, photocopying, recording or otherwise, without prior written permission from the publisher.
Authorization to photocopy items for internal or personal use is granted by Koninklijke Brill NV provided that the appropriate fees are paid directly to The Copyright Clearance Center, 222 Rosewood Drive, Suite 910, Danvers, MA 01923, USA. Fees are subject to change.

This book is printed on acid-free paper and produced in a sustainable manner.

*For my beloved daughter
Pavlina,
without whose constant encouragement
this book might never have seen the light of day.*

Contents

List of Figures   IX
List of Plates   XI
Abbreviations   XIV
Preface   XV
Note on Format   XIX

1   The Homeric Description of Boiotia: Mykenaian or Archaic or Both?   1

2   A Folk Story and the End of Amphiaraos   13

3   "Les Deux Béoties" in Archaic Times   24

4   The Origins of the Boiotian League   33

5   Early Boiotian Temples   61

6   Παιδοποιία in Archaic Thebai   77

7   Boiotian Connections with the Pontic and Propontic Area in Archaic to Hellenistic Times   88

8   The Spartan Occupation of Southern Boiotia   95

9   The Daughters of Skedasos and the Battle of Leuktra   136

10   The Sequel to the Spartan Occupation of Southern Boiotia   156

11   Further Thoughts on Late Classical and Hellenistic Defence Networks in Boiotia   172

12   A Valley in the Hills East of *Thívai*   208

13   An Unusual Hero Cult in East Central Greece   245

14   Another Boiotian Folktale   297

15   The Leuktra Epigram (*IG*vii 2462)   304
     S.M.L. Stringer

Bibliography   313

Indices
1A   Epigraphic Sources Quoted or Cited   327
1B   Ancient Literary Sources Quoted or Cited   330
2   Ancient and Modern Placenames   334
3   Ancient Personal Names, Human and Divine   340
4   Selected General Subjects   342

Figures

1. Table of identifications of Homeric and Heroic places in Boiotia   5
2. Places associated with the end of Amphiaraos   21
3. Map of "les deux Béoties"   25
4. Boiotia: imported Korinthian pottery 7th c. BCE   27
5. Distribution of archaic Boiotian *fibulae*   29
6. Boiotia: cities minting early coinage according to Head and followers   38
7. Boiotia: cities minting early coinage after reevaluation by Etienne & Knoepfler   38
8. Variations on letter *Heta*, taken from Etienne & Knoepfler, 1972: 384–385   44
9. Boiotia: cities minting early coinage; a new suggestion   45
10. Distribution of Herakles cults in Boiotia   47
11. *Oúngra*: temple plan   62
12. *Khóstia*: temple plan   66
13. *Mavrovoúni*: temple plan reconstructed   70
14. Temple of Artemis at Aulis   72
15. Temple of Apollon at the Ptoion Sanctuary   73
16. Temple of Hera (?) at Plataiai   74
17. Boiotian participation in colonisation   92
18. South West Boiotia   98
19. *Mavrovoúni*: general site plan   99
20. *Mavrovoúni*: distribution of polygonal masonry   102
21. *Mavrovoúni*: distribution of masonry types   103
22. *Mavrovoúni*: masonry types in building BA   112
23. *Mavrovoúni*: masonry types in building V   113
24. *Áyios Ioánnes Ikonostásion* plan   120
25. *Perakhóra* lighthouse fortification   125
26. Plan of the Áyios Nikólaos fortification at *Perakhóra*   126
27. The Spartan signalling network   129
28. The distribution of Artemis cults in Boiotia   132
29. The region of *Táteza – Xeronomí*   137
30. The defenses of South West and South Boiotia   157
31. The ruined chapel of Áyios Mámas and other structures as recorded in 1967   168
32. The *Skroponéri* area, A: the fortified sites   173
33. The *Skroponéri* area, B: the network   173
34. *Megálo Vounó, Kókkino*   183
35. *Kástron, Skroponéri*   186
36. The fort on *Sambáli*   189

37	The fort at *Kokkinóvrakhos* South	191
38	Map: the *Anaphorítes* system	200
39	Map: the area East of *Thívai*	209
40	Sketch of a lead figurine	237
41	Sketch of part of a bone or ivory seal	242
42	Distribution of horseman-hero relief carvings in Boiotia	250

Plates

1   *Voúliagma, Mourikíou*, general from South   13
2   *Voúliagma, Mourikíou*, detail of sinkhole from South West   14
3   *Oúngra*, temple: outer face of West wall   63
4   *Oúngra*, temple: inner face of North wall   63
5   *Khóstia*, general view of temple area from Akropolis wall looking North   66
6   *Mavrovoúni*, archaic antefix from temple   70
7   *Mavrovoúni*, South colonnade of temple from West   71
8   *Mavrovoúni*, threshold in temple doorway   71
9   Aulis, temple from South   72
10 Ptoion, temple of Apollon from Ptoion Fort above, looking West   73
11 *Mavrovoúni*, tower before the 1981 earthquake, from West   100
12 *Mavrovoúni*, West wall of the compound, outer face   103
13 *Mavrovoúni*, interior of building BA, detail of masonry   104
14 *Mavrovoúni*, gate in West wall of compound   105
15 *Mavrovoúni*, bottle-shaped cistern in Northern part of compound   106
16 *Mavrovoúni*, quarry   107
17 *Mavrovoúni*, polygonal masonry to immediate North East of temple   108
18 *Áyios Ioánnes*, North wall of tower   118
19 *Áyios Ioánnes* (*ikonostásion*), walling in Northern part of main complex   119
20 *Áyios Ioánnes* (*ikonostásion*), masonry in South wall of main complex, inside face   119
21 *Kalá Nisiá*, Southern tip of *Dhaskaleió* from the area of *Zoödhókhos Piyí*   122
22 *Kalá Nisiá*, Southern tip of *Dhaskaleió*, South wall running North-North-West   122
23 *Kalá Nisiá*, central plateau of *Dhaskaleió*, wall along North side   123
24 *Perakhóra*, the lighthouse fortification, general from East   124
25 *Perakhóra*, the Áyios Nikólaos fortification from the West   124
26 *Perakhóra*, the Áyios Nikólaos fortification, North wall from outside   126
27 *Perakhóra*, the Áyios Nikólaos fortification, South West wall from outside   127
28 *Perakhóra*, the Áyios Nikólaos fortification, cistern   127
29 *Tátiza*, triglyph block from circular building   141
30 *Tátiza*, another triglyph block from circular building   142
31 *Parapoúnyia*, the reconstructed trophy   143
32 *Khóstia*, trapezoidal masonry in Eastern part of North wall   158
33 *Khóstia*, ashlar masonry in central part of North wall   158
34 *Kakósi*, corner tower   159
35 *Alikí*, North wall, outer face, from below   159
36 *Livadhóstro*, East wall, outer face, from South East   160

37	*Áyios Mámas*, South side of tower from outside	162
38	*Pyrgáki/Episkopí*, general view of tower from East, below	162
39	*Pyrgáki/Episkopí*, detail of trapezoidal masonry in interior of tower	163
40	*Evangelístria*, South West corner of tower	163
41	*Vígla*, South rubble wall	164
42	*Palaiothívai*, rubble wall of Phase 2	164
43	*Kókkla* (Plataiai), North cross wall	167
44	*Áyios Mámas*, remains of original chapel, as seen in 1965	169
45	*Áyios Mámas*, Doric capital	170
46	*Áyios Mámas*, displaced blocks	171
47	*Áyios Mámas*, coping stone	171
48	*Pýrgos Paralímnis*, outer circuit, outer face on South West side	175
49	*Khelonókastro*, South East wall of inner circuit, outer face	175
50	*Khelonókastro*, North West wall of outer circuit, outer face	176
51	*Oúngra* South, North West wall, lower site in background with *Khelonókastro* (arrow) above	177
52	*Mouríki*, North West wall, detail of outer face (polygonal masonry)	178
53	*Mouríki*, rough masonry in another part of North West wall	178
54	*Pelayía*, East wall of circuit	180
55	Ptoion Fort and Ptoion below, from West-South-West	181
56	Ptoion Fort, mixed masonry in circuit wall	182
57	Ptoion Fort, more mixed masonry in circuit wall	182
58	*Megálo Vounó (Kókkino)*, line of circuit wall on West side	184
59	*Megálo Vounó (Kókkino)*, circuit wall, detail of masonry	184
60	*Megálo Vounó (Kókkino)*, entrance through circuit	185
61	*Megálo Vounó (Kókkino)*, tower in polygonal masonry	185
62	*Skroponéri* bay with *kástro* in foreground, seen from *Máli Dárdha*	186
63	*Skroponéri Kástron*, outer face of West wall by West corner	187
64	*Skroponéri Kástron*, detail of masonry	187
65	*Skroponéri Kástron*, entrance to circuit	188
66	*Skroponéri*, building remains on South slopes of *Kástron* hill	189
67	*Sambáli*, general from East	190
68	*Sambáli*, long South wall of circuit, detail of masonry in inner face	190
69	*Kokkinóvrakhos* South, line of circuit wall from inside	191
70	*Kokkinóvrakhos* South, detail of masonry in circuit wall	192
71	*Tsoukouriéli*, tower from West	193
72	*Tsoukouriéli*, tower from East	193
73	*Toúrlo* (arrow) at East end of Ptoion range, seen from plain of Anthedon	194
74	*Toúrlo*, walling on shoulder below flat peak	195
75	*Rákhis*, remains of circular building on Northern Peak	195

PLATES

76 *Rákhis*, North Peak, associated surface sherds   196
77 *Rákhis*, South Peak, remains of walling   196
78 *Pondíkia*, wall running South   197
79 *Brátzi*, South wall from outside   201
80 *Brátzi*, gate in South wall   201
81 *Sorós, Moustaphádhes*, general view of mountain from North West   202
82 *Thívai*, valley to East of the city, seen from South   209
83 *Parapoúnyia*, church of Saints Pétros & Pávlos; horseman-hero relief, *IG* vii 2153, *IThesp* 1193A–B   251
84 *Parapoúnyia*, church of Saints Pétros & Pávlos; horseman-hero relief, *IThesp* 1207   252

Abbreviations

AA	*Archäologischer Anzeiger*
AAA	Ἀρχαιολογικὰ Ἀνάλεκτα ἐξ Ἀθηνῶν /*Athens Annals of Archaeology*
ADelt	Ἀρχαιολογικὸν Δελτίον
AEph	Ἀρχαιολογικὴ Ἐφημερίς
AJA	*American Journal of Archaeology*
AM	*Mitteilungen des deutschen archäologischen Instituts, Athenische Abteilungen*
BAR	*British Archaeological Reports*
BCH	*Bulletin de correspondence hellénique*
BSA	*Annual of the British School at Athens*
BAAE	Βιβλιοθήκη τῆς ἐν Ἀθήναις Ἀρχαιολογικῆς Ἑταιρείας
EB	*Epigraphica Boeotica*
IG	*Inscriptiones Graecae*
IGBR	*Inscriptiones in Bulgaria repertae*
IThesp	Roesch, Paul†, edited Gilbert Argoud, Albert Schachter & Guy Votero, *Les inscriptions de Thespies*, 12 fascicules + indices (2007, revised 2009); available only on line at http://www.hisoma.mom.fr/production-scientifique/les-inscriptions-de-thespies
LGPN	*A Lexicon of Greek Personal Names*, details of various volumes given in bibliography
LSJ	Liddell, Henry George & Scott, Robert, 1940: *A Greek-English Lexicon* revised and augmented throughout by Sir Henry Stuart Jones *et all.* (Oxford, with a revised supplement added in 1996)
MUMCAH	*McGill University Monographs in Classical Archaeology and History*
RPhil	*Revue de philologie*
SEG	*Supplementum Epigraphicum Graecum*
TLG	*Thesaurus Linguae Graecae* available to online subscribers at www.tlg.uci.edu

Preface

In the last few years a number of books have dealt with Boiotia in antiquity so, the reader may ask, why one more? Most of the other books have dealt with the history of Boiotia without a real look at the physical setting in which that history took place whereas my own work has always started from the landscape of that country, a natural process for the son of two geographers. The only exception to this rule – and it is a distinguished one – is the work of my friend and colleague John Bintliff and his team. I can only claim to have spent even longer in the land of Boiotia than John and his cohorts have done for, while my own work has run for more than 50 years, theirs has a decade less of activity. After so many years and given the physical difficulties I now encounter it seemed worth drawing a final line to my work with this volume pulling together so much remaining material generated during half a century of exploring the Boiotian countryside. The pleasures of roaming the plains and climbing the hills and mountains of that area are now things of my past so it has been a sort of pilgrimage to go through the memory of them once more during the writing of this book, my Boiotian swansong.

My first acquaintance with Boiotia came in brief visits to *Thívai* in the summers of 1963 and 1964 as the result of a suggestion by Richard Hope Simpson that I might think of studying Boiotia for my graduate research. He made this suggestion knowing that I was interested in doing regional survey and he was aware of the richness of the Boiotian landscape as a result of his own explorations in company with his friend and colleague John Lazenby in preparation for their study of the Homeric *Catalogue of Ships*.

My real Boiotian life began in February 1965 when, as a graduate student of Birmingham University, I took up residence in *Thívai* and stayed there for the best part of the next two years, two of the most enjoyable years of my life. I explored Boiotia from end to end, large sections of it on foot. Returning in the spring of 1967 I had the use of a Landrover that allowed me to cover more ground than my previous reliance on feet and legs; the following two springs also allowed me to take advantage of vehicular transport before I emigrated from Britain to Canada to take up a teaching position at McGill University that was to be my base of operations until my retirement in 2000, after which, while being an Emeritus Professor of that institution, I became Curator of Archaeology at the Montreal Museum of Fine Arts, subsequently to end my professional career as its Emeritus Curator of Mediterranean Archaeology. During most of my years at McGill I continued my field researches in Boiotia and the neighbouring areas of Eastern Phokis and Opountian Lokris, as well as the Perakhóra peninsula across the Gulf of Korinthos to the immediate South of Boiotia. Indeed even after my move to the museum I still was able in Autumn 2004 to spend a last short season of travel based on the village of *Kaskavéli* a few kilometres to the West of *Thíva* (as it was then known in the demotic form unlike the katharevousa version of *Thívai* I had earlier known). My stay in *Kaskavéli* was much helped by the loan of his house in his native village by my old friend Níkos Kóllias; I am much in his debt. Even if my peregrinations in its landscape were to cease after 2004 Boiotia always occupied my thoughts and caused me to revisit notes and ideas I had set down from 1965 onwards.

The results of the various stages of my work in Boiotia were first published in several articles leading to *Topography and Population of Ancient Boiotia* (1988) that grew out of my doctoral thesis defended in January 1976; a volume *Papers in Boiotian Topography and History* (1990) in supplement to that monograph reprinted some of those articles. A year later *Epigraphica Boeotica I: Studies in Boiotian Inscriptions* (1991) published those of my previous articles on the inscriptions of the area together with a number of new studies; this was followed rather many years later by *Epigraphica Boeotica II: Further Studies on Boiotian Inscriptions* that brought to an end my investigations of the texts on stone (and pottery) from Boiotia, an area of study to which I had been introduced by the two mentors of my doctoral thesis at Université de Lyon II, the late Professors Jean Pouilloux and Paul Roesch.

In writing this book as a kind of swansong to my Boiotian researches I thought it perhaps useful to summarise their background. In fact it is inevitable that I shall continue to think about Boiotia since, with members of my team, we are continuing with the publication of our excavations of 1980 and 1983 at *Khóstia* in the South West corner of Boiotia but the present book will probably be the last study of the territory in general. I have, therefore, tried to include all the material remaining from my fieldwork in that area. Particularly is this the case with consideration of military activities represented by fortifications and what I have felt to be defence networks in the same way that I had explored similar situations in Eastern Phokis and Opountian Lokris; this sprang from ideas concerning the Spartan activities in Boiotia in the early 4th century BCE formulated after my work with Richard Tomlinson at *Mavrovoúni*, as also did some considerations of cults and temples.

During the many years of my fieldwork I had the help of several people and in finishing this *apologia pro vita mea in Boeotia* I recall, in no particularly chronological order, those whose company and help I most frequently enjoyed: my late wife Eléni Zoïtopoúlou, my late father Hubert Fossey, Roger Green, Nick Baykov, Ginette Gauvin, Jacques Morin, Mike Attas. During the preparation of my previous and present accounts I always received much help from the draughtsmanship of Ginette Gauvin and for the illustrations – both plates and figure – of this volume, in addition to using the base maps prepared by Ginette I have had a great deal of help from my friend George Kellaris who manages to do remarkable things with photoshop; my son-in-law, Scott Bédard with his expertise in computer-assisted design has managed to make sense out of some of the site plans which had been drawn in the field long ago; Renée Bouchard helped with finalising the appearance of several site plans herein. I also received much help in gaining access to certain publications in Greek from two friends, Christina Avronidaki and Yanis Kaliontzis. To all these friends and helpers I can only express my deepest thanks.

Very real thanks go also to my friends and colleagues at the publishing house of Brill. First must come Mirjam Elbers, senior collections editor for Classical Studies, and her assistant Giulia Moriconi; an especial debt at Brill is to Gera van Bedaf with whom I have worked frequently for over more than a decade on the production of volumes of the two series of which I serve Brill as Editor-in-Chief, *Monumenta Graeca et Romana* and *McGill University Monographs in Classical Archaeology and History* as well as on my previous book *Epigraphica Boeotica II*. A by-product of my working with Brill has been the frequent visits to its head offices in Leiden (Netherlands), a city I always enjoy and where I have acquired many other friends over these last years in addition to those at Brill; two of them in particular are Hanneke Kik and her husband Maarten Duinden, the hospitality of whose house and table has been generously and affectionately offered so often. Frequently, over the last period, it has been my assistant at the Montreal Museum of Fine Arts, Alexis Lemonde-Vachon who has coordinated electronic transfers between Montreal and Leiden of text and illustrations as well as information and up-dates. Alexis has also helped very much in getting hold of necessary bibliographic reference material. I also owe a big debt of thanks to my fellow Boiotologist Prof. Stepahnie Larson (Bucknell University) for her many suggestions.

This book sets out to see certain developments in the history of Boiotia in a geographic context and it is only appropriate that I recall the influence in my earlier years of my parents, both of them geographers. The geographic dimension of this work will immediately become very clear from the number of maps it includes. I hope that in some ways I have been able to see historical events in terms of the symbiotic relationship that exists between human societies and their physical environment. Human societies adopt a landscape, they adapt to it and they adapt it to their needs. Most of all can this be seen in furtherance of their strategies, economic and military. It is particularly military strategy that concerns several parts of this book – the way in which the inhabitants of ancient Boiotia made use of their mountains to place protective networks that take advantage of naturally strong positions to set their fortifications and to exploit natural lines of sight for control and communications

I am well aware that there will be readers who will disagree with various of my conclusions or suggested interpretations but there will be few of them who can claim the same close acquaintance with the Boiotian landscape that

I have acquired over the last half century. Close behind me, as already mentioned, has come John Bintliff and his team who have been fortunate enough to be able to make use of techniques and a sizable team; obviously GPS was not available to me, especially in the 60's and 70's when so much of my fieldwork was carried out and I never had a real team of people with me – most of my field work was "a one-man show".

Of the 15 chapters in this book nos. 1, 6 and 7 are reworked versions of earlier articles and 11 is a partial extract from another, again extensively reworked; much earlier versions of 3 and 9 were delivered orally at conferences but not published up to now and 13 is the continuation and expansion of a chapter in my last previous book. All the other chapters are completely fresh accounts of observations and interpretations not previously aired. Chapter 15 is, of course, the work of its author my friend Stephanie Stringer, an examination of the Leuktra epigram which she undertook at my request; I am very grateful to her for her collaboration and hope that this will be but the first of many academic works published by her.

It was a real pleasure to examine the ramifications of the three "modern" folk stories included herein that I heard during my Boiotian peregrinations and which always struck me as potentially having useful things to tell us with reference to a past more distant than their own apparent context. There are probably many other such stories to be recorded but it is hoped that this threesome may whet the reader's appetite for more; may it then encourage colleagues to be alert to possible ancient meaning in folk stories that appear superficially to be of recent genesis. In fact recording of such stories should be taken quite seriously; the account of the daughters of Skedasos reminds us that the key to its understanding was the word *tata* in Arvanitic; since that language is fast dying out so too can really be lost stories of this sort.

I have already thanked the various friends and colleagues who participated in the fieldwork and in the preparation of this volume but all that would have been as of little worth were it not for the influence and encouragement from my immediate family. As already mentioned, my late wife, Eléni Zoïtopoúlou, accompanied me on many of the later stages of my fieldwork and, as a fellow archaeologist, could always follow my reasoning. After her death in 2007 it was our daughter, Pavlína, who took up the torch constantly encouraging me to get back to my own work and being happy when things did work out and pages did get written. She and her husband Scott also added to my joy in these last years by giving me my two youngest grandchildren.

JMF
Montréal, December 2018

Note on Format

As in all my more recent publications I unrepentantly stick to a strict transliteration of toponyms and anthroponyms in both Ancient and Modern Greek. This is a matter of respect for Hellenism and for the Greek language. Greece is no longer a province (or group of provinces) of the Roman Empire and has not been for something like a millennium and a half; yet many scholars still insist on inflicting on Greek places Roman/Latin names that are completely irrelevant except when referring to an actual Roman text in Latin concerning some Greek subject. I never cease to be astounded at this disregard for the Greek language on the part of English-speaking people who have spent their lives studying the archaeology, history and language of that country; speakers of other languages offend much less in this either by transliterating often in German or by making a really French name out of it. My astonishment becomes greater when one of these scholars criticises the system that I have espoused! I treated this subject more extensively in the introductory notes to *Epigraphica Boeotica II*.

When Arvanitic place names occur they are produced in the regular phonetic spelling of Albanian proper; since Arvanitic has never been a written dialect but has the same phonetics as the related language of Albania itself it is only fair to use this system.

Apart from the fact that my own data were gathered over the span of some 50 years, material derived from the publications of others is basically good up to 2016 with some later items. As usual in my more recent publications footnotes are basically eschewed and references are given "in-text" in the manner of the Social Sciences; fuller details of publications referred to in the abbreviated form "(author, date: page[s])" can be retrieved from the consolidated bibliographies.

CHAPTER 1

The Homeric Description of Boiotia: Mykenaian or Archaic or Both?

For Boiotia, as for much of Central and Southern Greece, the Κατάλογος Νεῶν is the earliest "political document". The Boiotian section (*Ilias* ii, 494–516) is subdivided into two unequal parts, the first of which concerns the territory of the Boiotoi proper, while the second, smaller section deals with the area of the Minyans.

The first two lines list the leaders of the Boiotoi:

Βοιωτῶν μὲν Πηνέλεως καὶ Λήϊτος ἦρχον
Ἀρχεσίλαός τε Προθοήνωρ τε Κλονίος τε

and then follows a list of the communities from which contingents came:

οἵ θ' Ὑρίην ἐνέμοντο καὶ Αὐλίδα πετρήεσσαν,
Σχοῖνόν τε Σκῶλόν τε πολύκνημόν τ' Ἐτεωνόν,
Θέσπειαν, Γραῖάν τε καὶ εὐρύχορον Μυκαλησσόν,
οἵ τ' ἀμφ' Ἅρμ' ἐνέμοντο καὶ Εἰλέσιον καὶ Ἐρυθράς,
οἵ τ' Ἐλεῶν' εἶχον ἠδ' Ὕλην καὶ Πετεῶνα,
Ὠκαλέην Μεδεῶνά τ', ἐϋκτίμενον πτολίεθρον,
Κώπας Εὔτρησίν τε πολυτρήρωνά τε Θίσβην,
οἵ τε Κορώνειαν καὶ ποιήενθ' Ἁλίαρτον,
οἵ τε Πλάταιαν ἔχον ἠδ' οἳ Γλισᾶντ' ἐνέμοντο,
οἵ θ' Ὑποθήβας εἶχον, ἐϋκτίμενον πτολίεθρον,
Ὀγχηστόν θ' ἱερόν, Ποσιδήϊον ἀγλαὸν ἄλσος,
οἵ τε πολυστάφυλον Ἄρνην ἔχον, οἵ τε Μίδειαν
Νῖσάν τε ζαθέην Ἀνθηδόνα τ' ἐσχατόωσαν·

The last two lines record the numbers of the Boiotoi and their ships:

τῶν μὲν πεντήκοντα νέες κίον, ἐν δὲ ἑκάστῃ
κοῦροι Βοιωτῶν ἑκατὸν καὶ εἴκοσι βαῖνον.

The Minyan communities,

οἳ δ' Ἀσπληδόνα ναῖον ἰδ' Ὀρχομενὸν Μινύειον

are listed *before* the entry concerning their leaders (and the account of *their* origin):

τῶν ἦρχ' Ἀσκάλαφος καὶ Ἰάλμενος, υἷες Ἄρηος,
οὓς τέκεν Ἀστυόχη δόμῳ Ἄκτορος Ἀζεΐδαο,
παρθένος αἰδοίη, ὑπερώϊον εἰσαναβᾶσα,
Ἄρηϊ κρατερῷ· ὁ δέ οἱ παρελέξατο λάθρῃ·

The final line gives the number of Minyan ships involved:

τοῖς δὲ τριήκοντα γλαφυραὶ νέες ἐστιχόωντο.

The position that this section occupies in the whole Κατάλογος of *Ilias* ii has been the subject of much comment. The fact that it occurs as the first entry is out of accord with the negligible performance elsewhere in the *Ilias* of the Boiotian contingent (Leaf, 1886: 66). The details concerning Boiotia that are provided are also striking: this section occupies *one sixteenth* of the whole Κατάλογος, while there are *twenty-nine areas in all* to receive separate mention. The inordinate amount of space is reflected in the large number of communities listed: while the territory of the Boiotoi contains 29 named communities (and that of the Minyans a further two) the highest number recorded for any other district is twelve places belonging to Agamemnon; next come the ten ruled by Menelaos; there are less than ten in each of the other regions (cf. Page, 1963: 125).

It is clear that the composer or compiler of the Κατάλογος not only gave pride of place to the Boiotians, but was also far more knowledgeable about their territory than about that of any other part of the Greek world that he described. These facts, allied with the further point that catalogues are, by nature, an essentially Boiotian form (cf. also Page, 1955: 35–39), have led to the conclusion that that this section of *Ilias* ii may be of Boiotian origin (Willcock, 1970: 66; Kirk, 1965: 89 & 166; Page, 1963: 152). Such an origin may also be reflected in the title "Βοιωτία" given to the Κατάλογος in some manuscripts (thought this may simply come from the first word of the whole document, "Βοιωτῶν"). If this conclusion is valid, as I think it may well be, it gives the Κατάλογος a particular importance for Boiotia and Boiotia incidentally acquires thereby a considerable significance in consideration of some problems concerning the Κατάλογος.

In another respect too the Κατάλογος shows a special knowledge of Boiotia. For most of the twenty nine regions we are given the number of ships sent; for Arkadia (*Ilias* ii 610–611) and for Elis (*Ilias* ii 619) we are simply told that "many men embarked" on the ships, but only in the cases of Boiotia and the kingdom of Philoktetes (*Ilias* ii 719–720) are the actual numbers of these men indicated. In both cases this is done by saying how many men were in each ship. Here too Boiotia has a clear predominance, for while each of her fifty ships contained 120 men, each of Philoktetes' seven vessels carried only 50! Perhaps, however, this point should not be stressed too much for Thoukydides (ii. 10, 6) suggests that the poet's reason for giving only these two numbers was to show τὰς μεγίστας καὶ ἐλαχίστας; if such was the case, however, Boiotia still occupies an outstanding position within the Κατάλογος as the chosen example of the "largest".

Another contrast between the Boiotian section and the rest of the Κατάλογος is of particular interest here. Twenty seven of the contingents listed are led by a single king or by two brother kings; for the territory of the Boiotoi and the area of Elis (*Ilias* ii 620–624), however, the Κατάλογος gives two groups of commanders: in the case of Elis four commanders, Amphimakhos, Tholpios, Amarynkeïdes and Polyxeinos are mentioned and we are told that "δέκα δ'ἀνδρὶ ἑκάστῳ νῆες ἕποντο θοαί". For the Boiotoi five leaders are named, Peneleos, Leitos, Arkhesilaos, Prothoenor and Klonios, and we are told that these led 50 ships; perhaps it is more than coincidence that an equal division of these ships would also give *ten* to each commander, as for Elis.

With regard to the usefulness of the Κατάλογος, as a record of Boiotia (which we would expect to be good if there is any value in the suggestion of a Boiotian origin) it is important to note that of the 31 communities listed (29 of the Boiotoi and two of the Minyans), 27 bear names that belonged to places existing in Classical and later times. Of the four names, Graia, Arne, Mideia and Nisa, which are attested only in this early document, more will be said below, as also of certain important names, such as Tanagra and Khaironeia, that are noticeably missing from the Κατάλογος. It is sufficient at this stage to remark that the two Boiotian sections of the Κατάλογος Νεῶν provide us with an extensive, if sometimes eclectic account of Boiotia at an early date.

The exact significance of the Κατάλογος depends, naturally, on the date to which we may assign it. The Homeric texts in general refer to objects that can be archaeologically assigned to a variety of dates between the 15th and the 7th centuries BCE; for the Κατάλογος, however, a different criterion may be evoked. We are here dealing with a list of communities that ostensibly contributed contingents to the Troian expedition; the relevant evidence of archaeology, in this case, will be the distribution of settlements at various periods. Unfortunately by far the largest part of our archaeological knowledge of Boiotia is dependent upon the results of surface fieldwork alone; very few sites have been excavated and of these only four with relevance to the early period have had scientific examination and publication: Thebai, Eutresis, *Khóstia* and *Glá*. Obviously the results of field survey cannot be complete and can often be purely negative.

Over a quarter of a century ago I presented (Fossey, 1988: section II) my arguments for the identification of sites occupied in Classical times as well as during the Bronze Age and there I also summarized my conclusions concerning those which attest Bronze Age occupation only. The resultant table (Fig. 1) shows that, of the 31 communities listed in the Boiotian section of the Κατάλογος, 28 have been identified with sites producing Mykenaian pottery. The three names missing from the list are Skhoinos, Peteon and Okalee; for these I suggested identifications – in some cases rather tentatively – with sites that have not, as yet, produced LH material (Fossey, 1988: 229–232; 233–234; 314–318 respectively). It must, however, be remembered that no sherds at all have been recovered from *Evangelístria* (= Oaklee?) and very few from *Mouríki* (= Skhoinos?), while the site of *Metókhion Platanáki* (= Peteon?) has already produced EH and MH pottery. The absence, so far, of LH material from the last site, at least, may well be purely accidental, and the gap could be spanned at the other two sites if adequate sherds are ever obtained there.

Whether one follows my identifications of Bronze Age sites in the Kopaïs (Fossey, 1973/4 = 1990: 53–71) or prefers those proposed by German colleagues as the result of intensive work in the plain (e.g. Kalcyk & Heinrich, 1989), the same conclusion is reached, namely that whatever sites actually represent Homeric Mideia and Arne (as well as Eleusis found in other traditional contexts) they were all abandoned, at the latest, in the ceramic period of LHIIIC, probably as a result of the breakdown of the "Minyan" drainage system. The same result comes also from my identification of Homeric Graia with *Dhrámesi* (Fossey, 1970 = 1990: 27–52) but I will insist less on this than on the Kopaïs phenomenon since that does not rest purely on one individual and disputable identification (summarized Fossey, 1990: 52). The conclusion is inescapable that the Boiotian section the Κατάλογος refers to places that no longer existed after the end of the Bronze Age; that is, the *terminus ante quem* for the demography it describes is LHIIIC. A generally Mykenaian date for the Κατάλογος has long been accepted by many, but not all scholars; perhaps the best summaries of the evidence, although now out of date on details, are still those of Burr (1944) and of Hope Simpson & Lazenby (1970).

Ancient Name (+ epithet)	*Ilias* ii line	Site
Ὑρίη	496	*Tselonéri*
Αὐλίς (πετρήεσσα)	496	*Mikró Vathý – Áyios Nikólaos*
Σκῶλος	497	*Neokhorákion-Moustaphádhes*
Θέσπεια	498	*Erimókastro*
Γραῖα	498	*Dhrámesi*
Μυκαλησσός (εὐρύχορος)	498	*Rhitsóna*
Ἅρμα	499	*Lykovoúni*
Εἰλέσιον	499	*Khlembotsári*
Ἐρυθραί	499	*Dharimári*
Ἐλεών	500	*Dhrítsa*
Ὕλη	500	*Oúngra*
Μεδεών (ἐϋκτίμενον πτολίεθρον)	501	*Dhávlosis*
Κῶπαι	502	*Topólia*
Εὔτρησις	502	*Arkopódhi*
Θίσβη (πολυτρήρων)	502	*Kakósi*
Κορώνεια	503	*Palaiá Koróneia*
Ἁλίαρτος (ποιήενθ')	503	*Kastrí Mazíou*
Πλάταια	504	*Kókkla*
Γλίσας	504	*Sýrtzi*
Ὑποθῆβαι (ἐϋκτίμενον πτολίεθρον)	505	*Thíva*
Ὀγχηστός (ἱερός)	505	*Kazárma*
Ἄρνη (πολυστάφυλος)	507	*Magoúla Baloménou*
Μίδεια	507	*Kalámi*
Νῖσα (or Ἴσος) (ζαθέη)	508	*Pýrgos, Palaiometókhi*
Ἀνθηδών (ἐσχατόωσα)	508	*Loukísia*
Ἀσπληδών	511	*Polýyira*
Ὀρχομενός	511	*Skripoú*

A. Places named in the Catalogue of Ships and identified with Mykenaian Sites in Boiotia

Eleusis	=	*Agorianí*
Khaironeia	=	*Kápraina*
Tanagra	=	*Graïmádha*

B. Other places mentioned in Heroic Contexts and identified with Mykenaian Sites in Boiotia

FIGURE 1   Table of identifications of Homeric and Heroic places in Boiotia

Unfortunately but one indication of the *terminus post quem* exists; this concerns the entry of Ὑποθῆβαι (*Ilias* ii 505). It has frequently been remarked that the mention of the lower town of Thebai alone can only refer to the time after the destruction of the Kadmeia by the Epigonoi, a generation before the Troian War (Hope Simpson & Lazenby, 1970: 34). If the usual dating of that war in the second half of the 13th century BCE is accepted, the Epigonoi might be placed early in that century, i.e. early in the period of LHIIIB pottery.

Unfortunately again excavations at Thebai have complicated the archaeological picture rather than clarified it. Keramópoullos' excavations showed that the destruction of the "palace" occurred in the period of LHIIIA pottery, while the more recent excavators have suggested that this destruction occurred in fact at the beginning of the period of LHIIIB pottery "around 1300 BC"; in addition they found a later "palace" on a completely different orientation that had also been destroyed but at the end of that same period (Platon & Touloupa, 1964: a & b). The situation of the two palaces has been discussed at length by Symeonoglou (1985: 40–50); he places the first destruction late in the period of LHIIIA pottery.

The second destruction of the Kadmeia towards the end of the period of LHIIIB:1 pottery (Symeonoglou, 1985: 48–50) must be earlier than the destruction of *Glá* (Desborough, 1964: 120–121) and the abandonment of Eutresis (Caskey, 1960: 168–170), to say nothing of the apparent abandonment of many other sites not yet excavated – a phenomenon signalling the collapse of Mykenaian civilization during the period of LHIIIC pottery. On the basis of the usual chronology this destruction at Thebai might well accord with the tradition of the Epigonoi destroying Thebai a generation before the Troian War, and thus suggests that the entry of Ὑποθῆβαι refers to some time after the beginning of the period of LHIIIB pottery.

The indications outlined above would thus suggest that the Boiotian section of the Κατάλογος refers to a population geography in existence during the periods characterised by LHIIIB:2 and early LHIIIC pottery. That it was no later can be clearly shown but the *terminus post quem* leaves much to be desired; perhaps fuller publication of the many excavations at *Thívai* will ultimately throw more light on this matter. In general the Mykenaian date of this document is clear and there is also one other overall consideration that apparently endorses a date in LHIIIB; it is the period of the widest distribution of habitation sites and thus represents the period in which it is easiest to accommodate the situation described in the Κατάλογος. Further fieldwork may, however, modify this picture.

At the same time it must be observed that the Κατάλογος is not a *complete* record of Boiotian geography at the time of LHIIIB pottery. It is, however, possible to add to it a number of other communities referred to in other Heroic traditions. Ploutarkhos (*Ethika* 515c) talks of his hometown of Khaironeia in a Heroic context. Tanagra is definitely referred to as being in existence at the time of the Troian War (Fossey, 1970: 6–8 = 1990: 29–32). Boiotian Eleusis is represented in the traditions of the Late Bronze Age sites in the Kopaïs (Fossey, 1973/4: 14–15 = 1990: 61–62). The sites identified with these names (respectively *Kápraina*, *Graïmádha*, and *Agorianí*) have all produced adequate Mykenaian material. The omission of these three names is itself eloquent warning against considering the Κατάλογος as anything but eclectic. The omission of Hysiai or any other name to be identified with *Kriekoúki* is perhaps the most surprising for the mentions of Plataiai, Erythrai, Skolos and Eteonos show that the Κατάλογος is *au fait* with the geography of the Parasopia. Also surprising is the absence of a name (whatever it may have been) for the site of *Kháleia*.

Where these absences are concerned I am reminded of a point that Hope Simpson made a long time ago (in his London doctoral thesis, I believe, and subsequently repeated to me in discussion). Individual lines could so very easily have dropped out of the list or been omitted at some point and would not have been missed. The Boiotian section quoted at the beginning of this chapter demonstrates only too well how each line is an independent, and thus separable unit. It is interesting thus to compare the catalogue of troops taking part in an entirely mythical adventure as composed in the 5th century CE by the poet Nonnos of Panopolis who envisaged an expedition to India led by Dionysos and drew a great deal of material in general from the Homeric texts. Just like *Ilias* ii, so *Dionysiaka* xiii has a catalogue of contingents drawn from various regions of Greece; both of them begin with Boiotia. In his composition Nonnos follows the Homeric example by dividing Boiotia into two sections of which the first contains many ancient toponyms (xiii, 53–82), the second (xiii, 83–121) being limited to five: the Minyan places of Aspledon and Orkhomenos, as in the *Ilias*, but with the surprising additions of Hyria, Aulis and Harma. The inclusion of these places is strange since they are rather a long way from their home in Eastern Boiotia; the three of them constitute, nevertheless, a group of close neighbours, which may explain their common "migration" within the text, especially at the hands of a writer not well acquainted with the geography of Boiotia, a subject of which Nonnos may well have been ignorant, coming as he did from Panopolis in the Egyptian Thebaïs. It is the longer first part that provides the names of a large number of Boiotian homelands for the contingents: Thebai, Onkhestos, Peteon, Okalee, Erythrai, Arne, Mideia, Eilesion, Skolos, Thisbe, Skhoinos, Heleon, Kopai, Medeon, Hyle, Oropos/Oropia (referred to indirectly), Thespiai, Plataiai, Haliartos, and Anthedon, Askre, Graia, Mykalessos, Nisa, Koroneia (again referred to indirectly). This total of 25 places is only slightly less than the 29 of the main part of the Homeric Κατάλογος. If the misplaced group of Harma, Hyria and Aulis are added in here, two things will result: part two of Nonnos' list will have exactly the same two places as seen in the Homeric list; the first part of Nonnos will contain just 28 places in this list enriched with the Eastern group of three. At the same time, although there seems to be a sort of parity between the numbers of places in the longer first parts of the two lists (29 places for the *Ilias* and 28 for Nonnos), there are differences for Nonnos does not include Eteonos, Eutresis and Glisas but does add – in a fashion – Oropos. For all this a certain similarity between the two lists is apparent although the places named are not in the same order and not even combined in the same geographic way as occurs in the Homeric list. Thus Nonnos' text does not really help to explain the specific absences of Mykenaian places in the Homeric text as we have it today but it does suggest that they might have been present in a putative, variant version (or versions) of the Κατάλογος that might still have been available to readers in the 5th century CE. That Nonnos' catalogue is essentially derived from the Homeric one will, in fact, surprise nobody but this analysis gives a welcome indication that variant versions may have existed alongside each other for a very long time despite attempts to produce one (or more) canonical version(s) such as was intended by the Peisistratid recension.

A certain logic is nevertheless observable in some of the Homeric omissions. The Κατάλογος is noticeably ignorant of the South coast of Boiotia: *Livadhóstro* (ancient Kreusis), *Alykí* (ancient Siphai) and *Khóstia* (ancient Khorsiai) are all absent – as is *Záltza* (ancient Boulis) in the no-man's land between the South West extremity of Boiotia and the South East corner of neighbouring Phokis. This is in contrast with the apparently concentrated occupation along this coast in Mykenaian times, a phenomenon remarked long ago by Heurtley (1923–1925).

A similar gap seems to be noticeable for the North Kopaïs sites for, from this area, only *Topólia* (= ancient Kopai) is mentioned. At least four of the other sites in that zone are of a probably military nature and this might explain their absence from a list of communities but at least four other North Kopaïs Mykenaian *settlements* are absent from the Κατάλογος: *Pýrgos, Strovíki, Áyios Ioánnes* and *Ayía Marína*. At all four of these places the presence of tombs attests to their nature as settlements. [On the North East Kopaïs sites and their nature – settlement or military – cf. Fossey, 1980a = 1990: 72–89].

If then this account of Boiotia, as a picture of population centres, can reasonably be dated to the last two phases of Late Helladic pottery styles, what of the image it gives of the politico-military organization of the area? The most noticeable feature is the limited territory accorded to the Minyans of

Orkhomenos, although the traditions about the Kopaïs drainage – to say nothing of its archaeological remains – imply that in the later Bronze Age the whole basin would have been subject to Orkhomenos, her territory in the Κατάλογος is restricted to the North West bay of the Kopaïs. We may fairly presume that the second town in the Minyan section of the list, Aspledon, is envisaged as subordinate to Orkhomenos, since the two leaders of the Minyan contingent were joint brother kings of the latter city (Pausanias ix. 37, 7). According to the Κατάλογος the rest of Boiotia was in the hands of the Boiotoi.

It is interesting that the commanders of the Boiotoi (and of Elis) differ from those of all the other contingents in the Κατάλογος, in that they are five commanders (or four for Elis) and not a single king or two brother kings. I have suggested, on the analogy of the Eleians, that the five Boiotian leaders might each have commanded ten vessels, i.e. 1200 men. We have yet more information about this board of commanders for, according to tradition, Peneleos came from Thebai (Pausanias ix. 5, 15), Leïtos from Plataiai (Pausanias ix. 4, 3) and Arkhesilaos from Lebadeia (Pausanias ix. 39, 3), the latter here possibly meaning Mideia. The very distance separating the place associated with Arkhesilaos on the one hand and the places connected with Leïtos and Peneleos on the other strongly suggests that these commanders were sent on a regional basis and that perhaps the territory belonging to the Boiotoi was split up into a number of (possibly equal) districts. Unfortunately we have so little information about the other two commanders, Prothoenor and Klonios, that we cannot "locate" them, but it is tempting to suggest that one might have come from somewhere in the South East Kopaïs (perhaps from the important community of Haliartos) for otherwise there would be an enormous gap between Arkhesilaos and his brother officers in the East. For the fifth commander it is difficult to suggest – however hypothetically – an origin; the area of Thespiai has probably an equal claim with the area that later belonged to Tanagra.

I have suggested that the territory of the Boiotoi was split into at least five areas each contributing to the whole contingent an equal number of troops with a commander; this would present an interesting comparison with the constitution of the Boiotian League in later times. Yet another indication concerning this "board of commanders" is to hand. On one occasion (*Ilias* xiv, 489) the Theban Peneleos is accorded the title of ἄναξ, a title not conferred on the other Boiotian leaders at all, although Leïtos of Plataiai is similarly once referred to as ἥρως (*Ilias* vi, 35). What is more, Peneleos recurs seven times in the *Ilias* (xiii, 92; xiv, 487, 489 & 496; xvi, 335 & 340; xvii, 597), always a leading figure and all but once showing exemplary performance; in one instance (*Ilias* xiii, 92) he appears with Leïtos who has the next highest rate of appearances in the *Ilias* (four times: vi, 35: xiii, 91; xvii, 601 & 605). Leïtos, moreover, presents an interesting example of concurrence between the *Ilias* and local Boiotian tradition, for he is nowhere recorded in the *Ilias* as being killed, despite severe wounds, while Arkhesilaos of Lebadeia recurs but once (*Ilias* xv, 329) simply in order to be slain; the Boiotian traditions recorded that Leïtos brought back the remains of Arkhesilaos after the end of the Troian War. The two remaining Boiotian commanders, Prothoenor (*Ilias* xiv, 450) and Klonios (*Ilias* xv, 340) shared the ignominious fate of Arkhesilaos but nothing more is known of them. It is perhaps no more than coincidence that Theban Peneleos, who alone is ἄναξ, is mentioned the most number of times and the most creditably, but these facts, together with his position at the very beginning of the list of Boiotian commanders *might* suggest that he was the superior of the five (perhaps even similar arguments could give Plataian Leïtos something of a higher position?). It is perhaps worth adding that only Peneleos "son of Hippalkimos" and Leïtos "son of Alektor" are included by Apollodoros (iii. 10, 8) in the list of Helena's suitors, although all five leaders are recorded with their fathers' names in Diodoros (iv. 67) where they have essentially Thessalian connections.

This sort of political and military organization bears many similarities to that of the historical Boiotian confederations: a cooperative venture by regions of Boiotia each contributing equal forces and officers, often under some sort of Theban leadership. Does this then mean that the Boiotia of late Mykenaian times already knew such an organization? That is theoretically not beyond the bounds of possibility and it could even possibly have provided the model on which was based the structure of the Boiotian League of Archaic times when it emerged as one of the very earliest federal states. It is, therefore, possible to let the Boiotian section of the Κατάλογος stand as a thoroughly, if eclectically Mykenaian description or document. I would, however, like to suggest another possibility.

In a detailed examination of the Argive King List I have shown (Fossey, 1980b) how the essentially Mykenaian list of places in ArgoloKorinthia, as seen in that part of the Κατάλογος, has been adjusted to reflect the 6th century BCE political realities in the pattern of Argos' power increasing at the expense of the traditional pre-eminence of Mykenai. In the case of Argos it was possible to show how aspects of the traditional King List, another type of Κατάλογος probably reaching back also into Mykenaian times, had been subject to minor adjustments, in the form of fictitious marriage alliances, to make it correspond to the 6th century's political situation. The way in which *both* similar documents could be shown to have received similar treatment at a similar time led to further confidence in the reconstruction. The tradition of Athenian tampering with the Κατάλογος over the possession of Salamis (Kirk, 1965: 213–214) could be a more obvious example of the same phenomenon at the same sort of period.

When we turn to the Boiotian material we cannot perhaps help remembering that the 6th century is precisely the period of the genesis of the Boiotian League of Classical times. Exactly when in the 6th century we place this event depends upon a number of questions considered elsewhere in this book (chapters 3 & 4): when we date the battle of Keressos and the end of the Thessalian hegemony, and when we date the earliest coinage, including particularly that of Boiotia. We shall return to the question of precisely when in the 6th century we place these events. For now we can simply say that, whenever exactly these events did occur it is clear that it was before the last one or two decades of the 6th century at which time a Boiotian League existed and controlled (or *tried* to control, as Plataiai showed) all of the territory except for Orkhomenos – just like the situation described in the Boiotian section of the Κατάλογος. The similarity with the situation in the Argive section of the Κατάλογος leads me to suggest, then, that in the Boiotian section too a venerable list of Mykenaian communities associated with the Troian legends *vel sim.* has been adjusted to reflect the politico-military conditions of the 6th century – at least the later 6th century – after the repulsion of the Thessalians and the advancing organization of the Boiotian League.

The model of a Mykenaian list adjusted to the 6th century politics thus fits the two largest sections of the Κατάλογος Νεῶν, Boiotia and ArgoloKorinthia. Perhaps further examination may show that it fits other parts too but the problem is that, by their very nature, those other parts are much less detailed and thus much less informative. They are also less easy to subject to this sort of analysis.

Appendix

While I have tried to make this fresh examination of the question based upon the results of my own archaeological survey of Boiotia and thus have not wished to make extensive use of the work of previous students of the question to whom my sort of data was not always yet available, it is obvious that I cannot pass over in silence one particularly important attempt to give the Κατάλογος a post-Mykenaian date, the study by A. Giovannini (1969). At the same time I cannot, in the present context, do justice to this thought-provoking work; that would require a full-length review article of the book. I trust, therefore, that the author and other readers will forgive my brevity.

The principal point of Giovannini's work is to claim a concordance between the sequence of areas in the Κατάλογος and the geographic order of the Delphic lists of *theorodokoi*. This part of his thesis might even go in the same direction as my own thinking. With the rise to prominence of Delphoi in Archaic times, especially in the context of the increasing geographic awareness of the period of colonization, an influence of Delphic contacts upon the ordering of a disparate and – like all documents of oral tradition – not completely fixed Κατάλογος would not be surprising especially since it would fall, roughly speaking, into the time span of the "adjustments" we have looked at in the preceding pages and elsewhere (*à propos* of Argos). The problem is that this similarity between the Κατάλογος and *theorodokoi* lists has been shown to be a khimaira (Nachtergael, 1975). Even if the parallel did exist, to proceed from that to a complete dismantling of any original Mykenaian nature to the document is unnecessary and, to my mind, unjustifiable. Indeed, reading Giovannini's text, I have the impression that he starts off deliberately to disprove a Mykenaian origin rather than to look with a completely open mind at the incontrovertible dating implied by much of the evidence. In any case, without a detailed *personal* examination of the archaeological material he was bound simply to chew over the same cud that had already been pre-digested by many others. I would like to think that my preceding discussion, based as it is on a fresh and more detailed examination of the archaeological evidence than any conducted hitherto, has accordingly greater chance of getting nearer to the truth; in the final analysis it is archaeological evidence alone that can give any indications whatsoever for the dating of the original Κατάλογος.

CHAPTER 2

A Folk Story and the End of Amphiaraos

In the Northern part of the Theban Plain, a bit to the South-West of the village of *Mouríki* is an odd phenomenon in the physical landscape. A large, roughly circular depression in the ground, about 40m in diameter and as much as 5 meters deep, has vertical sides and gives the impression of a big sinkhole (Pll. 1–2). To place this phenomenon more precisely it should be said that it lies in a South-westwards prolongation of the *Tymbanókambos*, the plain composing the most cultivable part of the territory belonging to the ancient habitation site at *Mouríki* (= Skhoinos? Cf. Fossey, 1988: 229–232), itself situated on the North side. The place is just to the North of a rough road that runs Westward, across the South end of the *Sambáli* ridge (cf. chapter 11 below for an account of the fortifications on this ridge) to the church of Áyios Sóstis on the East bank of Lake *Likéri.* Such a strange phenomenon has naturally given rise to a story with a fantastic aspect to it; in short something like a recent myth has been created.

PLATE 1   *Voúliagma, Mourikíou*, general from South

PLATE 2   *Voúliagma, Mourikíou*, detail of sinkhole from South West

The story was first told to me by a Theban lawyer and old friend of mine, Ioánnis Gógos, who was once deputy mayor of *Thívai* and who possesses a small country house situated on the Eastern slopes of *Sambáli*, just to the West of the depression; the latter is appropriately called τὸ βούλιαγμα or τὸ βούλιαμα – "the sunken place" or "the swallowed place". When I heard the account I was immediately struck by certain similarities with ancient mythical stories of the death of Amphiaraos and it is this that I will now attempt to unravel.

The land in this part of the Theban Plain belongs to the 12th century monastery of the Metamorphosis of the Saviour (Metamórphosis Soteíros) on the peak of nearby Mount *Sagmatás* (747m = ancient Hypatos? Cf. Fossey, 1988: 223–225) on the site of what may have been a sanctuary of Zeus Hypatos. Below the monastery, at the South West foot of *Sagmatás*, sits the village of *Sýrtzi* (= ancient Glisas? Cf. Fossey, 1988: 217–223).

The current story goes that some of the monks from *Moní Sagmatá* wanted to till their lands here in the *Tymbanókambos* and set out from the monastery for that purpose despite being forbidden to do so by their superior on the grounds that it was the day of a holy festival. Because of the sacrilegious nature of their act the earth opened up, creating the *Voúliagma* that thus swallowed the monks, together with their plough and dray animals.

1 The Story of Amphiaraos

To investigate the similarities of the folk-story with that of Amphiaraos we may examine the mythical accounts of the Argive expeditions against Thebai.

1. À propos of the well-known Amphiaraon near Oropos in the very Eastern extremity of Boiotia, Pausanias (i. 34, 2) says:

   λέγεται δὲ Ἀμφιαράῳ φεύγοντι ἐκ Θηβῶν διαστῆναι τὴν γῆν καὶ ὡς αὐτὸν ὁμοῦ καὶ τὸ ἅρμα ὑπεδέξατο· πλὴν οὐ ταύτῃ συμβῆναί φασιν, ἀλλὰ ἐστιν ἐκ Θηβῶν ἰοῦσιν ἐς Χαλκίδα Ἅρμα καλούμενον

   It is said that, as Amphiaraos was fleeing from Thebai the earth opened up to swallow him and his chariot except that they say that this did not occur here (sc. at the Amphiaraon) but at the place called Harma on the road from Thebai to Khalkis.

2. In his account of the same Thebai-Khalkis road Pausanias (ix. 18, 1–19, 2) recounts several incidents in the story of the Argive attacks on Thebai:

   ἐκ Θηβῶν δὲ ὁδὸς ἐς Χαλκίδα κατὰ πύλας ταύτας ἐστὶ τὰς Προιτίδας. τάφος δὲ ἐπὶ τῇ λεωφόρῳ δείκνυται Μελανίππου, Θηβαίων ἐν τοῖς μάλιστα ἀγαθοῦ τὰ πολεμικά· καὶ ἡνίκα ἐπεστράτευσαν οἱ Ἀργεῖοι, Τυδέα ὁ Μελάνιππος οὗτος καὶ ἀδελφῶν τῶν Ἀδράστου Μηκιστέα ἀπέκτεινε, καί οἱ καὶ αὐτῷ τελευτὴν ὑπὸ Ἀμφιαράου γενέσθαι λέγουσιν (ix. 18, 1) ... πρὸς δὲ τῇ πηγῇ τάφος ἐστὶν Ἀσφοδίκου· καὶ ὁ Ἀσφόδικος οὗτος ἀπέκτεινεν ἐν τῇ μάχῃ τῇ πρὸς Ἀργείους Παρθενοπαῖον τὸ Ταλαοῦ, καθὰ οἱ Θηβαῖοι λέγουσιν, ἐπεὶ τά γε ἐν Θηβαΐδι ἔπη τὰ ἐς τὴν Παρθενοπαίου τελευτὴν Περικλύμενον τὸν ἀνελόντα φησὶν εἶναι (ix. 18, 6) ... ἐπὶ ταύτῃ τῇ λεωφόρῳ χωρίον ἐστι Τευμησσός· (ix. 19, 1) ... Τευμησσοῦ δὲ ἐν ἀριστερᾷ σταδίους προελθόντι ἑπτὰ Γλίσαντός ἐστιν ἐρείπια, πρὸ δὲ αὐτῶν ἐν δεξιᾷ τῆς ὁδοῦ χῶμα οὐ μέγα ὕλῃ τε ἀγρίᾳ σύσκιον καὶ ἡμέροις δένδροις. ἐτάφησαν δὲ αὐτόθι οἱ μετὰ Αἰγιαλέως ποιησάμενοι τοῦ Ἀδράστου τὴν ἐς Θήβας στρατείαν, ἄλλοι τε Ἀργείων τῶν ἐν τέλει καὶ Πρόμαχος ὁ Παρθενοπαίου.

   The road from Thebai to Khalkis runs through the Proitidian gate and along the way is pointed out the tomb of Melanippos, one of the best warriors of the Thebans; at the time of the Argive invasion this same Melanippos killed Tydeus and Mekisteus, one of the brothers of Adrastos, and he himself met his end at the hands of Amphiaraos ... close to the spring (sc. Oidipodia) is the tomb of Asphodikos. This Asphodikos is he who, in battle with the Argives, killed Parthenopaios the son of Talaos according to Theban accounts, although in the epic Thebaïs, where it speaks of the death of Parthenopaios, the text says that his killer was Periklymenos ... On this highway there is a place known as Teumessos ... turning left for seven stadia at Teumessos there are the remains of Glisas and in front of them to the right is a small earth mound shaded by wild and cultivated trees; here are buried those who joined Aigialeus, son of Adrastos in the march on Thebai, other Argives who were in the troop and Promakhos, son of Parthenopaios.

3. The role of Glisas in the tale of the Epigonoi is also referred to à propos of the 8th Pythian ode of Pindaros (line 68). Speaking of the double history of Adrastos leading the first unfortunate Argive attack (that of the Seven against Thebai) and then leading the second, successful one (that of the *Epigonoi*), the old scholiast says

πρότερον μὲν γὰρ ἐσώθη μόνος, κατὰ δὲ τὴν δευτέραν στρατείαν πάντων σωθέντων, αὐτὸς μόνος τὸν υἱὸν ἀπέβαλεν Αἰγιαλέα, ὥς φησιν Ἑλλάνικος λέγων ἐν Γλίσαντι τὴν συμβολὴν γεγενῆσθαι.

On the first time he alone escaped but in the second expedition he lost only his son Aigiaeus, as Hellanikos recounts it saying that the catastrophe took place at Glisas.

4. This sequence of the two Argive attacks on Thebai has already been recounted by Pausanias in the early part of his description of that city.

ἡνίκα ὑπὸ Ἀργείων μάχῃ πρὸς Γλίσαντι ἐκρατήθησαν, τότε ὁμοῦ Λαοδάμαντι τῷ Ἐτεοκλέους ὑπεξίασαν οἱ πολλοί. Τούτων οὖν μοῖρα τὴν μὲν ἐς τοὺς Ἰλλυριοὺς πορείαν ἀπώκνησε, τραπόμενοι δὲ ἐς Θεσσαλοὺς καταλαμβάνουσιν Ὁμόλην, ὀρῶν τῶν Θεσσαλικῶν καὶ εὔγεων μάλιστα καὶ ὕδασιν ἐπιρρεομένην. Θερσάνδρου δὲ τοῦ Πολυνείκους ἀνακαλεσαμένου σφᾶς ἐπὶ τὰ οἰκεῖα, τὰς πύλας διὰ ὧν τὴν κάθοδον ἐποιοῦντο ἀπὸ τῆς Ὁμόλης ὀνομάζουσιν Ὁμολωΐδας (ix. 8, 6–7) ...

When they (sc. the Thebans) were beaten by the Argives at Glisas many of them left with Laodamos, the son of Eteokles, a group of them avoided the journey to the land of the Illyrians by turning off into that of the Thessalians where they took possession of Homole, of all the Thessalian mountains the most fertile and the best watered. When, however, Thersandros, son of Polyneikes, summoned them to return to their homes they named the gate through which they passed the Homoloidan after the same Homole.

This sequence is stated a little differently a few lines later.

> τὸν δὲ πόλεμον τοῦτον, ὃν ἐπολέμησαν Ἀργεῖοι, νομίζω πάντων, ὅσοι πρὸς Ἕλληνας ἐπὶ τῶν καλουμένων ἡρώων ἐπολεμήθησαν ὑπὸ Ἑλλήνων, γενέσθαι λόγου μάλιστα ἄξιον (ix. 9, 1).
>
> ... γενομένης δὲ πρὸς τῷ Ἰσμηνίῳ μάχης ἐκρατήθησαν οἱ Θηβαῖοι τῇ συμβολῇ, καὶ ὡς ἐτράποντο, καταφεύγουσιν ἐς τὸ τεῖχος· ἅτε δὲ οὐκ ἐπισταμένων τῶν Πελοποννησίων μάχεσθαι πρὸς τὸ τεῖχος, ποιουμένων δὲ θυμῷ μᾶλλον ἢ σὺν ἐπιστήμῃ τὰς προσβολάς, πολλοὺς μὲν ἀπὸ τοῦ τείχους βάλλοντες φονεύουσιν αὐτῶν οἱ Θηβαῖοι, κρατοῦσι δὲ ὕστερον καὶ τοὺς ἄλλους ἐπεξελθόντες τεταραγμένοις, ὡς τὸ σύμπαν στράτευμα πλὴν Ἀδράστου φθαρῆναι (ix. 9, 2–3).
>
> ... ἔτεσι δὲ οὐ πολλοῖς ὕστερον ὁμοῦ Θερσάνδρῳ στρατεύουσιν τὰς Θήβας οὓς Ἐπιγόνους καλοῦσιν Ἕλληνες· ... (remarks on the allies of each side) ... καὶ μάχη πρὸς Γλίσαντι ἀπὸ ἀμφοτέρων ἐγένετο ἰσχυρά. τῶν δὲ Θηβαίων οἱ μὲν αὐτίκα ὡς ἡττήθησαν ὁμοῦ Λαοδάμοντι ἐκδιδράσκουσιν, οἱ δὲ ὑπολειφθέντες πολιορκίᾳ παρέστησαν (ix. 9, 4–5).

This war waged by the Argives I think must have been the greatest fought by Greeks against Greeks in the heroic period ...

In the battle at the Ismenion the Thebans got the worst of it and having lost ground took refuge within their city's walls. The Peloponnesians did not know how to fight over the walling and since they made many attacks in anger rather than with forethought the Thebans were able to kill many of them by throwing missiles from the wall and later to make a sortie and to deal with the rest of them thus destroying the entire force with the exception of Adrastos ...

A few years later those whom the Greeks call the "Epigonoi" marched against Thebai (note on allies); the battle at Glisas was hard fought by both sides. Some of the Thebans, immediately after their defeat, retreated under the leadership of Laodamos; those who remained were taken by siege.

The Periegetes had made brief reference (ii. 23, 2) to the end of Amphiaraos in connection with latter's charioteer, Baton:

> γενομένης δὲ τῆς τροπῆς ἀπὸ τοῦ Θηβαίων τείχους χάσμα γῆς Ἀμφιάραον καὶ τὸ ἅρμα ὑποδεξάμενον ἠφάνησεν ὁμοῦ καὶ τοῦτον τὸν Βάτωνα.

When they were driven away from the walls of Thebai a gap in the earth swallowed up Amphiaraos and his chariot, together with this Baton.

5. In the even longer account by Diodoros Sikeliotes (iv. 64–67, 2) it is briefly said that

Ἀμφιάραος δὲ χανούσης τῆς γῆς ἐμπεσὼν εἰς τὸ χάσμα μετὰ τοῦ ἅρματος ἄφαντος ἐγένετο (65, 8).

When the earth gaped open Amphiaraos having fallen into the hole with his chariot was lost to sight.

6. In his 9th Nemean ode Pindaros refers to the story of the Seven (see no. 3 above for the relevant *skholion*). The expedition against Thebai is described as ill-fated, with Zeus urging the Argives not to set out (lines 18–20):

ἐσ ⟨λὸν ἐς⟩ ἑπταπύλους Θήβας ἄγαγον στρατὸν ἀνδρῶν αἰσιᾶν
οὐ κατ' ὀρνίχων ὁδόν· οὐδὲ Κρονίων ἀστεροπὰν ἐλελίξαις οἴκοθεν
    μαργομένους
στείχειν ἐπώτρυν', ἀλλὰ φείσασθαι κελεύου.

Once they led against seven-gated Thebai a mighty host of hopeful men despite the lack of good auguries for the journey and the fact that the son of Kronos, by the whirling of his lightening, did not encourage them to set out from home in their fury, but rather to desist from the journey.

After describing the pomp of their expedition the poet goes on to describe their ends (lines 22–27):

Ἰσμηνοῦ δ' ἐπ' ὄχθαισι γλυκὺν
νόστον ἐρεισάμενοι λευκανθέα σώμασι ἐπίαναν καπνόν·
ἑπτὰ γὰρ δαίσαντο πυραὶ νεογυίους φώτας· ὁ δ' Ἀμφιαρεῖ σχίσσεν
    κεραυνῷ ταμβίᾳ
Ζεὺς τὰν βαθύστερνον χθόνα, κρύψεν δ' ἅμ' ἵπποις,
δουρὶ Περικλυμένου πρὶν νῶτα τυπέντα μαχατὰν
θυμὸν αἰσχυνθῆμεν.

On the banks of the Ismenos they left their sweet longing to return home and their pale bodies fed the smoke for seven funeral pyres consumed the young men, except for Amphiaraos for whom Zeus cleft the deep bosom of earth with his almighty thunderbolt and hid him with his horses before the spear of Peryklymenos could dishonour the warrior by striking him in the back.

Pindaros refers to this end of Amphiaraos on two other occasions:

A. in a shorter version (*Nemean* x, 8–9):

γαῖα δ' ἐν Θήβαις ὑπέδεκτο κεραυνωθεῖσα Διὸς βέλεσιν
μάντιν Οἰκλείδαν, πολέμοιο νέφος

In the Theban land, being struck with the thunderbolts of Zeus, swallowed the prophet son of Oikles, the cloud in battle.

B. yet again, in reference to Adrastos' lament for the loss of Amphiaraos, (*Olympian* vi, 12–14):

ὃν ἐν δίκᾳ
ἀπὸ γλώσσας Ἄδραστος μάντιν Οἰκλείδαν ποτ' ἐς Ἀμφιάρηον
φθέγξατ', ἐπεὶ κατὰ γαῖ' αὐτόν τέ νιν καὶ
φαιδίμας ἵππους ἔμαρψεν,

That which was said in justice by Adrastos concerning the seer Amphiaraos son of Oikles when the earth had seized himself and his shining horses.

(Obviously there it is no specified place where the earth swallowed him up, just as occurs in a brief incidental reference made by Euripides [*Hiketides* 925–927].)

7. Not only was the expedition ill-fated but also considered accursed as Aiskhylos (*Hepta epi Thebas* 785–787) reminds us, saying of Oidipous:

τέκνοις δ' ἀγρίας
ἐφῆκεν ἐπικότους τροφᾶς,
αἰαῖ, πικρογλώσσους ἀράς,

On his children, when they grudged him support, he hurled bitterly spoken curses.

(The same theme is found in the long speech of Oidipous' curse in Sophokles' *Oidipous epi Kolono* 1354–1396.)

8. Continuing to describe the road from Thebai to Khalkis coming Eastwards after Teumessos and Glisas, the *periegetes* adds a detail:

> ἑξῆς δὲ πόλεων ἐρείπιά ἐστιν Ἅρματος καὶ Μυκαλησσοῦ· καὶ τῇ μὲν τὸ ὄνομα ἐγένετο ἀφανισθέντος, ὡς οἱ Ταναγραῖοί φασιν, ἐνταῦθα Ἀμφιαράῳ τοῦ ἅρματος καὶ οὐχ ὅπου λέγουσιν οἱ Θηβαῖοι.
>
> PAUSANIAS ix. 19, 4

Thereafter are the ruins of the cities Harma and Mykalessos, the former of which was so named because this is where, according to the Tanagrans, the chariot of Amphiaraos disappeared and not where the Thebans claim.

9. The identification of Harma as the place of Amphiaraos' end occurs in Strabon (ix. 404):

> περὶ δὲ τοῦ Ἅρματος τοῦ Βοιωτιακοῦ οἱ μέν φασιν ἐκπεσόντος ἐκ τοῦ ἅρματος ἐν τῇ μάχῃ τοῦ Ἀμφιαράου κατὰ τὸν τόπον, ὅπου νῦν ἐστὶ ἱερὸν αὐτοῦ, τὸ ἅρμα ἔρημον ἐνεχθῆναι ἐπὶ τὸν ὁμώνυμον τόπον·

Concerning Boiotian Harma there are those who say that Amphiaraos fell out of his chariot during the battle at the place where there is now his sanctuary, and that the empty chariot was dragged to the place that bears this same name.

(This recurs in a passage – for what it is worth – by Pseudo-Ploutarkhos [*Synagoge Historion Parallelon Hellenikon kai Romaikon* 6]:

> τῇ δ' ὑστεραίᾳ πολεμούντων κατ' ἐκεῖνο κατεπόθη ὁ Ἀμφιάρεως ἅμα τῷ ἅρματι, ἔνθα νῦν πόλις Ἅρμα καλεῖται.

The following day as they were fighting Amphiaraos, was swallowed up together with his chariot there where is now the city called Harma.

Obviously the nature of the place-name itself was a strong attraction.)

10. Describing the sequence of places along the coast of Attike and into that of Boiotia, Strabon (ix. 399) provides another witness:

> μετὰ δὲ Μαραθῶνα Τρικόρυνθος, εἶτα Ῥαμνοῦς, τὸ τῆς Νεμέσεως ἱερόν, εἶτα Ψαφὶς ἡ τῶν Ὠρωπίων· ἐνταῦθα δέ που καὶ τὸ Ἀμφιαραεῖόν ἐστι τετιμημένον ποτὲ μαντεῖον, ὅπου φυγόντα τὸν Ἀμφιάρεων, ὥς φησι Σοφοκλῆς,

"ἐδέξατο ῥαγεῖσα Θηβαία κόνις,
αὐτοῖσιν ὅπλοις καὶ τετρωρίστῳ δίφρῳ" (= Sophokles, fragment 873 [Nauck]).

After Marathon comes Trikorynthos, then Rhamnous with the sanctuary of Nemesis, then Psaphis in the land of the Oropians; here is the Amphiaraion. Once an honoured prophetic shrine to which Amphiaraos was fleeing when he was, in the words of Sophokles, "received by the split Theban soil together with his arms and his four-horse chariot".

2   Discussion

For the geography of the area in question cf. the map, Fig. 2.

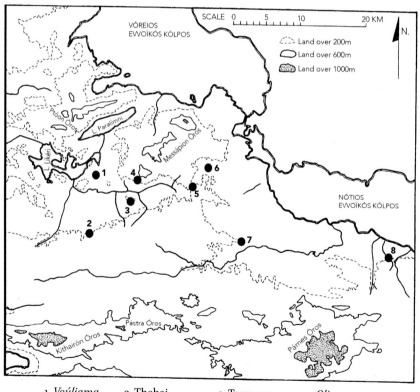

1. *Voúliama*   2. Thebai   3. Teumessos   4. *Glisas*
5. Harma   6. Mykalessos   7. Tanagra   8. Amphiaraion

FIGURE 2   Places associated with the end of Amphiaraos

A. The expedition of the Seven and that subsequently undertaken by the *Epigonoi* against Thebai seem to have been overshadowed by curse and foretold doom. It was with the second that Amphiaraos met his end.
B. Although there was a healing and one-time prophetic sanctuary of Amphiaraos in Oropia, it is only Strabon (no. 10 above) who attempts to identify the Amphiaraion as the site associated with the death of the hero. Two conflicting local traditions wish to place the scene of his end much further West at locations nearer to Thebai in one of two positions, in the Western end of Tanagraia or in the adjacent North East part of Thebaïs, neither of which locations lies anywhere near the Amphiaraion. These two traditions agree to the extent of ruling out the Oropian Amphiaraion as the place of his end. The question of whether the Amphiaraion, as a prophetic shrine was always in the same location is, thus, not relevant here (cf. Schachter, 1981: 22–23). We are here concerned with myth not history.
C. Of these two other locations, the one in the West end of Tanagraia based its claim on its very name Harma (= chariot) since the hero's end came with being swallowed up together with his chariot.
D. The rival location in North Eastern Theban territory seems to have the stronger traditional support and ties in with the consistent placing at Glisas (in North East Thebaïs) of the final conflict in the expedition of the Epigonoi. The accounts of Amphiaraos' flight as being the sequel to this conflict underline the fact that, apart from his personal loss, the whole fight constituted a success for the Peloponnesian force.
E. A possibly "learned" tradition arose to explain the two locations by saying that the one was where Amphiaraos fell off his chariot, the other, further from Thebai, where the driverless chariot itself ended up. This runs counter to the near uniformity of most of the *testimonia* that said that he was swallowed up together with the chariot.
F. One obviously local tradition, recounted by the Theban poet Pindaros himself, attributed the swallowing up of man and equipment to the act of Zeus throwing a thunder-bolt to cleave the earth.

3 Comparison and Conclusion

It will be obvious from the preceding summaries that the two stories have several elements in common. The forbidden and cursed nature of the expeditions bring together the role of Zeus and the superior of the *Sagmatás* monastery which is, let us remember, taken to stand on the site of an ancient sanctuary of none other deity than Zeus. It is even clear that that sanctuary would so dominate the whole *Sírtzi-Mouríki* area as to make it an easy association with Zeus hurling a bolt to save Amphiaraos from being killed from behind.

We have seen that the majority of sources place the event of Amphiaraos' end in Theban territory and the connection again with adjacent *Sírtzi* (ancient Glisas) indicates that the scene is not out of place at the *Voúliagma*.

The large, unnatural hole in the ground and the legend that it was the site where men and horses together with equipment (chariot or plough) were swallowed up is surely too much to be dismissed as mere coincidence and can leave little doubt that the *Voúliagma* was the site where in antiquity there was located a myth concerning the disappearance of Amphiaraos and his horses and chariot.

CHAPTER 3

"Les Deux Béoties" in Archaic Times

The late Pierre Guillon was perhaps the first to refer specifically to the phenomenon of "two Boiotias" in the first lines of his book *La Béotie antique*:

> Quand au terme de défilé sinueux qui monte d'Athènes et d'Eleusis à travers le Cithéron par l'antique passé des Têtes-de-Chênes, on débouche au sommet de la muraille abrupte qui tombe sur le village de Kriekouki et sur Kokkla, l'antique Platées, on discerne aussitôt deux Béoties.
> GUILLON, 1948: 17

He is referring to the distinction between the Boiotia of the Central, Southern and Eastern plains on the one hand and the Boiotia of the Kopaïs on the other. If this distinction is valid in our days how much more so was it in antiquity? In antiquity the Kopaïc Plain was in fact largely a lake; while its exact limits to the South and the West may have varied with the cyclic blocking and unblocking of the swallow holes at the opposite side, to North and East, its waters would normally have lapped fairly constantly around the feet of the mountains that descend sharply into it. Even to the South and West peripheral marshes and the near approach yet again of ridges running out from the surrounding mountains caused the splitting of the terrain into at best small parcels of land controlled each by one of the smaller Boiotian cities; to North and East the fragmentation of the land and the exiguous size of cultivable areas was even more marked. The Kopaïs was thus the land of the smaller members of what became the Boiotian confederation while the plains of the Centre, South and East with their extensive arable lands gave rise to the large cities which were to dominate that league – Thebai, Thespiai, Thisbe, Plataiai, Tanagra and even Oropos. This is not to say that the distinction is absolute in all its terms for there are smaller cities also in the South, Kreusis, Siphai and Khorsiai, each of which controlled a tiny parcel of land trapped between mountains and sea, but for all three of these immediate communications were with the larger cities of the interior, especially Thisbe and Thespiai. Even Anthedon on the North coast and thus in the non-Kopaïc zone, for all its isolation, had quite extensive cultivable land and good grazing areas on the slopes around.

The actual line of demarcation between these two Boiotias is constituted by the two principal mountains within the terrain, Helikon and Ptoon, together

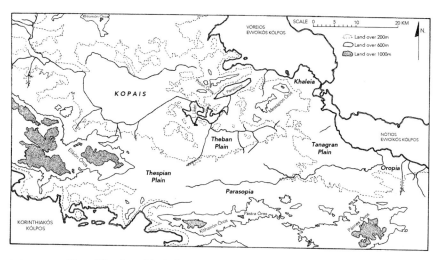

FIGURE 3   Map of "les deux Béoties"

with the mass of Sphinx mountain (*Phagás*) that connects them (cf. map, Fig. 3). To the Northwest of this line were cities so small that (with the sole exception of Orkhomenos which may, at times, have exercised some sort of suzerainty over many of her neighbours) two and even three of them had to be combined to produce voting districts in the confederation of Classical times. To the South and East lay the large cities each of which, for the most part, represented on its own at least one voting district, and often even two.

Apart from the historic differences just mentioned this line of demarcation can be seen in the archaeological record of Late Geometric–Early Archaic times. Two different types of evidence show the distinction: the patterns of imported Korinthian pottery and the distribution of certain works of Boiotian bronze smiths, the incised *fibulae* of the (Attiko-)Boiotian type, type IX.a in the classification of Blinkenberg (1926).

1   Protokorinthian Imports

In publishing the pottery from the *Mavrovoúni* site on the South Boiotian coast I had concluded that "Corinthian Material was imported into Boeotia from the beginning of the seventh century" (Tomlinson & Fossey, 1970: 251 = Fossey, 1990: 130) but this statement was overgeneralized and in fact applies only to the larger area of Central, Southern and Eastern Boiotia. When we examine the overall distribution of Korinthian pottery found in Boiotia we come across a different situation in the Kopaïs.

The main sites at which imported Korinthian pottery has been found in properly published contexts are few but a consistent picture does emerge nevertheless. At *Mavrovoúni* (no. 4 on the map, Fig. 4) the earliest imported material dates to the Middle Protokorinthian period starting around the beginning of the 7th century. From the Ismenion at Thebai (no. 1) apparently come Korinthian sherds with "subgeometric decoration" that should date to the early 7th century (Keramópoullos, 1917: 70). The picture at *Rhitsóna* (no. 2) is quite clear (Ure, 1934): apart from a single example of "Argive" monochrome ware in grave 134, the earliest imported material appears to be Middle ProtoKorinthian, the very earliest aryballos being transitional between the bellied and ovoid forms but found in a grave of early 6th century date which may give it the nature of an heirloom; it is, however, followed by many instances of both the ovoid and piriform shapes that cover most of the first three quarters of the 7th century. At Tanagra (no. 3) illegal digging has uncovered large quantities of pottery – and, of course, the famous terracottas – and local sources have clearly described to me examples of aryballoi of both ovoid and piriform shapes, covering the same time span as that which we have just seen at *Rhitsóna* (cf. also the Middle Protokorinthian aryballos from Tanagra illustrated in the *Jahrbuch* for 1887, Plate II; more recent official excavations in one part of the nekropolis only produced Ripe Korinthian: Andreioménou, 2007: pin. 4, 5, 13–25, 27, & 32–33). Unfortunately no material of these periods is known from the Parasopia; from the recent partial excavations at Plataiai (Konecny, 2013: 454–455) we have only Ripe Korinthian but much of the site and, in particular, of its cemeteries, remains to be investigated. When, however, we turn further to the West the story picks up again. In the area around the two smaller lakes of Boiotia, at *Oúngra* (no. 5, which I have equated with the ancient city of Hyle; Fossey, 1988: 235–243) and at both the Ptoian sanctuary (no. 6) and the neighbouring city of Akraiphiai (no. 7) the earliest imported pottery dates to the end of the Middle and to the beginning of the following Late Protokorinthian period, that is from the middle of the 7th century (for *Oúngra* cf. *ADelt* 1966: Plate 205; for the Ptoion cf. Ducat, 1971: 56, pl. IX nos. 31032 and Johansen, 1923: 88 for Akraiphiai cf. Andhreioménou, 1974: pl. 5). In the Valley of the Muses (no. 9) to the immediate South of the Kopaïs the earliest material belongs to the Ripe Korinthian (de Ridder, 1922: 287–291). The same applies to Haliartos (no. 8) in the South Kopaïs (Austin, 1926–7: 130 & 1930: 192) and to Orkhomenos (no. 10) at the West end of the basin (de Ridder, 1985: 182–188, cf. Johansen, 1923; 88).

To this picture of excavated material may be added what can be derived from examples drawn from less secure proveniences and the resultant picture remains essentially the same. In several museum collections there are quite many vases in Korinthian fabric with "provenances" in Boiotia, mostly

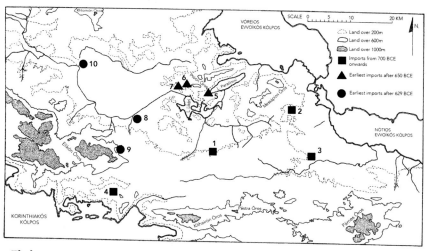

1. Thebai 2. *Rhitsóna* 3. Tanagra 4. *Mavrovoúni* 5. *Oúngra* 6. Ptoion
7. Akraiphiai 8. Haliartos 9. Valley of the Muses 10. Orkhomenos

FIGURE 4   Boiotia: imported Korinthian pottery 7th c. BCE

Thebai and Tanagra. These are preceded by a few Late Geometric and Proto-Attic Athenian vases said to come from Thebai (Mannheim Cg.78; Ashmolean 1927. 4058; Heidelberg G.9 & G.11) and there are many that follow from Late Geometric Korinthian (Heidelberg G.1; Johansen, 1923: Pl. I.3 & Pl. i.3) but the main sequence begins with a plethora of Middle ProtoKorinthian aryballoi (e.g. Louvre L.2; Ashmolean 504; Louvre CA 617; MFA Boston, 95.10; British Museum 89.4–18.1 etc.) and this occurs also, but less frequently with Tanagran "provenances" of Middle and Late ProtoKorinthian material (e.g. *CVA Baltimore MD* Pl. xiv, 1 & 4; Louvre L 28 & 153). For the rest of Boiotia ("Levadheia", "Ptoion", "Khaironeia") the earliest pieces are Ripe Korinthian. Only one apparent exception is known to me and that is an ovoid aryballos in Reading (*CVA Reading* I, Pl. iii, 8) said to be from the Kopaïs; it dates to the mid-7th century but comes from a private collection, proveniences for the objects in which are, in fact, far from sure and reliable; this piece cannot thus be taken to disprove on its own what has already been said.

When these data are summarized on the distribution map (Fig. 4) it appears quite clearly that, while Protokorinthian pottery was arriving in South, Central and Eastern Boiotia from the beginning of the 7th century BCE, it was only seen in the Kopaïs at the earliest in the last quarter of that century; there is a small group in the area of the lesser lakes, and thus lying between the two Boiotias of which we speak, where it began to arrive from the middle of the century, a little before reaching the Kopaïs proper.

2 *Fibulae*

Fibulae of the Attiko-Boiotian type were first really defined by Blinkenberg (1926). Subsequent work, especially by Keith DeVries (1970), defined subcategories within the large class and it is possible to recognize specifically Boiotian products. We may quote an interesting preliminary summary by DeVries of the results of his work:

> It has proved possible to distinguish three major groups as being Boeotian with one of the three being specifically Theban, in all probability. Two other groups can be considered Thessalian – or at any rate "Northern" – and there are some Attic classes (the latter relatively early).

It is important to remember that DeVries was working on all the Late Geometric and Subgeometric *fibulae* with incised decoration that thus included also those of Blinkenberg's Thessalian type. This gives extra meaning to the continuation of his summary:

> ... there are some striking historical implications in the patterns of distribution. The Thessalian, or Northern, types occur monopolistically in West and East Lokris, Phokis and the Thessalian regions, thus perhaps suggesting a Thessalian dominance in this whole area already during the late eighth and early seventh centuries BC. The true Boeotian *fibulae* have not so far been found in those neighbouring regions to the west and north (though the Boeotian pieces certainly did exert a strong influence on the northern metalworkers); instead the Boeotian *fibulae* (and presumably Boeotian interests and Boeotian travellers) normally went southwards and in particular to the Argolid.
>
> DEVRIES, 1971

In fact these *fibulae* are only found in the Southern, Central and Eastern parts of Boiotia, that is in just the one of our two Boiotias. They are known from Thisbe, Thespiai, Thebai, *Oúngra*, the Ptoion, Plataiai, *Rhitsóna* and Tanagra (cf. map, Fig. 5), in addition to examples from Eretria on nearby Euboia, from Attike and from the Peloponnesos etc. (for full lists of these cf. DeVries and the older, fundamental work of Hampe, 1936; for *Oúngra* cf. Spyrópoulos, 1971, fig. 9); the Tanagra material is, however, unpublished being based on information given to me by the same local sources as were able to identify the types

"LES DEUX BÉOTIES" IN ARCHAIC TIMES

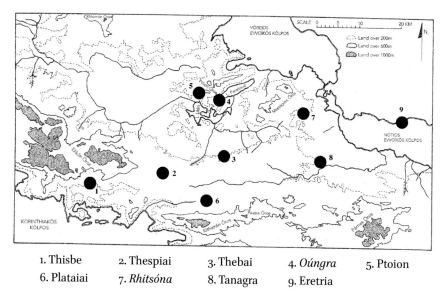

| 1. Thisbe | 2. Thespiai | 3. Thebai | 4. *Oúngra* | 5. Ptoion |
| 6. Plataiai | 7. *Rhitsóna* | 8. Tanagra | 9. Eretria |

FIGURE 5   Distribution of archaic Boiotian *fibulae*

of Korinthian pottery found during illegal excavations in the extensive ancient cemeteries of the city).

Again Western Boiotia, like the surrounding districts mentioned by DeVries, does not produce any examples and, again, the area of absence in Boiotia is identical with that which does not produce imported Korinthian pottery in the same period, late eighth and first half of the seventh centuries BCE. Just as with the pottery, there appears to be one exception to this rule for a single example of one of these incised *fibulae* is said to come from Khaironeia at the very Western end of the Kopaïs (no. 40 in Hampe's catalogue, currently located in the museum at *Thiva*). This brooch is, however, strange. Unlike all other *fibulae* of its type it is not of one piece; in fact it is clear that the bow, the shaft and the spring (and obviously the now missing pin) are reused from another such artefact; the end of the bow opposite the spring has been cut into along its vertical axis in such a way as to receive an inserted catch plate with incised decoration; this plate has been reused from another *fibula*. In short, not only is the object isolated geographically, it (or rather both of its constituent parts) must be presumed to have had a long life (or long lives); since it can, therefore, have arrived in Khaironeia – always assuming the provenience to be in any way reliable – long after the date of original manufacture and first currency of each part, it cannot be used to invalidate the otherwise clear distinction in distribution between frequent presence in the other Boiotia and absence in the Kopaïs.

3   Discussion

What then can be the explanation of this distinction between the Kopaïs and the rest of Boiotia – over and above the obvious geographic separation – specifically at this point in time, namely the late eighth century BCE and the first half to three quarters of the following century? DeVries' own words may point us in the right direction for he makes a distinction between Boiotian and Thessalian. This distinction recalls rather forcibly the matter of the Thessalian hegemony that reached as far as the East side of the Kopaïs and no further into Boiotia; in effect the Thessalian hegemony controlled exactly that part of Boiotia in which Middle Protokorinthian pottery and incised *fibulae* of the Boiotian type are absent. I stress the word "exactly" for the Thessalian hegemony reached as far as but was finally cut short in the battle at Keressos; Keressos, wherever exactly it was located (cf. Fossey, 1988: 145–146), lay in the territory of Thespiai and to the West of that city, i.e. in the direction of the Kopaïs. If indeed we are to look to the Thessalian hegemony for an explanation of these differential distributions a particular detail of the pattern acquires its own specific logic for if the Thessalians controlled the very Western part of Thespian territory this could explain why the Valley of the Muses, normally part of Thespian territory, but seemingly further West than any possible site for Keressos, should follow the Kopaïc pattern rather than that of the plains which included the city of Thespiai itself.

The only problem with this suggestion is one of chronology for the dating of the Thessalian hegemony has long been a subject of discussion and dispute; unfortunately previous discussants have made little or no use of the archaeological evidence. It is this evidence that may enable us to cut through a basic complication that arises from the all-too-thin literary record. At the heart of the problem is the fact that the only point recorded and "dated" for this obscure event is the battle of Keressos which put an end to the Thessalian domination (Buck, 1979: 108–112) but this is further complicated by the fact that the only ancient authority who does "date" this battle, Ploutarkhos (himself a Boiotian, let it be remembered) does so twice but gives a very different date each time. In one passage (*Ethika* 866e) he dates the battle to "shortly before" (ἔναχος) the second Persian invasion, that is a little before 480 BCE; in the other account (*Kamillos* 19) he dates it to "more than two hundred years before the battle of Leuktra" (πρότερον ἔτεσι πλείοσιν ἢ διακοσίοις), in other words well before 571 BCE. The imprecision in Ploutarkhos' wording about these two dates seems to indicate lack of detailed knowledge which would be more easily understood if it reached back before the coming into existence of anything approaching written history, a thought that encourages support for the earlier of the two dates. Obviously, in any case, the two dates cannot be reconciled but, although there may be many reasons for discounting the later date, Buck (*loc. cit.*), not entirely without reason, observed that this does not necessarily mean that we must automatically espouse the earlier one. Buck (1972), while convinced that the formation of the Boiotian League and the Thessalian invasion "must be closely associated" also argued that numbers are more easily corrupted in manuscript tradition than are words, thus taking up the position adopted by Sordi (1958: 87, repeated in 1993) who felt that σ′ (= 200) and could easily be confused with ρ′ (= 100) thus adducing a date more than one hundred years before Leuktra, i.e. before 471 BCE. It is not easy, however, to see such a mix-up occurring early in the manuscript tradition since *rho* and *sigma* are quite distinguishable in majuscule or uncial writing and one might feel it a little strange if the battle of Keressos was so close to the Persian Wars and yet was ignored in sources for that period, notably Herodotos. In short the original choice must remain between "more than 200 years before Leuktra" or in the times of the Persian Wars and since the latter is otherwise completely and inexplicably unattested this should strengthen support for the earlier date back in the later 7th (at a pinch the early 6th) century.

In a lengthy article Schachter (1989) attempts to draw out some meaning from the rare indications, principally literary, partly archaeological and finally in part epigraphic, to reconstruct something of the history of 6th century Boiotia. While he too sees a distinction between the two Boiotias, his comparison of them to each other on archaeological questions goes completely contrary to what I have outlined above for the preceding 7th century. This is in part because he did not consider the evidence from the sanctuary site at *Mavrovoúni* on the mountain range of the South coast (where the history begins in Late Geometric times). In general he did not use the information that comes from surface exploration and this is what shows abundantly well that, even if there was some expansion of settlement activity in the Kopaïs in the 6th century, this was on a lesser scale than that seen in the Boiotian plains from Late Geometric through archaic times (cf. Fossey, 1988: Plates VII and VIII); this gives, if anything, the distinct impression that matters in the Kopaïs were simply trying to catch up with Central, East and South Boiotian plains albeit on a lesser scale because the territory involved is much smaller. Schachter also avoids commenting on any Boiotian artefacts (the sort of information that was available to me concerning the material found during illegal digging in the cemeteries of Tanagra) other than the occasional piece of sculpture found in a sanctuary. Overall he concentrates too much on the developments at certain sanctuaries – natural given his long-time concentration on the cults of Boiotia but setting completely aside the importance of settlement patterns which show where people were really active. His choice of inscriptions to treat was by his own admission personal ("dealing only with those which I think may have a bearing on the history of this period"). I will turn to other aspects of his paper in the next chapter but of particular relevance here is his statement that "the battle of Keressos, *whenever it happened*, need not have been connected with the formation of the league" (my italics), thus choosing to avoid facing this critical problem.

Despite the attempts by others to down date Keressos, it remains a fact that a date **more** than 200 years before Leuktra could well take us to the late 7th century and we might then see the incorporation of Kopaïc Boiotia into what was going on in the rest of the territory some time during the last quarter of that century as a consequence of this putative battle of Keressos.

Since I have never been convinced that the origin of the Boiotian league is to be placed as late as the latter part of the 6th century, I am really tempted to see in this pattern of artefact distribution an indication that Ploutarkhos' early date is to be retained and, with Keressos thus put into the late 7th century, to see the initial formation of the Boiotian league as taking place around the end of that century or early in the following one, building upon the foundations of a common and successful resistance to the Thessalian advance by the Boiotians of the Centre and East. If I am right, however, there is one further corollary: the distributions of pottery and artefacts should then imply that the Thessalian hegemony was not some brief adventure but a condition of some duration, perhaps even the best part of a century during which the line across the Boiotian mountains divided two Greek worlds, the Northern, Thessalian dominated part and the Central/Southern free zone of independent city states, some of which were subsequently to merge into the earliest recorded federal state of the Western world. If I am right it is archaeology, rather than texts, that can best illuminate this singular event of human history, military and political.

CHAPTER 4

The Origins of the Boiotian League

We have just observed that there is reason to look for the beginnings of the League in the resistance to the Thessalian hegemony. We have thus seen that certain archaeological evidence (imported Korinthian pottery and incised Attiko-Boiotian *fibulae*), combined with a single date indication from the Boiotian author Ploutarkhos, allows us to suggest that the battle of Keressos, which saw the end of the Thessalian domination, may be placed late in the 7th century BCE. This seems then to have been followed by a short period during which the cities of North Western Boiotia, i.e. the Kopaïs that had until then been under Thessalian control and thus isolated from cultural trends in Southern Greece, now entered the sphere of activities seen in the rest of Boiotia; this cultural "liberation" of North West Boiotia does not necessarily mean that Orkhomenian interests would have ended immediately or have been drawn politically into the world of the Eastern plains. It could mean, however, that many Boiotian cities in general might have been reflecting on the lessons from the preceding period and considering the value of common efforts such as those brought about by the combined actions of several of them in the face of the Thessalian occupation and the threat of its expansion. It might thus have been a time when a hitherto unknown type of formal association could well have come into being and brought about the emergence of the earliest example of a federal state in the Western world. Since this organization – at whatever point in the 6th century it came into being – was, by its nature, an experiment without precedent we can imagine that it was not created in a day; it may have evolved over a period of time before reaching its full form. On the basis of the suggestion that Keressos was in the late 7th century we can allow that some of that development took place over the last years of that century and the first years of the 6th. Such a sequence is in accord with the evidence of imported Korinthian pottery and the distribution of the incised *fibulae*.

1 Early Boiotian Coinage

In a rather pessimistic article published many years ago Jean Ducat (1973) opined that we have little material on which to construct any understanding of the genesis and development of this unique political experiment. For him the only real source of information – and not very precise information at that – was the early coinage; he was perhaps correct but we are faced with the same question about the coinage as we are with the origins of the League, i.e. are we looking at a date in the early or in the late 6th century? The question concerning the date of the beginning of coinage in the East Mediterranean world has been much debated in recent years and those who prefer a date later in the 6th century will be led to see the first tangible attestation of the existence of a Boiotian League, the early coins, as dating from that time. Perhaps we can cut through this conundrum by looking rather at the Boiotian context itself and then moving from that to the date of the first specifically Boiotian coins, always remembering that the federation could very well have existed clearly **before** the minting of any coins; *i.e.* the minting of the coins could perfectly well have been the act of a federation that already existed (perhaps had even done so for some while) and that was following the current idea of producing a systematic coinage. It is even worth remembering a series of events in recent history that can provide a very pertinent parallel. The European Economic Community (EEC) was first formed with just six members in 1957; in 1993 the European Union (EU) was founded and the EEC was incorporated into it; its economic zone then included 15 countries; the currency, known as the Euro was officially so named in 1995 but only came into circulation at the beginning of 1999 and even then the 19 states that form the Eurozone where that currency circulates do not include all states within the European Union, Great Britain being the most obvious absentee. In short a union that has been developing over nearly two thirds of a century (and still develops) only produced its currency after nearly the first half century of its existence, and that was in a world where monetary systems had been known for so many centuries; how much more easily can we understand a federation of some sort that had come into being with the end of the Thessalian domination sometime around the end of the 7th/beginning of the 6th century BCE (cf. previous chapter) only taking the step of introducing coinage perhaps as much as three quarters of a century later, in a world that had, until very recently, had no experience of a monetary system. Even the case of Britain in the EU/Eurozone may caution against being too surprised at absences from the list of cities participating in the system of that coinage.

In short the date of the earliest coinage, even if we knew it, may very well be nothing more than a *terminus ante quem* for the inception of the league or at least for some sort of cooperative effort by those Boiotian cities that lay outside the Thessalian controlled Kopaïs zone; from a cooperative act of this sort may well have developed over time an increasingly formal collaboration, ultimately a federation. Our best candidate for that inception must remain the battle of Keressos not far from 600 BCE. Wherever Keressos is located exactly it is worth noting that, since the Thespians are said to have twice taken refuge in the stronghold of Keressos, the second time being after the battle of Leuktra and the first when besieged there by the Thessalians they were clearly part of the Boiotians implying that their city itself may not have been under Thessalian control. (ἔστι δὲ ἐχυρὸν χωρίον ὁ Κερησσὸς ἐν τῇ Θεσπιέων, ἐς ὃ καί πάλαι ποτὲ ἀνεσκευάσαντο κατὰ τὴν ἐπιστρατείαν τὴν Θεσσαλῶν. Pausanias ix. 14, 2.) The further implication is that Keressos should probably have stood in Western Thespike (the only part of that territory that really has any naturally defensible positions). This would bring us near to the Kopaïs and we might reflect that once the Thessalians had really passed out of the marshy land around the lake their redoubtable cavalry would have been able to operate freely in the plains of Central, Southern and Eastern Boiotia. Keressos might thus be seen as the best single position to block the Thessalians.

Having thus disassociated the coinage from the inception of the league, let us see just what we do know about those early coins from themselves. Their most quoted classification is that published long ago by Head (1881; 1884: xxxvi–xlv & 32–93; 1910: 343–355); this has almost always been followed subsequently, all too often in a slavish, unquestioning manner. The dates that Head assigned to the different classes in his scheme have fortunately been followed less slavishly but have, nonetheless, sometimes had results. It is regrettable that students of the history of the Boiotian League have not asked sufficient questions about the early coinage for it may be that it can possibly tell us something more than implied by Ducat's assessment. In what follows I shall try to ask some of those questions that have not really occurred to others and, while the results of my thinking may not find favour with all readers, at least these questions will finally have been asked.

Whatever the exact dating of different issues, it seems that, from the very start, Boiotia witnessed the emissions of two quite distinct series, easily recognizable by a different symbol on the obverse of each; despite this distinction, both these coinages were minted on the same "Aiginetan" standard.

The larger of these two series included a rich variety of coins whose obverse bore the "Boiotian" shield, a device that was to be a constant of Boiotian coinage over several centuries but which left little room for variation through time and so not allowing any real discernment of typological development and thus relative dating. The second distinct series comprises a smaller number of coins clearly identified by the grain of corn on their obverse that subsequent issues were to demonstrate as undoubtedly belonging to Orkhomenos; again this is a symbol that seems to show little change over time thus not allowing much observation of any development. The existence of two distinct series is somewhat reminiscent of the existence of two Boiotias, one in the plains, the other in the Kopaïs (cf. preceding chapter). It seems that the existence of these two distinct series shows that an apparently old rivalry between Orkhomenos and the more Easterly parts of Boiotia, Thebai in particular, was reflected by an Orkhomenian "separatist" coinage.

Both series of coins show some similarity in development. At the beginning we have in the two completely anepigraphic issues where the reverse is simply a "mill-sail" incuse square of so-called Aiginetan type. In the next stage(s) one or two letters are added onto the coins, always using the epichoric forms that, with variations, were to continue in use in Boiotia until the first part of the 4th century BCE. At the start the letter(s) is/are placed on the obverse, in the case of the Orkhomenian pieces the letter(s) either to one side or on both sides of the grain of corn, in the case of the "Boiotian" issues the letter occurs in both the side cuts of the shield. In this second stage the reverse of the Orkhomenian pieces shows the incuse square divided by thin ridges into five quite unequal compartments; the other series remains faithful to the mill-sail motif. The third stage for the shield issues sees the letters move to the reverse being inserted in the cut-out centre of the mill-sail; there also begins to be a greater number of different letters used. The following stage is the logical extension of this move of attention to the reverse for now the incuse square disappears in favour of a circular sunken area occupying almost the entire surface of the flan; the reverse also begins to sport more than just a letter; rather is quite a variety of motifs seen together with several letters. In fact some instances remain of use of the letters on the obverse in the Orkhomenian issues but the motifs on the reverse are quite elaborate representations of a whole ear of corn thus doubling the significance of the obverse type.

The early inscribed Orkhomenian coins bear the letter *epsilon* later expanded to *epsilon* + *rho* (the original name of the city was Ἐρχομενός not Ὀρχομενός); thus the place of minting of the corn issues is clear. With the really Boiotian shield series it is the variety of letters seen on the early inscribed pieces that begins to give us some indication of places of minting. On the analogy of the Orkhomenian issues it is always logically assumed that these letters also represent the initial letter(s) of place names and it is this aspect that may be said to begin our (very lacunary) knowledge of the early stages in the development of the Boiotian confederation.

The first inscribed coins of the "Boiotian" shield with the letters in the cut-outs of the shield on the obverse indicate but two names, one with the letter(s) *tau* (or *tau-alpha*), the other with the letter *heta*. Of immediate interest to us here are those that have the letter *tau* once or twice on the obverse; especially is this noticeable in the examples where two letters of *tau* are placed antithetically in the cut-outs on either side of the shield and when there occurs a similar antithetical arrangement of the letters *tau* and *alpha*. These *tau*-coins (or *tau-alpha* coins) have always been taken – quite logically – to represent the city of Tanagra, since it is the only Boiotian city whose name begins with that letter or with those two letters.

If indeed we accept that these characters are the initial letters of city names we can see the immediate logic of assigning those infrequent ones that bear the letter *mu* to the town of Mykalessos since, again, it is the only Boiotian settlement whose name begins with that letter. At the same time, there is a further question that arises for when we first encounter Mykalessos in literary sources it is part of the territory of Tanagra, one of a group of settlements known as the *tetrakomia* of Tanagra (Strabon ix. 405 – ἔστι δὲ τῆς τετρακομίας τῆς περὶ Τάναγραν, Ἐλεῶνος, Ἅρματος, Μυκαλησσοῦ, Φαρῶν). This, in itself, will prompt other thoughts shortly. [There is also, surely, just the possibility that the *mu*, if rotated through 90°, could be seen as a four-bar *sigma*; that might refer to the only Boiotian city whose name begins with that letter – Siphai – though, theoretically at least, Skaphlai in the Parasopia (see below) and Skhoinos at *Mouríki* might be included for consideration. I do not personally set much store by this idea but the question must logically be asked for, since the letter is always in the centre of an incuse square, who is to say which is the top or bottom or sides of this square in order to orientate the letter?]

Apart from *tau* and *mu* we have several other letters appearing: *alpha, heta, theta, qoppa* and *phi*. Continuing with the assumption that each letter represented the initial(s) of the minting city's name, as at Tanagra, Mykalessos and, of course, at separatist Orkhomenos, these letters led to the assignment of their issues to Akraiphiai, Haliartos, Thebai, Koroneia and Pharai respectively. The distribution of minting cities was thus assumed to be as shown on the map (Fig. 6); it is a remarkably uneven distribution within Boiotia. For example the complete absence of any mint across the whole of Southern Boiotia is striking. Then there is a large cluster in the East while the Centre shows but a few minting cities.

When we turn to those coins that bear the letter *heta* (the only one other than the first Tanagran pieces to have the letter, once or twice, on the obverse and subsequently on the reverse) the situation becomes more interesting. These have received more attention than those with the other letters for Etienne and Knoepfler, in their monograph on *Hyéttos de Béotie* (1976: 215–226; cf. their detailed catalogue of many examples on pages 383–390 + 400) examined the question of the archaic pieces with this letter and concluded that they should be assigned to the city of Hyettos, the city remotely positioned in the mountains North of the Kopaïs that was the subject of their own fieldwork and researches at the time. The distribution that this creates is shown on the next

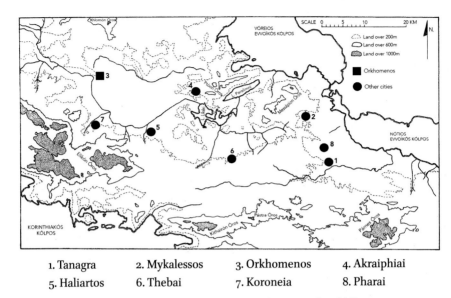

1. Tanagra   2. Mykalessos   3. Orkhomenos   4. Akraiphiai
5. Haliartos 6. Thebai   7. Koroneia   8. Pharai

FIGURE 6   Boiotia: cities minting early coinage according to Head and followers

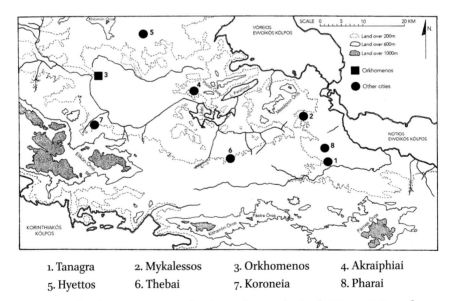

1. Tanagra   2. Mykalessos   3. Orkhomenos   4. Akraiphiai
5. Hyettos   6. Thebai   7. Koroneia   8. Pharai

FIGURE 7   Boiotia: cities minting early coinage after reevaluation by Etienne & Knoepfler

map (Fig. 7); it too has its oddities in that the West is now even more thinly represented while the Eastern cluster remains inviolate.

There is, in addition, a variety of different forms of the letters *heta*, *theta* and possibly *qoppa* that occur on these issues and nobody appears ever to have asked if this variety might not have its meaning; i.e. is it impossible that the different forms, rather than being simply variants used in a meaningless way (as is usually assumed), were deliberately used to distinguish coins issued by different towns whose names happened to begin with the same sound? This question appears not to have been faced by any of Head's successors:

1. Robert J. Buck (1972: 97; summarised also by him in 1979: 111–112) speaking of the anepigraphic issues says "The statement in Herodotus (5. 79) about Thebes and its long-associated allies points to an original membership of Coronea, Haliartus, Thespiae, Tanagra, and Thebes for the military league. It should be these members that struck the earliest League coinage, with shield but no cities specified, about 520 or very shortly before."

2. Jean Ducat (1973: 61–62), although his paper only came out a year later, was able to take the first of Buck's two discussions into consideration. He shows five letters for the first enepigraphic issues, *heta*, *alpha*, *phi*, crossed *theta* and *epsilon* (I leave on one side those with *beta* inside a circle that are usually, not without reason, taken to be panboiotian). He identifies these letters as representing the cities of Akraiphiai ("plus vraisemblement qu'Aulis"), Koroneia, Haliartos, Mykalessos, Pharai (? "L'existence meme de cette cité parait problématique"), Tanagra and Thebai alongside the separate coinage of Orkhomenos. We may repeat his final remark: "Pour Thespies, il n'y aurait pas de monayage archaïque; ce qui étonne, vu l'importance de la cité".

3. Etienne & Knoepfler (1976), as we have just seen, did approach the question of the initial letters but only in so far as concerned *heta*. While they do consider other Boiotian place names with initial aspirate they were primarily interested in possible relevance to the site of Hyettos that was the subject of their own fieldwork and research. Thus, important as it is, their slight opening of the window on these lettered coins leaves us wanting more.

4. Meidani (2008), in a study too often just following previous suggestions unquestioningly, says simply "la constitution de cette confederation dans le dernier quart du VIe siècle serait prouvée par l'émission d'une monnaie dont le type était identique dans cinq cites: à Thèbes, à Coronée, à Hyettos (ou à Haliarte), à Thespies et à Tanagra". One wonders where the coins with *mu*, with *alpha*, with ligatured *alpha-kappa* and with *phi* have been lost and how she is able to list two cities whose names begin with *theta* without any evidence despite the obvious temptation shared by others. [A particular example of how Meidani is removed from knowledge of reality occurs later on the same page: "les Orchoméniens, grâce aux deux ports qui étaient à leur disposition: Larymna et Anthédon,.... avaient la possibilité de constituer un centre d'exportation des produits béotiens"; I have never understood how it could possibly seem logical to

envisage Anthedon as a port for Orkhomenos, except by someone without any knowledge at all of the actual topography of Boiotia and the sort of terrain through which such commerce would have to travel. What is more, one is tempted to ask, if Opountian Larymna is considered a possible port for Orkhomenos, why is not the equally Opountian coastal city of Halai? This is not just a criticism of Meidani but also of the previous scholars whom she follows.]

5. Beck (2014: 34) devotes only about five lines to the meaning of the coins and is essentially referring to the enepigraphic issues. We may quote him in full: "The literary record appears to be supplemented by a large volume of coin emissions that bear the Boeotian shield on the obverse and incuse stamped monograms with the initial of the minting *polis* on the back. Uniformity in weight and style seems to indicate some sort of cooperation between the communities that participate in those emissions." The uniformity of weight implies nothing peculiar to Boiotia since the same "Aiginetan" standard was in wide use, including, for example, almost all of the Peloponnesos (with Korinthos as the sole exception); it is similarity of style that says something about Boiotia but even the identity of the minting communities is omitted from Beck's ultra brief reference.

6. Mackil (2014: 46) publishing in the same volume as Beck, accords a little more space to the early coins of Boiotia. "In this period (*sc.* the late 6th century) the famous 'Boeotian shield coinage' begins to be produced first by Thebes, Tanagra, and Hyettos, followed shortly after by Akraiphia, Koroneia, Mykalessos, and Pharai". She then goes on to doubt the value of this coinage as evidence for political history, but averring that "it is an excellent one for economic history". Nobody will dispute the last part of her statement but regarding her doubt as to the political information to be deduced therefrom she plainly flies in the face of a substantial number of people who have studied the question; she terms it a "cooperative" coinage that signifies a voluntary participation in a process to aid commercial interchange (previously stated at length by her, in collaboration with van Alfen [2006]). In fact the participation of so many areas of the Greek world in use of the same Aiginetan standard, obviously in order to facilitate commercial exchange across all sorts of borders, is really the example of a "cooperative coinage", not the issues by a series of cities in the same geographic and restricted area which are differentiated from those of other cities and areas by use of a particular obverse type proper to them alone, the Boiotian shield. What is more it is difficult to follow her separating out an earlier stage with Tanagra and Hyettos AND Thebes for while *tau* and *heta* find themselves on the obverse in the cut-outs of the

shield, I have yet to see *theta* so placed. We will return to the question of the *heta* coins below.

7. Schachter (1989) returned to his earlier interest in Boiotian coinage when discussing 6th century Boiotia; in a recently published new version of that paper (2016) he specifically reworked the section where he discussed the early coinage of the area and it is to this later version that reference should be now made. In the recent flurry of papers on the early Boiotian League his is the only one to treat the coins in detail. He says "it is assumed" that the anepigraphic coins of the earliest group on Head's classification were minted at Thebai; that this has long been assumed is all too true and may explain the mistake of Mackil just mentioned but the assumption is just that – an assumption without any solid basis. He unquestioningly follows Etienne and Knoepfler's reassignment to Hyettos of the *heta* coins and, of course, accepts the Tanagraian origin of the *tau* and *tau-alpha* issues. He then turns to the second series in the Head scheme saying "the mint marks in Head's second group are to be assigned to Akraiphia or (H)aliartos (A)" [Akraiphiai being a suggestion of Etienne and Knoepfler subsequent to their disposal of the *heta of Haliartos*] "Koroneia (Q) Mykalessos (M), Tanagra (T/TA), Thebes (Θ/ΘΕΒΑ) and Thespiai (Φ)". Although he is again able to refer to Etienne and Knoepfler to justify the assignment to Thespiai of coins marked with what seems, in all truth, to be *phi*. An open mind should perhaps be kept on this latter point; Pharai may be a somewhat elusive Boiotian settlement (cf. Fossey, 1988: 96–98) but there is no reason to disallow the possibility of coins being minted there since there are later coins, dated by Head to c. 387–374 BCE, that bear the Boiotian shield on the obverse and, on the reverse, an amphora with the letters *phi* and *alpha* one to each side.

8. Stephanie Larson (2007: chapter 3) tends to accept a date in the later 6th century for the introduction of Boiotian coinage but she also judiciously quotes the principal scholar on the subject, Kraay (1976: 109), stating that Boiotian shield coins could have been minted "at any time after about 550, but there is little evidence from which to determine the actual date". She also finds the suggested reference to the cult of Herakles by use of the shield motif on the obverse a "possibility". What is more she has underlined the circular nature of much argumentation concerning the dies of earlier stages in the history of Boiotian coinage. Unfortunately she follows unquestioningly Étienne and Knoepfler in assigning the *heta* coins to Hyettos.

It has always been assumed that the many coins bearing *theta* should be assigned to Thebai but we should perhaps remember that two other Boiotian cities had names starting with *theta*: Thespiai and Thisbe. Just because Thebai was later to be frequently the dominant city in the area, often with extensive coinage, why do we necessarily retroject this situation onto a period for which we know so little? Is there, then, any possible significance in the fact that the letter has the internal cross sometimes positioned vertically (i.e. like a St. George's cross) and sometimes in oblique position (i.e. like a St. Andrew's cross)? Obviously the two forms could easily still be confused at first sight but this variation might, nevertheless, have served to distinguish coins with the letter *theta* that had been minted at two separate cities. At the same time, given the independent stance of Thespiai during the Persian Wars at the beginning of the 5th century, it is not difficult to conceive of that city being still independent of Thebai in the 6th and so far free from her expansionist policies, as we shall see might be the situation of Plataiai. By extension this might also have been the status of Thisbe and the rest of South West Boiotia, all of which would be completely isolated from Theban territory and the Eastern plains of Boiotia by the intervening position of precisely Thespiai. At the same time the possibility that the two forms of *theta* were intended to distinguish between issues of Thebai and those of Thespiai or, theoretically at least, Thisbe cannot be summarily discounted though we shall see below that the omission of the latter two would give a comprehensible distribution.

In their monograph on Hyettos, Etienne and Knoepfler (1976: 384–385) show the large variety of forms of the letter *heta* encountered on the coins and argued forcefully for abandoning the old assignation to "Haliartos". Although they prove that "Haliartos" never bore an initial aspirate (*pace* several Roman writers) – apparently rightly though we are faced with the problem of the aspirate indicated by the phrase ποήενθ' Ἀλίαρτον in the Homeric κατάλογος (cf. chapter 1) – and further pointing out that the *heta* coins cannot thus belong to Aliartos (as it should perhaps consequently be written), all this is far from proving that they must have been issued by Hyettos. On the contrary, the same authors also remind us that, in addition to Hyettos, there were several other places in Boiotia whose names began with an aspirate: Hysiai, Hyria, Hyle, Harma and perhaps Heleon (whose initial aspiration they gently question). I am not sure that we have any real reason to retain the candidacy of Hyria, for which I have had to propose identification with an essentially prehistoric site (Fossey, 1988: 75–76). The others, however, merit further consideration.

Hysiai would pose an interesting possible presence in the line-up of candidates for these early coins; as we have just remarked, noticeably missing from that line-up of minting places is any representation from the entire Parasopia of South Boiotia, just as is the South West (Thespiai etc. cf. preceding paragraphs).

While the absence of the best known city of the Parasopia, Plataiai, is indeed striking, it seems that other settlements in the Parasopia, later regarded as more like villages, may have had city status in archaic times (cf. Fossey, 1991: 181–189 for the case of Erythrai, recalling also the case of Skaphlai first signalled by Koumanoúdhis, 1961). Was then Hysiai a city in the Parasopia minting its own coinage and thus filling the gap? Perhaps, but we may remember that the Parasopia was definitely a bone of contention between Thebai (in her attempt to enrol Plataiai and area in her league) and Athenai in late archaic times; it is not illogical to suggest that the South Parasopia might have come rather under Athenian control or influence in archaic times. [We may even note that the present border between the *nomoi* of *Attikí* and *Voiotía* in the same sort of way defies all geographical logic in that it makes a completely strange loop Northwards from the natural boundary constituted by the Kithairón-Pástra mountain range; it does so in order to place that part of the Southern Parasopia that contains *Kriekoúki* (ancient Hysiai quite wrongly now renamed *Erythraí* cf. Fossey, 1988: 112–115) in *Attikí*.]

The question of small independent cities of archaic times in the Parasopia reminds us that something of the same sort seems to have pertained in what would later be the Tanagrike, the territory of Boiotia's major Eastern city, Tanagra (Fossey, 1991: 188–189). That city itself was the product of some early fusion of smaller settlements (ἔτι τῆς Ταναγρικῆς κατὰ κώμας οἰκουμένης; Ploutarkhos, *Ethika* 299c where it appears that two of the villages may have been called Stephon and Poimandria; cf. discussion at Fossey, 1988: 53–56). It is here that we come to two of the other place names with initial aspirate, Harma and Heleon (ἔστι δὲ τῆς τετρακωμίας τῆς περὶ Τάναγραν, Ἐλεῶνος, Ἅρματος, Μυκαλησσοῦ, Φαρῶν; Strabon, ix, 405). Should we now entertain the possibility that, at the time of these early coins the members of what was to be known as the *tetrakomia* of Tanagra were all independent cities each with their own coinage; Mykalessos is already given this status and the fourth member, the elusive Pharai (Fossey, 1988: 96–98), has often been accorded it with the attribution there of the coins bearing the letter(s) *phi* (or *phi+alpha*); indeed Pharai is the only ancient place name known in Boiotia that begins with *phi* (or *phi+alpha*).

What is more, there really is a considerable variety of forms of *heta* (more than shown in the table of Jeffrey, 1961: 89): I count at least eight quite distinct forms in the discussion by Etienne & Knoepfler (1976: 384–385); all have two vertical *hastae* between which cross bars follow very different arrangements, either with three parallel but decidedly *sloping* lines (sloping in either the one direction or the other) or some cases with two, some with three *horizontal* cross bars, or again some with a single crossbar and yet others where *horizontal*

FIGURE 8   Variations on letter *Heta*, taken from Etienne & Knoepfler, 1972: 384–385

top and bottom bars close off an oblong across the centre of which runs a single cross bar (occasionally two parallel cross bars placed close together), again *horizontal*. For the full range of letterforms cf. Fig. 8. This is amply sufficient a variety to accommodate the names of both Harma and Heleon (in addition even to Hyettos and Hyle should that be deemed necessary). It is interesting to note that it is the type of *heta* with the three *sloping* cross bars that occurs, like the *tau* of Tanagra, in the side cuts of the shield in what may be the earliest inscribed issues, leaving the reverse still anepigraphic; this may incline us to see these issues as coming from a town connected with Tanagra such as Harma and perhaps particularly Heleon. It may be that finds during the current excavations by the Canadian Institute at *Dhrítza* (which I identify precisely with Heleon cf. Fossey, 1988: 89–95, an identification that seems to be frequently followed by others) will do something to elucidate this question for it has always been obvious to me that this was a particularly important site throughout antiquity (Fossey, 1988: 460). Since the case of Hyettos has already been dealt with, we may return to the final aspirated candidate, Hyle, shortly.

Pharai is indeed the only known Boiotian place name to begin with the letter *phi* but the site remains elusive and my attempt to identify it with *Áyios Pandeleîmon* (Fossey, 1988: 96–98) could be stronger. If, however, we leave it with the *phi* coins then all members of the *tetrakomia* are possibly of the same status. We have already pointed to the existence of later coins inscribed *phi+alpha*.

There remain the coins marked with *alpha* and with *qoppa*. While it might now seem logical to assign them respectively to Aliartos (the possibly mistaken aspirate being "corrected") and Koroneia thus filling out the South side of the Kopaïs, it is clear that some coins must still be assigned to Akraiphiai since there are those with *alpha* and *kappa* ligatured and the only city whose name begins with that letter combination is indeed Akraiphiai. This then prompts two questions: was the existence of the ligature a deliberate attempt to distinguish between emissions of two cities whose names both began with *alpha* (Aliartos and Akraiphiai?) and why assign the *qoppa* coins to Koroneia when it was not the only Boiotian city whose name could be initialised with that letter for there was also Kopai, a neighbour of Akraiphiai whose candidacy we have just had to approve? If we remove both Aliartos and Koroneia from the list of places minting coins with the "Boiotian" shield we leave the entire South and

THE ORIGINS OF THE BOIOTIAN LEAGUE

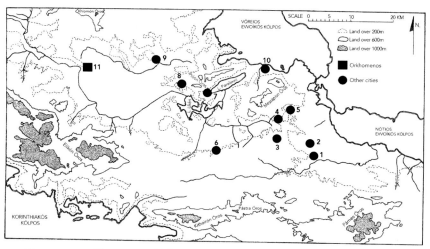

1. Tanagra 2. Pharai 3. Helaion 4. Harma 5. Mykalessos 6. Thebai
7. Hyle (?) 8. Akraiphiai 9. Kopai 10. Anthedon 11. Orkhomenos

FIGURE 9   Boiotia: cities minting early coinage; a new suggestion

West Kopaïs perhaps under the leadership of Orkhomenos, a not illogical situation; at the same time, as we have just seen, it might be possible to envisage both Aliartos and Akraiphiai minting, together with Kopai, thus limiting the blank Kopaic area simply to the Western parts that may be seen even more logically as under Orkhomenian control.

If then we consider giving *alpha-kappa* coins to Akraiphiai and the *qoppa* ones to Kopai they make another small cluster, being connected to Central Boiotia and the Theban area perhaps by the outstanding potential *heta* city, Hyle, that I have identified, for its pre-Hellenistic phases, with the site at *Oúngra* at the South West end of Lake *Paralímni* (Fossey, 1988: 235–244). Finally, if the ligatured *alpha-kappa* is intended to distinguish emissions of Akraiphiai from those some another *alpha* city I would have to express my long-standing surprise that the possibility of seeing Anthedon on the North Boiotian coast as producing its own early coins has never been suggested. Why not? It may, however, seem more convincing to opt for Aliartos.

After all these thoughts and suggestions it may be interesting to survey the distribution of cities that I have either endorsed or suggested as more acceptable candidates for mints. This distribution is shown on the next map (Fig. 9) and it has a remarkable logic to it. The cities in question form a continuous zone from Tanagra, through all the members of her later *tetrakomia*, to the North-Central plains with Thebai and (possibly) Hyle, on to the North East Kopaïs with Akraiphiai and Kopai. This distribution leaves empty the entire zone of South Boiotia from the Parasopia through Thespike and Thisbe (including the smaller cities of Kreusis, Siphai and Khorsiai). There is a similar empty zone encompassing the South and West Kopaïs, although we have outlined a possible solution to this concerning Aliartos; I am less convinced of this so have omitted that city from the map. In the West (or South West) Kopaïs it is possible to envisage the circulation of Orkhomenian coins while, for the South zone, we are constrained to entertain the idea of Athenian control or domination, not impossible or illogical given the stance of the two main towns in that zone (Plataiai and Thespiai) in face of the Medizing by the rest of Boiotia during the Persian invasions.

2   The Early League

If I am at all right in this hypothesis – and I am well aware that many will not be convinced, just as I myself am not convinced of many previous attempts to identify the minting cities of early Boiotian coinage – what might this say about the origins of the Boiotian League?

While the original impetus to cooperation between the Boiotian cities of the South, Centre and East may have been provided by a necessary common resistance to the Thessalian hegemony around the end of the 7th century BCE something must have changed in the 6th century (and presumably before the minting of the earliest coins where no candidate for the city of Koroneia is seen and the case of Aliartos is dubious); as a result there was created a second separate zone in the entire South, in addition to that in the West (and South) Kopaïs. The latter zone of possible Orkhomenian leadership may always have existed, even in the days of the Thessalian domination, but the Southern blank should be something new. We might consider Athenian influence as a very logical cause but must also entertain the possibility that the beginning of Theban attempts at domination lay behind it, those attempts which came to a head in the dispute with Plataiai (519 or 509 BCE; cf. Herodotos vi. 108; Thoukydides iii. 55 & 68; Fossey, 1991: 177). It might even be possible to see in the apparent commemoration of a 6th century Theban victory over Hyettians (cf. discussion by Etienne and Knoepfler, 1976: 215–218) a particular stage – and a more successful one than that over Plataiai – in the Theban attempts at expansion (here at the expense of Orkhomenian authority?). It may thus seem that the parts of Boiotia that Medized in the first two decades of the 5th century BCE could have been those represented in the zone of minting states, according to my previous suggestions.

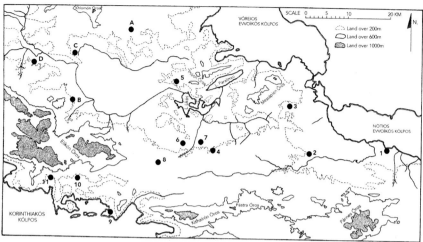

A. Hyettos	B. Mt. Laphystion	C. Near Orkhomenos	D. Khaironeia
1. Oropos	2. Tanagra	3. Mykalessos	4. Thebai	5. Akraiphiai	6. Teneric Plain
7. Near Kabeirion	8. Thespiai	9. Siphai	10. Thisbe	11. Khorsiai

FIGURE 10 Distribution of Herakles cults in Boiotia

3   The Boiotian Shield and the Cult of Herakles

It is interesting to compare the distribution of Herakles cults in Boiotia with those distributions that we have already explored concerning Boiotian *fibulae* and imported Korinthian pottery. This distribution is shown on the map (Fig. 10). It is readily clear that the distribution of Herakles' cults corresponds quite closely to that of the *fibulae* and the Korinthian imports for, with a few outliers, Herakles' cults are attested mostly in the Centre, South and East of Boiotia.

We may look briefly at the four outliers noting that at least two of them are rather peculiar cults of the hero:

A. The one, completely isolated from the rest in the mountains North of the Kopaïs, is attested at Hyettos where he is described as a source of healing, a most unusual rôle for him; his "image" is also unusual – ὄντος οὐχὶ ἀγάλματος σὺν τέχνῃ, λίθου δὲ ἀργοῦ κατὰ τὸ ἀρχαῖον (Pausanias ix. 24, 3; N.B. the late Hellenistic inscription, SEG xxvi 524, cited by Schachter, 1986: 2 does not specifically mention Herakles);

B. A second, with the epithet Χάροψ, is attested high up on Mount Laphystion between Koroneia and Lebadeia, on a spot where οἱ δὲ Βοιωτοὶ λέγουσιν ἀναβῆναι τὸν Ἡρακλέα ἄγοντα τοῦ Ἅιδου τὸν κύνα (Pausanias ix. 34, 5) and where a late 3rd century BCE series of slave manumissions by consecration to the hero were recorded (cf. discussion by Schachter, 1986: 3–10; Darmezin, 1999: nos. 122–135), yet another unusual function for Herakles;

C. Little is known of the third sanctuary a very short distance West-North-West of Orkhomenos except that its cult image was small (Pausanias ix. 38, 6 cf. Schachter, 1986: 10–11) although a possible candidate for it may have been found by excavation (de Ridder, 1895: 150–155, 160 ff.; cf. the convenient summary by Frazer, 1913: 193–194);

D. Even less is known about the fourth; at Khaironeia a single inscription (*IG*vii 3416 – now lost but apparently of Roman date) attests a cult of Herakles under the epithet Apalexikakos otherwise unknown in Boiotia and a Herakleion associated with the battle of 338 BCE is mentioned by the local writer Ploutarkhos (*Demosthenes* 854D–E cf. Schachter, 1986: 2).

The set of Herakles' cults in South, Central and Eastern Boiotia presents a much longer list:

1. Oropos (possibly at the city itself as shown by a single votive inscription, *IG*vii 436, of perhaps Hellenistic or early imperial times and certainly at the Amphiaraion as recorded by Pausanias i. 34, 3 in Roman times [Schachter, 1986: 11]);
2. Tanagra, identified by inscribed votive vases of Archaic and later date found in a votive pit located in one of the ancient cemeteries (Schachter, 1986: 12; Andhreioménou, 2007: 31–43);
3. Mykalessos with Herakles as an Idaian dactyl, supposedly responsible for closing the temple of Mykalessian Demeter every night and reopening it on the morrow, attested to only by Pausanias (ix. 19, 5 & 27, 8) and with no indication of earlier dating (such an association is occasionally attested at other locations in Greece [cf. Farnell, 1920: 124–131, esp. 128] but never is it seen elsewhere in Boiotia);
4. Thebai itself, home to the traditions of the hero's birth and youth, housed a major sanctuary in his honour, frequently attested, including a reference to it by the Theban poet Pindaros (*Isthmian* iv. 61) that seems to infer a long history (Schachter, 1986: 14–30); the site has recently been discovered and partly excavated at the South East edge of the city but is not yet completely published (cf. beginning of chapter 12);
5. Akraiphiai, in fact attested only in early imperial times by two inscriptions (cf. Schachter, 1986: 1 – he lists three inscriptions but one, *IG*vii 2736, is erroneous);
6. Another place where the cult was observed with the epithet "Rhinokoloustes" lay in the open between Thebai and the Kabeirion and here, as in the following case, the aitiology suggests a long history (Pausanias ix. 25, 4);

7. A further location also not yet precisely identified is described as a large sanctuary of Herakles with another intriguing epithet – "Ἱπποδέτης" – in the Western Teneric Plain and thus near to the Kabeirion (Pausanias ix. 26, 1) where the association with the early Orkhomenian-Theban conflict may suggest a history reaching quite far back in time (cf. Farnell, 1920: 147);

8. Thespiai observed a cult of Herakles that is again richly attested at least as far back as the earlier 5th century BCE (cf. detailed account by Schachter, 1986: 31–36);

9. Siphai/Tipha was always a small city where the Herakleion was the only thing noticed by Pausanias (ix. 32, 2, very brief: Ἡρακλεῖόν τε Τιφαιεῦσίν ἐστι καὶ ἑορτὴν ἄγουσιν ἐπέτειον); it might possibly be located at the small Roman temple in Korinthian order noticed in 1968 at the South end of the beach at *Aliki* (Fossey, 1988: 170 & 173, just a tentative suggestion), remains which now seem to have disappeared;

10. Thisbe had a sanctuary of Herakles and celebrated an associated festival but this is only attested briefly by Pausanias (ix. 32, 2) and by one probably Hellenistic inscription associating Herakles with Hermes (*IG* vii 2235; cf. Schachter, 1986: 37 who also refers to another inscription, *IG* vii 2359 which he takes to refer to a virgin priestess of the cult but the inscription bearing that number is completely different and I could not locate any text that would correspond to his indication);

11. Khorsiai had a small temple whose identification with a Herakleion is assured by a votive graffito found in it during our excavations of 1983 (Fossey, 1986a: 128); this building, which dates from Archaic times according to other votive material found within it, is not attested in other epigraphic or literary sources. Like the temple of the Hero Ptoios near Akraiphiai this temple is not only small but aperipteral and with only a single axial colonnade in the interior suggesting that this might be a typical plan for a Boiotian temple to a hero.

[To the preceding list Schachter (1986: 11–12) would suggest adding just possibly Plataiai and the Ptoion; this is very uncertain and no dating is available. Accordingly these two vague suggestions are not convincing and thus are omitted from our map, Fig. 10. In any case, at least where the Ptoion is concerned the fact that the cult existed close-by, at the main city of the area, Akraiphiai, means that nothing significant would be added to the distribution by including this suggestion on the map.]

From the preceding it is obvious that a goodly number of the South-Centre-East group of Herakles cults can be seen to have an early date in at least Archaic times (Tanagra, Thebai, Thespiai and Khorsiai) or in times relating to the traditions of an even earlier situation (the two sites toward the Teneric plain and the Kabeirion). This does invite consideration in the context of the growth of the Boiotian confederation, especially in view, not only of the distributions of imported Korinthian pottery and the incidence of incised *fibulae*, but also of the indications that the earlier Boiotian coinage – whatever its exact date within the 6th century – is most at home in East and Central Boiotia.

There seems to have long been a rivalry between Orkhomenos (with the Kopaïc area?) and Thebai (with much of Eastern, Central and Southern Boiotia?) to the context of which two of the cults in the second list are attached (nos. 6 & 7). It is possible to see reasons for suggesting that one stage in this rivalry may have been terminated towards the very end of the Bronze Age when a breakdown in the drainage system in the Kopaïc basin led to the reflooding of much of the otherwise rich agricultural land on which Orkhomenos and the other cities of that basin would depend for their cultivation (Fossey, 1990: chapter 6). The rich agricultural value of the Kopaïc plain may very well be responsible for the Orkhomenian choice of the grain or the ear of corn as the symbols on its coinage. A rôle in bringing about the Kopaïc reflooding was attributed mythologically to Theban Herakles who supposedly blocked the *katavóthres* to which the waters of the inflowing rivers were channelled around the periphery of the plain and by which they were drained to the sea and possibly to the neighbouring lakes *Paralímni* and *Likéri* (cf. discussion in Fossey, 1990: 86–87; the effect of such flooding is also discussed on the preceding pages, 60–66). As we have seen, a division of Boiotia into two parts, the Kopaïs on the one hand and, on the other, the Eastern, Central and Southern plains may reflect also a reality of archaic times in the context of the Thessalian hegemony (chapter 3).

Is it possible that the involvements of Herakles may explain the symbolism of the Boiotian shield? Perhaps it is no coincidence that one of the works in the Hesiodic *corpus*, with its clearly Boiotian connection, is that called "Ἀσπις", a poem perhaps dating to the early 6th century BCE, of which the main part (lines 139–317) is a description of the shield of Herakles in the context of his battle with Kyknos. This description, obviously intended as an epic parallel for the description of the shield of Akhilleus in the *Ilias* (xviii, 478–608), makes reference (lines 270–272) to a city with seven gates, in itself a fairly clear allusion to Thebai, thus reinforcing the Boiotian connection.

4   The Parasopia Revisited

The events of 519 BCE (or 509? cf. How & Wells, 1958: 2, 109–110), as recorded by Herodotos (vi, 108), tell of an attempt by the Thebans to bring the Plataians under their leadership – πιεζεύμενοι ὑπὸ Θηβαίων οἱ Πλαταιέες ("the Plataians being hard-pressed by the Thebans") – a face-off between Athenian troops supporting Plataiai and a Theban force send in reaction to the Plataian submission to Athenai was arbitrated by some Korinthians who οὔρισαν τὴν χώραν ἐπὶ τοισίδε, ἐὰν Θηβαίους Βοιωτῶν τοὺς μὴ βουλομένους ἐς Βοιωτοὺς τελέειν ("divided up the area with the condition that the Thebans should leave alone those Boiotians who did not wish to join a common Boiotian entity"). The Korinthians then departed and the Athenians started to set out for home when they were attacked by the Boiotians [i.e. Thebans] whom they defeated; as a result the Athenians took further action: ὑπερβάντες δὲ οἱ Ἀθηναῖοι τοὺς οἱ Κορίνθιοι ἔθηκαν Πλαταιεῦσι εἶναι, τούτους ὑπερβάντες τὸν Ἀσωπὸν αὐτὸν ἐποιήσαντο οὖρον Θηβαίοισι πρὸς Πλαταιέας εἶναι καὶ Ὑσιάς ("the Athenians, having crossed the boundary which the Korinthians had established for the Plataians, they set up the Asopos as the boundary of the Thebans in the direction of Plataiai and Hysiai").

It is worth noting that Herodotos specifies that the Asopos was established as the boundary for the people of Plataiai *and* those of Hysiai making clear the independence of the latter. In this connection we may remember that there are indications that Erythrai also in the Southern Parasopia was independent around 500 BCE (Fossey, 1991: 181–189, *EB*i 78) and that yet another settlement of the Parasopia was independent within the living memory of expatriots buried at Eleusis during the 4th century BCE. The last mentioned settlement bore a name with variant spellings Skaphe/Skaphle/Skarphe; we do not know very much about this place except that it was earlier called Eteonos, that it was situated on a hill *and* that it was in the Parasopia (Fossey, 1988: 130–131). In view of the similarity of the cases of independence of Plataiai, Hysiai and Erythrai I am tempted to hesitate before looking further for Skaphle in the Northern Parasopia and to suggest that it too may have lain South of the Asopos though there appears to be no candidate there to suggest itself; at least none has yet been noticed.

From time to time scholars have considered a certain fragment of the 4th century BCE historian Ephoros of Kyme preserved in the writings attributed to the 4th century CE grammarian Ammonios of Alexandria (*on the Difference of Similar Words s.v. Θηβαῖοι καὶ Θηβαγενεῖς*), and what they feel this fragment may tell us of the position of the Southern Parasopia in Archaic times. The passage reads as follows:

Θηβαῖοι καὶ Θηβαγενεῖς διαφέρουσιν, καθὼς Δίδυμος ἐν ὑπομνήματι τῶι πρώτωι τῶν Παιάνων Πινδάρου φησίν· "καὶ τὸν τρίποδα ἀπὸ τούτου Θηβαγενεῖς πέμπουσιν τὸν χρύσεον εἰς Ἰσμηνίου πρῶτον". Τίς δ' ἐστι διαφρορά Θηβαγενέων πρὸς Θηβαίους, Ἔφορος ἐν τῆι δευτέραι φησί· "οὗτοι μὲν οὖν συνετάχθησαν εἰς τὴν Βοιωτίαν· τοὺς δὲ τοῖς Ἀθηναίοις ὁμόρους προσοικοῦντας ἰδίαι Θηβαῖοι προσηγάγοντο πολλοῖς ἔτεσιν ὕστερον, (δέ) οἳ σύμμικτοι ἦσαν πολλαχόθεν, ἐνέμοντο δὲ τὴν ὑπὸ Κιθαιρῶνα χώραν καὶ τὴν ἀπεναντίον τῆς Εὐβοίας, ἐκαλοῦντο δὲ Θηβαγενεῖς, ὅτι προσεγένοντο τοῖς ἄλλοις Βοιωτοῖς διὰ Θηβαίων".

Thebans and Thebageneis are different, as Didymos says in his commentary on the first Paian of Pindaros: "for this reason the Thebageneis send the golden tripod first to the sanctuary of Ismenian (Apollon)." What then is it that makes the Thebageneis different from the Thebans? Ephoros in his second book writes "these were, therefore, incorporated into the Boiotians and many years later the Thebans in particular pulled in those who lived close to the borders of the Athenians; they were a mixed group deriving from many parts who inhabited the land along the foot of Kithairon and the country opposite Euboia and they were called Thebageneis because their incorporation with the other Boiotians had been brought about by the Thebans."

Although we have the text of what has been identified as the first Paian of the Theban poet it is difficult to understand what point in it would have called for a comment of this sort other than the general mentions of Apollon and Thebai.

Pindaros' eleventh Pythian Ode, was written for the young Theban sprinter Thrasydaios who had won the race of his class in the games at Delphoi in 474 BCE. At the beginning of the ode the poet addresses the daughters of Kadmos, Semele and Ino:

ἴτε σὺν Ἡρακλέος ἀριστογόνῳ
ματρὶ πὰρ Μελίαν χρυσέων ἐς ἄδυτον τριπόδων
θησαυρόν, ὃν περίαλλ᾽ ἐτίμασε Λοξίας
Ἰσμήνιον δ᾽ ὀνύμαξεν, ἀλαθέα μαντίων θῶκον
PYTHIAN X. 3–6

come with Herakles' mother of noble birth
to Melia and the inner chamber with the golden
tripods that which Loxias honoured above all others
and named the Ismenion, seat of unerring prophecies

The old skholion on this passage comments on its meaning:

ἴτε εἰς τὸν ἄδυτον, ὅς ἐστι χρυσέων τριπόδων θησαυρός.
πυκνῶς δὲ τίθησιν ὁ Πίνδαρος κατὰ τὸ ἀρσενικὸν τὸν ἄδυτον.

προσκαλεῖται δὲ τὰς Θήβησιν ἡρωΐδας εἰς τὸ Ἰσμήνιον ἥκειν,
ἐν ᾧ τὸ τοῦ Τηνέρου ἱερόν ἐστι χρηστήριον. τριπόδων δὲ εἶπε
θησαυρὸν τὸ Ἰσμήνιον διὰ τὸ αὐτόθε πολλοὺς ἀνακεῖσθαι
τριπόδας· οἱ γὰρ Θηβαγενεῖς ἐτριποδοφόρουν ἐκεῖσε.

*Go to the adyton that is a treasury of golden tripods.
Frequently Pindaros treats "adyton" as masculine.
He invites the heroines at Thebai to go to the Ismenion,
where the sanctuary of Teneros is an oracle. He called the Ismenion
a treasury of tripods because there many tripods are deposited,
for there the Thebageneis would carry their tripod.*[1]

The Thebageneis are briefly mentioned by Diodoros (xix. 53, 4) in a mythical context:

μετὰ γὰρ τὸν ἐπὶ Δευκαλίωνος κατακλυσμὸν Κάδμου κτίσαντος τὴν ἀπ' αὐτοῦ προσαγορευθεῖσαν Καδμείαν συνῆλθεν ἐπ' αὐτὴν λαὸς ὅν τινὲς μὲν Σπαρτὸν προσηγόρευσαν διὰ τὸ πανταχόθεν συναχθῆναι, τινὲς δὲ Θηβαγενῆ διὰ τὸ τὴν ἀρχὴν ἐκ τῆς προειρημένης πόλεως ὄντα διὰ τὸν κατακλυσμὸν ἐκπεσεῖν καὶ διασπαρῆναι.

After the flood of the time of Deukalion when Kadmos was building the city which was named after him people came to join him there; by some they are called Spartoi since they had been gathered together from all over, by others (they are called) Thebageneis because they, although originally from the aforementioned city, had been driven out by the flood and scattered.

The late R.J. Buck (1979: 80) wrote: "In eastern Boeotia the distinction between the Thebaioi and the Thebageneis shows that some of the older inhabitants remained in some way segregated from and in a status subordinate to the new comers; these distinctions were still felt in the fifth century". 20 pages later he again refers briefly to this question: "Inhabitants of Boeotia who were not of Boeotian stock had, it seems, not too pleasant a time, if one may draw an inference from the Theban attitude towards *Thebageneis* as opposed to *Thebaioi*. These inhabitants would include the Ionic speakers of the Asopos valley and probably the Thracian groups on Helicon. They were not a class like the helots, but they were at the worst perioeci, at the best independent". It has always seemed to me that my late friend was reaching too far in this interpretation.

---

[1] Here, as elsewhere in this book, I avoid translating *adyton* (cf. Hollinshead, 1999).

Because of the role of the tripod Nassos Papalexandrou (2005: 41) was led to comment rather more fully: "The basic structure of this motif informs a Boiotian ritual, the performance of which actualized values of territorial sovereignty. Known as the *tripodephoria* of the Thebageneis ('the carrying of the tripod by the Theban-born'), this rite features once again the tripod, which is of pivotal importance as an explanans of its motivation [footnote with reference to the first Paian of Pindaros and Wilamowitz' argument that the principal theme of the paian was the aition of the *tripodephoria* of the Thebageneis]. The principal *dromenon* of this rite focused on the ceremonial transference and deposition of a tripod by the Thebageneis to the sanctuary of Apollon Ismenios at Thebes. It is known from Ephoros that the Thebageneis were a racially mixed group of people who inhabited the borderland between Boiotia and Attica along the Asopos river [*FGrH* 70 F 21 – see above]. They were originally independent but at some point they were annexed by the Thebans as part of the Boiotian League. The ancient sources do not contain any indications regarding the date of the annexation of the Thebageneis, but the fact that the theme was treated by Pindar suggests that the custom had been well established by his time. The transference of material and symbolic value in the form of a tripod from the annexed territory to Thebes by the Thebageneis amounted to no less than a ritually endorsed transposition of their spiritual and political autonomy – a public affirmation of their dependent status. By depositing a tripod in Thebes and not in a local sanctuary, these marginal elements acknowledged Thebes as the core of their existence".

Returning three years later to the subject of tripods and Boiotia Papalexandrou (2008) gives an account of the history of the artefact type in Boiotia from the 7th century BCE to the Roman imperial period. He outlines the importance of these objects in a religious context as reflections of the status of the dedicants, whether they were dedicated by individuals as symbolising prestige and social status or by communities as collective gestures affirming their own territorial definition of themselves. He also stresses the costly nature of these objects, calling them "expensive, monumental constructions" in terms of their materials and size, combining poros stone with bronze. He looks further at the question of the Thebageneis where he summarises the limited evidence presented here above concerning them and their taking a tripod to the sanctuary of Ismenian Apollon which he compares to the *tripodephoria* of the Thebans to Dodona. He admits that the two cases are opposites but are they? The carrying of a tripod to the Ismenion from the South Parasopia is a short distance while transporting one from Thebai to Dodona is an altogether different undertaking; at the same time if there is any similarity between the two stories it must mean that, just as it was the Theban body civic that went to Epeiros there should have been some sort of collectivity to the Thebageneis and this is perhaps further indicated by the specification that the tripod that went to the Ismenion was made of gold, a rare, precious and costly material in a country that itself had no natural sources for it. Surely a community, however spread out, that could expend this sort of effort and did so apparently more than once if we take into account the imperfective meaning of ἐτριποδοφόρου suggesting that this may have been a not infrequent act. Schachter (1981: 83) suggests in fact that this may have been a regular ritual but then supposes that it was "performed in recognition of the hegemony of Thebes". Again the fixation with an act of subservience to Thebai that Papalexandrou (2008: 268) has termed as dramatizing "the political surrender of the Thebageneis to the authority of Thebes".

Francis Vian (1963: 197 + n. 3) many years earlier in tracing the myth of Lykos and Nykteus concluded that there is reason to see them as the Thebageneis. The most telling phrase in his brief discussion is "mais quelle valeur historique faut-il accorder à ce texte?". If it means anything this is not clear despite the use made of the story to promote a particular view of Theban expansion. Papalexandrou (2008: 267 n. 56) writes that "in Theban propaganda, the origins and ethnic constitution of the Thebageneis fluctuated in the 5th and 4th centuries BC, reflecting the political interests of Thebes as leader of Boiotia". This is surely an exaggeration since the only sources we have are Didymos and Ephoros both dating apparently to the 4th century if we remember that their words are preserved for us by Ammonios a fellow writer of approximately the same date. What do we know of the situation in the 5th century BCE? Nothing really.

I do not see anything in the very few ancient sources that we have which supports the idea of a forceful take-over of the Thebageneis by the Thebans. Since Papalexandrou has been at pains to demonstrate a territorial or identity significance in the dedication of tripods why can we not imagine for a moment the existence of a group of people scattered along the South side of the Asopos who considered themselves "expatriots" of Thebai and who stressed their Theban origin by regular dedication of valuable tripods in a sanctuary of Thebai precisely thus reminding the rest of the world (and even themselves) of their Theban heritage? In the phrase attributed to Didymos by Ammonios the verb προσηγάγοντο could mean simply that the Thebans, many years after others συνετάχθησαν εἰς τὴν Βοιωτίαν, accorded a welcome to the Thebageneis thus acknowledging their claims to Theban origin; the persistence of the latter and thus their tripod dedications may thus have borne fruit.

While it might be tempting to put the incident of the Thebageneis in the context of the formation of the Boiotian federation it is difficult to do so. In the first place there is no clear way of knowing when this event occurred. Secondly if the Thebageneis were so spread out that they were to be found all the way from Kithairon to the Oropia they were not the same sort of territory as the other settlements of the South Parasopia. Thirdly the mere facts that they claimed a Theban origin and that it was supposedly the Thebans who "led" them into Boiotia despite any propinquity suggests a different situation where the Thebageneis can be envisaged as expatriot Thebans who were spread across a long strip of land; there they may have lived mixed in with other peoples such as the inhabitants of Erythrai but who had a particular sense of unity sufficient to undertake the traditional act concerning the tripods. In addition to that sense of unity they had to have sufficient resources to be able to afford for the tripods to be of gold. It may be that this mix with other populations that can account for the word σύμμικτοι in the all too brief account we have of them.

The situation resembles a little that of the Poseidonians according to a the mid-4th century BCE philosopher Aristoxenos of Taras as recorded by Athenaios of Naukratis writing over half a millennium later in the late 2nd or early 3rd century CE:

> διόπερ Ἀριστόξενος ἐν τοῖς Συμμίκτοις Συμποτικοῖς ὅμοιον, φησί, ποιοῦμεν Ποσειδωνιάταις τοῖς ἐν τῷ Τυρσηνικῷ κόλπῳ κατοικοῦσιν, οἷς συνέβη τὰ μὲν ἐξ ἀρχῆς Ἕλλησιν οὖσιν ἐκβεβαρβαρῶσθαι Τυρρηνοῖς ἢ Ῥωμαίοις γεγονόσι, καὶ τήν τε φωνὴν μεταβεβληκέναι τά τε λοιπὰ τῶν ἐπιτηδευμάτων, ἄγειν δὲ μίαν τινὰ αὐτοὺς τῶν ἑορτῶν τῶν Ἑλληνικῶν ἔτι καὶ νῦν, ἐν ᾗ συνιόντες ἀναμιμνῄσκονται τῶν ἀρχαίων ἐκείνων ὀνομάτων τε καὶ νομίμων καὶ ἀπολοφυράμενοι πρὸς ἀλλήλους καὶ ἀποδακρύσαντες ἀπέρχονται.
>
> ATHENAIOS, *deipnosophistai* xiv.632a

> *Thus, in his* Drinking Medley *Aristoxenos says "We are behaving like the people of Poseidonia who live on the Tyrrhenian Gulf, to whom it happened, despite their being originally Greeks, that they were completely barbarized becoming Tuscans or Romans and that their speech was changed together with their other habits. Yet, to this day, they celebrate a certain one of the Greek festivals at which they gather together and recall those ancient words and customs; then, having grieved and wept in company they leave for home."*

The situation so described could find parallels with the cases of many immigrant groups particularly into English-speaking countries where they lose their language by the third generation though sometimes retaining rather longer other aspects of their origins (especially religion) although these too die out as a result of intermarriage and other social mixings. The Poseidonians and the Thebageneis have in common that both are said to have lived among other peoples and thus to have lost much of their identity but both maintained one traditional institution; in the case of the Poseidonians it was a particular (but unspecified in the sources) festival while the Thebageneis kept their tradition of the *tripodephoria* to the Ismenion. In both cases the preserved institution served to underline their origins

5   Summary

At the end of this somewhat disjointed discussion what emerges potentially? Starting from the preceding examination of the phenomenon of the "Two Boiotias" we arrive at the picture of a division of the territory between the Orkhomenos-dominated Kopaïs and the plains to East and South, two zones that seem to be quite distinct in much of the 7th century BCE, a separation that may have decreased gradually in the last quarter of that century before the attempt of the Thessalians to extend their control from North West Boiotia (the Kopaïs) into the main plains was curtailed at the battle of Keressos in the very late 7th/early 6th century.

The defeat of the Thessalians may have involved a concerted effort by several of the Boiotian cities of the South, Central and Eastern plains but by a time somewhat later in the 6th century a reduced alignment seems suggested by the distribution of Herakles cults, especially if we accept the possibility that the Boiotian shield of the earliest confederacy's coinage may draw its inspiration from the shield of Herakles, harking back to the time when Herakles, in myth, was the supporter of Thebai and the plains against the pressure of the Orkhomenian Kopaïs. If this construction is at all correct the earliest confederation seems to have been centred in the Eastern plains, especially at Tanagra and the members of its *tetrakomion*, with Thebai and possibly a region to her North West being outliers of the kernel. The beginning of a separatist area in the South Parasopia and South West Boiotia was to lead to the resistance of Plataiai and Thespiai to attempts by Thebai to enrol them in the federation of which Thebai had, in the meantime, begun to try to take over control. The climax of the push onto the South Parasopia came in either 519 or 509 BCE with the battle between the Boiotians and the Athenians over Plataiai (Herodotos vi. 108: Thoukydides iii. 55 and 68). Here the Thebans lost and Plataiai retained her independence. We may wonder whether the absence of any indication about attentions to Thespiai at this time does not simply imply that the

Theban drive was already curtailed by the defeat at the hands of the Athenians and that Thespiai was accordingly spared such attention; however that may be, certain it is that in 480 BCE both Plataiai and Thespiai refused to follow the Medizing line of Thebai and the rest of Boiotia in the Second Persian War.

A defeat of people from Hyettos somewhere in the later 6th century indicated by a Theban dedication at Olympia (cf. Etienne & Knoepfler, 1976: 215–218 with reference to *Olympia-Bericht* viii [1967] 99, fig. 34.2 – "Θεβαῖοι τὸν Ηυετίον") might reflect a push North West by Thebai and the Boiotians of the plains; since the transitional position we have previously remarked (in terms of Korinthian imports, cf. preceding chapter) for the area of the lakes and Akraiphiai – and possibly Kopai – shows that, by around the middle of the 7th century and thus well before Keressos, the North East corner of the Kopaïs was already part of the Boiotia of the plains rather than belonging with the Western (Orkhomenian) zone; this might then have been a logical point of departure, something like a century later, for a push into the mountains North of the Kopaïs in an attempt to curb the strength of the continuing independence of Orkhomenos and thus to extend the control of the Boiotian confederacy. It may be that such an apparently successful campaign in the North West, if it occurred (shortly?) before the struggle between Thebai and Athenai over Plataiai (dating the dedication at Olympia by letter forms is hardly more accurate than suggesting simply the later 6th century), encouraged further adventures of this sort until the defeat over Plataiai. Thus the Olympia dedication would fit the most conveniently into the third quarter of the 6th century. [We should, of course, be wary of assuming that the battle – or skirmish or whatever it was – from which came the material dedicated at Olympia was necessarily fought just in the mountains North of the Kopaïs; we have no reason to exclude the possibility that a troop of Hyettians was part of some other army (e.g. Orkhomenian?) that met a Theban force on a field of battle elsewhere.]

The possible case of Hyettos and certainly that of Plataiai, together with the stance of Orkhomenos during the Persian invasions, shows, at least, that the process of creating a unified Boiotian federal state was not complete by the beginning of the 5th century BCE. Several steps in that direction had, however, been made and the early coinage, whatever its exact date of inception in the 6th century, shows perhaps the beginnings of the federation in the Eastern Boiotian plains extending through Thebai to the North East Kopaïs. I must stress again the simple fact that, whatever the dating of the earliest Boiotian coinage it can only testify to the *existence*, not to the *beginning* of the federation at that point in time.

6   "Cooperative Coinage"

Before leaving completely the question of the origins of the Boiotian League it is necessary to return briefly to the early coinage and another interpretation. Mackil and van Alfen (2006) coined (pun intended!) the expression "Cooperative Coinage", a concept they examined particularly in connection with Boiotia (pages 226–231) and Akhaia (231–235). It is, of course, to the former that we turn our attention.

We may remark some possible correctives needed in their "review in broad outlines (of) the main stages in the historical development of the Boiotians' cooperative coinage".

For the earliest stage which they date in the last quarter of the sixth century they state that three *poleis* began issuing silver coins with a cut out shield on the obverse and an incuse punch on the reverse; the three places in question are Thebai, Tanagra and Hyettos (or possibly Haliartos) and at this stage it is said that "the first letters of the *polis* responsible for each issue appear on the obverse in the shield cut-outs. We have seen above that there do not appear to be any coins with the letter *theta* for Thebai occurring in cut-outs, only *tau* and *heta* for Tanagra and "Hyettos". It seems to be merely an assumption that attributes the very early, completely anepigraphic Boiotian issues to Thebai, as we have already said. Hyettos is a different matter: had Etienne and Knoepfler not excavated at Hyettos it is doubtful that anyone would have considered proposing that the *heta* coins were minted by that small and isolated city in the mountains North of the Kopaïs. Again Mackil and van Alfen follow the traditional outline in saying that the second stage soon saw four more *poleis* – Akraiphiai, Koroneia, Mykalessos and Pharai – minting coins; at this stage the initial letter was transferred to the centre of the incuse punch on the reverse. We have previously pointed out that the attributions to Akraiphiai and Koroneia are open to question; only Mykalessos and the enigmatic Pharai do not provoke such doubts. This stage Mackil and van Alfen feel runs to the middle of the 5th century and there we may leave the story since we have no reason to doubt that by then there was really some sort of Boiotian union.

Mackil and van Alfen seem impressed by the fact that, although they minted on the same standard each city declared its independent role by the use of initial letters. If we, once again turn to the European Union we can find a good parallel, in that most member countries strike coins of the same values but independently. Thus Euro coins originally minted in France, Germany or Greece etc., and clearly identified as being produced there, circulate alongside each other with exactly the same value everywhere in the territory of the EU.

So there is no surprise to be felt about the same sort of situation in ancient federated states. Their other surprise was that "there appears to have been no arrangement for specialization by particular *poleis* in the minting of particular denominations". This is, of course, *argumentum a silentio* since in all of such matters we depend on what has actually come to hand. It is a fair estimate that for every example of a particular coin issue there are probably enormous numbers of parallel pieces still underground. The sample we have is too small to be statistically significant. A further thought on this is that, since a goodly number of such coins as we do have come from funerary contexts we should expect a much larger representation of the small coins, obols and divisions thereof, since there does appear to be some reality behind the history of the obol as the fee for Kharon. The vagaries of coin representation were brought home to me with my excavations at *Khóstia*/Khorsiai where, despite wide sampling of different parts of the site, we found virtually no coins at all. In chapter 12 we shall look at a series of coins from *Thíva* and will see that it is indeed only small denominations that are represented.

CHAPTER 5

Early Boiotian Temples

My programme of fieldwork in Boiotia in the later 1960's and the 1970's led to the recognition of a small number of hitherto unknown ancient religious sites.[1] Comparison of these sites with each other and with a few other sites known more or less imperfectly from excavations permits some general considerations of Boiotian temple architecture to be outlined here. Unfortunately no structural remains, except for the ash-altar, have yet been found at the recently discovered sanctuary of Herakles at Thebai (cf. beginning of chapter 12) so we do not know how things functioned; architectural fragments attest to the existence of buildings and two possible temples have been suggested as well as place for celebration of the games to Iolaos. Similarly the sanctuary of the same hero found during our excavations at *Khóstia* awaits publication in the series of volumes devoted to that project. As a result we still have only one published temple clearly dedicated to a hero in Boiotia, that of the hero Ptoios near to Akraiphiai; it appears to have similarities with our *Khóstia* heroon in that both are small aperipteral buildings with only a single axial colonnade inside. In conclusion, for the present we can only consider here temples apparently dedicated to deities although the actual dedications of the temples presented is not sure in some cases.

1   *Oúngra*

The most striking of these new temples is that at *Oúngra* at the South West end of Lake *Paralímni*. A surprising drop in the level of the lake's water during 1965 and 1966 revealed the traces of a whole sunken ancient town. Publication of this site as a whole was planned in 1966 by Sarántis Symeónoglou and myself; this, however, was never realized and a few years later "investigations" were carried out there by Th. Spyrópoulos (1971) but – as usual – not properly published. In the meanwhile I published an account of the site in general, including a brief mention of the temple (Fossey, 1988: 235–238). I there argued

---

1 A preliminary version of this paper was presented to the December 1970 annual meeting of the Archaeological Institute of America in New York. In that version I used frequently the word "adyton"; here the word has been replaced with "inner room" in view of the evidence that "adyton" could be used for a multiplicity of purposes and locations (Hollinshead, 1999).

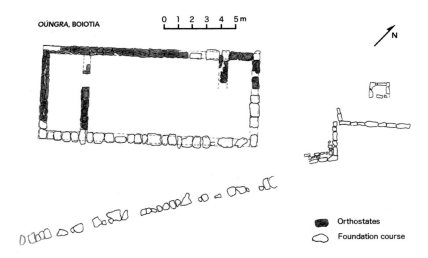

FIGURE 11 *Oúngra*: temple plan

that the site at *Oúngra* should represent the original location of the town of Hyle that was abandoned apparently in the later 4th century BCE according to the surface finds; possibly this could have occurred in the situation of *stasis* prevailing among (some) Boiotian cities at the time of Alexandros the Great (Strabon ix. 407). The town seems then to have moved to the more isolated and thus perhaps more defensible nearby site of *Klimatariaí* on the North side of the neighbouring Lake *Paralímni* (Fossey, 1988: 238–243). The *Oúngra* site surrounds what was always the Western end of the lake and has a very high akropolis hill near its Easterly extremity on the North side of the lake, where the peak of *Khelonókastro* dominates the whole area. On the much lower hills at the East end of the site on the South side of the lake, and even at the lower edge of their slopes right by the lake, is a cemetery of Archaic date. More tombs (apparently robbed) lie at the foot of *Khelonókastro* just beyond what seemed to be a circuit wall through which passed a road leading Eastwards out of the city and coming from the temple along the South side of which it ran.

Much of the plan of the temple (Fig. 11) was clearly discernible even among the large stones surrounding it, result of the fact that, for a good part of a century it had been a lake bed after the draining of the adjacent lake Kopaïs (Pl. 3). The plan is that of an aperipteral temple with *pronaos*, *cella* and *inner room*. The building, orientated roughly East-West and with its *pronaos* to the East, measures 15.21 × 6.43; the *pronaos* is 1.80 deep, while the *inner room* at the other end is 2.40. Thickness of the walls is 0.50 and the very well preserved North wall, in fine masonry, has an evenly levelled top (Pl. 4), as preserved, suggesting that, above the two courses of dressed stone, the wall was constructed of mud brick. Nothing is preserved to indicate the columnar arrangement in the

EARLY BOIOTIAN TEMPLES

PLATE 3   *Oúngra*, temple: outer face of West wall

PLATE 4   *Oúngra*, temple: inner face of North wall

pronaos although the continuation of the long walls demonstrates clearly that it was *in antis*; the small size of the building suggests strongly that it would have been distyle *in antis*.

The dimensions with a length to width ratio of 2.37:1 appear to identify this as being of the characteristically elongated shape of an archaic temple. The dimensions might also suggest a building unit ("foot") of 30.95cm. With the superstructure probably in mud brick it may well be that any columns in both *pronaos* and *cella* were of wood. The number of columns in the *cella* is unclear. While the door between *pronaos* and *cella* was not clearly defined, that between the latter and the rear *inner room* was unmistakable. Of the building's upper structure, apart from the indication of mud brick walls, there survive only some fragments of roof tile; these do not have to have belonged to the initial stage of the building, of course.

A long wall, immediately to the South of the temple, seems to indicate the presence of an earlier building; this is shown on the plan (Fig. 11). Mykenaian sherds found among the stones of this wall may indicate quite an early date for the building that preceded the archaic temple. Dating the temple itself is less obvious since it had not actually been excavated, at least when I last saw it. The supposed mud brick upper parts of the structure could take us back to the 7th century and indeed Korinthian sherds of the 7th and 6th centuries do abound in the area of the building but so too do other sherds running down to, but not later than the 4th century BCE as elsewhere on the site. Since there is no evidence of rebuilding in stone we must presume that the temple preserved its original plan during its lifetime, even if upper parts were renovated in mud brick (which would leave no traces, of course). Thus we assume that this archaic building plan remained in use here until the end of the Classical era.

From his photographs it is difficult to be sure that the temple Spyrópoulos describes (1971) excavating is the same as that discussed here, though it seems most likely. At the time of the photography the building was plainly not being excavated since it was still flooded. Spyrópoulos dates his temple to Late Geometric and says that it produced 12 bronze *phialai* and *pinakia* of early archaic date, an undated terracotta idol, a Late Geometric cup and an engraved *fibula* of Boiotian type dating to the end of the Geometric period and the beginning of the Archaic.

2 *Khóstia*

Another temple recognised by surface work is found on an apparently natural terrace of land just outside the North wall of the fortifications at *Khóstia/*

ancient Khorsiai (cf. preliminary discussion in Fossey [ed.], 1981: 20–23). It is a large building constructed with some quite considerable blocks (Pl. 5). Although there is some thin soil cover around, little was observed in the nature of surface sherds except that a fragmentary seated female figurine in terracotta lay just to the West; this is of a type known in Boiotia during the 6th century BCE. The central part of the level area of the building has been made into a threshing floor in recent times. No doubt the construction of this feature has led to some deterioration of the ancient building itself, yet where anything is preserved above regular foundation blocks, it is consistently only one course and the level upper surface that this presents strongly suggests once again that this was all the stone structure the building ever knew. This is not the only reason for positing a mud brick – perhaps with timber – structure above this level: in the entire surrounding area of the building there are virtually no pieces or blocks of building stone to be observed except for such as are incorporated into the threshing floor and even these can hardly account for more stone than would be required to complete the walls to this single course height above foundation level. This single course was intended to project only some centimetres above ground surface to judge from the dressing preserved, for example, at the South East corner. A further argument for envisaging a very simple structure above the stone base is the complete absence of even tile sherds in the whole area suggesting possibly a roof of perishable materials. The solid nature and heavier weight of tile fragments usually causes them to turn up even where smaller pieces of fired clay may be missing. If my suppositions concerning this structure are correct it is logical to suggest again an archaic date for the construction of this temple. If we look at its clearly preserved plan (Fig. 12), we can see that this building, just like that at *Oúngra*, was aperipteral with a porch and an *inner room*; here the proportions are, however, even more elongated than at *Oúngra*. The length is 26.735m with a width of 7.825m, giving a ratio of 3.42:1. Taken by itself this would concur with the indications already outlined in suggesting an archaic date for the construction and it might even suggest an earlier date than that of the *Oúngra* temple; I hope, however, to show that the proportions of the ground plan are less valuable as a dating criterion for temples in Boiotia than for those in at least some other areas of Greece. We may finally note that the two corner blocks at the Western end show on their upper surfaces settings for what may have been wooden *anta* facings. In its turn this suggests that the deeper "room" at the Western end was the porch and that the smaller Eastern one was the *inner room*. The two internal walls, although their lines are clear, are so ill preserved that the positions and dimensions of both doorways cannot be recovered. We notice the use of thicker, more substantial foundations at the Western end. There the depth of soil is greater and, at the same time, the ground starts to slope away; the heavier foundations would give

PLATE 5   *Khóstia*, general view of temple area from Akropolis wall looking North

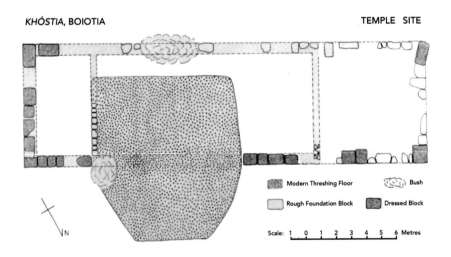

FIGURE 12   *Khóstia*: temple plan

this part of the building an accordingly greater stability. As at *Oúngra*, there are no signs to indicate reconstruction at any period after its original building, although renewal of any mud brick superstructure would obviously leave no real trace; we may thus conclude that the plan, as reflected in the stone base, must have been the same for the building's life, i.e. down to at least the 1st century BCE when the site seems to have been destroyed, probably in the course of the Mithridatic Wars.

A well-known 4th century BCE inscription from *Khóstia* (the most important critical edition is that of Taillardat & Roesch, 1966; *editio princeps* = Platon & Feyel, 1938; now *IThesp* 38) provides a list of objects deposited by Thespians in the "Heraion". A lot of perhaps unnecessary discussion has occurred concerning this Heraion: one of the original editors (Platon) thought it should be the temple of Hera at Plataiai; Schachter (1981: 238–240, 242–251) has been led to suppose the existence of Heraia at Siphai and Kreusis since dedications by Thespians at both those places are also listed (although without any specification involving a Hera cult centre). In fact there is no mention of Plataiai and no reason whatsoever to suppose that the Heraion there was so important that dedications there by Thespians should be listed in an inscription found at *Khóstia*/ancient Khorsiai; there is no mention of which sanctuaries at Siphai and Kreusis – if they were indeed sanctuaries – were the recipients of the Thespian deposits mentioned briefly in the very last lines of the inscription and supposing that they too were centres for the cult of Hera is utterly unnecessary (just as is Schachter's other opinion that the epithet of Hera at Khorsiai might be "Kithaironia", as at Plataiai). It seems perverse to suggest that the Heraion in question was anywhere other than the site where the inscription was found, namely at Khorsiai; in fact the only logical alternative that might – *in extremis* – be envisaged at all would be that the sanctuary of Hera in question might have been at Thisbe, the immediate neighbour of Khorsiai and which is perhaps noticeable for its absence from the text of the inscription; if, however, that were to be suggested, for a *pierre érante* travelling from Thisbe to Khorsiai would not theoretically be impossible – though why should it travel to another ancient site at which no building activity calling for *spolia*, has taken place since antiquity – the question then would have to be turned around asking why was it precisely Khorsiai that was absent. Khorsiai, Siphai and Kreusis are, after all, the three coastal cities of Southern Boiotia so why would two be mentioned in the inscription and not the third. In short there should really be no question that the Heraion mentioned in the inscription was to be found at Khorsiai/*Khóstia*. Indeed it can very well be argued that it is the very absence of the name of Khorsiai from the inscription that implies that the inscription stood originally at the site of that city and so its name was unnecessary, unlike the cases of the other two cities actually named; citing the Heraion was quite sufficient in the context. If anything this is reinforced by the existence of another such list, albeit much more fragmentary (*IThesp* 39; a recent discussion by Iversen is summarised in *SEG* lx 523), this time from the site of Thespiai itself and apparently carved in the same hand, showing that more than one document, apparently referring to the same situation, was required within the relevant cities; Schachter's suggestion (1994: 387) that the Thespian text may refer to "an urban sanctuary of Hera?" is unnecessary although the cult is indeed attested at Thespiai; there is no indication whatsoever that all the materials were deposited in temples of the same deity and it is much more logical to suppose that they would be deposited in whatever happened to be the main sanctuary of each city. The disparity between the paucity of objects referred to as deposited at Siphai and Kreusis and the considerable variety of those deposited in the Heraion is striking; given the obvious importance of the Heraion to take so many varied dedications, it seems logical to posit that the Heraion in question should be the large temple at *Khóstia* that we have just been describing and that seems to have been the principal sanctuary of ancient Khorsiai.

[Before we leave the subject of the Hera temple at Khorsiai we may note that the temple of the same deity at Plataiai also has elongated "archaic" proportions and according to Herodotos (ix. 52) stood πρὸ τῆς πόλιος, a description that could also fit the large temple at *Khóstia*, lying outside the city walls and on the line of approach to the site from inland. The temple at Plataiai will be further considered below.]

In sum, just as at *Oúngra*, so here at *Khóstia* we have an aperipteral temple of elongated proportions with a *pronaos* distyle *in antis* and with an *inner room* behind the *cella*. Again there are reasons to think that this construction long continued in use, perhaps with renovation of the mud brick superstructure but maintaining its archaic proportions, until late Hellenistic times. Interestingly enough, the dimensions of this temple suggest again a unit of measure ("foot") with the length of 30.95cm.

3   Mavrovoúni

The third temple has already been described in our publication (Tomlinson & Fossey, 1970) of the site in which it lies. The site is that of *Mavrovoúni* on the Southern coastal ridge where the large and complex site, taken by us to be a base for the Spartan invasions of Boiotia in 370's BCE, enclosed within its circuit an archaic sanctuary (cf. chapter 8); this sanctuary may possibly have been dedicated to Artemis Agroteira, although it is always possible that her cult was there introduced later into the cult context of another deity whose identity is so far unknown to us. Surface finds indicate that the site began its life in the Late Geometric period and continued through to and including the Hellenistic era, but there are no finds to indicate any continued existence into Roman times. Architectural fragments allow us to postulate at least two stages in the building of the temple. The earliest of these phases belongs to the early 6th century and is represented by an antefix fragment (Pl. 6); of course it is perfectly possible that there may have been an even earlier structure on the site of which we could find no obvious traces. The actual remains of the temple visible today appear to belong to a 5th century stage, judging from the many Korinthian roof tiles of that date that lie around. Not a great deal can be seen without excavation but the porch end is fortunately clear (Pl. 7); the end colonnade with settings for the *antae* shows this to have been again an aperipteral temple with a *pronaos* distyle *in antis*. The fall of the ground makes it perfectly possible to recover the full length of the building allowing us to see that the overall dimensions are 19m × 8.20m, giving us a ratio of about 2.4:1, just as at *Oúngra*. The reconstructed plan of the temple (Fig. 13) shows the overall picture; the details of the *inner room* are left blank since that end of the building is essentially under soil cover. The depth of the *pronaos* was also made clear by the finding of the threshold block for the doorway into the *cella* (Pl. 8). The temple's *pronaos* was distyle *in antis* with an interaxial spacing of 2.3m; a portion of a column drum showed that the *antae* terminated with engaged ¾ columns. The width of 8.20m and the 2.30m interaxial column spacing together suggest a unit of measure ("foot") here of 0.328m, respectively 25 "feet" and 7 "feet"; the width of the door, 1.42 measured by the same unit gives us 4.3 "feet", just as the depth of the *pronaos*, 4.70m gives us 14.33 "feet". Obviously there seems not to have been one standard unit of measure in Boiotia.

4   Discussion

At these three sites we have the same plan of an aperipteral temple with porch distyle *in antis*, *cella* and *inner room*, even if the latter cannot be clearly measured at *Mavrovoúni*. In all three the elongated archaic proportions appear to have been retained through the classical period and even later, in one case actually being *rebuilt* with those proportions in the 5th century. Is this just a coincidence? Perhaps not. It may be objected that all three examples that I have so far discussed are located in Eastern and Central Boiotia, as are the excavated sites to which I shall refer shortly. This is true and perhaps this chapter should better have been titled "Early Temples in Central and Eastern Boiotia", thus avoiding the other Boiotia of the Kopaïs (cf. chapter 3). This small group of temples found during my topographic work does not stand alone. Close similarities are to be observed at three previously excavated Boiotian temples and some comparison may be made with others but, even so, these others are also equally in Central and Eastern Boiotia.

MAVROVOÚNI, BOIOTIA

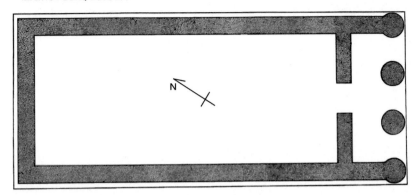

FIGURE 13 *Mavrovoúni*: temple plan reconstructed

PLATE 6 *Mavrovoúni*, archaic antefix from temple

Most striking is the temple of Artemis at **Aulis** (Pl. 9). The plan (Fig. 14) is that of Hellenistic and Roman times. We may note the elongated proportions preserved down to the Roman Period. This temple, again aperipteral, has the usual arrangement of *pronaos*, *cella* and *inner room*. The similarity, moreover, does not end there; until a rebuilding in the Hellenistic period the *pronaos* had also been distyle *in antis*. We can see that the truncated *antae*, as left after the Hellenistic rearrangement, turned the porch into one that was tetrastyle,

EARLY BOIOTIAN TEMPLES

PLATE 7
Mavrovoúni, South colonnade of temple from West

PLATE 8   *Mavrovoúni*, threshold in temple doorway

PLATE 9   Aulis, temple from South

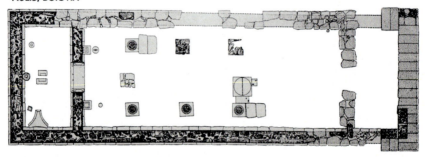

FIGURE 14   Temple of Artemis at Aulis
ADAPTED FROM *ADELT* 1961/2, KHRON. PL. 162 (THREPSIÁDHIS).

hemi-prostyle. Here at least is one example where the continued popularity of, or respect for the "archaic" elongated proportions well into the Hellenistic period is clearly demonstrated by excavation.

A slightly less clear example is the temple of Apollon at the **Ptoian** sanctuary (Pl. 10). The plan (Fig. 15) shows that this too was a temple with archaic features. It was on account of these that Orlandos (1915: 107) suggested that the preserved building of the 4th century replaced a predecessor of the 6th century or even earlier. Things would be more straightforward if the site had

EARLY BOIOTIAN TEMPLES

PLATE 10   Ptoion, temple of Apollon from Ptoion Fort above, looking West

PTOION, BOIOTIA

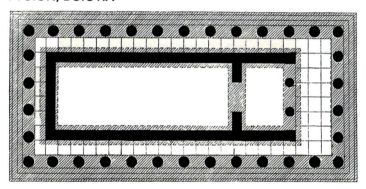

FIGURE 15   Temple of Apollon at the Ptoion Sanctuary
ADAPTED FROM *ADELT*. 1915: 94-110, PL. 6 (ORLÁNDHOS).

benefitted from full publication but what is clear is that, whether the temple was built for the first time in the 4th century or was then rebuilt, the archaic elongated plan is there, although surrounded by an exterior colonnade (24.72m × 11.65 according to Orlandos [1915: 103]). If we leave to one side this colonnade we see that what we have inside it is the same plan as in our other temples, an elongated structure (*c.* 19m × *c.* 7m = 2.7:1) with a very deep porch, distyle *in*

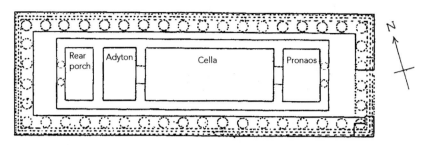

FIGURE 16   Temple of Hera (?) at Plataiai
ADAPTED FROM AJA 1891, PL. XX (WASHINGTON).

antis. True the rear *inner room* is apparently absent, as is the rear false porch or *opisthodomos* which one would normally expect in a regular peripteral temple; the absence of the latter element makes all too obvious the way in which much of the building's plan is based on that of Boiotian aperipteral temples. Ducat (1971: 40–46) indicates much of the difficulties surrounding the many periods of French excavations at the Ptoion but also illustrates and describes in the body of his book the rich haul of finds dating to Late Geometric and Archaic times to show that the sanctuary existed here already well before Classical times; concerning the date of the temple itself he is very cautious (1971: 41 n. 2), simply opting to call it "classique".

Recent work at **Plataiai** (Konecny *et all.*, 2013: 141–144) has led to a re-evaluation of the temple, usually assumed to be that of Kithaironeian Hera poorly excavated by an American team in the late 19th century and not properly published (Waldstein & Washington, 1891). The building is that of a peripteral temple and thus is not another example of the aperipteral plan we have just been considering (Fig. 16). At the same time it too presents the elongated proportions usually taken to be typical of archaic temples. It measures 49.90m long on its nearly East-West orientation by 16.70, giving a ratio of 2.99:1, or virtually 3:1. Its internal plan shows a main room preceded by a fairly deep *pronaos*; to the rear, and separating the main room ("*cella*") from the rear (presumably false) porch, is a smaller room, presumably an *inner room*, entered from the former. A further particularity is the way in which both porches are closely crowded by the side lines of the peristyle but set back nearly the equivalent of their own depths from the end exterior colonnades. The dimensions allow for the possibility that a foot of *c.* 0.31m was again the unit of measurement in this building, similar to the situation at *Oúngra* and *Khóstia*.

There is no real indication of stratigraphy in and around the temple; in fact the excavation seems to have been rather an exercise in "chase the walls". It is, however, tempting to question whether we may not be looking at a case similar to that of the Ptoion. In short is it possible that the remnants of an earlier aperipteral temple may have been reconstructed and incorporated into a later peripteral one, thus preserving the "archaic" dimensions. In any case the recent detailed examination of the site of Plataiai by Andreas Konecny and his colleagues has demonstrated that there is indication of some unknown activities in the building's area in the 6th century BCE although the textual evidence examined suggests that the presence of such a temple at the time of the Persian wars is difficult to consider. A further conclusion arrived at suggested that the temple found by the Americans cannot be identified with the *hekatompedon* built in 426 BCE; for that temple can only have come into existence after the Peloponnesian War and accordingly it appears that the building discussed probably was constructed rather after 338 BCE with the rebuilding of the city; it thus follows that there was a decision to adopt a known archaic plan to replace the *hekatompedon* built by the Thebans. A compromise position is, however, possible, namely that an earlier "archaic" aperipteral *hekatompedon* was in fact located at this position and that remnants of it, with their elongated plan, were reconstructed in mostly new masonry – Konecny views the temple's masonry as similar to that of the city's circuit walls that his investigation has dated to late Classical or early Hellenistic times – with the addition of a surrounding colonnade of 6 × 18 columns.

However this all may be, it is clear that the latest examination of the building suggests either a) that this was a building of later date than its elongated plan would normally be taken to imply or b) that it is indeed a building of late Classical times – or even a little later – and thus, in either case, that the Plataian temple shows another example of the elongated plan long outliving the archaic period in Boiotia. In fact Konecny indicates other examples of this phenomenon outside Boiotia: the elongated temple of Apollon at Thermos in Aitolia was built at the turn of the 3rd to 2nd centuries BCE and Konecny further points out that the temple at *Kalapódhi* built in the late 5th century is also elongated. These are two interesting comparisons but they do not preclude the idea that the elongated plan may have remained especially popular in Boiotia a lot later than elsewhere; in any case *Kalapodhi* is very close to Boiotia.

Less valuable comparison can be made with a fourth excavated example, the temple at the **Kabeirian sanctuary** just West of Thebai. Here again the plan shows in Hellenistic times an elongated aperipteral building with a *pronaos*; the rest of the temple's plan is less clear. Even less clear still is the plan of the temple, possibly dedicated to Athena, at **Haliartos**.

Of the two earlier temples at the **Theban Ismenion** so little has been preserved that we have no means of reconstructing the plans, though a new program of excavations may ultimately clarify matters; in the meanwhile we are left with the plan of the third stage (4th century) of temple building on the Ismenion hill consisting in a peripteral building of unusual plan. It is hexastyle at both ends but with just 12 columns on the long sides, a porch – apparently distyle *in antis* – leading to a long *cella* behind which the rear porch (also distyle *in antis*) is little short of symbolic for it is so shallow that the two columns almost touch the rear wall of the *cella*. It is difficult to make any comparison with the buildings I have presented above.

5 Conclusion

There would seem good reason to think that at five Boiotian sanctuaries was preserved, sometimes even through re-buildings, a certain archaic plan with elongated proportions down to at least later Classical times and, in some cases, even later still. The five are *Oúngra, Khóstia, Mavrovoúni,* Aulis and the Ptoion while the Kabeirion may even perhaps be added; this is quite a large percentage of the total number of Boiotian temples known to us.

This elongated plan is taken, elsewhere, to be an essentially archaic concept. Here in Boiotia its continued popularity into much later times seems to be perhaps another example of that spirit of conservatism in Classical Boiotia that could produce, among other things, black figure decoration on pottery well into the 4th century and which resulted in a very restricted taste for the subsequent red figure style. For these and other aspects of the phenomenon cf. my paper written some many years ago (Fossey, 1990: chapter 15).

CHAPTER 6

Παιδοποιία in Archaic Thebai

νομοθέτης δ'αὐτοῖς (sc. Θηβαίοις) ἐγένετο Φιλόλαος περὶ τ'ἄλλων καὶ περὶ τῆς παιδοποιίας, οὓς καλοῦσιν ἐκεῖνοι νόμους θετικούς· καὶ τοῦτ' ἐστὶν ἰδίως ὑπ' ἐκείνου νενομοθετημένον, ὅπως ὁ ἀριθμὸς σῴζηται τῶν κλήρων.

Philolaos became legislator for the Thebans in regard to various matters, particularly concerning paidopoiia, what the Thebans call laws of adoption; about this especially he set up legislation, in order that the number of the lots of land should be preserved.
ARISTOTELES, *Politika* ii, 1274b

∴

The actions of Philolaos at Thebai, mentioned by Aristoteles, are not infrequently referred to *en passant* by historians of antiquity but some aspects of the question are perhaps deserving of a fuller examination for what they may tell us of early Theban institutions.

The exact dating of Philolaos, and also of his legislation, is disputed (e.g. Cloché, 1952: 26; Moretti, 1957: 61. 13 & 1962: 101; Asheri, 1963: 8; Buck, 1979: 95 & 103 n. 72; Snodgrass, 1980: 120) but overall a date in the late 8th or 7th century BCE seems acceptable. If we cannot be more exact as to his date, Philolaos' origin at least seems indisputable for Aristoteles himself (*Politika* ii, 1274a) clearly states that he was a Korinthian. This origin prompts two different observations: one that refers back to the question of dating and the other that concerns related legislation at Korinthos itself. The importation of Korinthian pottery into Eastern and Central Boiotia (cf. chapter 3) from the beginning of the 7th century BCE, while not conclusive in itself, might suggest that very century, rather than the late part of the preceding one, as a more appropriate time for the presence of a notable Korinthian being active at Thebai. In any case we shall have reason to consider that the comparison of Philolaos' legislation with the condition reflected in Hesiodos is such as to suggest that this legislation should postdate the Boiotian poet and thus be placed rather in the 7th century. Philolaos' Korinthian origin also obliges us to compare our initial text with another entry a few pages earlier in in the same treatise:

ἄτοπον δὲ καὶ τὸ τὰς κτήσεις ἰσάζοντα τὸ περὶ τὸ πλῆθος τῶν πολιτῶν μὴ κατασκευάζειν, ἀλλ' ἀφεῖναι τὴν τεκνοποιίαν ἀόριστον ... μᾶλλον δὲ δεῖν ὑπολάβοι τις ὡρίσθαι τῆς οὐσίας τὴν τεκνοποιίαν ὥστε ἀριθμοῦ τινὸς μὴ πλείονα γεννᾶν ... τὸ δ' ἀφεῖσθαι, καθάπερ ἐν ταῖς πλείσταις πόλεσι, πενίας ἀναγκαῖον αἴτιον γίνεσθαι τοῖς πολίταις, ἡ δὲ πενία στάσιν ἐμποιεῖ καὶ κακουργίαν. Φαίδων μὲν οὖν ὁ Κορίνθιος, ὢν νομοθέτης τῶν ἀρχαιοτάτων, τοὺς οἴκους ᾠήθη δεῖν διαμένειν καὶ τὸ πλῆθος τῶν πολιτῶν, καὶ εἰ τὸ πρῶτον τοὺς κλήρους ἀνίσους εἶχον πάντες κατὰ μέγεθος.

It is also strange that while maintaining equal the number of properties there is no attempt to regulate the number of the citizens, but the birth-rate is left uncontrolled.... It might instead be thought that it is the birth-rate rather than properties that should be restricted, so as not to allow the birth of more than a certain number of children ... leaving that question alone, as happens in most states, will inevitably lead to poverty among the citizens, and poverty produces revolt and crime. Therefore Pheidon the Korinthian one of the earliest legislators, thought that households and citizen population ought to remain at the same numbers, although in origin the estates of all were unequal in size.

ARISTOTELES, *Politika* ii 1265a–b

Since Pheidon must also be assigned an early date (Ure, 1922: 182–183; Salmon, 1984: 63–65) he becomes either a contemporary or an immediate predecessor of Philolaos; this, allied with their common Korinthian origin and the similarity of the subject matter of their legislations, led Will (1955: 317) to consider their two laws as essentially the same. Indeed both legislative acts are plainly concerned with maintaining the number of κλῆροι and can be seen as part of a much more widespread phenomenon in archaic Greece, a preoccupation with land-possession and inheritance; over half a century ago this subject was examined at some length in an important article by Asheri (1963).

For all the common content, the two passages present some differences. Perhaps the most striking is the use of different words. In the case of Pheidon at Korinthos his legislation is referred to in a context concerning τεκνοποιία while Philolaos' legislation at Thebai is termed "περὶ τῆς παιδοποιίας". Although both of these words can bear essentially the same meaning, "procreation of children" (LSJ[9] s.v. παιδοποιία and τεκνοποιία), it is worth noting that the two initial roots παιδο- and τεκνο- can contain slightly different nuances. This difference can be seen sometimes in the tragedians. For example Euripides calls Orestes

Ἀγαμέμνωνος παῖ καὶ Κλυταιμνήστρας τέκνον
Iphigeneia en Taurois 238

while Akhileus is addressed as

ὦ τέκνον Νηρῇδος, ὦ παῖ Πηλέως
Iphigeneia en Aulidi 896

It is clear that in these passages παῖς signifies the offspring of the father, τέκνον that of the mother – the latter being hardly surprising given the meaning of the cognate verb τίκτω *to give birth*. In later Greek any clear distinction between the two words seems to have been lost, the word παιδί(ον) [< παῖς] having become the generic word for "child" in modern Greek and τέκνον having been largely abandoned with the demise of *katharevousa*; it is, however, still worth noting that the latter is sometimes used in ecclesiastical contexts, continuing a tendency reaching back to the church fathers and thus perhaps reflecting a concept of relationship to *mother*-church and constituting a vague reminiscence of a much earlier distinction. At the same time it is obvious that, although the tragedians of the later 5th century BCE retained a knowledge of this distinction and could exploit it when occasion required that they do so, in other contexts the same tragedians can reflect the assimilation of both words to a single meaning:

(Deineira to her son Hyllos) ὦ τέκνον, ὦ παῖ
SOPHOKLES, *Trakhiniai* 61

(Philoktetes to Neoptolemos) ὦ τέκνον, ὦ παῖ πατρὸς ἐξ Ἀχιλλέως
id., *Philoktetes* 26

(Hekabe to her daughter Polyxene) ὦ τέκνον, ὦ παῖ δυστανοτάτας (ματέρος)
EURIPIDES, *Hekabe* 171–172

The varied contexts of these three examples illustrate a possible interchangeability of the two words.

The different nuance implicit in the two Euripidean passages previously cited is reflected a little earlier in the 5th century by Herodotos. The "father of history" only uses three times one or other of our two words "creation of children" but the contexts are clear: twice he uses the phrase "γυναῖκα τεκνοποιόν"

(i. 59, 8; v. 40, 7) and in the third passage he says "ὅ τε λόγος πολλὸς ἐν Σπάρτῃ ὡς Ἀρίστωνι σπέρμα παιδοποιὸν οὐκ ἐνῆν" (vi. 68, 11). The distinction between mother/τέκνον and father/παῖς is again clear. Another example takes us back a little earlier still; while the text of the Gortyn Law Code (*IC* iv 72) in which it occurs, dates, like Herodotos, to the 5th century Willetts (1967) has shown that the contents must go back to the 6th century. The code, as a whole, usually uses the word τέκνον for child – and this is hardly surprising given the many vestiges of matriarchal society reflected in its legal forms (Willetts, 1967: 18); on three occasions, however, the word παιδίον is used and in one case there is a contrast with the usual τέκνον:

αἰ δέ κα μὲ δέκσεται ἐπὶ τôι
πάσται ἔμεν τὸ τέκνον τôι τ-
ᾶς ϝοικέας, αἰ δὲ τôι αὖ-
τιν ὀπυίοιτο πρὸ τô ἐνιαυτ-
ô τὸ παιδίον ἐπὶ τôι πάσται
ἔμεν τôι τô ϝοικέος
    Gortyn Code IV, 1–6

In Willetts' translation this passage (with my emphases added) reads as follows:

and if he do not receive it the child (τέκνον) shall be in the power of the female serf; but if she should marry the same man again before the end of the year, the child (παιδίον) shall be in the power of the master of the male serf.

Again it is clear that the word παιδίον is used for the child when the law concerns or recognizes descent through the male; τέκνον is used of the case when the child is seen only in relation to its mother.

The legislative context of the distinction in the Gortyn Code is of particular interest for our present purposes. The legislation at both Korinthos and Thebai that is our current focus seems to date to the period of Bakkhiad control of the former city and we are specifically told that the νομοθέτης at Thebai, Philolaos, was not merely from Korinthos but was in fact a member of the Bakkhiad clan. That clan was endogamous and matrilineal (Thompson, 1954: 201–202) and it may be more than coincidence that it is precisely the legislation of Pheidon at Bakkhiad Korinthos that is spoken of in terms of τεκνοποιία, a word whose initial root enshrines the matrilineal concept. In Thebai, on the contrary, we may presume that the dominant groups, in whose context Philolaos legislated, were patrilineal – the case of the Bakkhiads seems, indeed, to be unique at this late date – hence the word παιδοποιία with its nuance of male descent at Thebai. It is unlikely that Aristoteles himself was particularly conscious of the difference for he normally talks indiscriminately of τεκνοποιία – *Politika* ii, 1274b is in fact the only occasion when he uses the word παιδοποιία – just as his predecessor Platon always writes of παιδοποιία. This makes it all the more likely that where a contrast does occur, as in the present case, it is beyond coincidence. This solitary instance of παιδοποιία in the whole surviving Aristotelian corpus reminds us that the scholar had compiled detailed information concerning the various Greek constitutions before writing his *Politika* and leaves us in little doubt that the Theban law was officially called περὶ τῆς παιδοποιίας with its stress on patrilineal descent.

The main purpose, in any society, of determining line of descent is the definition of property rights and inheritance – made clear in our present cases by the references to the κλῆροι. We may note, before moving on, that the importance of this whole concern, the preoccupation of archaic Greece to which reference was previously made, is perhaps indicated by the fact that of the 20 instances of the word in the Aristotelian corpus (21 if we include the *hapax* παιδοποιία), 11 (12 with παιδοποιία) occur in the *Politika* alone, that is in precisely that work of his that was so much based on earlier constitutions.

Even if consciousness of the different nuances of τέκνον and παῖς was slipping by the second half of the 5th century BCE and had, in effect, disappeared by its end, realisation that earlier Greek societies had known varyingly patrilineal and matrilineal systems still existed in the middle of that century for it is the conflict between these two and the victory of the patrilineal principle that is the central motif in yet another "legalistic" situation, namely the trial scene in Aiskhylos' *Eumenides* (Thompson, 1946: 287–289). In his argument against the matrilineal (and matriarchal) principles Apollon is quite specific in his use of vocabulary:

οὐκ ἔστι μήτηρ ἡ κεκλημένη τέκνου
τοκεύς, τρόφος δὲ κύματος νεοσπόρου

*The so-called "mother" is not a parent of the child,
only the nurse of the newly-begotten embryo.*
Eumenides 658–659

That this use of the word τέκνον with its matrilineal nuance is no mere coincidence, but is rather deliberate, is stressed by the plentiful alliteration of its two principal consonantal sounds, *tau* and *kappa* in the surrounding words.

Apart from the different lines of descent and thus of inheritance involved there are other distinctions between the Korinthian and Theban legislations. Whereas the latter is specific only as to maintenance of the number of κλῆροι, the legislation at Korinthos talks of the number of households and the number of citizens, and all this in a context of advocating control over the number of births (ἀριθμοῦ τινὸς μὴ πλείονα γεννᾶν) to avoid poverty and the resulting political instability. The Korinthian legislation seems thus much farther reaching than the Theban.

At Korinthos plainly the laws were aimed at birth control as such and at resultant population control. A study published quite some years ago (Jöchle, 1971) demonstrated all too clearly that the Greeks in antiquity used a considerable variety of methods of birth control; essentially these were of two categories: on the one hand the use of a variety of ointments and suppositories in the vagina were strictly contraceptive in nature while, on the other, the taking of various medications by mouth was intended to cause either infertility (both temporary and long term) or premature *menses*, the latter being methods of **birth** control rather than contraceptive; moreover, ancient texts, both medical (Galen xix) and legal ([Lysias], *kat' antigenous ambloseos* and Cicero, *pro Cluentio* 11 à propos of a woman from Miletos) refer quite specifically to the practice of abortion. In view of this evidence we need hardly be surprised that an ancient legislator felt able to call for birth control although we may wonder how effective some of these methods could be in reality and thus how justified his confidence might be. However this may have been, the Theban legislation is not said to involve population control as such; at the same time this may be a logical deduction *a silentio* for it is specifically stated that Philolaos' law aiming at maintenance of the κλῆροι (which is Aristoteles' main concern) was just one of a group of related laws introduced by him; what these other laws stipulated, we do not know.

One thing that we do know about Theban law is that another potential method of population control was specifically illegal:

νόμος οὗτος Θηβαϊκὸς ὀρθῶς ἅμα καὶ φιλανθρώπως κείμενος ἐν τοῖς μάλιστα ὅτι οὐκ ἔξεστι ἀνδρὶ Θηβαίῳ ἐκθεῖναι παιδίον οὐδὲ εἰς ἐρημίαν ῥῖψαι θάνατον αὐτοῦ καταψηφισάμενον

This law at Thebai, both correctly and very humanely at the same time, provided that a Theban was not allowed to expose his child or leave it in deserted land to cause its death.

AILIANOS *poikele historia* ii, 7

In addition to forbidding the exposure of unwanted children this same law went on to allow "ἐὰν ᾖ πένης τὰ ἔσχατα ὁ τοῦ παιδὸς πατήρ" he (the father) may hand over the child to the magistrates to be sold but the very terms of the passage make it all too clear that this was but a last resort and thus rarely to be invoked. Apart from the fact that this law makes clear the patriarchal/patrilineal nature of society at Thebai (note again the use of the words παιδός and πατήρ combined), all told we have the impression that in that city there was no attempt, at state level, to control population size – if anything the contrary is implied by the respect for children. We have thus good reason to see in Philolaos' legislation an attempt to control inheritance only. We may then understand why this passage of Aristoteles has been considered as indicating an alternative meaning for παιδοποιία – that of "adoption" (LSJ[9] s.v. παιδοποιία) for the other side of the problem of maintaining the number of households and κλῆροι was what to do in the case of absence of an heir. One other text is adduced in support of this meaning although it is much later in date:

τότε γὰρ καὶ εἰς παιδοποιίαν ἀναχθέντες ἀλλότρια κληρονομοῦσι

Foe then they are put up for adoption and inherit the estate of others
PTOLEMAIOS *tetrabiblos* iv. 2[174]

Indeed the existence of this mechanism at Athenai is well known and there is no intrinsic reason to discount its possible presence at Thebai (Asheri, 1963: 8–9); it is even worth noting that the provision in Attic law applied specifically and exclusively to the case of the head of a household who was ἄπαις, the term again using the root of παῖς to designate descent in the male line.

Just as is the case for most Greek states, our information about the laws of Thebai (and even more so about those of other Boiotian cities) is extremely scarce; even in the Hellenistic period with the wealth of documentation concerning many aspects of the Boiotian confederation our knowledge even of federal laws is very limited (Roesch, 1972). Apart from the two Theban laws that we have already examined, that of Philolaos and that concerning exposure and sale of children, we know of just one other:

τὴν δὲ μετάδοσιν γίνεσθαι τῷ πλήθει τοῦ πολιτεύματος ἤτοι καθάπερ εἴρηται πρότερον, τοῖς τὸ τίμημα κτωμένοις, ἢ καθάπερ Θηβαίοις, ἀποσχόμενος χρόνον τινὰ τῶν βαναύσεων ἔργων

When the people get a share in governing it should happen either in the previously stated way and recipients should be those who have the property

qualification or, as is the practice at Thebai, participation should go to people who, for some while, have abstained from manual labour.
ARISTOTELES, *politika* 1321a, 26–29

As Aristoteles informs us, Philolaos' legislation περὶ τῆς παιδοποιίας was but one of a group known as the θετικοὶ νόμοι, a phrase that is not, in itself, altogether clear. Edouard Will (1955: 317) comments "lois successorales – c'est ce qu'il faut entendre par θετικοὶ νόμοι; 'lois concernant l'adoption'" (cf. LSJ⁹ s.v. θετικός II) but this interpretation is derived purely from the Aristotelian context for there does not appear to be any parallel to the expression. It is, of course, true that cognate words such as θέτος can have meanings connected with adoption, just as compounds such as διατίθημι and διαθήκη have meanings involving inheritance but it remains a fact that the principal significance of θετικός is that of the Latin *positivus* (cf. *TLG ad loc.*). An ancient gloss is more precise still:

Θετικός, τὸ ὀφειλόμενον γενέσθαι (Hesykhios).

This reminds us possibly of the distinction between the first two of the Ten Commandments and the remaining eight: the distinction between "thou shalt" and "thou shalt not", that is between laws which are of obligation and those which are of prohibition, between *positive* and *negative,* between the meaning of θετικός and that of ἀρνιτικός (*cf. TLG*).

Seen in this light it would be logical to consider the θετικοὶ νόμοι as those that laid out obligations as to what must be done, in the present case the obligation to provide an heir to an estate (κλῆρος) in such a way as to ensure a single line of inheritance and thus the specified maintenance of the plots, one of the ways of providing such an heir being explicitly by adoption. In this way we might expect that the θετικοὶ νόμοι might contain other expressions of obligatory acts and duties, perhaps beyond the simple matter of land control but including such matters as hoplite service that was related to the possession of the κλῆρος. The logical extension of this would be that the citizens of Thebai knew also a set of ἀρνητικοὶ (*vel sim.*) νόμοι containing prohibitions; the other two laws of which we know (forbidding exposure of children and forbidding access to magistracies by members of the commercial class) fit admirably into this postulated second class. Such prohibitive legislation may also have contained provisions against the sale of the κλῆρος, except *in extremis*, just as occurred in Lokris according to Aristoteles (*politika* 1266b). It is unclear which was the Lokris in question but if it were, by chance, Eastern or Opountian Lokris it would represent a parallel from a neighbour whose history was often intertwined with that of Boiotia.

Asheri (1963), following upon the various observations of Aristoteles shows at length that this sort of property control was characteristic of moderate régimes, be they democratic, aristocratic or oligarchic. We may thus see at Thebai an indication that the oligarchic system was of a moderate nature. It may have been its very moderate nature that led to the basic popularity of the oligarchic system in Boiotia and even to its influential role in the development of Greek oligarchic theory as indicated by the late Robert J. Buck (1985). The hoplite class (based upon property qualification) was a *sine qua non* for the functioning of an oligarchic constitution, as he rightly observes. If then constitutional structures of Boiotian type may have influenced the development of oligarchic ideas elsewhere – why not also the Boiotian modalities for ensuring the continuance of those structures?

One of the most important of oligarchic theorists was undoubtedly Platon. Is it then possible that in his writing we may find a hint as to the solution to the problem of inalienable and indivisible κλῆροι (i.e. maintenance of their number) and absence of population control? Platon does indeed outline a system for dealing with this problem:

ὁ λάχων τὸν κλῆρον καταλείπετω ἀεὶ ταύτης τῆς οἰκήσεως ἕνα μόνον κληρονόμον τῶν ἑαυτοῦ παίδων.

The proprietor of the land plot shall always leave behind him as sole legatee of his home one son, whichever he pleases.
Nomoi v. 740b–c

The other children, if they be girls will be given in marriage and, if boys, be given to families that lack sons, continues the philosopher. The second half of the latter statement might indeed be seen as the other aspect of the adoption implied by παιδοποιία. Perhaps preferable, however, and not the least so because it is more straightforward, is the system operating in fact in some other cities as indicated for us by Platon's pupil Aristoteles, whose writings lie behind much of what we have already said:

μετέβαλε δὲ καὶ ἐν Κνίδῳ ἡ ὀλιγαρχία στασιασάντων τῶν γνωρίμων αὐτῶν πρὸς αὑτοὺς διὰ τὸ ὀλίγους μετέχειν καί, καθάπερ εἴρηται, εἰ πατήρ, υἱὸν μὴ μετέχειν, μηδ' εἰ πλείους ἀδελφοί, ἀλλ' ἢ τὸν πρεσβύτατον.

At Knidos also the oligarchy was disturbed since the notables split into factions opposing each other, because few were active in government, and

according to the stated rule, if a father took part his son was excluded, and if there were several brothers only the eldest could participate.
  Politika v, 1305b

Aristoteles has just referred to similar systems in existence at Massalia, Istros and Herakleia and it is worth remembering that Herakleia was in part a Boiotian colony (cf. Fossey, 1988: 436–437) founded well after Philolaos' activities at Thebai and thus a logical place at which to find echoes of his legislation. At a much later date, moreover, but in a context of traditional ideas we find a specifically Boiotian writer, Ploutarkhos, referring to a system of this sort by which family plots remain constant even in the presence of more than one son:

τὰ φίλα καὶ προσήκοντα λαμβάνοντα καὶ διδόντας οἴεισθαι τὴν ἐπιμέλειαν νέμεσθαι καὶ τὴν οἰκονομίαν, χρῆσιν δὲ καὶ κτῆσιν ἐν μέσῳ κεῖσθαι κοινὴν καὶ ἀνέμητον ἁπάντων.

Let them feel, as they give and take what is appropriate to each and chosen by each, that what is really being shared it is the care and maintenance of the estate, and that it is neither used or owned individually but is left unassigned and undivided for them all in common.
  ethika 483d = *peri philadelphias* 11

If then Aristoteles and Boiotian Ploutarkhos give us a straightforward solution to the problem does this mean that we should treat Platon's remark as nothing but abstract philosophy? The need, on occasion, of παιδοποιία *qua* "adoption" in order to guarantee an heir to a family without a son, thus solving that particular problem, could, at the same time, if uncontrolled, lead to other problems in that the same person might be the natural heir to one κλῆρος and become the adopted heir to another; this problem was not unknown in Attike (Asheri, 1963). If, however, in Boiotia, or indeed elsewhere, it was specifically provided that *only* those who were not natural heirs in their own family might be adopted as heirs into another family we have a practical and practicable restrictive modality invocable only in specific circumstances that lay behind Platon's general and plainly impracticable rule. Although we have no evidence as such that this modality was in fact observed in Boiotia it is pleasing to speculate upon the possibility that another part of Philolaos' θετικοὶ νόμοι might logically have contained this sort of provision since the oligarchic structures enjoyed a long life at Thebai and in Boiotia and that this refinement of the system of παιδοποιία may lie behind Platon's writing, just as Boiotia contributed much else to oligarchic theory.

Finally we may return to the date of Philolaos' activity. We have seen that the Archaic period witnessed a general concern with limiting the disposal of property, in part so as to maintain the number of κλῆροι and thus the size of the enfranchised hoplite class. Philolaos' law(s) constituted a particular example of this preoccupation, but it is specifically in Boiotia, though not actually at Thebai, rather in the neighbouring lands of Thespiai, more specifically at Askre, that we know from the native Hesiodos that in his day the κλῆρος was not, in fact, always inalienable (*erga kai hemerai* 341) and that the presence of more than one son in a household – as was Hesiodos' own case – led to a dismembering of the family's resources (*erga kai hemerai* 376–378). If this problem had indeed begun to be felt in Boiotia around 700 BCE it becomes easier to understand the impetus for legislation such as that of Philolaos in the following 7th century BCE. At the time when full-scale expansion of settlement in the Boiotian landscape, the phenomenon of "internal colonization", had got well under way (Fossey, 1988: 434–436) the need was felt to make sure that newly gained land, and the increased hoplite numbers it supported were maintained.

In summary, then, what do we learn and what can we deduce from Aristoteles about early Theban (and Boiotian) institutions? The extensive growth in population and resultant expansion of settlement in Late Geometric and Archaic times created a need to organize and ensure continued control of the economic basis of society and its structures; in an area such as Boiotia where the economic basis must always have been agricultural the unit of organisation was the family plot, the κλῆρος that Philolaos' legislation rendered inalienable and indivisible. One of the modalities involved in that legislation was adoption to provide a male heir, for descent and inheritance were measured in patrilineal terms. Other modalities may have insisted upon the recognition of only one heir per family although there is no indication of attempts at birth control, rather the contrary, and – more speculatively – may have defined eligibility for adoption. The whole structure is that of a moderate oligarchy that may have provided the model for many subsequent constitutions and legislations. By getting in "on the act" so early in the history of land problems, Boiotia, and rather more specifically Thebai, may have made more than one significant contribution to Greek ideas on inheritance as well as oligarchic theory. While I think that Buck (1979: 92) was wrong to regard Aristoteles' theory as "late analogy from colonial practice" it is interesting to speculate that the origin of the idea may indeed have lain in a form of colonization, the internal variety as practiced in Boiotia.

CHAPTER 7

Boiotian Connections with the Pontic and Propontic Area in Archaic to Hellenistic Times

The evidence for Boiotian immigration to the Black Sea littoral is disparate in nature and scattered in location.[1] When, however, it is assembled it provides a consistent picture of Boiotian involvement in the colonization of certain parts of the Pontic and Propontic coasts and it is from this participation that must begin any consideration of the relations between the two areas. Some of this disparate evidence was first gathered more than a quarter century ago in a thesis written under my direction (De Angelis, 1991).

In general Boiotia participated but little in the great colonizing movement (Fossey, 1988: 436–437, where I perhaps underestimated the case). In good part this may be the result of the earlier extensive loss of population over the several generations of the Aiolian and Ionian migrations in which Boiotians appear to have taken a considerable part (Fossey, 1988: 428–430). A rather thin level of population may well account, moreover, for the fact that when she *did* participate in colonization, it was more-or-less consistently as a partner with neighbouring Megaris; it would seem that she did not have the numbers to "go it alone" and so joined forces with another state that was heavily involved in the colonizing movement. Like Megara, Boiotia may have been involved on an odd occasion in Westwards colonization but the presence of Boiotian migrants in *Magna Graecia* and Sikelia is a somewhat hazily remembered thing and thus not so easily examined although my friend Duane Roller (n.d.) made a serious attempt to unravel the matter; in any case it is perhaps the exception that proves the rule for otherwise Boiotia's efforts in colonization were exclusively directed towards the Propontic and Pontic areas.

There is perhaps a sort of historical continuity to be seen in this concentration. Despite recent questions raised about the nature of the Aiolian Migration

---

1   This paper was originally intended for the Vani conference in 1994; it was delivered there in part only and by someone else and so was without my authorization. The unauthorized version read at Vani was published under the title "Boiotia and the Pontic Cities in the Archaic to Hellenistic Periods", in the Proceedings of that Symposium (O. Lordkipanidzé & P. Lévêque, edd., 1999: 35–40). It had, in the meanwhile, been published under the same title in full in John M. Fossey (ed.), 1994: *Boeotia Antiqua* iv (Amsterdam): 107–115. It is here republished with changes to update or ameliorate the previous authorized version but it is the present text that should be considered to be the final one and the others should be discarded.

(Rose, 2008 & Parker, 2008), there seems to be quite an amount of evidence for early Boiotian involvement in population movement and colonization to Northern and Central Anatolia. Aiolis itself was later referred to as "Βοιωτική" (Strabon ix. 402) and "Boiotians" were specifically counted among Aiolians (Stephanos of Byzantion s.v. Ἰτωνία) while Thoukydides (iii. 2, 3: vii. 57, 3), writing in the later 5th century BCE, records the memory of special ties between Boiotia and the Aiolian island of Lesbos. In addition to all these indications of Boiotian involvement in settlement of the North East Aigaion, there are traditions (Strabon ix. 401) that the "Aiolian Migration" set out from the Boiotian port of Aulis, following the example of the earlier expedition against Troia. It seems clear that in Greek antiquity reasons abounded for positing an important Boiotian participation during the "Dark Ages" in a movement that brought contact with not only the North East Aigaion but thus with the approaches to the Propontic/Pontic area. Should we also perhaps look for another possible connection of which we are reminded by the allusion to Aulis? The tradition is that Iphigeneia, saved at the eleventh hour from being sacrificed by her father at Aulis was transported thence to serve her saviour Artemis in the Tauric lands on the North side of the Euxinos Pontos. This Boiotian connection with the Pontos proper, over and above connections with the approaches to the Propontis, takes up an earlier mythological connection between Boiotia and the Euxinos: the tradition that the steersman of Iason and the Argonautes was none other than the eponymous hero of the Boiotian port of Siphai/Tipha, i.e. Tiphys whose grave was traditionally located on the Black Sea's South coast (Apollonios of Rhodos ii. 854), but to whose city the *Argo* herself was supposed to have returned from Kolkhis (Pausanias ix. 32, 4). Tiphys' role must have some "historical" significance since the location of his place of origin on the *South* coast of Boiotia does not lend itself to ready association with the North East Aigaion; I take it that this means at least that there was some sort of real memory of even South Boiotian involvement in early contacts with, or voyages to the Black Sea.

After this accumulation of apparently (Late) Bronze Age and Dark Age contact with the North East Aigaion and the Pontic area, Boiotians resumed travels in the same direction perhaps around the end of the 8th century BCE. Astakos, founded on the East side of the Bosporos perhaps c. 711 BCE, was a Megarian colony but already some Boiotian participation may be indicated since Memnon (*FGrHist* 434F 12. 2–3) derives the city's name from that of one of the "Spartoi" of Kadmos, providing a possible connection with Thebai. Even if this association seems a little tenuous in itself we must remember a different indication of Boiotian contact with the North East Aigaion: the movement from Kyme in Aiolis to Askre in Boiotia – we may note *en passant* **South** Boiotia – by the father of Hesiodos must be placed around this time and can hardly be seen as a completely isolated phenomenon. In any case, in the first quarter of the following 7th century – Eusebios gives the date as *c.* 684 BCE – the Megarians placed another colony on the East side of the Bosporos, at Kalkhedon. Again possible Boiotian participation is indicated by the name of one of the city's tribes, *Asopodoreis* (*IKalkhedon* 7, line 16); the name seems to be derived from the area of the Asopos river, the "Parasopia", that part of Southern Boiotia which directly abuts Megaris and would be the most obvious area upon which to draw in a neighbourly cooperation. Even if this association still seems tenuous the foundation of Byzantion about a quarter century later, perhaps *c.* 658 BCE, provides clearer evidence for, although the only literary mention of Boiotian cooperation in the venture is late, its author, Konstantinos Porphyrogenitos, was a prominent local citizen of the 10th century CE who may be presumed to be well informed about the traditions of his own city. In any case there is a collection of other indications. One of these is the existence at Byzantion of a cult of Amphiaraos (cf. the discussion by Hanell, 1934: 189, who also lists the ancient sources); another, yet more obvious instance is the presence again at Byzantion of an official body of 30 "Βοιωτοί" (Diodoros Sikeliotes xiv. 12, 3); finally two of the months in the city's calendar seem to reflect Boiotian cults – Makhaneios (cf. Zeus Makhaneus at Tanagra, *IG*vii 548) and Eukleios (cf. Artemis Eukleia throughout Boiotia – and Opountian Lokris – Ploutarkhos, *Aristeides* xx. 6; Fossey, 1990b: 151–152).

With the foundation of Kalkhedon and Byzantion, reinforced by Astakos possibly, Megara and her Boiotian partners could control passage through the Bosporos and thus to the Euxinos Pontos proper and their *subsequent* expansion into that sea's coasts is a logical sequel to the Propontic settlements and to the preceding involvement in the North East Aigaion. In fact Boiotia's first possible participation in colonisation of the Euxine littoral is again an exception to confirm the rule for it concerns cooperation with a state other than Megaris, but it is still a cooperative act, as were all her other colonial attempts. Sinope was founded, possibly in 631 BCE, by Miletos, the city that was reputed to have founded 90 colonies (Plinius, *naturalis historia* v. 112) and which was certainly responsible for the establishment of very many Euxine settlements; there are, however, indications that Miletos may not have acted completely on her own and that Boiotians may have been involved. The very name of Sinope has Boiotian associations for it is that of a daughter of the Asopos whose area we have already encountered in connection with Kalkhedon; the other offspring of that river gave their names to uniformly Boiotian toponyms: Thebe, Tanagra, Thespeia, Asopis, Ismenos (Bowra 1938). A case has even been made for regarding the colony's *oikistes*, Habrondas, as a Boiotian (Bilabel, 1920: 33 & 151) and, whatever one may think of that, there are two toponyms East of Sinope that point backwards to Boiotia: the city of Kabeira (Hemberg, 1950: 153–158) may relate to the Boiotian cult centre of the Kabeirion just outside Thebai, while nearby flowed the river Thermodon whose name finds its only parallel in the homonymous river that was located between the territories of Thebai and Tanagra (Fossey, 1988: 222–223). There are, then, some indications of Boiotian interest in the South East Pontos and thus incidentally close to Kolkhis, which might bring us back to the involvement in the *Argonautika*.

The culmination of the story comes in c. 559 BCE with the foundation of Herakleia Pontike. Here a plethora of *testimonia* leaves no doubt whatsoever as to Boiotian collaboration in this Megarian foundation (Burstein, 1976: 15–18). The very name of the city reflects its dedication to Herakles, whose cult is widely attested in Boiotia (cf. chapter 4 above) but completely absent from Megaris; people from the East Boiotian city of Tanagra are specifically located at Herakleia (Pausanias iv. 26, 7); Herakleides Pontikos, a native of the colony, claimed descent from a certain Damis who is said to have led a Boiotian contingent to the foundation (*Suda* H451); the previously mentioned cult of Tiphys indicates a connection with Siphai and perhaps – by extension – with the neighbouring large city of Thespiai for which Siphai frequently served as a port. The picture is consistent with that implied by the children of Asopos in the case of Sinope: the connections are with the Eastern, Central and South Western parts of Boiotia where there are reasons to postulate the genesis and initial growth of the earliest Boiotian League (cf. chapter 4), exactly those parts of Boiotia, moreover, where the cult of Herakles, who gave his name to the colony, was first widespread – in the Archaic period (again cf. chapter 4).

Once Herakleia was well established she began to take control of the surrounding territory at the expense of the indigenous Mariandynoi (cf. Saprykin, 1986: 31 for a map). The territory that she eventually came to control contained several smaller Greek towns, including her own secondary colony of Kieros, later renamed Prousias, at which one tribal division was called "Thebaïs" (*IPrusias* 1–8; 10–12; 14), another memory of Boiotian origins; yet one more of these smaller settlements was called Krenides, plainly associable with the homonymous gate at Thebai. Herakleia also sent out true secondary colonies beyond her own territory; there is some indication that one of these – location unknown (Asheri, 1972: 14) – was called Panelos (Stephanos of Byzantion *s.v.* Πάνελος) and may refer to (a descendant of?) the specifically Theban hero (*Ilias* ii 494, cf. discussion in chapter 1). Three other secondary colonies of Herakleia are, however, more important than the hazy Panelos. In the later 6th century BCE she founded the city of Kallatis on the West coast of the Euxinos Pontos; frequent depictions of Herakles on that city's coinage may

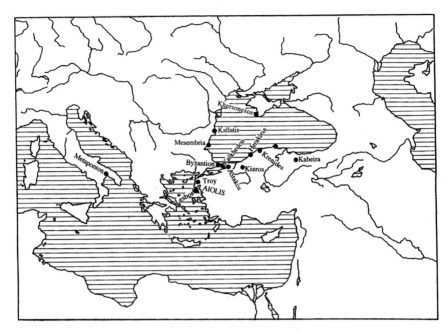

FIGURE 17   Boiotian participation in colonisation

underscore an original Boiotian connection of the mother city. Around the same time, or just slightly later, and again on the West Euxine coast, acting in conjunction with Megara, Kalkhedon and Byzantion – an almost incestuous group – she founded Messembria which was to provide a *proxenos* for Boiotian Oropos in the 3rd century BCE (*IG*vii 281). Messembria, following her mother city's example, was to expand her control over a strip of coastal territory and to plant within it a tertiary colony, at Naulokhos a little to the North. This model of territorial expansion was also followed by the last, and in some ways best known of Herakleia's secondary colonies, Khersonnesos Taurike, founded in 421 BCE on the North side of the Euxinos Pontos; she thus came to control much of the Western Crimea. Khersonnesos brings us back full circle to the connection with Aulis implied by the legend of Iphigeneia.

At the end of this whole process, during the last quarter of the 5th century BCE, a pattern had emerged of Boiotian connections, direct and indirect, with the Bosporos and South West Pontos, as well as several enclaves further along its West and South shores, and an important outlier on the North side, as well as more tenuous contacts with Kolkhis on the East. The situation is outlined on the map (Fig. 17).

In this context it is easier to understand certain events of some 50 years later. During the short-lived Theban hegemony, in her attempt to weaken Athenai, the Boiotian League built a fleet (for the only recorded time in her history; cf. chapter 13 below) and in 366–363 BCE, with the support of Byzantion – and thus with control of the Bosporos – sought to impede Athenian corn supplies coming from the area of the modern Ukraine (cf. Roesch, 1984; Fossey, 1990b: 185–199 & 2014: 3). If we look at the potentially pro-Boiotian zone that extended beyond Byzantion on both sides of the approach to the Bosporos we can see that Boiotian connections could exercise quite a decisive stranglehold on the Athenian corn convoys. In this context it is worth recording that my late friend, Velizar Velkov once suggested to me that an Athenian settlement at, or in the neighbourhood of modern Akhtopol might be Periklean in origin; as the architect of the Athenian policy of abandoning the countryside immediately surrounding their city and feeding its population on cereal imported from abroad, Perikles would indeed be a likely person to foresee the potential cut-off by a hostile alignment in the South West Euxinos.

For all this potential it is doubtful that military considerations lay behind the original Boiotian involvement in these Pontic settlements. What then was the cause? I hope to have disposed of the idea that colonization was often a way of exporting surplus population (Fossey, 1996) and, in any case, given the continued and considerable expansion of settlement in Boiotia that was possible for centuries after the colonizing movement (Fossey, 1988: chapter III.1), it is hardly likely that her cities or their league felt any need to relieve overpopulation or land-shortage.

In a certain way the answer may be suggested by a later situation. Elsewhere I have attempted (Fossey, 2014: chapter 1) to show the consistency with which most of the *proxenoi* of the Boiotian cities in the Hellenistic period resided in various cities of the North East Aigaion and the South and West Euxine seaboards. The situation is remarkably reminiscent of the concentration of colonies and pre-colonial contacts that we have just examined. If we take it that the *proxenoi* of Hellenistic times served a largely commercial function then we may incline to think that commerce may have lain behind Boiotia's Pontic interests from the start. It can, however, hardly have been of the same nature as the later commercial interests of Athenians in the Euxinos for Boiotia, with her very rich plains and obviously agricultural economy, would surely not usually need corn imports. What she was chronically short of, like many other areas of Greece of course, was metals, and I am forced, yet again, to the conclusion that it was the search for metals, and perhaps for knowledge of metal technology, that led to her involvement as a partner in colonization; this would do much to explain the quasi exclusivity of her movement towards the Euxinos with the metal traditions of the Thrakians, the Skythians and the Kolkhians and Khalybes. Unfortunately, when it comes to the reciprocal question of what the Boiotians might have exported to these same regions in return, I have no answer; plainly it could not be agricultural produce of which they both had an abundance.

As a final footnote to this story we may remember another indication of the connections between the South West Pontos and Boiotia. In the Hellenistic period and well down into Roman times, we notice an unusual concentration in Boiotia of heroising horseman reliefs on tombstones (Fossey, 2014: chapter 7, cf. also chapter 13 below); the indebtedness of these to the Thrakian horseman-hero reliefs is plain. It is noteworthy that these reliefs are not spread across the entirety of Boiotia but rather are concentrated in the East, Central and particularly the South West parts of the territory – precisely those parts that appear to have been the most involved in the colonization of the South and West Pontos.

CHAPTER 8

The Spartan Occupation of Southern Boiotia

In the 1970 volume of the *Annual of the British School at Athens* Richard Tomlinson and I published an account of the work that we had carried out in spring 1968 on the crest of Mount *Mavrovoúni* overlooking the South coast of Boiotia (Tomlinson & Fossey, 1970; republished in Fossey, 1990: chapter 11). In that article we attempted to show that, while the site had seen four phases of use, the most extensive second one was related to the Spartan presence in Boiotia between 378 and 375 BCE; remains of the first phase had been included in this larger second phase, while the third phase, lying a short distance to the West of the main enclosure represented a fairly immediate sequel to the second. The small fourth phases was separated in time by perhaps nearly a millennium from the rest, although built in one of its corners; it serves, nevertheless, to underline the strategic position of the place.

My own repeated visits to the site in the years between 1976 and 1992 have allowed me to add in many details not observed in 1968. These are incorporated in the description and plan that follow.

1 Historical Background

The 1970 article analyses in detail the sources and the historical context in which we sought to situate the *Mavrovoúni* site; it bears summarizing here since it applies to a number of aspects of the South coast area of Boiotia and not to *Mavrovoúni* alone. The original sources on which the following brief narrative is based are given in the article mentioned above.

Boiotia had belonged to the Spartan alliance against Athenai and her empire in the Peloponnesian War. Thus in 404 BCE she shared in the Spartan victory and was one of the Spartan allies to demand – unsuccessfully – the destruction of Athenai.

Such were the vagaries of alliance that less than a decade later, in 395 BCE, Boiotia was allied with Athenai and Korinthos against Sparta in the "Korinthian War". This war was finally terminated in 386 BCE by the intervention of the Persian king on the side of Sparta. One of the terms of the "King's Peace" involved the disbanding of the Boiotian League and, thereby the loss to Thebai of her control over her neighbours – a control that she had struggled hard to assert for well over a century, and the struggle which had probably been the prime reason for her original alliance with Sparta in the Peloponnesian War [just as it may have been the cause of her Medizing in the earlier 5th century in search of a chance to use the Persian forces' strength to bring pro-Athenian elements such as Thespiai and Plataiai to heel].

For all this effect of the Peace, the reduction of Thebai to the simple state of an individual Spartan ally was not sufficient reassurance for Sparta, and, in 382 BCE the akropolis of Thebai, the Kadmeia, was captured by a Spartan force under Phoibidas, working in concert with a pro-Spartan faction among the Thebans. Although Phoibidas was fined back at home in Sparta for breaching the treaty by this hostile act towards a technical ally, the Spartan garrison that he had installed in Thebai was not withdrawn.

Three years later, in 379 BCE, a group of Thebans under the leadership of Pelopidas, setting out from their refuge in Athenai, were able to move into Boiotia, to recapture the Kadmeia by subterfuge and then to oust the Spartan garrison. In the face of impending Spartan reprisals Pelopidas and his colleagues, to whom was added the hitherto seemingly unknown Epameinondas, had to organize their defences quickly.

In the winter of 379–378 BCE the Spartan king Kleombrotos invaded Boiotia and campaigned fruitlessly in Theban territory. He then set up a Spartan garrison at Thespiai (reinforcing her long held opposition to Thebai). Although he had entered Boiotia through the passes over Mt. Kithairon, the easiest land route from the Peloponnesos into Central Greece, he now withdrew by a hazardous route around the coast to Megaris, being embarrassed by the presence of a formally neutral Athenian force at Eleutherai. Wherever exactly we place ancient Eleutherai – and most people seem to place it at the fortified site of *Yiphtókastro* at the South entrance to the main pass (Kynoskephalai?) between North West Attike and South Boiotia – it is easy to see his reason for choosing the difficult coastal route.

In 378 BCE the other Spartan king, Agesilaos, secured the Kithairon passes and moved by that route into Boiotia, where, using Thespiai as his base, he raided Theban territory. He fortified Thespiai and then withdrew across Kithairon. Shortly afterwards the Thebans attacked Thespiai, killed the garrison's commander and pressed it so hard that reinforcements had to be sent from Sparta. It may be significant that these relief troops were sent *by sea*. This could mean that the Kithairon passes could not be used, but it could also mean that it was considered faster to transport them by sea since the situation was pressing.

In fact in the following year, 377 BCE, Agesilaos did use the Kithairon passes again, having ordered the garrison at Thespiai to secure them for him in advance. It is to be noted that two ruined towers with black glazed tile sherds associated have been observed by the two roads across Kithairon from the fortress at *Yiphtókastro* (one of the candidates for ancient Eleutherai, as just mentioned) to both Plataiai and the *Pantánassa* site (= ancient Hysiai?; cf. Fossey, 1988: 112–115) in the Parasopia (Pritchett, 1957: 17). Is it possible that these towers played some role in control of these passes either during or after the Spartan invasions? However that may be, after this invasion of Boiotia Agesilaos was also able to withdraw across the mountain but this was the last time that Spartan troops could move easily across Kithairon for, in the following year, 376 BCE, Kleombrotos was turned back in the mountains by the Boiotians. From that point on the Spartans had to send troops and supplies into Central Greece by sea, across the Gulf of Korinthos. The Thebans were increasingly on the attack and Spartan concern in 375 BCE was far more the defence of her ally Phokis than the further harassment of Thebai. The latter, in fact, now regained control over most of Boiotia and inflicted a telling defeat on a Spartan force at Tegyra in the extreme North West of Boiotia; the sites proposed for ancient Tegyra and the battle itself were examined in detail by the late John Buckler (1995).

In general, as the difficulty of using the Kithairon passes increased, the Spartans must have realized more and more the importance of using their mastery of the Korinthian Gulf and this is where *Mavrovoúni* enters the story but, as we shall shortly see, not *Mavrovoúni* alone. Peace was patched up in 375 BCE but lasted not more than a year. In 374 the Thebans, with the bit well between their teeth, invaded pro-Spartan Phokis and in 373 they finally regained control of Thespiai and Plataiai; now Orkhomenos remained the only recalcitrant Boiotian city outside the reformed League.

In 371 BCE the Athenians tried to negotiate a renewal of the King's Peace but the Thebans were this time too strong to be coerced into acquiescing in the disbanding of their league and so refused the terms of the Peace. Within a matter of weeks Kleombrotos, with a large Spartan force, advanced against Boiotia from Phokis. This advance which culminated in their crushing defeat by the Boiotians at Leuktra was the turning point and from now on, not only were the Spartans unable again to invade Boiotia; rather it was the turn of the Boiotians to invade the Peloponnesos and of the Spartans to be on the defensive. We shall return below to the aftermath of this brief period of Spartan interference actually in Boiotia.

2   *Mavrovoúni*

Mavrovoúni is the Western outlier of the conical Mt. *Korombíli* that dominates the Eastern part of the Boiotian South coast. The land slopes gradually

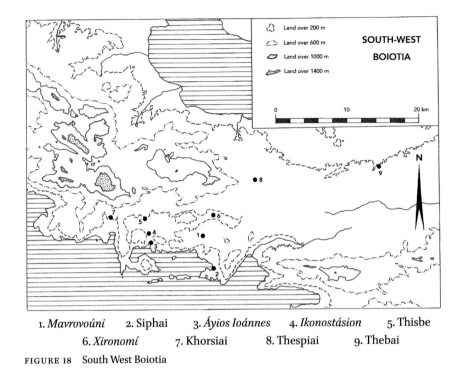

1. *Mavrovoúni*   2. Siphai   3. *Áyios Ioánnes*   4. *Ikonostásion*   5. Thisbe
6. *Xironomí*   7. Khorsiai   8. Thespiai   9. Thebai

FIGURE 18   South West Boiotia

Westwards down from the summit of *Korombíli* until it reaches 440m above sea level; at this point it levels out for several hundred meters before recommencing its Westwards down slope. On the virtual plateau formed on the level part is located an extensive ancient site. Along its East side passes the modern unsurfaced road from the small coastal village of *Alikí* near the ancient city of Siphai, to the larger inland village of *Xeronomí*. The geographical situation is shown on the map (Fig. 18). [It must be stressed that there is absolutely no reason, and no textual or other indication for calling *Mavrovoúni* "Ano-Siphai" as proposed by the German archaeologists who investigated both sites (Schwandner, 1977a: 516–519). Unfortunately this unjustified appellation begins to be adopted by others (e.g. Farinetti, 2011: 348) and should in future be eschewed.]

2.1   *Bibliography*
Lolling, n.d.: 82–84.
McCredie & Steinberg, 1960.
Tomlinson & Fossey, 1970 (reprinted in Fossey, 1990: 130–156).
Schwantner, 1977a & b.
Fossey, 1988: 173–174.

MAVROVOÚNI, BOIOTIA

FIGURE 19 *Mavrovoúni*: general site plan

2.2   *Structural Remains*

The plateau is not quite flat but presents a very gentle and even slope (1 in 13.2 or 7.5%) from the actual watershed towards the South. Most of its extent is covered by the second and largest of the four structural phases of the site's history. For a general plan of the remains cf. Fig. 19.

The earliest observable structural phase was located on the watershed itself, where the ubiquitous *pournária* disappear and an isolated field – still cultivated until fairly recent times – reveals a greater soil depth; the phase within and around this field consisted of a sanctuary with two temples and a variety of associated buildings; we have already referred to the one temple (cf. chapter 5). For the time being, however, we may point out that some earlier use of the site, going back at least to Late Bronze Age times, is indicated by surface sherds collected in this Northern part of the site. Other surface sherds seem to show that the first observable structural phase, the sanctuary, began its life in Late Geometric times and ran down through the Hellenistic period; particularly telling in this regard are the sima fragments of painted plaster and, most of all,

PLATE 11   *Mavrovoúni*, tower before the 1981 earthquake, from West

an antefix in the same medium found by the late Paul Roesch and shown to me by him in 1969 on a colour slide.

It was into this long period of the sanctuary's life that was interjected the second, most extensive observable structural phase; this phase incorporated the sanctuary into its North West corner and consisted of a large enclosure spilling Southwards from the watershed and enclosing a series of smaller buildings mostly composed of one, two or three rooms. Before proceeding to a description of this second phase it may be pointed out that there are two more observable structural phases, much reduced in size but still making use of this strategic position. A little to the North West of the large enclosure, the third phase is represented by a square watch tower built in coursed trapezoidal masonry that was well preserved (Pl. 11), until somewhat destroyed by the earthquake of February 1981; we shall also return to this structure later but its state of preservation implies that it dates after the construction of the large enclosure since it might otherwise have been expected to provide a source of building material for the latter. The fourth and final structural phase occupies the North East corner of the large enclosure and is built into the walls of this earlier construction. This final phase is a small square fort with round corner towers; the remains of a tiny Christian chapel in the interior, together with the general plan of the fortlet, testify to its Late Roman date. It may well be that this site served as an outpost to protect the town of Siphai on the coast below; if so it serves to underline the strategic nature of the position on *Mavrovoúni* but, at the same time, we may note that other lines of approach to Siphai from inland are not, it seems, similarly defended. In any case this part of the site's history will not concern us further since it is far removed in time from the rest of the account.

In the Southern parts of the large enclosure, that is those parts lying outside the areas both of the sanctuary and of the late fortlet on the watershed, the surface sherds consist only in some black-glazed pottery fragments and pieces of red- and black-painted roof tiles. These all indicate a 4th century BCE date and the latter show that the internal buildings – presumably all – may have been fully roofed. A single *caveat* must, however, be expressed: the German Institute's archaeologists had excavated some of the internal buildings the contents of which do not appear to have ever been published; publication of the pottery and other objects found in those buildings would have done much to elucidate the history of this second, extensive phase of the site's use. Unfortunately responsibility for this material was accorded to the then *ephor* of prehistoric and classical antiquities in Boiotia, Dr Angelikí Andreioménou, whose record of publication even of her own excavations leaves much to be desired. Will this information remain forever lost? It appears, in fact, that, apart from the actual sanctuary buildings on the watershed, several of the internal buildings in the lower Southern parts may also in fact relate originally to the life of the sanctuary since they are constructed in the same polygonal masonry (cf. detailed plan, Fig. 20). It may thus be that, when the large enclosure was constructed, thus extending the area of the site Southward, in addition to creating many more new internal buildings, all in the same rough masonry, it enclosed several pre-existing buildings in polygonal masonry probably associated with the sanctuary, just as it incorporated the sanctuary itself. Enclosure of the sanctuary, we will argue, was deliberate in several senses and presumably at least some other associated buildings – now become internal – were still serviceable or required minimum maintenance to be habitable; the conjunction of polygonal and rough walling seen in several other internal buildings seems to represent the sort of reconstruction work that may have been needed in places but basically one has the impression that, while they did not attempt to imitate the quality of the construction technique of pre-existing buildings, the builders of this extensive second phase were concerned to reuse a lot of substantial walling that remained from the earlier use.

The large enclosure, built in rough dry-stone technique (Pl. 12) is nearly square measuring *c.* 185m North-North-West – South-South-East by *c.* 175m West-South-West – East-North-East (for a detailed plan of this phase cf. Fig. 21). The North and West walls dating from the first building phase joining at a (rounded) right angle, the slight irregularities in wall alignment are found on the other sides. The East wall diverges slightly from the orientation

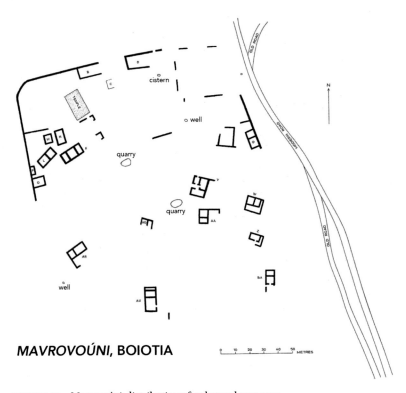

FIGURE 20   *Mavrovoúni*: distribution of polygonal masonry

of the opposite, West, side causing the South end of the site to be a little wider than the North; possibly this was caused by a desire to incorporate on its internal face a pre-existing building (G) whose alignment might thus have determined that of the circuit wall. The South side is, moreover, not a single line but consists of a long South-West stretch and a much shorter South East segment which meet in a very obtuse angle creating a slight outward bulge beyond the basic square; one may wonder if this was determined by the wish to incorporate within the enclosure two of the pre-existing, still well-preserved, buildings (Schwantner, 1977b) in polygonal masonry (AU and BA; for latter see Pl. 13) which ended up abutting the circuit wall, in one case (BA) doing so at a very odd angle. Several of the buildings in the central and West parts of the enclosure are in such a ruinous state or are concealed under such thick bush cover as to render their masonry unclear though one suspects that they are probably of rough construction; some other buildings enclosed in the circuit are in good polygonal masonry, while others are definitely in the rough masonry seen in the circuit wall. To the latter category belong most of the buildings built onto or against the circuit wall. It is noticeable that, while there is a goodly number

PLATE 12   *Mavrovoúni*, West wall of the compound, outer face

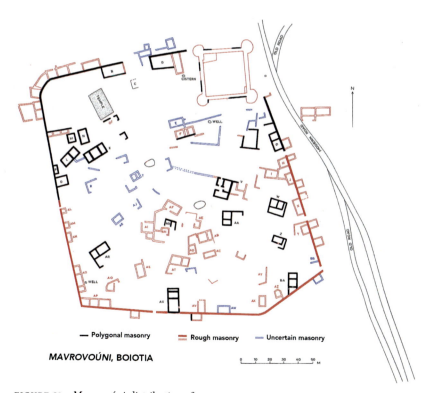

FIGURE 21   *Mavrovoúni*: distribution of masonry types

PLATE 13   *Mavrovoúni*, interior of building BA, detail of masonry

of such buildings, many of them just single rooms, built against the outer face of the circuit on the North and East sides of the circuit and just a few on the South, the West side has no such excrescences. On the other hand the inner faces of both the East and the West circuit have long sequences of buildings – again usually single rooms – constructed against them while this sort of construction is much less frequent along the South wall.

The line of the circuit wall is broken by several entrances. What was the state in the North East corner is not known since that part is concealed under the Late Roman fortlet but otherwise we see two entrances spaced out along the East wall with a third at the very South East corner, two more fairly evenly spaced along the South wall but only one in the whole run of the West wall. The North wall's line presents many difficulties with confusions of individual bits of polygonal and then rough walling. What is noticeable is that these are all simply entrances, not gateways and that they are not provided with any extra protection such as flanking towers *vel sim.* (cf. gate in West wall, Pl. 14). The overall impression is that the wall served essentially to define space rather than constituting a defence.

It seems an obvious suggestion that the buildings in polygonal style should be seen to go with the sanctuary while those in rough masonry should be associated with the bulk of the circuit wall. The relative sequence of these two phases is perhaps indicated by the way the apparently later complex AF-AI-AH

PLATE 14   *Mavrovoúni*, gate in West wall of compound

(rough masonry?) seems to have destroyed or overlain part of the pre-existing building AG (polygonal walling). So we will discuss these two phases separately and in that order.

Before that detailed examination we may make one general observation. Whatever the purpose of the large enclosure and the many buildings associated with it by style of construction, if it was to house in any way the number of people that the buildings suggest, just like the smaller accumulation of polygonal buildings of the posited earlier stage, water would be a problem on the top of this barren mountain ridge. Thus we notice, in the Northern part of the site, and adjacent to the Late Roman fortlet both a bottle-shaped cistern and a well (as seen in 1968, Pl. 15; now blocked up). It is tempting to see these as going with the sanctuary. In the central parts of the large enclosure there are two large depressions in the ground surface (Pl. 16). Examination of these showed that they had started life as quarries for building stone and that they had then been lined with plaster to make them waterproof to hold collected rain-water as open-air cisterns; given that the stone does not seem to have been cut in anything like squared or shaped blocks (there are no long cutting lines) it would seem that the rough pieces extracted here were intended for walls of the second phase (the large enclosure) while there are no indications as to the source of the stone used in the polygonal walls. Finally in 1968 another well could be seen inside the South West corner but was no longer visible in 1992;

PLATE 15   *Mavrovoúni*, bottle-shaped cistern in Northern part of compound

PLATE 16   *Mavrovoúni*, quarry

since there are a few buildings in polygonal masonry in the South part of the enclosure it is possible that a well in this position might also go, like its fellow to the North by the Late Roman fort, with the sanctuary but nothing is certain.

2.2.1   Sanctuary

As the general plan (Fig. 19) shows, the field in the North West part of the site is largely free of building remains except for an elongated temple with a portion of wall in front of it and similarly aligned parallel to its front (perhaps a platform of some sort or an altar, though, in either case it is very close to the temple). This temple, whose life seems to have run from at least the Archaic period, possibly from the Late Geometric, through the Hellenistic but not into Roman times, belongs to a group of archaic and archaizing temples in Boiotia that present the same appearance (aperipteral and distyle *in antis*) and that are the subject of another chapter (5) in this book. The boundary wall running along the North side of the field is mostly of fine polygonal work (Pl. 17), as is the Northern part of the West wall. Although these sections of wall were incorporated into the circuit of the large enclosure they contrast very much with its generally much rougher construction and this contrast is underlined by the curved nature of the North West corner itself; all other corners in the large enclosure are angled, not rounded. This polygonal work continues in parts of

PLATE 17   *Mavrovoúni*, polygonal masonry to immediate North East of temple

the North wall of the Late Roman fort so if we were correct to suggest in 1970 that this all constituted the remains of a *temenos* wall, the implication is that the sacred area extended a considerable distance West-East. There is, at the same time, no way of determining its North-South dimension for, although there are buildings in polygonal masonry, as we have already observed, as far South as that side of the large enclosure there is no indication of any substantial cross wall to delimit the supposed *temenos* in this direction and, in general, the polygonal work is less and less present as one proceeds Southwards. In particular we notice that in the Southern half of the site all the buildings that back onto the circuit wall, with the exception of the two long ones AU and BA (Schwantner, 1977b), are all in rough masonry.

The plan (Fig. 20) summarises as much of the presence of polygonal masonry as could be clearly distinguished during my several visits to the site subsequent to our original survey work of Spring 1968. I was also able to distinguish that the small building in polygonal masonry, K, near to the large temple presented evidence that it might in fact be seen as yet a second, though much smaller temple and it is noticeable that it is aligned both at right angles (East-West) to the North-South axis of the large temple and that both of them are aligned on a further square structure (unnumbered on our original plan and only preserved at foundation level), leading to the thought that this structure might have been a common altar for both temples; we may remember that the Heraion on Samos, by the end of the 6th century, seems to have had three temples all orientated towards the same altar (cf. discussion by Berquist, 1967: 44–47). The reconstructed plan of building K given by us in 1970 (Tomlinson & Fossey, 1970:

254, fig. 5; Fossey, 1990: 142) should be emended since small portions of walling at its West end, not noticed in 1968, show the existence of a shallow *adyton* behind the main room which itself is preceded by a deeper porch on the East; it is this *adyton* that distinguishes the building from the sort of secondary buildings seen in many sanctuaries where the small ones may often be rectangular buildings with a front porch but no internal divisions.

At least one deity worshipped in the sanctuary must at some stage have been Artemis Agroteira according to the dedicatory inscriptions of two Hellenistic statue bases found on or near the site more than half a century ago (*SEG* xviii 166–167). There is, however, no clear indication whatsoever of this or any other dedication in pre-Hellenistic times and whether it was the larger or the putative smaller temple in which her cult was housed is not clear; nor is there any indication as to who might be the dedicatee of this suggested smaller temple. Given the small dimensions of the latter it might have been intended to house a hero cult. Similar pairings of a temple and a heroon do occur elsewhere in Boiotia, like the sanctuary of Ptoian Apollon and the shrine of the hero Ptoos outside Akraiphiai and the suggested temple of Hera with the heroon of Herakles at *Khóstia*, though distance between the two is a bit less here at *Mavrovoúni* than at *Khóstia* and much less than that which occurs at the Ptoion where the two are separated by a wide stretch of land including a stream bed. Concerning the dedication(s) perhaps we should entertain two different possibilities: 1. that the sanctuary was originally dedicated to some other divinity and that Artemis, with or without the epithet, was a later introduction; 2. that Artemis may have originally been worshipped at the sanctuary and that the epithet Agroteira was introduced later. Should the smaller temple (if such it indeed was), have housed a hero cult it would follow, that the large temple might have housed the cult of Artemis at some stage but the identity of such a putative hero remains lost. A further possibility that must be born in mind is that specifically the builders in the phase of the large enclosure may have introduced the cult of Agroteira to a pre-existing sanctuary of Artemis (with or without some other epithet) or possibly even brought the cult of Artemis Agroteira as such into the sanctuary of a completely different deity. The evidence does not allow us to decide and the dedications plainly date some time after the second large construction phase.

In addition to the second possible temple, examination of the other remains in polygonal masonry outside the immediate area of the sanctuary field reveals that there are several showing variations on a simple plan. Building W is a good example of this (Tomlinson & Fossey, 1970: 254, Fig. 6 – note that this detailed plan shows the dividing wall between the two rooms in the North West part of the building, a wall which is missing in the general site plan of our Fig. 1). This plan is essentially two rooms with a partial or complete enclosure (courtyard *vel sim.*) across one side of them; it can be seen in buildings Z, AR, AA and – with some subsequent remodelling – V, as well as in AG as it might have been before it was, as we have already seen, partly demolished by the construction of AF, AH and AI.

Looking at the plan of the distribution of these buildings in polygonal masonry I am reminded of what happens at the land just across the water from *Mavrovoúni* in the buildings on the upper plain towards the end of the *Perakhóra* peninsula (Tomlinson, 1969: esp. 172–192 + Plate 50). Separated by some distance from the possibly double sanctuary of Hera by the harbour and in the small valley leading down thereto, the end section of the peninsula has other structural remains in the upper plain which runs East-West from Lake *Vouliagméni* nearly to the end of the peninsula and the Heraion. Excavations in this area in 1964 produced a small temple (not, unfortunately, excavated properly but cleaned simply in order to clarify the plan) opening to the East, a feature that led R.A. Tomlinson to suggest that it might be a temple of Artemis; he also postulated that it might have been distyle *in antis*. The date of this temple is not clear on account of the lack of real excavation of it; Tomlinson tried to date it to the later 5th century BCE but this dating is only a hypothesis and cannot be confirmed. Given the indications that many of the small buildings scattered around in the neighbourhood of this temple started their lives in the Archaic period there is good reason to propose that a temple may have stood here from that time onward, if not the actual temple revealed in 1964, at least a predecessor or predecessors. It is the surrounding buildings that catch attention, some of them having a plan consisting in two rooms fronting onto an enclosed area or courtyard (especially buildings ZI and ZII), just as occurs at *Mavrovoúni*. It is this similarity which leads me to suggest that, just as was surmised for *Perakhóra*, the structures in polygonal style at *Mavrovoúni* may be adjuncts to the temple(s) and may have served people attending festivals at the sanctuary(ies). We shall have other reasons to look at *Perakhóra* in connection with *Mavrovoúni* in later pages but for the time being we may note that both are sanctuaries in isolated locations; it must be assumed that provision for housing pilgrims, especially making available facilities for ritual feasting, and providing water was a necessity. That buildings at *Mavrovoúni*, just as at *Perakhóra*, may have had quite long lives can be deduced from the fact that some of them, at least, show signs of remodelling while construction was still being carried out in polygonal masonry and presumably, therefore, before the changes that some were to undergo when the time for construction in the more hurried rough masonry arrived. There are doorways blocked and benches (for feasting?) subsequently inserted especially in buildings BA and V, two of the best preserved of these internal structures and the ones that were examined in detail by the German archaeologists in the 1970's.

In summary we can see at *Mavrovoúni*, from the later 8th century BCE onward, the development of a sanctuary ultimately with perhaps two temples, both possibly aligned on a single altar, and surrounded by a possible *temenos* wall (though much of this latter remains to be demonstrated) and with other buildings scattered on the slopes to the South to provide feasting and other facilities for visitors to the sanctuary. The existence of such areas gathered around but not in the immediate area of the cult centre itself has been explored by Birgitta Bergquist (1967: 100–107) and found by Tomlinson (1977) to correspond to the situation at *Perakhóra*; these more separated buildings are especially called by both scholars "οἴκοι", such as those used as dining rooms (or, for larger groups "oikoi complexes").

As we have seen the cult of Artemis Agroteira was observed in this sanctuary at least by the 3rd century BCE (Schachter, 1981: 102–103). Given the idea of a second temple is it altogether too audacious to suggest that another divinity here at *Mavrovoúni* just possibly might have been Apollon (it should be noted that I do not hold to this very strongly); this natural brother-sister pairing is generally not unknown in Boiotia but, what is more, although she does also appear at Lebadeia as "Agrotis" (*IG* vii 3100), the only other occurrence of Artemis with the specific epithet "Agroteira" in Boiotia is at nearby Thisbe where she is clearly associated with her brother (*IG* vii 3564):

['Ἀπόλλ-]
ωνος
Ἀρτάμι-
[δ]ος Ἀγρο-
[τ]έρας.

We shall return to the question of Artemis Agroteira/Agrotis in Boiotia further on but for the moment will remark simply that the inscription at Thisbe might give a certain logic to the proposition of a similar pairing here at *Mavrovoúni*. [On other possible Boiotian occurrences of the specific "Delian" couple cf. Schachter, 1981: 49, 100.]

2.2.2 The Large Enclosure

Into the setting of this sanctuary was introduced in the 4th century BCE (as it appears from the surface sherds of black-glazed pottery) the large enclosure and many more buildings in and around it. The circuit wall is observable in all its extent, except in the North East corner where it was covered over by

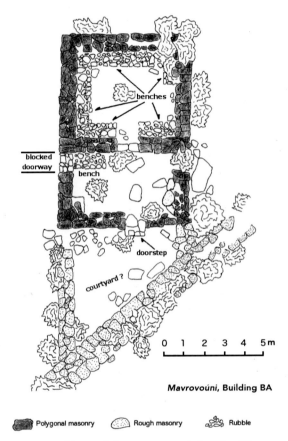

FIGURE 22 *Mavrovoúni*: masonry types in building BA

the Late Roman fortlet. This circuit was described above. Obviously some at least of the existing structures in polygonal style were incorporated deliberately within the enclosure wall; we have already suggested that the course of the South wall might have been in part determined by the desire to incorporate several buildings, notably BA (Fig. 22) and AU, and it is noticeable that, with the exception of the rather complicated situation around the North West corner, there is effectively no polygonal masonry left outside the circuit.

Some of the existing buildings in polygonal masonry were extended into something larger and more complex. Thus a small square building at BA (Fig. 22) with an oblong room in front of it to the South had the side entrance to this South room blocked and this permitted the insertion into that smaller room of yet another bench to the side of the doorway between the South room and its main partner to the North which was (at the same time?) equipped with benches around most of its sides, albeit with a striking gap in the Southern

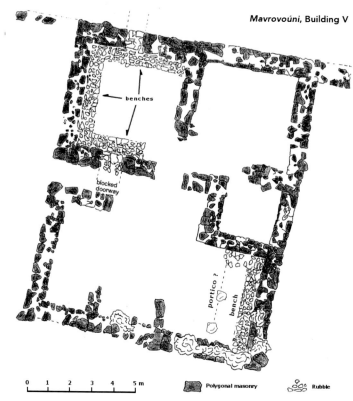

FIGURE 23 *Mavrovoúni*: masonry types in building V

part of the East wall. The entrance to the resulting two-room sequence was by a doorway with an elevated step almost at midpoint in the South wall, not quite aligned with the similar doorway between the two rooms themselves. The area immediately to the South of the South room was enclosed by a wall on the West, and another much shorter one on the East, both in rough masonry, continuing approximately the East and West walls of polygonal masonry so as to attach the resulting building to the inside of the circuit wall in the same sort of rough masonry. This small area was entered through a doorway in its North West corner and gives the appearance of a small nearly triangular courtyard.

In a similar way another small structure with two rooms and front yard at V (Fig. 23) was reorganized into a whole ensemble. The Westerly of the two rooms that originally had entrances through both its North and South walls now saw these doorways closed with rubble masonry thus allowing the insertion of benches around most of the interior. The front yard now had a bench added on its East wall with a possible portico protecting it (and showing that the rest of the space really was some sort of unroofed yard); a short corridor from the West side provided the only entrance to the complex.

The relative sequence of the walling styles is clearly shown by the way in which the rough masonry walls of AF, AH, AI – and incorporating possibly part of AE – replaced the partially destroyed AG in polygonal masonry. The group formed by E and F reused some polygonal walling with the addition of more walls in rough masonry to create another larger complex. An entirely new, also complex group of walled spaces was created by AB, AD and possibly AC, though this has some resemblance to the earlier concept of two rooms fronting onto an enclosed space; AT in rough masonry, also looks very much like one of the buildings in polygonal masonry with the same two-room-and-yard ensemble.

It was not possible to determine the masonry of some of the smaller interior buildings but it seemed likely that their ruinous state was probably the result of their being built in a somewhat less durable masonry and thus probably not in polygonal work and perhaps not even in the rough but fairly solid building seen in so many parts of the site. Many of the indeterminate buildings were apparently single rooms, rather like almost all those tacked onto the inside (and sometimes the outside also) of the circuit wall; the only exceptions here are the two three-roomed structures in rough masonry built against the inner face of the circuit wall to either side of the South West corner (AO and AP).

There is a single independent external building, in rough masonry again, with two large rooms and a partly enclosed area in front of the one; separated from the main site by the modern road, its West end has been destroyed as the result of road-widening activities. It is theoretically possible that other remains lie in this area which is much more heavily overgrown than the land to other sides of the circuit but we were not able to see any.

It is the extensive enclosure with its plethora of varied internal buildings – the latter resulting from at least two construction phases (polygonal and rough, though with modifications certainly in the former and seemingly in the latter too) that we identified as a Spartan base for the invasions of Boiotia in the first years of the 370's BCE. In this it would have been like the fort that the same Spartans just a decade earlier had proposed to erect on the frontiers of their old enemy, Argos and Argolis (Xenophon, *Hellenika* iv.7, 7); the latter idea had to be abandoned because of bad omens (cf. comment by Pritchett, 1971: 113) but it seems that *Mavrovoúni* did not incur the same sort of wrath of the gods!

In a reaction against our conclusion that *Mavrovoúni* was a Spartan base, A.W. Lawrence (1979: 181) refers to the remark by Xenophon (*Lakedaimonion Politeia* xii. 1–2; he incorrectly says only "1", although he is about to misuse something from 2):

Διὰ μὲν γὰρ τὸ τὰς γωνίας τοῦ τετραγώνου ἀχρήστους εἶναι εἰς κύκλον ἐστρατοπεδεύσατο, εἰ μὴ ὄρος ἀσφαλὲς εἴη ἢ τεῖχος ἢ ποταμὸν ὄπισθεν ἔχοιεν. φυλακάς γε μὴν ἐποίησε μεθημερινὰς τὰς μὲν παρὰ τὰ ὅπλα εἴσω βλεπούσας· οὐ γὰρ πολεμίων ἕνεκα ἀλλὰ φίλων αὗται καθίστανται.

Given that the corners in a square are useless he (Lykourgos) encamped in a circle unless in the rear there was a secure height or a wall or a river. He caused sentries to be posted in the daytime looking inward over the arms for these are placed not on account of the enemy but because of their fellows.

Summarizing this, he writes, "Xenophon commends a regulation in Spartan armies, put into effect wherever the terrain permitted, that their camps should be circular in outline and centered on the stacked weapons". He further draws the "apparent implication" that other Greeks observed no ideal plan. We may first observe that, in fact, Xenophon nowhere seems to specify that the arms were either stacked or in the centre, simply that they were, not illogically, "inside" the camp. We should then remark that Xenophon himself outlines several situations that could cause departure from the circular ideal, one of which was a wall, presumably a wall that might be reused. At *Mavrovoúni* our putative Spartans found not one but many walls, remaining from the earlier building phase of the sanctuary; this is very clear from the Northern side and the Northerly parts of the East and West walls and we have even suggested that the irregularity of the South wall might have been caused by the desire to incorporate pre-existing buildings. What Lawrence did not take sufficiently into account was that there was clearly a building phase that predated the enclosure. This is such a clear example of precisely the sort of situation that Xenophon himself envisages as possibly causing departure from the circular ideal.

In a chapter devoted to "Fortified Camps" the late Kendrick Pritchett (1974: 133–146) also quoted the description by Xenophon of the Lykourgan camp referring at the same time to an earlier scholar, Gilbert (*non vidi*), who apparently wrote "that the camp was surrounded by palisades may be concluded from the consideration that we cannot well think of a circular-shaped camp without them". At *Mavrovoúni* we are plainly not thinking of temporary palisades but of built, stone walls intended for more than ephemeral occupation.

Lawrence was quite right to point out, as we had already done in any case, that the nature of the gateways argues against this being a defensive fortification just as the buildings attached to the enclosure wall both on the inside and on the out cannot by any stretch of the imagination be seen as towers to strengthen the wall for defensive purposes. He does not, however, consider that these aspects support our view that the site had an offensive nature rather than a defensive one and that this is much more consistent with being the creation of an invading, mobile force rather than a defensive and essentially stationary local one.

3   The Spartan Network

Obviously forts on the borders of enemy territory were in the frame of Spartan military thinking in the first quarter of the 4th century BCE. The question of bad omens left aside, there is a considerable difference between establishing a fort on the border of enemy territory when the other side of that border is your own territory, as would have been the case of a Spartan fort on the border of Argolis. Obviously enough, having home territory adjacent can considerably simplify the question of transporting reinforcements and supplies. This is not the case when the fort is at considerable remove from home territory, as would have been the case with a Spartan base on *Mavrovoúni*. If our earlier argument was in order, namely that the establishment on *Mavrovoúni* was created to facilitate Spartan operations at a time when use of even the passes through the mountains along the South side of Boiotia was blocked and when reinforcements and supplies had to be transported across the Korinthian Gulf, it is clear that for a Spartan force based in Boiotia stable communications with home or friendly lands would be essential.

It was this latter thought that led me to look into the possibility of other places of Spartan presence on the South Boiotian coast and one candidate did soon emerge. It had, in fact, been noticed by a single previous traveller although his description is misleading in some ways. Leake (1835: vol. ii: 507) wrote:

> The port of *Thisbe*, which is now called Vathý, is a beautiful little harbour surrounded by woody hills. On the ridge looking down upon it, which separates the plain of *Thisbe* from the coast, are the remains of a Hellenic tower and station, similar to that upon the ridge above Alikí, and evidently a fortified point and signal post on the road from *Thisbe* to its port. There are said also to be some remains of a fortress on the side of the harbour.

The nearly landlocked bay of *Dhómvraina* presents an excellent natural harbour at modern *Alikí* (ancient Siphai) below *Mavrovoúni* but this is not the only natural harbour in the extensive bay. Further West there are two more such places (Fossey, 1988: 182–183); of these the first is the small fishing harbour of today at *Áyios Ioánnes*, the simplest place of access to the sea for the modern settlements at *Kakkósi* (ancient Thisbe) and *Dhómvraina*; these two formerly independent villages have today been amalgamated into the single centre of the δῆμος Θισβέων whence a road to *Áyios Ioánnes* runs straight across the plain or natural *polje* of *Dhómvraina* on the top of an ancient dyke which would easily have supported a roadway also in antiquity (Fossey, 1988: 182; cf. Knauss, 1992). This road descends gently to the small harbour in a series of curves. To the West of *Áyios Ioánnes* is another, much deeper harbour, appropriately called *Vathý* ("deep"); from here a very steep natural climb to the ridge separating coast from *polje*, follows the torrent bed; despite the difficulty of this ascent, there are indications that a road cut into bedrock was engineered in antiquity to rise to the top of the ridge. Photographs of the latter were kindly provided to me some years ago by my colleague and friend Klaus Fitschen, then Director of the German Archaeological Institute in *Athína*; a brief description of remains observed here is also given by Gregory, 1992: 28–29. It seems that both these harbours must have been used by Thisbe in antiquity since the *senatus consultum* of 170 BCE concerning the city (*IG* vii 2225) mentions "harbours" in the plural (περὶ λιμένων) and these two seem to be the only possible candidates (Farinetti, 2011: 350 summarises some previous observations at both harbours). The routes from both harbours cross the ridge at more or less the same point where an *ikonostásion* of *Áyios Ioánnes* stands on the West side of the modern road.

Some 200m further back from the road, on a gentle slope overlooking it from the West, there is another ancient site not previously recorded in the archaeological bibliography, apart from the incidental mention by Leake. Since it has no toponym of its own, as far as I am aware, I have simply dubbed it *Ikonostásion Ayíou Ioánnou* or *Áyios Ioánnes ikonostásion*. It should be noted that the site is not as easily approachable from the road nowadays, as it was in the 1970's when I explored it; a large, deep channel has been cut through the ridge to the East of the site. The channel, I was told, was to permit the transport of bauxite to the harbour at *Vathý*.

This is presumably the Hellenic "station" mentioned by Leake but the tower cited in the same phrase by him must be either the one in a very ruined condition by the road on a small headland before it finishes its descent to *Áyios Ioánnes* or one that has completely disappeared (cf. Gregory, 1992: 28), just as the one by the road is ruined down to one course of stones; the "fortress" said to be by the harbour can only be the substantial short stretch of walling down by the beach at *Vathý* (known to me only from photographs, again provided by Klaus Fitschen), a structure hardly meriting the appellation "fortress". The ruined tower closer to *Áyios Ioánnes* is in the same coursed trapezoidal masonry

PLATE 18   *Áyios Ioánnes*, North wall of tower

(Pl. 18) that we shall encounter in many watch towers that dot much of the landscape of Boiotia (cf. chapter 10) whereas the masonry at the *ikonostásion* site on the ridge (Pll. 19–20) is of the same solid but rough type seen in the large enclosure at *Mavrovoúni*. Leake's confusion in this area is perhaps explained by his phrase "there are also said"; we may legitimately question whether on this occasion Col. Leake was a little less meticulous in his search than was his wont. What he may have written at this point was the result of a misinterpretation of some garbled remarks by guides or other villagers. Not only are the three separate structures confused; there is no way in which the normally very observant colonel could have described the *ikonostásion* site as similar to that on *Mavrovoúni* from any point of view except the type of masonry.

This site by the *ikonostásion*, as the plan (Fig. 24) shows, despite being built in the same sort of rough masonry as seen in the large enclosure at *Mavrovoúni*, has a different and more complex layout than the latter. Understanding the plan has been complicated by the very rough building up in more recent times of certain walls (and the addition of an extra one), especially in the South part, presumably to serve as sheep-pens. It appears to be organized in three sections succeeding each other in a North-South line. Possibly the large central section ("rooms" VI, VII, VIII and IX, together with "corridors" 1 and 2) was the initial part built, followed by the equally large South section ("rooms" I, II, III and IV, together with "courtyard" V); the uneven junction of these two at the South

PLATE 19   *Áyios Ioánnes* (*ikonostásion*), walling in Northern part of main complex

PLATE 20   *Áyios Ioánnes* (*ikonostásion*), masonry in South wall of main complex, inside face

East corner of "room" IX is what suggests the order of construction; the smaller section to the North ("rooms" XII and XIII) looks rather like an afterthought. The more recent building work has left some spaces or "rooms" apparently without doorways.

Apart from a single separate building lying to the East, just as at *Mavrovoúni*, this site does not present separate structures but is simply a concatenation of spaces/"rooms" of varying sizes and shapes, mostly approximating to rectangles – in some cases, large rectangles with one or two much smaller "rooms" set into a corner – but obviously not measured in the more precise

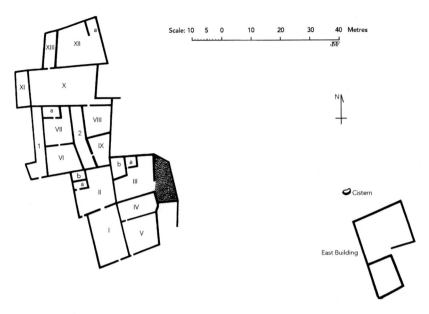

FIGURE 24 *Áyios Ioánnes Ikonostásion* plan

way seen in most of the buildings at *Mavrovoúni*. No potsherds were recovered making it look as though the site was not heavily inhabited, although the presence of numerous red- and black-painted tile-sherds shows that much of the structure, like the East Building, was roofed and the presence of a cistern by that same East building demonstrates provision of this necessary life support. It is the tile sherds, together with comparable position (by a road from harbour to hinterland) that suggest a dating and context for this site similar to those of *Mavrovoúni*. If they do indeed belong together it is clear that their functions and purposes must have been rather different. My suggestion would be simply that this second site may have been a supply depot; the shorter ascent from the sea would have facilitated the transport of supplies landed by boat, while its remote position would guarantee some security for those supplies, added to the fact that the force postulated to have been positioned at *Mavrovoúni* had visual control over the routes which might lead hostile Boiotian troops in the direction of *Áyios Ioánnes ikonostásion*, and could thus protect its "quartermasters' store", if such it was. We shall return to further reasons for seeing this site as connected with *Mavrovoúni* and with the Spartan occupying forces in the early 4th century BCE.

Keeping a sizeable force supplied while situated near the edge of hostile territory and far from home would necessitate good communications between these two putative Spartan invasion bases and Sparta itself. It is, in fact, possible to envisage a signal network with archaeological candidates at points along it.

In the Halkyonic Gulf, the Northern branch of the larger Korinthian Gulf, is a group of islands, once perhaps known as the Halkyonides but nowadays called the Καλά Νησιά. Today there seem to be four islands, two of them large and close together, the other two being much smaller and situated a bit further away to the West. The two small barren ones, called *Prasonísi* to the North and *Glaronísi* to the South do not seem to need our attention any further but the two larger ones are indeed very close to each other and, when we visited them in 1979, we were told that the strait between them is so shallow that it was possible to wade through the sea from the one to the other. The North West edge of the largest island, *Zoödhókhos Piyí*, perhaps so named after the fresh water well by the deserted monastery of the Theotókos (Mother of God) that lies by the small bay at the same North East end of the island is connected by this ford to the South point of the slightly smaller island of *Dhaskaleió*. What the situation is today, after the earthquake of February 1981, I do not know but when visiting the Καλά Νησιά two years before that earthquake, whose epicentre was exactly at this same group of islands, I was told that locals considered that the two had originally been one continuous island; indeed at the very South end of *Dhaskaleió* (Pll. 21–22) we found remains of a settlement of at least Late Helladic and Archaic date which appeared to continue under water onto the floor of the ford. If the two were indeed connected the rest of the space between them would form a natural harbour opening to the North and this is indeed the line of approach for boats sailing into the small modern harbour next to the monastery. Apart from an exiguous plain by the monastery and harbour, the island of *Zoödhókhou Piyí* is rather barren and rocky whereas *Dhaskaleió* slopes gently up from the area of the beach that continues the line of the postulated original harbour, and is surmounted by a large fairly flat area with remains of walls in solid rough masonry using large blocks (Pl. 23) in which the existence of an open cistern has been noted. Unfortunately the visit in 1979 was extremely brief with no possibility of planning or measuring before the boat's siren summoned us back to the harbour for immediate departure. The visit of a Greek colleague, I. Papakhristodhoúlou (1968) led to another all too brief account. [It may be noted that this colleague mentions a small site with walls and a rock-cut staircase at the South end of the island, a stair case which we also observed carved into the rock; this is obviously the Mykenaian site we have already mentioned although the colleague only cites finding archaic Korinthian pottery. Also recorded were indications that the church of the

PLATE 21 *Kalá Nisiá*, Southern tip of *Dhaskaleió* from the area of *Zoödhókhos Piyí*

PLATE 22 *Kalá Nisiá*, Southern tip of *Dhaskaleió*, South wall running North-North-West

Theotókos might have replaced a Palaiochristian basilica, implying perhaps a long history for this as a cult site and indications of ancient tombs noticed would show that habitation here was not just some ephemeral incident.]

The conclusion of the colleague regarding the walls on *Dhaskaleió* may be quoted:

> ἡ δὲ προχειρότης τῆς κατασκευῆς τῶν τειχῶν ὑποδηλώνει, ἴσως, ὅτι ἀνηγέρθησαν ἐσπευσμένως κατὰ τὴν διάρκειαν πολεμικῶν ἐπιχειρήσεων.

If this conclusion of hasty building in a military context seems plausible, given also the similarity of the walling style observed here with that seen in the large

PLATE 23   *Kalá Nisiá*, central plateau of *Dhaskaleió*, wall along North side

enclosure at *Mavrovoúni* and at the site by the *Áyios Ioánnes ikonostásion*, it is logical to consider the possibility that all of them might be connected.

Just as the *Kalá Nisiá* lie due South of the Bay of *Dhomvraína*, at a slightly smaller distance further in the same direction comes the North coast of the *Perakhóra* peninsula. Here we can find other possibly connected sites. At the very end of the peninsula are two fortified sites with walls in the same rough masonry already discussed for the preceding sites (Wiseman, 1978: 33). The one fortification surrounds the small peak at the very point of the peninsula, the peak that is occupied by the lighthouse (Pl. 24). The other is a bit smaller still and stands on a higher peak to the East (Pl. 25) that dominates both the entire Heraion valley and the upper plain to whose cult buildings, investigated in 1964 we have already referred; this site is marked by the presence within the ancient walls of a chapel of Áyios Nikólaos, next to the back of which is an ancient open cistern.

The lighthouse fortification (cf. plan, Fig. 25) is difficult to understand at first sight because it has been damaged in parts by the construction of the lighthouse and its outbuildings, together with the creation of a proper track leading up to it from the flatter part of the peninsula end where there is a rudimentary modern car park. In several stretches the lighthouse peak falls away in steep, near-vertical cliffs and so there a natural defence is provided; this applies in particular to the highest, Eastern part of the peak where the lighthouse itself is situated but also to the continuation of the South side of the hill where it overlooks the Heraion and the harbour. It is along part of the South side, after the cliffs cease towards the East, and also at the narrow East end where fortification walls are needed. The wall on the South side is cut across by a doorway wherein is preserved even a carved socket for the lower corner of a

PLATE 24   *Perakhóra*, the lighthouse fortification, general from East

PLATE 25   *Perakhóra*, the Áyios Nikólaos fortification from the West

door to swing open and closed; from this doorway a rather steep path leads down in the direction of the harbour. Immediately to the East of the path a higher rock outcrop bears traces of a well-constructed angular wall turning the outcrop into a sort of flanking tower to protect the door. At the East end proper, in addition to a short stretch of defence wall there is, further down the slope, a long stretch of wall in the same masonry and on a roughly parallel alignment

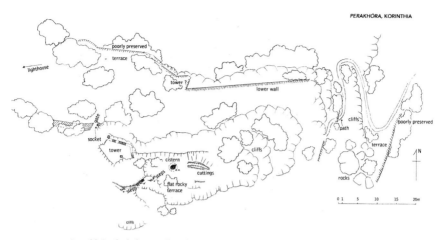

FIGURE 25 *Perakhóra* lighthouse fortification

providing a terrace wall to support the path (together with adjoining small terraces) that leads up from the aforementioned flat area of the current car park. There are no clear indications of internal structures but on the Eastwards continuation of the "tower" outcrop there are more steps, several cuttings and a cistern. The surface of the site does not provide much in the way of pottery pieces but, in any case, we would expect the peak to have seen some sort of use, fortified or not, at more or less all times during the life of the Heraion sanctuary, that is from Middle Geometric times through to the Roman period.

The Áyios Nikólaos fortification (cf. descriptions by Robinson, 1938: 43–45 and Tomlinson, 1969: 241–242) is simpler and encloses a smaller space than that at the lighthouse (cf. plan, Fig. 26). On another rocky spur, this time to the East of the Heraion valley, its position is strong by nature with steep sides all around except where a narrow path leads up from the sanctuary area of the upper plain. In plan it presents an elongated triangle, the short West side being a roughly straight line, while to North East (Pl. 26) and South East (Pl. 27) long approximately straight defining lines are composed of combinations of cliffs and fortification/retaining walls in the usual rough masonry. Within the acute Eastern angle a higher zone is offset again by a combination of walls and especially cliffs. On this higher zone is situated the chapel of Áyios Nikólaos to the immediate South of which is a short stretch of ancient walling with more modern extension upwards; this is the only sign of internal building except for the chapel itself. Behind the North East corner of the chapel more walls in the rough masonry define a narrow path that leads to a rock carved cistern (Pl. 28), beyond which the steepness of the hill's slope provides natural protection. Perhaps this cistern carved into the bedrock is the "cave" noticed by an early traveller, Dutroyat, cited by Col. Leake (1830, vol. iii: 399) and which was

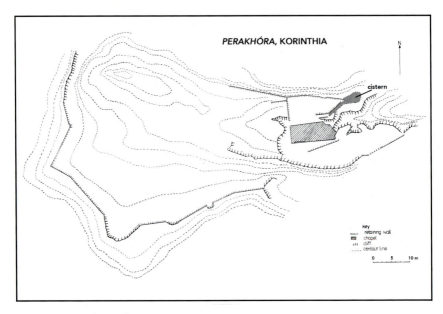

FIGURE 26   Plan of the Áyios Nikólaos fortification at *Perakhóra*

PLATE 26   *Perakhóra*, the Áyios Nikólaos fortification, North wall from outside

thought to be possibly the site of a supposed oracle of Hera; even Robinson (1932: 44) repeated this suggestion for the "cave". At the North West corner another higher zone of the bedrock appears to have been artificially smoothed down to form a flat top at about the same level as the chapel terrace. To the East of the enclosure the rocky spur rises steeply on all sides, completing the natural protection of the fortified site. Again little is obvious in the way of surface

PLATE 27   *Perakhóra*, the Áyios Nikólaos fortification, South West wall from outside

PLATE 28   *Perakhóra*, the Áyios Nikólaos fortification, cistern

potsherds although the existence of the cistern shows, once more, provision for more than merely ephemeral occupation of the fortification if necessary. Such surface sherds as were noticed here were of Classical, Hellenistic and possibly Roman date.

It is now the moment to see why I termed all of this a "network". Virtually all the sites just described are in visual contact with each other. From *Mavrovoúni* can be seen the site by the *ikonostásion* of *Áyios Ioánnes*, the *Kalá Nisiá* and, in clear weather, are visible also the lighthouse point of *Perakhóra* together with the North Peloponnesian coast West of Korinthos; all that is not directly visible at any time is the Áyios Nikólaos *kástron* on the *Perakhóra* peninsula. Similarly from the *ikonostásion* site one can see *Mavrovoúni*, the *Kalá Nisiá*, and, again in clear weather, the *Perakhóra* lighthouse and the Northern coast of the Peloponnesos including Akrokórinthos. From the *Perakhóra* lighthouse both *Mavrovoúni* and the *ikonostásion* site are visible in clear weather, while the North Peloponnesian coast and the *Kalá Nisiá* are virtually always visible, as is, of course, the nearby Áyios Nikólaos fortification. From the latter, by reason of its higher elevation, the North Peloponnesos is clear, as is, naturally, the lighthouse site and, dimly to be sure, the *Kalá Nisiá*.

It will be clear from the foregoing that the position of the *Kalá Nisiá* is crucial since the lines of sight most affected by unclear weather are those between the sites on the South Boiotian coastal ridge (*Mavrovoúni* and the *ikonostásion*) and the *Perakhóra* peninsula which represents the connection to the Peloponnesos. Many of the lines of sight mentioned above I have been able to check during very frequent visits at different times of the year and under different weather conditions to *Mavrovoúni* in particular but also to the *ikonostásion* site. My visits to *Perakhóra* were less frequent in terms of variety of weather conditions but still in the 1960's the lighthouse had a resident crew and I was able to check with its members who could remember virtually no occasions when both the *Kalá Nisiá* and the North Peloponnesian coast were not visible. These lines of sight are summarised on the map (Fig. 27) and it is merely the direct lines from the South Boiotia sites to *Perakhóra* and the North Peloponnesos that should be regarded as questionable in bad weather.

The remaining question then is, what would have been the role of the Áyios Nikólaos *kástron* in this supposed network of communication? First of all it is clear on the ground that the lighthouse can be approached by a hostile force unseen to within less than half a kilometre (perhaps even nearer depending on forest cover), whereas the Áyios Nikólaos *kástron* controls from above that line of approach and is thus in a position to give advance warning to whoever was at the lighthouse fort. It also provides an even clearer view to and from the North Peloponnesos than does the lighthouse site as well as doubling in the direction of the *Kalá Nisiá*. Thus, I suggest, the two sites in the end of the *Perakhóra* peninsula should be seen to function as a pair for defence and with some possibility of reinforcing signals in certain directions. The flattened rock surface at the West end of the Áyios Nikólaos *kástron* would have served well as a platform for fire signals.

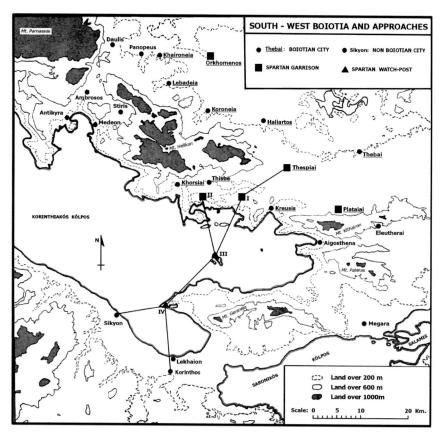

FIGURE 27   The Spartan signalling network

4   Note on Fire Signals

It has always surprised me, when discussing such communication networks, to be questioned by fellow classicists about the reality of the use of fire signals in antiquity. It is indeed noticeable that several modern studies of ancient military affairs pay scant if any attention to this important consideration (e.g. Adcock, 1957; Engels, 1978; Hanson, 1989). This is not the place to go into details on this matter; suffice it to say that there is plenty of textual evidence – in addition to the existence of networks such as that discussed here, whose existence and nature presuppose some such form of signalling depending upon intervisibility. First we may mention the famous "beacon speech" in Aiskhylos' *Agamemnon* 280–314; an Athenian audience in 458 BCE might well have wondered about the actual distances traversed by the beacon message from Troia to Argolis but they would obviously not find anything strange about the method of communicating especially since use of such signals had already been experienced a couple of decades earlier, during the Persian Wars (Herodotos vii. 183, 1 and ix. 3, 1 – in both cases the use of "πυρσοί" has a clear meaning), and recurred during the subsequent Peloponnesian War (Thoukydides ii. 94, 1; iii. 22, 7; iii. 80, 2) – this last is particularly significant in that it specifies that the information transmitted from Leukas was detailed to the extent of saying that the signal sent the information that 60 Athenian vessels were approaching Kerkyra – and iv. 111, 2 – "τὸ σημεῖον τοῦ πυρός", where in other cases Thoukydides speaks rather of "φρυκτωρία". In the 2nd century BCE Polybios was to devote a few chapters to the subject (x. 43–47) where he developed a whole alphabetic system following on the work of the otherwise unknown "Kleoxenos and Demokleitos"; this complex system (cf. explanation of Walbank, 1967: 259–260) is favourably contrasted with earlier, less sophisticated methods to which he refers in terms of "πυρσεία", "πυρσῶν χρεία". In early Hellenistic times there is a clear example of such a network organised by Antigonos Monophthalmos – αὐτὸς (sc. Antigonos) δὲ πᾶσαν τὴν Ἀσίαν ἧς ἦν κύριος διέλαβε πυρσοῖς καὶ βυβλιαφόροις δι' ὧν ὀξέως ἤμελλεν ὑπηρετεῖσθαι πάντα (Diodoros Sikeliotes xix. 57, 5). It is obvious that signalling by fire (and smoke) was far more sophisticated in antiquity than was thought by Donaldson (1988: 350) when he discussed signalling even much later on, in the Roman military world.

5   The Cult of Artemis

We have already remarked on the cult of Artemis Agroteira at *Mavrovoúni* and have indicated that the only other location for this cult in the whole of Boiotia is at nearby Thisbe. This then prompts the question as to whether it is not more than mere coincidence that this particular cult should occur exclusively at or near the two points of Spartan military entry into Boiotia from the South that we have just suggested – *Mavrovoúni* itself and the *Áyios Ioánnes ikonostásion* to the immediate South of Thisbe.

I have elsewhere examined the role of Artemis Agroteira in Spartan military affairs, especially when the Spartan army was abroad (Fossey, 1987). It was shown that a number of Artemis cults was concentrated in Western Argolis, always near or on passes and routes through or by which the Spartan army entered into its rival's territory between the 7th and the 5th/4th centuries BCE. It is ironical to reflect that on many of those occasions Sparta's entry into Argolis lead to the defeat of her army, just as was eventually to be the case with her repeated incursions into Boiotian lands in the 370's all of which culminated in the crushing defeat at Leuktra in 371. In my treatment of the Argolic distribution of Artemis cults it was the presence of cults, specifically that of Artemis Orthia, which focussed my thinking on Spartan military involvement since that cult was particularly important in the military *agoge* of young Lakedaimonians.

In the present case the Spartan military connection is yet clearer since the epithet of Artemis here is Agroteira at or near both of the proposed Spartan bases. In my previous study of the Artemis-Sparta connection I outlined the ancient accounts of Spartan military procedures when setting out for, or being already on campaign abroad: rituals attended the army all the way to the borders of Lakonia (Xenophon *Lakedaimonion Politeia* xiii); the kings who commanded the army on such manoeuvres were always accompanied by a flock of sheep led by she-goats for sacrifice before battle and for taking the omens (Pausanias ix. 13, 4); the sacrifice might include also the goats (Xenophon *Lakedaimonion Politeia* xiii. 8 cf. Ploutarkhos, *Lykourgos* xxii, 4). Most telling of all, however, is another passage of Xenophon (*Hellenika* iv. 2, 20):

σφαγισάμενοι οἱ Λακεδαιμόνιοι τῇ Ἀγροτέρᾳ ὥσπερ νομίζεται,
τὴν χίμαιραν, ἡγοῦντο ἐπὶ τοὺς ἐναντίους.

The Lakedaimonians, having sacrificed a she-goat to Agrotera,
as is their wont, led off against the enemy.

Indeed sacrifices of goats specifically to Artemis *Agrotera* are noted elsewhere in ancient Greek sources (Aristophanes, *Hippeis* 660–661 & Ailianos, *Poikile Historia* ii. 25, 5) but the passage quoted above from Xenophon – a well informed source on Spartan affairs – makes it very difficult to consider as pure coincidence the attestation of the cult of Agroteira at *Μαυροvoύνι* (SEG xviii 166–167) and at Thisbe near the *ikonostásion* of *Ἁγίου Ἰωάννες* (*IG* vii 3564).

We may even take the story one stage further for, while the only attestations of Agrotera in the whole of Boiotia are indeed these two (always omitting the completely unfounded suggestion of an instance in the (H)Aliartia, advanced by Schachter, 1981: 99), there is one lone instance of the shorter form of the epithet in the attestation of Artemis Agrotis at Lebadeia (*IG* vii 3100); Lebadeia was, of course, the other point of entry into Boiotia used by the Spartans when they came from the allied territory of Phokis at the beginning of the incursion that ended at Leuktra. Is this too to be seen as a coincidence? I believe not, though it must be added that the attestation at Lebadeia is itself of Roman

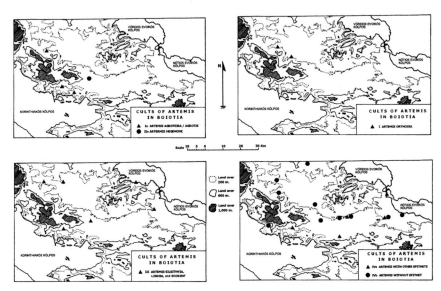

FIGURE 28   The distribution of Artemis cults in Boiotia

Imperial date, much later, that is, than the 4th century/Hellenistic date of the attestations on the South coast.

From the series of distribution maps (Fig. 28) can be clearly seen the exclusive concentration of these attestations of the cult at just the three points of Spartan entry to Boiotia but they also show something else. The Spartan cult of Artemis *par excellence* was that of Artemis Orthia to which we have already referred; this also, with the epithet in the form *Orthosia* (a form also attested in the spelling ϝορθοσία at the very sanctuary of Artemis Orthia in Sparta itself, *BSA* 1907–1908: 25), occurs with another very restricted distribution in Boiotia: merely Lebadeia again (*ADelt* 1917, 421–423, 6) and Koroneia (*AA* 1940: 188 & *Chiron* 1976: 18–19, no. 11), that is the point of Spartan entry to Boiotia from Phokis in 371 BCE and then the next stopping point on that advance, the point, in fact, of turning back after finding that the Boiotians had blocked the passage through the narrows East of Koroneia (Fossey, 1990: chapter 13, cf. 1993: 112–114). Again the exclusive nature of the restricted distribution does not encourage any suggestion of coincidence.

One other incidence that shows on the distribution maps is the sole presence in Boiotia of a cult of Artemis Hegemone, appropriately at Thespiai (*BCH* 1926: 409, 24) the principal place of Spartan military presence in Boiotia; this cult too is attested at Sparta (Pausanias iii. 14, 6). On its own this lone occurrence might not provoke much further thought but in the context of the placements of the cults of Agrotera and Orthosia, it should undoubtedly be added here at least tentatively. The contrast with the wide distribution of other Artemis cults in general within Boiotia highlights the special distributions of Agrotera and Orthosia, possibly together with Hegemone. This general distribution of Artemis cults in Boiotia is, in fact, less wide than we might have expected for Ploutarkhos, himself a Boiotian of course, has a potentially interesting remark about her presence:

τὴν δ' Εὔκλειαν οἱ μὲν πολλοὶ καὶ καλοῦσι καὶ ὀνομάζουσιν Ἄρτεμιν, ἔνιοι δέ φασιν Ἡρακλέους μὲν θυγατέρα καὶ Μυρτοῦς γενέσθαι, τῆς Μενοιτίου μὲν θυγατρός, Πατρόκλου δ' ἀδελφῆς, τελευτήσασαν δὲ παρθένον ἔχειν παρά τε Βοιωτοῖς καὶ Λοκροῖς τιμάς. Βωμὸς γὰρ αὐτῇ καὶ ἄγαλμα κατὰ πᾶσαν ἀγορὰν ἵδρυται, καὶ προθύουσιν αἵ τε γαμούμεναι καὶ οἱ γαμοῦντες.

Most people call Eukleia Artemis and so address her but others say that she is the daughter of Herakles and Myrto (the daughter of Menoitos and sister of Patroklos) and that when she died still a virgin she was honoured by the Boiotians and the Lokrians. There is an altar and a statue set up for her in every agora and brides and bridegrooms offer preliminary sacrifice to her.
PLOUTARKHOS *Aristeides* xx

Seen in this light, while the situation does indeed occur in Lokris (Fossey, 1990: 151–152), the Boiotian presence is not really so widespread. In particular we may note that the cult of specifically Artemis Eukleia is only attested, independently of Ploutarkhos, at Plataiai (*AJA* 7, 1891: 405–421) and Thebai in the whole of Boiotia (Schachter, 1981: 102 & 104–105, respectively plus another of unspecified location p. 106). Although the last sentence of the passages quoted is often taken to indicate that there was an altar and statue to her in every agora of Boiotia and Lokris Ploutarkhos does not, in fact, specify just where all these agorai were and we may wonder if he simply means in Lokris, the Lokrians being the people mentioned at the very end of the preceding sentence. Thus Ploutarkhos' text and archaeology would be in agreement. So I am inclined to recant of my earlier statement that "this text clearly states that the cult of Artemis Eukleia was widespread in Lokris *and Boiotia*, but I can still stand by the reasons I gave for taking the text to refer to just Opountian Lokris (Fossey, 1990: 151). The custom referred to in this last sentence is also reminiscent of the tradition I heard in the village of *Koláka* in the South part of Opountian Lokris concerning the *Kamíni* spring (Fossey, 1990: 54).

In some ways the best attested cult of Artemis is that with the epithet Aulideia but this owes its importance solely to its association with the setting-out point of the Troian expedition; otherwise it is a purely local cult not attested anywhere else in Boiotia. The most common Boiotian epithet of Artemis in Hellenistic and Roman times is, in fact, Eileithyia, which occurs at several locations (cf. Schachter, 1981: 94–106): Anthedon, Khaironeia, Orkhomenos, Tanagra, Thebai, Thespiai, Thisbe and – according to a not very convincing hypothesis of Schachter (1981: 101–102) – possibly at the Amphiaraion and also at Lebadeia (in the guise of the Praiai; cf. *IG* vii 3101). In this role as the goddess of childbirth she also recurs with the epithet Soodina at Khaironeia (*IG* vii 3430) and with that of Lokhia at Thespiai (*BCH* 26, 1949: 291, no. 2). [Given a natural concern with safe childbirth in just about any society the long list of places where this protectress is attested does not surprise us, though some noticeable gaps – the Parasopia and most of the Kopaïc cities – are striking.] The one remaining epithet – omitting from consideration an unsupported suggestion of Monogeneia at Koroneia by Pappadhákis (*AEph* 2, 1916: 233 cf. Schachter, 1981: 100) – is Soteira, so far only attested at Thespiai (Schachter, 1981: 105) and Thisbe (*IG* vii 2232) where proximity of the sites may suggest some particularly local reason for such a restricted occurrence (Fossey, 1992: 48–49). At the same time we may remember that it is not an epithet peculiar to Artemis for, in feminine and masculine forms it is applied to several other divinities.

Although, in our hypothesis they would have been introduced by a hostile invading force, the continued existence of these cults of Agrotera and Orth(os)ia in later times – the bulk of the attestations we have just looked at fall between the 4th century BCE and earlier Hellenistic times – should not surprise us for they would subsequently have been respected by the local people, as Thoukydides (iv. 98, 2) reminds us:

τὸν δὲ νόμον τοῖς Ἕλλησιν εἶναι, ὧν ἂν ᾖ τὸ κράτος τῆς γῆς ἑκάστης, ἤν τε πλέονος ἤν τε βραχυτέρας, τούτων καὶ τὰ ἱερὰ αἰεὶ γίγνεσθαι, τρόποις θεραπευόμενα οἷς ἂν πρὸ τοῦ εἰωθόσι καὶ δύνωνται.

The law of the Hellenes was that whoever held the power in any land, whether of greater or lesser extent, the sanctuaries were theirs as well, which were cared for in every way practiced before this, as far as they could.
Translation: LATTIMORE, 1998: 233–234

Before we leave the subject of Artemis there is one more possible aspect we may consider. The present theory postulates the presence of Spartan forces not only at *Mavrovoúni* and the *ikonostásion* but also on the *Kalá Nisiá* and in the end part of the *Perakhóra* peninsula so can we trace Artemis there too? The possibility is tenuous in the extreme but we may recall that Tomlinson suggested that, because of its orientation, the temple that we cleaned in the upper plain at *Perakhóra* in 1964 may have been dedicated to Artemis. The possibility is, actually, reinforced by the fact that the chapel in the *kástron* immediately above it is, as we have just seen, dedicated to Áyios Nikólaos, a saint whose churches often replace former sanctuaries or shrines of Artemis. So Artemis at *Perakhóra* is not unlikely and thus could be a Spartan importation. What then of the *Kalá Nisiá*? Here the position is yet more tenuous and can only be argued very tentatively by pointing out that the monastery church is that of the Theotókos, the virgin mother of God, and then remembering that Artemis, similarly a virgin, had the function of caring for mothers and childbirth. Does this take matters too far? Perhaps, but it should still be mentioned here for completeness of the discussion.

CHAPTER 9

The Daughters of Skedasos and the Battle of Leuktra

The two main ancient towns of South West Boiotia were Thespiai and Thisbe, the former being the more important of the two. The natural route way linking these places starts from the ancient site of Thespiai, lying to the South of the twin villages of *Erimókastro* (today *Thespiai*) and *Kaskavéli* (today *Leondári*) that dominate it from the hills on the other, North side of the *Kanavári* stream (Fossey, 1988: 135–140). Not far from Thespiai the road crosses the *Áskris* river which, at this point, changes direction from the South Easterly line that has brought it from its headwaters in the Valley of the Muses (rather West of Thespiai; Fossey, 1988: 141); it now turns almost due West towards the *polje* of *Dhómvraina* into the East side of which it empties. The road follows this river, passing through the villages of *Karandás* (now *Ellopía*) and *Xeronomí* and continuing to run along the slopes on the Northern side of the *polje* and dropping down into the village of *Dhómvraina* whence it reaches, a little further along the Northern slopes, the village of *Kakósi* (modern *Thísvi*) lying in the centre of the ancient city site of Thisbe (Fossey, 1988: 178–182). At the point where the road from Thespiai crosses the *Áskris* a branch road cuts due West and re-joins the main road a little beyond the village of *Xeronomí*. This branch road is only roughly surfaced although it is more direct than the main road just described, since it does not today pass through any settlements. In previous times, however, it did pass through the now deserted hamlet of *Táteza* (for which I suggested an identification with the ill-attested ancient Donakon; Fossey, 1988: 147–149). Of that hamlet there only survive two apparently disused buildings on the North side of the road and, almost directly across from them but set back a little from the road so as to nestle into the hillside, the church of the Ayía Triádha (Fossey, 2014: 275). For the geography of the area cf. the map Fig. 29.

[The church was apparently in ruins when seen by Leake (1835: 500–501) early in the 19th century; he describes it as "built of ancient fragments, among which are some heroic monuments like those already described. Here are also two plain tombstones, with single names in the nominative, in archaic characters". It is likely that the last two inscriptions may be *IG* vii 2045 and 2052 (republished by me as *EB* ii 54 and 53 respectively); consequently the "heroic monuments" could very well be the horseman hero reliefs at one time (when the church at *Táteza* was rebuilt?) gathered together at *Xeronomí* and more

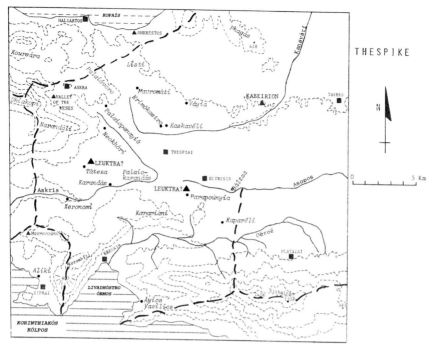

FIGURE 29   The region of *Táteza – Xeronomí*

recently moved to the Museum at *Thívai* (for a discussion of these stones cf. Fossey, 2014: chapter 7 and now chapter 12 here below). Since these stones appear to have been already gathered at *Xeronomí* when seen by Körte (1878) we must assume that the church at *Táteza* may have been restored some time in the second quarter or middle of the 19th century. Their collection at *Xeronomí* is altogether logical for, even when *Táteza* was an inhabited "hamlet", Leake describes it as "dependant on Xeronomí"; to this day lands at *Táteza* are farmed by villagers from *Xeronomí*. Leake (1835: 501–502) describes *Xeronomí* as having a large ruined church and continues "here are several heroic monuments, bearing figures of a man and horse", a little later he continues "one only of the heroic monuments, and apparently more ancient than the others, is inscribed". The last remark makes obvious that the group of horseman reliefs formerly in the small ruined church of Áyios Yeóryios at *Xeronomí* seen and photographed by me in 1965 and 1967 (Fossey, 2014: chapter 7) simply cannot be those mentioned here by Leake for *all* of them were inscribed. Farinetti, 2011: 340 gives an account of more recent observations at *Táteza* and *Xeronomí*; she thinks that there may have been ancient settlements with cemeteries at both. For *Táteza* she lists EH, LH, Classical, Hellenistic, Roman and Late Roman material, a much fuller picture than resulted from my earlier observations (Fossey, 1988: 147–148). It seems, however, that for *Xeronomí* she only adduces the inscribed and sculpted stones just mentioned and I am aware of no other ancient material derived thence.]

In autumn 1965 the origin of the toponym *Táteza* was explained to me by an elderly villager in *Karandás*. The story is that some girls (the number of them was not specified) were attacked by some marauding Turks – a traditional bogeyman for Greek children – and ran off into the woods shouting "Táta, táta" which in the local Arvanitic dialect means "Dad, dad". There the story ended. Despite its brevity this story is reminiscent of the ancient myth concerning the daughters of Skedasos.

Ploutarkhos, himself a Boiotian from Khaironeia, in addition to his parallel biographies, collected all sorts of curious histories, five of which are grouped together as Ἐρωτικαὶ Διηγήσεις. Unlike modern "Love Stories" these do not have happy endings but three of them (1, 3 and 4) do refer to Boiotia. It is the third and longest of these stories (Ploutarkhos, *ethika* 773c–774d) that tells of the daughters of Skedasos.

Skedasos was a poor man of Leuktra with two beautiful daughters. Two young Spartan men travelling to Delphoi were given hospitality by Skedasos and fell in love with the daughters but did nothing about it in the presence of the father. On their way back from Delphoi, however, they took advantage of the absence of Skedasos himself to rape the girls; because of the latters' distress at what had happened to them the girls were afterwards murdered by the youths or they took their own lives. The story of Skedasos continues with his vain attempts to get retribution in the aggressors' native Sparta and his ultimate suicide. He had in the meanwhile buried his daughters:

ἐν τῷ Λευκτρικῷ πεδίῳ τὰ σήματα τῶν τοῦ Σκεδάσου θυγατέρων, ἃς Λευκτρίδας καλοῦσι διὰ τὸν τόπον

In the plain of Leuktra are the grave-markers of the daughters of Skedasos who are called the Leuktridai from the name of the place.
PLOUTARKHOS, *Pelopidas* xx. 4

The story has, however, a sequel much later when Skedasos is said to appear in a dream to Pelopidas on the eve of the battle of Leuktra encouraging him, despite bad omens, by saying that the Spartans were coming to Leuktra to pay the penalty for the act towards himself and his daughters:

παραγίνεσθαι γὰρ εἰς Λεῦκτρα Λακεδαιμονίους, αὐτῷ καὶ ταῖς θυγατράσι δώσοντας δίκας

> *For the Lakedaimonians were coming to Leuktra to give just retribution to him and his daughters.*
>
> PLOUTARKHOS, *ethika* 774d

The part played by Skedasos and his daughters in the battle of Leuktra is again recounted by Ploutarkhos in his life of Pelopidas (xx, 3–xxii, 2) with differences in certain details that do not concern us here. This sequel to the story occurs also in Pausanias (ix. 13, 5–6); he alone provides us with the names of the two Spartan youths (Phrourarkhidas and Parthenios; cf. Poralla, 1985: nos. 735 & 589. Note that Poralla incorrectly implies that Ploutarkhos also gives these names). The *periegetes* also gives the names of the two outraged girls as Molpia and Hippo, whereas Ploutarkhos in the "love story" gives them as either Hippo and Miletia or as Theano and Euxippe. Hippo is common to both accounts and Miletia could simply be a misunderstanding of Molpia (or *vice versa*) in textual or oral tradition but it is also worth noting that, from Ploutarkhos' alternative pair of names again one, Euxippe, like Hippo in the first pair, is an anthroponym involving the word for horse (ἵππος); Pelopidas eventually sacrificed a white horse to the girls in order to obtain success in the battle (Pausanias mentions only sacrifices by Epameinondas) – is this role precisely of a horse mere coincidence?

There is a brief reference to the Leuktridai, but without their names or appellation in the account of the battle given by Xenophon:

πρὸς δὲ τούτοις παρεθάρρυνε μέν τι αὐτοὺς καὶ ὁ χρησμὸς ὁ λεγόμενος ὡς δέοι ἐνταῦθα Λακεδαιμονίους ἡττηθῆναι ἔνθα τὸ τῶν παρθένων ἦν μνῆμα, αἳ λέγονται διὰ τὸ βιασθῆναι ὑπὸ Λακεδαιμονίων τινῶν ἀποκτεῖναι ἑαυτάς.

> *In addition they were somewhat encouraged by the oracle which recounted that the Lakedaimonioi were destined to suffer defeat exactly there where stood the monument to the maidens who are said to have killed themselves because they had been raped by some Lakedaimonians.*
>
> XENOPHON, *Hellenika* vi. 4, 7

The story of the girls is a little more detailed in the account of Leuktra by Diodoros:

προσῆλθον δὲ τῷ Ἐπαμεινώνδᾳ καὶ χρησμολόγοι τινὲς ἐγχώριοι, λέγοντες ὅτι περὶ τὸν τάφον τῶν Λεύκτρου καὶ Σκεδάσου θυγατέρων μεγάλη συμφορὰ δεῖ περιπέσειν Λακεδαιμονίοις διὰ τοιαύτας αἰτίας. Λεῦκτρος ἦν, ἀφ' οὗ τὸ πεδίον τοῦτο ἔσχε τὴν προσηγορίαν, τούτου θυγατέρας καὶ Σκεδάσου τινὸς ὁμοίως κόρας πρέσβεις Λακεδαιμονίων ἐβιάσαντο· αἱ δὲ ὑβρισθεῖσαι τὴν συμφορὰν οὐκ ἐνέγκασαι, τῇ πατρίδι τῇ πεμψάσῃ τοὺς ὑβριστὰς καταρασάμεναι τὸν βίον αὐτοχειρίᾳ κατέστρεψαν.

And certain local soothsayers approached Epameinondas saying that the Lakedaimonians were fated to suffer a great disaster by the tomb of the daughters of Leuktros and Skedasos for the following reasons. Leuktros was the person from whom the plain took its name. Ambassadors of the Lakedaimonians raped his daughters and also those of a certain Skedasos. These outraged (girls), unable to bear their mistreatment, cursed the country that had sent out those who had outraged them and then took their lives with their own hands.
DIODOROS SIKELIOTES XV. 54, 2–3

Diodoros has given us the first mention of Leuktros as parent of the raped girls but Ploutarkhos, in contrast with his accounts quoted above, does elsewhere have a brief mention of Leuktros:

καὶ τοὺς θεοὺς ἀβέλτερα ποιεῖν λέγωμεν, ὑπὲρ τῶν Λεύκτρου θυγατέρων βιαισθεισῶν μηνίοντες Λακεδαιμονίοις....

Let us say then that the gods commit folly when they are angered by the Lakedaimonians for the raped daughters of Leuktros.
PLOUTARKHOS *ethika* 856f

It is not clear whether Leuktros should be regarded as an original element of the story or whether the girls being called "Leuktridai" simply from the place thus bore a name with the appearance of a patronymic suggesting a father with the name Leuktros but Skedasos may seem to have the greater claim, perhaps even more so if we invoke the old rule of *praestet difficilior lectio*. In collecting all the *testimonia* regarding the "Leuktrides", Schachter (1986: 122) has pointed out that pairs of girls with posthumous protective powers for their homeland are a motif known elsewhere in ancient Boiotian cult practice.

It is obvious that we have somewhat more information for the ancient damsels than for those supposedly of the Ottoman period. For the latter we do not have, apparently names or even a number, nor do we have the name of their father and there seemed to be no mention of their further fate – at least in the version told to me by my elderly informant in 1965. So why then do I compare the two here?

At *Táteza* I observed (Fossey, 1988: 148) worked stones, including three Doric metope and triglyph blocks from a circular monument (Pll. 29–30), obviously

PLATE 29   *Tátiza*, triglyph block from circular building

similar to the *tropaion* associated by everybody with the field of Leuktra which has been reconstructed from ancient material (Pl. 31) in the plain below, and to the North West of the village of *Parapoúnyia*. [Originally three villages, *Dhéndra, Siákhani* and *Tziakhanáni* (Píteros, 2008: 588, n. 33) were combined into one village that has now been renamed *Lévktra*!]

The architectural blocks in question lay a short distance to the East of the two houses that remain of the hamlet of *Táteza* and right next to the North side of the road. Furthermore in the ploughed fields that rise in the slope to the immediate North of this monument it was possible in 1965 to observe very many pieces of human bone. I am not for one minute saying that these human bones come from the battle of Leuktra since Greek armies usually were punctilious about seeking or granting a truce for gathering up the dead (Pritchett, 1974: chapter xiii) but it is an aspect in a complete description of the site. The important phenomenon, though, is the circular monument. Two monuments of the same nature in such close proximity to each other may seem too much of a coincidence, especially since historically we know of only one candidate for a battlefield in that area. Were there then **two** *tropaia* for the battle of Leuktra? We shall return to that question later but, in the meantime, the story of the

142 CHAPTER 9

PLATE 30   *Tátiza*, another triglyph block from circular building

PLATE 31   *Parapoúnyia*, the reconstructed trophy

girls being attacked at *Táteza* must, with its basic similarity to the story of the daughters of Skedasos, give some support to the possibility that the circular monument at *Táteza*, with its similarity to that near *Parapoúnyia* may be another commemoration of the battle of Leuktra. It is noticeable that the epigram concerning the commemoration of that battle (*IG* vii 2462; Tod, 1948: no. 130; cf. Beister, 1973: 65–66 for a list of some other publications of the text) refers to victory monuments (τροπαῖα) in the plural, not once but twice:

Ξ ε ν ο κ ρ ά τ η ς,
Θ ε ό π ο μ π ο ς,
Μ ν α σ ί λ α ο ς.
Ἁνίκα τὸ Σπάρτας ἐκράτει δόρυ, τηνάκις εἷλεν
Ξενοκράτης κλάρῳ Ζηνὶ τροπαῖα φέρειν.
οὐ τὸν ἀπ' Εὐρώτα δείσας στόλον οὐδὲ Λάκαιναν
ἀσπίδα, "Θηβαῖοι κρείσσονες ἐν πολέμῳ"
καρύσσει Λεύκτροις νικαφόρα δουρὶ τροπαῖα,
οὐδ' Ἐπαμεινώνδα δεύτεροι ἐδράμομεν.

> *Xenokrates,*
> *Theopompos,*
> *Mnasilaos*
> *When the spear of Sparta dominated then it came*
> *to Xenokrates by lot to carry trophies to Zeus.*
> *Having no fear of the fleet from the Eurotas nor of the Lakonian*
> *shield, "the Thebans are more mighty in war"*
> *declare by spear the trophies at Leuktra*
> *and we were not behind Epameinondas in running.*

As J.G. Frazer (1898: III, 435) commented "the inscription is in verse, and somewhat awkwardly expressed". The reference to δουρί in the last line is odd except that it might be a take up from δορύ at the beginning of the epigram in line 4; the use of the word στόλος in the sixth line surprises. On the other hand, of the three men listed at the beginning Xenokrates is recorded as being one of the *boiotarkhontes* at Leuktra who voted with Epameinondas to go straight away to battle (cf. Koumanoúdhes, 1979: 3148¹) and Theopompos is known to have been a close associate of Pelopidas (Koumanoúdhes 1979: #917) but Mnasilaos is only mentioned in this inscription although a homonymous Theban leader of the mid-3rd century BCE could be assumed as a possible descendant (Koumanoúdhes, 1979: ## 1362 & 1363). We also know the story of the shield of Aristomenes and its part in the run-up to Leuktra as it is told to us by Pausanias who quotes an oracle from the Trophonion in Lebadeia which – together with others from the Apolline sanctuaries of Thebai (Ismenion), Ptoion and Delphoi that he does not record in detail – was delivered to the Thebans shortly before the battle of Leuktra:

> πρὶν δορὶ συμβαλέειν ἐχθροῖς, στήσασθε τρόπαιον,
> ἀσπίδι κοσμήσαντες ἐμῇ, τὴν εἵσατο νηῷ
> θοῦρος Ἀριστομένης Μεσσήνιος. αὐτὰρ ἐγώ τοι
> ἀνδρῶν δυσμενέων φθίσω στρατὸν ἀσπιστάων.

> *Before you come within spear's length of the enemy set up a trophy*
> *decorating it with my shield, which was placed in the temple*
> *by the impetuous Aristomenes, the Messenian, and I*
> *will destroy the army of shield-bearing hostile men.*
>   PAUSANIAS iv. 32, 4–6

While the use of the plural (τροπαῖα) in the fifth line of *IG* vii 2462 needs special pleading it might just possibly be judged appropriate in the context of

Xenokrates bringing the shield of the Spartan-hating Aristomenes – perhaps with other elements – from the sanctuary of Trophonios in Lebadeia. What really needs explaining is the use of the same plural in the eighth line: is it deliberate and could it, in fact, mean that there was more than one victory monument, as the archaeological remains might suggest? In his concluding translation of the epigram, Beister (1973) both times renders the word as "Tropaion" in the singular. A fuller discussion and analysis of the use of the word τροπαῖα in the Leuktra epigram and elsewhere will be found in the last chapter of this volume; it was kindly prepared for me by my friend Stephanie Stringer.

At the risk of repeating the frequent observations of others who have studied the monument, it is probably best to start with a brief consideration of the reconstructed monument lying below the village of *Parapoúnyia*, since this is often taken as a *pointe de depart* for discussions of the battle.

Piterós (2008: 589, nn. 34 & 37) gives a useful summary of the history of the monument's discovery and the stages of its eventual reconstruction. To this may be added an observation of Kendrick Pritchett (1965: 51). It seems that Orlandos' excavations in the area of the monument had revealed the foundations of a Byzantine church several feet below the modern soil level; frequency of ploughing in this deep alluvial accumulation may explain how parts of the monument could still be discovered in the 1990's at certain distances (e.g. 2km and 500m) from its position but one architectural piece discussed by Piterós (2008: 590, item listed as β), a curved metope block – τμῆμα ἐλλιπῶς σωζόμενου καμπύλης μετόπης – has dimensions that make clear that it belongs to a slightly smaller monument (of the same type) "προφανῶς προέρχεται ἀπό ἀλλό μνημείο". This find in itself indicates that our suggestion of more than one monument in this area is not without independent support. Even the last line of the epigram could well be seen as indicating geographically separate engagements in the area of Leuktra, saying that the leaders in one part of the overall battle (Xenokrates, a *Boiotarkhon*, together with his adjutants) played an equal part to that of the leader (Epameinondas, also a *Boiotarkhon*, apparently with a certain seniority) in a separate engagement elsewhere in the area – οὐδ' Ἐπαμεινώνδα δεύτεροι ἐδράμομεν.

[By a nice coincidence Boiotia provided, some years after my own observations at *Táteza*, a further instance of a plurality of trophies for different parts of a single battle. The victory commemorated is that of Sulla against the forces of Mithridates near Khaironeia in 86 BCE when two permanent trophies were set up made of sculpted statuary (Camp et all., 1992).]

The question of the route followed by the Spartan army of Kleombrotos has caused the spilling of much ink and the sources themselves upon which the discussions have been based are extremely laconic and lacunary. Essentially we depend on three ancient sources:

a. οὕτω δὴ ἄγει (sc. ὁ Κλεόμβροτος) τὴν στρατιὰν εἰς τὴν Βοιωτίαν. Καὶ ᾗ μὲν οἱ Θηβαῖοι ἐμβαλεῖν αὐτὸν ἐκ τῶν Φωκέων προσεδόκων καὶ ἐπὶ στενῷ τινι ἐφύλαττον οὐκ ἐμβάλλει· διὰ Θισβῶν δὲ ὀρεινὴν καὶ ἀπροσδόκητον πορευθεὶς ἀφικνεῖται εἰς Κρεῦσιν, καὶ τὸ τεῖχος αἱρεῖ, καὶ τριήρεις τῶν Θηβαίων δώδεκα λαμβάνει. Ταῦτα δὲ ποιήσας καὶ ἀναβὰς ἀπὸ τῆς θαλάττης, ἐστρατοπεδεύσατο ἐν Λεύκτροις τῆς Θεσπικῆς.

So [Kleombrotos] led the army to Boiotia. He did not, however, enter that country where the Thebans expected him to and where they had occupied a narrow pass but, passing by way of Thisbe along a mountainous and unexpected route, he came to Kreusis, captured its fortification and took twelve Theban triremes. After that and having marched up from the sea he camped at Leuktra in Thespike.
XENOPHON, *Hellenika* vi. 4, 3–4

b. οὗτοι (sc. οἱ Λακεδαιμόνιοι) μὲν οὖν προάγοντες ὡς ἧκον εἰς Κορώνειαν, κατεστρατοπέδευσαν καὶ τοὺς καθυστεροῦντας τῶν συμμάχων ἀνέμενον. (52, 1)

So they [the Lakedaimonioi], having advanced as far as Koroneia, they camped to wait for those of their allies who were delayed.

... εὐθὺς γὰρ προαγαγὼν τὴν δύναμιν (sc ὁ Ἐπαμεινώνδας), καὶ προκαταλαβόμενος τὰ περὶ τὴν Κορώνειαν στενά, κατεστρατοπέδευσεν. (52, 7)

For [Epameinondas] straightway led forward his force and, having occupied the narrows about Koroneia, he pitched camp.

ὁ δὲ Κλεόμβροτος πυθόμενος τοὺς πολεμίους προκατειληφέναι τὰς παρόδους, τὸ μὲν ταύτῃ ποιεῖσθαι τὴν διέξοδον ἀπέγνω, πορευθεὶς δὲ διὰ τῆς Φωκίδος, καὶ διεξελθὼν τὴν παραθαλαττίαν ὁδὸν χαλεπὴν οὖσαν, ἐνέβαλεν εἰς τὴν Βοιωτίαν ἀκινδύνως· ἐν παρόδῳ δέ τινα τῶν πολισματίων χειρωσάμενος δέκα τριήρων ἐγκρατὴς ἐγένετο. μετὰ δὲ ταῦτα καταντήσας εἰς τὰ καλούμενα Λεῦκτρα κατεστρατοπέδευσε καὶ τοὺς στρατιώτας ἐκ τῆς ὁδοιπορίας ἀνελάμβανεν. (53, 1–2)

Kleombrotos having learned that the enemy had occupied the passes decided against forcing his way through there and instead he marched through Phokis and following a coastal and difficult route he entered Boiotia safely. On his way he took possession of some of the small cities and captured ten triremes. After this, having reached the place called Leuktra, he pitched camp and let his soldiers have a respite after the march.

DIODOROS SIKELIOTES, XV. 52–53

c. ὡς δὲ ὁ Λακεδαιμονίων καὶ Θηβαίων ἐξῆρτο ἤδη πόλεμος καὶ οἱ Λακεδαιμόνιοι δυνάμει καὶ αὐτῶν καὶ τῶν συμμάχων ἐπὶ τοὺς Θηβαίους ᾖεσαν, Ἐπαμινώνδας μὲν ἔχων τοῦ στρατοῦ μοῖραν ἀντεκάθητο ὑπὲρ τῆς Κηφισίδος λίμνης ὡς ποιησομένων ταύτῃ Πελοποννησίων τὴν ἐσβολήν, Κλεόμβροτος δὲ ὁ Λακεδαιμονίων βασιλεὺς ἐπὶ Ἀμβρόσσου τρέπεται τῆς Φωκέων· ἀποκτείνας δὲ Χαιρέαν, ὃς φυλάσσειν διετέτακτο τὰς παρόδους, καὶ ἄλλους σὺν αὐτῷ Θηβαίους, ὑπερέβη καὶ ἐς Λεῦκτρα ἀφίκνειται τὰ Βοιώτια.

When the war between the Lakedaimonians and the Thebans broke out and the Lakedaimonians, with a combined force of their own men and of their allies, was pressing the Thebans, Epameinondas with a unit [moira] of the army occupied a position above the Kephisian lake to block the Peloponnesians from making their passage there as he had expected them to do. The Lakedaimonian king Kleombrotos, however, turned towards Ambrossos in Phokis. Having killed Khaireas who had been ordered to guard the passes and having crossed the high ground, he reached Leuktra in Boiotia.

PAUSANIAS ix. 13, 3

Such is the scant evidence concerning the route taken by Kleombrotos and his army. A few points are clear:

a. The Theban force, described only as a *moira* of the city's army, occupied a position, "the narrows" on the Kephisian or Kopaic lake near to Koroneia; this seems correctly identified as the *Palaiothíva-Vígla* ridge and the passes that it controls at both its ends (Fossey, 1990: 169–184). It was from here that the Spartans turned back towards Phokis. Tuplin (1987: 72) puts into question the emendation by Wesseling of Χαιρώνεια to Κορώνεια in the text of Diodoros xv. 52, 1 saying that this is the only relevant source and thus discounting Pausanias (and even Xenophon) for Koroneia can best qualify for straits ὑπὲρ τῆς Κηφισίδος λίμνης, a phrase which can plainly not apply to Khaironeia since, in no way, can that city be described as lying above the Kopaic (or Kephissian) *Lake* only above the *river* Kephissos. On the subject of the *Palaiothíva-Vígla* Cooper (2000: 181 n. 133) dismisses our "attractive but unsupportable suggestion that a set of small walled forts on the perimeter of the Copaic Basin were emplacements for defense against the pre-Leuktra maneuvers of Kleombrotos"; he would have been fairer to call it "unproven" for it is definitely not "unsupportable" as the circumstantial evidence we adduced makes all too clear.

b. The Spartans made for Ambrossos, the present *Dhístomon* in Eastern Phokis (Fossey, 1986: 30–31), whence they moved towards Boiotia.

c. Somewhere along the way they managed to kill Khaireas and a group of Thebans who had been sent to occupy "the passes"; the sources give absolutely no indication as to where this occurred, nor what was the nature/size of the Theban contingent under Khaireas. [The passage of Pausanias is rather short at this point, leaving the impression that something is missing from the text covering the Spartan movements between Ambrossos and Leuktra.]

d. The Spartans are said to have taken a coastal road to enter Boiotia but does this necessarily imply that their entire transit followed the coast or may it simply mean that just a particular part of it did so and it was that part that specifically received attention because of its difficulty? No clear answer is forthcoming from the texts.

e. The next point to be clearly indicated is that the Spartans came to Thisbe (modern *Kakkósi*, cf. Fossey, 1988: 177–182).

f. It is not clear whether Thisbe was one of the πολισμάτια seized at some point(s) during the transit; were the other(s) seized before or after Thisbe or some before and some after? Various candidates for these other small cities can be proposed – Boulis, a mostly isolated and independent town located between South East Phokis and South West Boiotia at modern *Záltza*, Khorsiai at modern *Khóstia* (Fossey, 1988: 187–194), possibly even some small settlement at Thisbe's harbour on the bay of Ἁyios Ioánnes-Vathý (Fossey, 1988: 182–183; cf. chapter 9) and Siphai on the bay of *Alikí* (Fossey, 1988: 168–173) but not one is specifically mentioned in the ancient sources. It may be added that the one of the potential πολισμάτια that has been partially excavated – *Khóstia* – showed no signs of hostile activity in the first quarter of the 4th century, although a destruction of this city later in that century (347/6 BCE) is recorded by Diodoros Sikeliotes (xvi. 58 & 60). [In fact the only destruction of the site attested *archaeologically* dates to the 1st century BCE possibly during the Mithridatic wars.]

g. Passing through Thisbe they moved towards Kreusis by another route classified also as difficult – ὀρεινὴν καὶ ἀπροσδόκητον; here also lay some of the small cities listed under f. above, especially Siphai.
h. At Kreusis they appeared to have captured ten or twelve battle triremes of the Thebans.
i. From Kreusis they clearly ascended mountain slopes to arrive at the fateful plain of Leuktra in the territory of Thespiai. Tuplin (1987: 72–77) has a lengthy discussion of exactly the line followed by the route chosen;[1] while he rightly says the starting point (Kreusis) is clear, the end point (where Kleombrotos' forces pitched camp) is less clear and no decision by a scholar today can be really safe.

Similarly the impossibility of reconstructing the route used between Ambrossos and Thisbe and again between Thisbe and Kreusis is well illustrated by Beister's map (1970: 73) showing five different routes proposed by five different scholars all basing their suppositions on exactly the same evidence – *quot homines tot sententiae*! The truth is that we will never know. Perhaps, however, we should look briefly at one aspect of the question that seems rarely to have detained the thoughts of those who have examined this problem. Almost all seem to have believed that the Spartan army's movements were monolithic, that is that the whole force moved together and hardly ever has the possibility been aired that the force could have been split. If, however, I am right in seeing indications that there may have been more than one battle monument, implying more than one single engagement, then the idea that the Lakedaimonians may have divided their forces becomes a greater possibility.

It is also a fact that, in seeing that sort of monolithic movement, scholars have not really considered the problem of moving such an enormous force at one go. Thus Buckler (1980: 58–59) could blithely refer to the climb from Steiris to the upper reaches of Helikon as doable in three hours and that from Kreusis to the *Áyios Mámas* col from which to descend to the Thespian plain as also achievable in three hours but these estimates were the result of his own climbs as one person, not the time taken by a force of thousands of men (all carrying armour and weapons moreover). For example, one can readily envisage the entire force retiring in ranks from Koroneia to Ambrossos and even as far as Steiris before the ascent of the West flank of Helikon, but expecting a force of this size to arrive together at Kreusis is another matter. Whether one approaches

---

1   It is to be noted in passing that Tuplin refers to the church a little to the West of *Parapoúnyia* as Ag. Petros; in fact it is the church τῶν Ἁγίων Παύλου καὶ Πέτρου. On the ancient material built into its walls to which he refers cf. Fossey, 2014: 244–275.

Kreusis around the coast from Siphai or down the slopes of *Korombili*, or even down the bed of the river Oëroe (completely dry in summer time[2]), these are all routes where, in many places, no more than two or three men can march side-by-side; there are even places on some of the routes where single file is necessary. What is more, the case of an approach by the whole Spartan army to Kreusis around the coast from Siphai would mean that, marching in single file, as it would have to, the vanguard would arrive at Kreusis while the rear was still not far from Siphai; the vanguard would, moreover, be in such thin numbers that even a very small group of defenders within the walls at Kreusis would easily have held up the Lakonian advance for long enough to have had a chance to save the ten or twelve triremes supposedly captured; this, in its turn, may make us wonder how real an achievement was the "capture" of Kreusis and we will return to this question in the following paragraphs. In general the account by the late John Buckler of the travels of Kleombrotos' force is much more a work of fiction than anything based on documentary evidence.

It is incumbent upon us, in light of all this, to accept the possibility that the Spartans may well have split their forces up; given their superior numbers they had no intrinsic need to feel any danger in doing so. We must also remember that, if the identification of the site on *Mavrovoúni* as the principal base for the Spartan invasions of Boiotia just a very few years earlier (Tomlinson & Fossey, 1970; reprinted Fossey, 1990: 130–156) is correct, the topography of Southern Boiotia was well known to the Lakedaimonian forces and their high command.

This latter observation even raises the question of how much effort would really have been required to "take" the πολισμάτια, since Southern Boiotia, perhaps under Thespian lead, had often tended to be anti-Theban and thus, on occasion, pro-Spartan. We might accordingly then wonder just how much a force within Kreusis, a fortification in Thespian territory, would really have tried to protect triremes specifically called Theban. We can even remember that Epameinondas, quite rightly as it was to turn out, doubted the reliability of Thespians in his army at Leuktra:

---

[2] There is no need here to add to the ink that has already been spilled concerning the largely unimportant question of the exact date of the battle since most scholars agree at least on placing it in July–August when the streambed would be completely dry. This date is examined in terms of the Boiotian calendar by Roesch (1982: 37) since it is the specifically Boiotian Ploutarkhos (*Kamillos* xix. 2; cf. discussion of Tuplin, 1987: 77–84 who seems unaware of Roesch's study) who gives its date as 5th Hippodromios, the eighth month of the Boiotian year, noting that in earlier times on the very same date Thebans/Boiotians had also won an important victory against a different invader, the Thessalians. 5th Hippodromios thus saw Boiotians put an end to the *hegemonia* first of the Thessalians and, later on, that of the Spartans!

τῷ δὲ Ἐπαμινώνδᾳ καὶ ἐς ἄλλους Βοιωτῶν ὕποπτα ἦν, ἐς δὲ τοὺς Θεσπιεῖς καὶ περισσότερον· δείσας οὖν μὴ σφᾶς παρὰ τὸ ἔργον προδῶσιν, ἀποχώρησιν παρεῖχεν ἀπὸ στρατοπέδου τοῖς ἐθέλουσιν οἴκαδε· καὶ οἱ Θεσπιεῖς τε ἀπαλλάσσονται πανδημεὶ καὶ εἴ τισιν ἄλλοις Βοιωτῶν ὑπῆν δύσνοια ἐς τοὺς Θηβαίους.

But Epameinondas was suspicious of some other Boiotians and especially of the Thespians. Fearful, therefore, that they might behave treasonably during the engagement, he gave leave to depart from the camp to all who wished to go home. The Thespians left en masse as did any other Boiotians who had a grudge against the Thebans.

PAUSANIAS ix. 13, 8

The Boiotians certainly had – as we know – split their smaller forces up, with one *boiotarkhon*, Bakkhilidas, guarding the Kithairon passes with obviously some forces under his command, until the very eve of Leuktra, with another force (of unknown size but possibly small) detached under Khaireas blocking "the passes" and with the troops under Epameinondas described at Koroneia as merely a *moira* of the whole army. The Boiotians, with their generally inferior numbers actually had more cause to hesitate in dividing their strength but, nevertheless, did so; why not then the Spartans? There is no valid reason not to posit the idea that, forces being split on both sides, different engagements, separated even by a few kilometres, may have constituted parts of a technically single battle of Leuktra fought on the one day. In this way we can more easily understand the existence of a plurality of monuments seen both physically and in the epigram.

In his study of victory monuments Pritchett (1974: 246–275) shows instances at least as early as during the Peloponnesian War when more than one *tropaion* was erected for separate engagements in one battle. He cites Diodoros on tradition regarding Greek trophies:

τίνος γὰρ χάριν οἱ πρόγονοι πάτων τῶν Ἑλλήνων ἐν ταῖς κατὰ πόλεμον νίκαις κατέδειξαν οὐ διὰ λίθων, διὰ δὲ τῶν τυχόντων ξύλων ἱστάναι τὰ τροπόπαια; ἆρ' οὐχ ὅπως ὀλίγον χρόνον διαμένοντα ταχέως ἀφανίζηνται τὰ τῆς ἔχθρας ὑπομνήματα;

For what reason did the forebears of all the Greeks demonstrate that trophies for victories in war should be constructed, not of stone but with any wood that came to hand? Was it so that, since these would last but a short while and that thus the memorials of hostility should speedily disappear?

DIODOROS SIKELIOTES xiii. 24, 5–6

This intentionally temporary nature of victory monuments received comment from Cicero (*de inventione* 2.23) who tells the story that, because they had set up a trophy of bronze (it is assumed that a bronze figure surmounted the stone monument at which we have been looking), the Thebans were accused before the Amphiktyonic council of having acted improperly especially since their permanent monument recorded a quarrel between Greeks. It is this story that has led to the assumption that Ploutarkhos, at the end of his account of Greek practice over only temporary trophies, out of his native Boiotian sensitivity, fails to name specifically the Thebans in his final phrase:

οὐδὲ γὰρ παρ' Ἕλλησιν οἱ πρῶτοι λίθανον καὶ χαλκοῦν στήσαντες τρόπαιον εὐδοκιμοῦσιν.

For neither among the Greeks are those much respected who first set up a trophy of stone and bronze.
PLOUTARKHOS *ethika* 273c–d

If indeed the Thebans did set up not one but two trophies and both were constructed of stone, i.e. intended to be permanent, this criticism becomes all the more comprehensible: they had doubly transgressed tradition in twice commemorating this turning point in Greek history. The implication should be that twice, in what was essentially the same battle, they had caused the Spartans to turn – τροπαῖον being derived from τροπή, *turn*. One might assume that the Thebans were led to make this unusual move of erecting permanent memorial(s) of their defeat of Sparta at Leuktra partly because they were aware just how much they had changed for good the politico-military landscape of Greece and had done it with much inferior numbers of troops and perhaps had made it a double victory. Of the five archaeologically attested trophies in Boiotia listed by Kalliontzis (2014: 349–359) only that at Leuktra – obviously he thinks of only one – dates before the period of Roman involvement in matters Greek; three others concern the activities of Sylla in the Western Kopaïs and the last, also probably of the 1st century BCE, is likewise located at the museum of Khaironeia.

One should not be tempted to explain (cf. Beister, 1973) the plural τροπαῖα of the epigram in terms of the story recounted by Pausanias (iv. 22, 5–6) that concerns the Theban ruse with the shield of Aristomenes preceding the battle; we have already discussed the epigram. The whole account of this τροπαῖον – a story that Pausanias makes clear came to him from specifically Theban sources (ἃ δὲ αὐτὸς ἤκουσα ἐν Θήβαις) – shows beyond any doubt that this *tropaion* was of the normal temporary type although erected **before** the victory was won; especially is the temporary nature assured since the main component was removed immediately after the battle was won and returned to the Trophonion (ὡς δὲ ἐγένετο ἡ νίκη Θηβαίοις, ἀποδιδόασαν αὖθις τῷ Τροφωνίῳ τὸ ἀνά, θημα); it was, thus, not of a sort to have produced critical reaction of the nature discussed above. It was, then, the final monument(s) that was/were held in disrepute and we are thus still free to retain the idea of more than one **durable** *tropaion* as shown by the physical remains of two.

The final question seems to be one that must perhaps remain unanswered – where was Leuktra itself? Was it near modern *Parapoúnyia* and the reconstructed monument or was it at or near *Táteza* and the second, not reconstructed, monument **and** the story of the daughters of Skedasos with its more recent echo? Again Pritchett (1965: 49–52) has looked at the question of what was the nature of Leuktra, merely a πεδίον, just a τόπος, or a κώμιον. He came, quite rightly – for that moment – to the conclusion "unless archaeological evidence is discovered, we must entertain uncertainty, especially because of the references in Xenophon and Diodoros, as to whether any village existed in 371". My own view is that, since only very sparse remains of antiquity (sherd scatters) have in fact been found at or near *Parapoúnyia* while quite a lot more has been observed at *Táteza* (Fossey, 1988: 147–149, cf. Farinetti, 2011: 341–342) and since we now have the parallel for the daughters of Skedasos at *Táteza*, it is this latter that must be considered to have the somewhat stronger claim to be the site of any possible ancient settlement called Leuktra. Accordingly I am tempted to abandon completely my previous very tentative suggestion that *Táteza* might just possibly be the ancient Donakon that Pausanias (ix. 31, 7) placed (somewhere) in the land of the Thespians.

In this discursive chapter I have tried to combine historical, archaeological and topographic evidence together with an element of folklore. The two starting points in my thinking were the local story of *Táteza* and my observation there of the remnants of a second circular monument. As a result of this holistic approach I hope to have shown reason to posit the occurrence of two separate military engagements that were effectively parts of the same crucial battle, a battle that constituted a major turning point in Greek military and political history, the battle of Leuktra. In consequence it has been possible to suggest that the Spartan army would have advanced in separate units between West Phokis and Leuktra; we have also seen reason to suggest the correct location of the ancient toponym of Leuktra itself. The next chapter will lead us to consider some of the politico-military results of the Spartan loss and the Theban victory.

Afterthought: And the Triremes?

Before continuing the story and considering the aftermath of the Boiotian victory at Leuktra we may pause a moment to consider the matter of the Theban triremes captured by the Spartans at Kreusis. As we saw earlier on both our principal sources mention them:

> Of these two sources Xenophon is just a little fuller: ἀφικνεῖται εἰς Κρεῦσιν, καὶ τὸ τεῖχος αἱρεῖ, καὶ τριήρεις τῶν Θηβαίων δώδεκα λαμβάνει.
>
> Diodoros is briefer and does not even specify where the boats were captured nor even that they were Theban: ἐν παρόδῳ δέ τινα τῶν πολισματίων χειρωσάμενος δέκα τριήρων ἐγκρατὴς ἐγένετο.

Three questions arise: a. how many were they (10 or 12)?; b. how were they captured given the difficulties we have already seen concerning the route of the Spartan forces along the coast to Kreusis?; c. what happened to them after their capture?

The question of the number probably need not detain us very long. It is most easily understood that the δέκα in the second *testimonium* should be the result of a simple haplography in the manuscript tradition of Diodoros resulting from the presence of *delta* twice and in very close proximity in Xenophon's δωδέκα. Whichever of the two numbers we may prefer it is clearly a few ships if we keep in mind the size of the fleet built by the Thebans c. 366–363 BCE, i.e. just a few years later:

> ὁ δῆμος ἐψηφίσατο τριήρεις μὲν ἑκατὸν ναυπηγεῖσθαι, νεώρια δὲ ταύταις ἴσα τὸν ἀριθμόν
>
> > DIODOROS XV.79.1
>
> *The assembly voted for the building of a hundred triremes and an equal number of shipsheds.*

If the matter of the number of vessels can be disposed of quickly the means of their capture is not the same case. We have seen that, if the entire Spartan force came around the coastal path from Siphai to Kreusis it would have had to move in single file and could hardly take by surprise any garrison at Kreusis since the straggly line would be visible long before it reached the fortification and coastal plain beyond. If, however, we posit that the army was divided into different companies, as we have just seen reason to do, it becomes much more convincing to envisage at least one company having moved inland and thus having proceeded down the valley of the Oëroe. The valley is always dry out of the winter season and today actually carries a rough road wide enough to drive a regular automobile along. The width of route would allow soldiers to move at least three abreast and out of sight of Kreusis until arriving at the beginning of the coastal plain about a kilometre from the fortification and the beach (for the situation see the map given in our previous account of *Livadhóstro* [Fossey, 1990: 159]). A sudden rush of men already in groups of at least three would not only take people in the fortification by surprise but it would also take by surprise any crew members and guards by the ships which, one must remember, had to have been drawn up on the beach since there are not any remains of a harbour large enough to take ten or twelve ships at Kreusis/*Livadhóstro*; the only harbour that can be seen is a small one at the foot of the fortification large enough to house a couple of fishing boats. Obviously it takes longer to launch beached ships than it does to cast off ropes mooring vessels in port. Thus a surprise attack from the direction of the valley can have so easily captured the ships before their crews would have had time to set sail. We can, in fact, wonder if troops moving along the coastal path would have played any part at all in the action: if there actually were troops coming along the coast they might have served at most to distract guards and crew members thus rendering support for the sudden surprise attack from the valley.

If the preceding paragraph has succeeded in showing how the boats could have come into Spartan possession we still must wonder what subsequently happened to them. Their capture was obviously seen as important by Xenophon; otherwise why would he specify even their number when he has in the immediately preceding words dismissed rather cursorily ἐν παρόδῳ δέ τινα τῶν πολισματίων χειρωσάμενος (*on the way having captured some of the small towns*)? Obviously without fresh textual evidence the question will always remain in the air but we may still ask what were possibilities. Was it the intention of Kleombrotos to add them to his country's naval resources for transporting men and supplies from the Peloponnesos to the traditionally friendly Southern Boiotia should he succeed in establishing a re-occupation of the sort suggested for a few years earlier? Were they then of some use during the ignominious retreat after the defeat at Leuktra? Did they possibly serve to transport the dead (including Kleombrotos himself?) gathered after the defeat? Were they joined by other Spartan vessels from further West that had supported the king's troops when on garrison in Phokis? There may well be other possibilities that can be suggested by colleagues. If I touch on this matter it is because it was a natural question after dealing with the other two questions about the triremes.

CHAPTER 10

The Sequel to the Spartan Occupation of Southern Boiotia

After the operation of the Spartan network in the first half of the 370's and the suggested abandonment of *Mavrovoúni* by the Spartans, the Thebans spent the 3–4 years following the important defeat of a Spartan force at Tegyra in 375 BCE in consolidating their position in Boiotia and in reforming the Boiotian League under their leadership. Both then, and even in the years immediately following the victory at Leuktra, they must have recognised that the South coast and the Western extremities of their territory constituted a "backdoor" for an invading force, particularly given the all-too-often anti-Theban spirit of the cities in those two areas, especially Thespiai to the South and Orkhomenos to the West. That they had not only learned the lesson of recent history but also wanted to forestall any repetition thereof may explain the existence of a remarkable phenomenon in the Boiotian landscape. That phenomenon is the presence of city circuit walls with square towers and then similar individual towers in between those cities, all the walls and towers being constructed in the same coursed trapezoidal masonry and, in so far as concerns the towers, even with very similar dimensions as well as the same corner drafting. These constructions give quite definitely the appearance of belonging to a coordinated system; a preliminary account of this was given a couple of decades ago (Fossey, 1993: 114–117; an earlier and more brief note was reprinted in Fossey, 1990: 148–149).

As the map shows (Fig. 30), the system links, by lines of sight, all of which I have personally checked, seven of the cities of South West Boiotia (thus classing temporarily Kreusis as a "city" although its actual status is not clear) and six watch-towers all of them in the same coursed trapezoidal masonry with the same corner dressings. Incorporated into this group were two fortifications in rough masonry that already existed, being those by which the Boiotians turned back the Spartan army before the final advance to Leuktra and – more tentatively – two other pre-existing dominant sites. We may now consider briefly each of these sites according to their category.

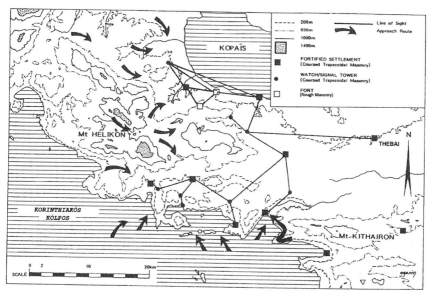

FIGURE 30   The defenses of South West and South Boiotia

1   **The Cities**

1. KHORSIAI (*Khóstia*) – Fossey, 1988: 187–194 with earlier bibliography; add Fossey (ed.) 1981 and Fossey & Morin, 1986.
   The circuit wall has parts in trapezoidal masonry (Pl. 32) but the towers and much of the circuit are in regular ashlar (Pl. 33) and date probably to the reconstruction of the site after the Phokian destruction of its defences in 347/6 BCE (Diodoros Sikeliotes xvi. 58 & 60). The towers (at least the two well preserved ones in the South corner of the site) are in this ashlar masonry too and do not have the accurate square plans seen elsewhere in the ones constructed in trapezoidal masonry; they are, moreover, somewhat smaller than what we shall see in city walls of the trapezoidal group: *c.* 5m × 5.65 and *c.* 4.8 × 5.65.
2. THISBE (*Kakósi*) – Maier, 1958; Fossey, 1988: 178–182; Gregory, 1992: 26.
   One of the best preserved fortifications of the group; the lower of the two circuits – that on the plateau – is pretty well exclusively in trapezoidal masonry with square towers at regular intervals, all showing the customary corner dressing (Pl. 34). These square towers are consistently (with only the very slightest variation of 1 or 2cm) 6.4m on each side.

PLATE 32   *Khóstia*, trapezoidal masonry in Eastern part of North wall

PLATE 33   *Khóstia*, ashlar masonry in central part of North wall

3. SIPHAI (*Alikí*) – Fossey, 1988: 168–173, but more fully Schwantner, 1977a. Pl. 35
Where the wall can be traced, partly along a crest on the Northern side and then on the East side of the akropolis, it is seen to be in the usual coursed trapezoidal work with interval towers in the same style.

4. KREUSIS (*Livadhóstro*) – Fossey, 1988: 157–163 and, in more detail, Fossey, 1990: 157–168 (a rewrite of the original published with Ginette Gauvin). The curtain wall is in the same trapezoidal masonry seen elsewhere, as

PLATE 34   *Kakósi*, corner tower

PLATE 35   *Alikí*, North wall, outer face, from below

    are the two visible towers on the long West and North-West wall (Pl. 36); the towers measure 6.5 × 7.5m and *c.* 6 × 6m.

5. THESPIAI (*Erimókastro*) – Fossey, 1988: 135–140; it is clear that no comparable fortification walls seem to be preserved at this site, although a small *enceinte* using many *spolia* and probably dating to Late Antiquity was in fact preserved until French archaeologists destroyed it in the 19th century in order to recover the sculpted and inscribed stones built into it.

PLATE 36   *Livadhóstro*, East wall, outer face, from South East

It is, however, basically unthinkable that a main site such as this would not have featured in such a network and it is thus included only on the basis of topographical logic.

6. (H)ALIARTOS (*Kastrí Mazíou*) – Fossey, 1988: 301–312 with a summary of the observations of R.P. Austin (1925/26: 81); no photographs were included and Austin did not mention any towers at all, although he specifically did describe parts of the fortifications as being in exactly the same masonry as the *Pyrgáki* tower (= Askra, see below). Although no dimensions can be used to compare with towers elsewhere, the walling masonry renders the inclusion of the site in this list entirely logical: the presence of isodomic trapezoidal masonry (as indeed of Kyklopaian, polygonal, isodomic ashlar, and Late Antique) has been confirmed recently by the work on the site by John Bintliff (2016: 5–7) and his team, although he now tends to view several of the styles, except Kyklopaian and Late Antique, as possibly contemporary; obviously our thoughts on this latter question differ and I am of the opinion that the question can only be really answered by making more small sondages across examples of all types at a wide variety of sites, such as my team did at *Khóstia* in 1980; ultimately this sort of study needs to be carried out not just in Boiotia, of course. Meanwhile we may note that the distinction made by Bintliff and his colleagues between "isodomic trapezoidal" and "isodomic ashlar" is not clear at least on the plates provided with the description (11 and 12).

7   KORONEIA (*Palaiá Koróneia*) – Fossey, 1988: 324–330; again no photographs are available but trapezoidal masonry was observed at points along the Western wall of the circuit.

2   The Towers

A. *Áyios Ioánnes* – Despite its poor preservation (only, at most, a couple of courses surviving), the trapezoidal nature of the masonry is obvious (Pl. 18) and the dimensions are also clear: 5.5m in (approximately) East-West direction × 6.1m.
B. *Mavrovoúni* – Fossey, 1990: 148–149 & pll. 68a & 68b (reprint of article originally published with R.A. Tomlinson); Schwantner, 1977a: 516–519 & Figs. 4 & 5. Cf. herein our pl. 11. The tower measures 6.1 × 6.1m.
C. *Áyios Mámas* – Pritchett, 1965: 55, pll. 56a & b. Although the masonry is clearly of the same type as in the other sites listed here (Pl. 37), this tower is unusual in that it is circular in plan (diameter of 8~8.1m) and thus does not present any corners, drafted or otherwise. It is only preserved up to two/three courses in height and many blocks have been removed over time and lie, some near to the tower but others, still in 1965, scattered in various directions over the flattened area on this ridge. The tower lies a very short distance (in Pritchett's estimate about 100m) East of the chapel of Áyios Mámas, a ruined tiny shrine when I first saw it in 1965 but now replaced with a larger church (see appendix to this chapter).
D. *Pyrgáki/Episkopí* (ancient Askra) – Fossey, 1988: 142–145; Roux 1954: 45–47, cf. Schwantner, 1977: Fig. 5, Snodgrass, 1985 and Gauvin & Morin, 1992: 9–11, Pll. 4–6 & 9. This tower occupies the highest point of the hill site normally identified with ancient Askra. Built in the usual masonry with drafted corners measuring 7.7 × 7.7m, and preserved to as much as 13 courses high (Pll. 38–39), it is centred on the small peak in the North West corner of an earlier circuit wall in rough masonry that surrounds the entire hilltop and is pierced by three small entrances. That small peak itself is mostly surrounded by a retaining wall in rough polygonal masonry; it thus encloses a much smaller space than the circuit in rough masonry encircling the whole hilltop. Close to the Eastern foot of the peak (and thus within the enclosure formed by the circuit in rough work) is an extensive ancient quarry, source of the building material of the tower at least, if not also of the polygonal and perhaps even the rough circuit walls.
E. *Evangelístria* (ancient Okalea?) – Fossey, 1988: 314–318; Kallet-Marx, 1989: 304–305. Most of this tower is badly destroyed but its South West

PLATE 37　　*Áyios Mámas*, South side of tower from outside

PLATE 38　　*Pyrgáki/Episkopí*, general view of tower from East, below

    corner survives to four courses in height and shows both the trapezoidal masonry and the drafted corner seen on other sites in this list (Pl. 40). I measured the tower as 6.8 × 7.4m, but Kallet-Marx urges caution since he feels that in the destroyed larger part of the tower the collapse of the blocks may have led them to shift sideways; he, therefore, thinks that it was probably closer to 6.6 × 6.6m.
F.　*Rákhes* – For this I am dependent upon the observations of John Camp (1991).

PLATE 39   *Pyrgáki/Episkopí*, detail of trapezoidal masonry in interior of tower

PLATE 40   *Evangelístria*, South West corner of tower

3   The Sites Walled in Rough Masonry

i.   *Vígla* – Fossey, 1990: 174–176, pll. 1, 8–10. Pl. 41.
ii. *Palaiothíva* – Fossey, 1990: 172–174, pll. 2, 4–6. Pl. 42.

PLATE 41   *Vígla*, South rubble wall

PLATE 42   *Palaiothívai*, rubble wall of Phase 2

iii. *Lykóphio* – Kallet-Marx, 1989: 305–307. I only know this site from Kallet-Marx who provides a useful plan but no photographs; I have no reason to question his description of the walls as being in rough masonry and thus similar to the two preceding ones and others in another group to which we shall return shortly. Here the plan shows a long curved wall penetrated by two gates cutting off on the North a nearly oval area the rest of whose limits are defined by cliffs that obviated any need for walling; Kallet-Marx estimates the dimensions as *c.* 35 × 15m with the longer axis running East-West. In the interior he only found badly worn, undatable pottery fragments but noted a flat "platform" near the North East limit that could have served as a signal point.

4   Earlier Sites Added

a. *Máli* – Fossey, 1990: 93–99 (reprint of the text originally published with Ginette Gauvin). All walls, including circuits appear to be "Dark Age" in date but it is clear that some building remains saw later use; part of the site could thus have been reused in the sort of circumstances predicted by the fortifications network, especially given its commanding view in several directions. It is thus included for reasons of topographic logic.
b. *Áyios Ioánnes ikonostásion* (cf. above, chapter 8)
c. Thebai. The map (Fig. 30) also shows a line of sight to Thebai from the Askra tower without the need of any intermediate signalling station. The fortifications at Thebai, while their lines can be fairly well established, have not had the detailed treatment that would have been optimally desired: all that shows clearly today is the Elektra Gate and the adjacent wall, all in regular isodomic masonry (Symeonoglou, 1985: 117–122, pll. 19–20). At the same time it would be unthinkable that a system covering the whole of South West Boiotia in this way should not be linked to the main city of the territory so inclusion of Thebai is logical in just the same way as Thespiai even though both of them do not today preserve fortifications that can be assigned real dates.

5   Summary of Network

Independent dating of the component parts, and thus of the system itself is problematic and has often been based on historical deduction rather than direct archaeological evidence. For example, Schwantner (1977a: 546–550) wished to place the walls of Siphai between 363 and 330 BCE. Our excavations at ancient Khorsiai, modern *Khóstia*, were designed in an attempt to obtain more direct dating; they suggest that the walls were in existence there in time to be destroyed by the Phokians in 347/6 BCE. For the moment we may, then, envisage the period of this work by the new Boiotian League as taking place between 362, when, after Mantineia and the death of their principal military leader Epameinondas, their Peloponnesian adventures drew to a close and they could thus concentrate more on reconstruction at home; this work should have been accomplished before the Phokian attack on *Khóstia* in 347/6 BCE. I have elsewhere argued (Fossey, 1992: 122–123) that, if the Boiotian network was, in fact, completed by 353 BCE this would allow for it to inspire perhaps the development of a similar network in Eastern Phokis constructed in the same coursed trapezoidal masonry and with the same corner dressings, also in the late 350's.

Finally a passing thought needs to be expressed. Walling of a very similar trapezoidal masonry is to be observed at *Kókkla* (= ancient Plataiai) with projecting square towers showing the sort of drafted corners we have seen in the cities and signal towers of the South coast area (Pl. 43). How does this fit into the scheme just outlined, given that the walls of that city were destroyed by the Thebans in 373 BCE? The obvious answer to that question must be that, for some while, this remained a possible building style for fortifications not hurriedly constructed in a rough masonry; thus when Plataiai was refortified in 338 BCE, after the defeat of the Thebans and their allies by Philippos II at Khaironeia, the new walls could be constructed in the same masonry style; this was, in fact, only a mere 15 years after the end of the period which we have argued for the construction of the Southern trapezoidal masonry sites. Since this period must also have seen the rebuilding of the fortifications at *Khóstia* it may well be that the trapezoidal and ashlar styles coexisted for a while in the second half of the 4th century. It is even noticeable that the front dimension of at least two of the Plataian projecting towers is 6.1~6.2m, like several of the sites in that network. With this later addition of Plataiai the defences of Boiotia become a little more comprehensive, extending to the East. At the same time, although it is negative evidence, we must remember that there is no clear occurrence in the rest of the Parasopia of other sites with the same sort of fortifications as at Plataiai. This apparent gap may seem a little surprising in light of the frequent hostility of the Athenians but necessity can make for strange bed-fellows as the combined Atheno-Boiotian resistance precisely to Phillipos II was to show. At least we may add that Plataiai has lines of sight to the *Áyios Mámas* tower and to Thebai itself thus allowing it to function as part of the Southern network.

PLATE 43   *Kókkla* (Plataiai), North cross wall

Two possible Eastwards extensions of the signalling and fortifications network that we have just been analysing are presented in the next chapter.

6   Conclusion

If the series of hypotheses presented above holds good we can suggest that the active Spartan presence in Boiotia only seems to have lasted at most 4–5 years in the first half of the 370's BCE but that it left its legacy on the Boiotian physical landscape in the form of the many city walls and intervening watch towers in which the territory abounds to this day – like some other parts of Central and Southern Greece. It is even ironical to think that the idea of connecting these by lines of sight for the transmission of fire (and smoke) signals may have reflected the fact that the Spartans themselves could have done this briefly during the years of their short residence. That residence seems also to have left its mark on the religious landscape in the form of certain cults of Artemis respected by the local inhabitants long after the hostile importer of them had departed.

Appendix: Áyios Mámas

In addition to the circular tower discussed above other material has been observed on the flattened area near to it. Pritchett (1965: 55) recorded many of these but his account can be filled out a little; this is particularly useful since the appearance of the area has been much changed in the process of building a new church in 1973. This new church lies a short distance to the West-South-West of the original chapel of Áyios Mámas.

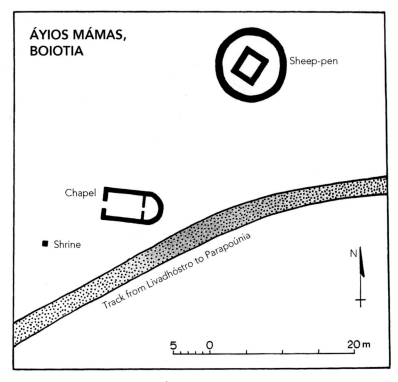

FIGURE 31   The ruined chapel of Áyios Mámas and other structures as recorded in 1967

In Fig. 31 I give a rough plan of the area of the old ruined miniature chapel of Áyios Mámas as I still found it in 1968 (and again in 1970). The chapel (Pl. 44) was only preserved in parts to a single masonry course in height and even that course was not entirely visible although several blocks were of large dimensions. It measured about 8m long and about 4m across and had a narrow door in the centre of its West end while the apsidal sanctuary at the East end was separated from the main body of the chapel by a thinner wall, similarly crossed by a small central doorway; this inner wall may have been intended to support a reduced *ikonostásion*. A functioning shrine to the saint stood about 9m West-South-West of the chapel's South West corner; this shrine is all that has been left intact by the remodelling of the area around the new church. Fortunately the tower was far enough away to be spared.

In the earlier 1960's Pritchett (1965: Pl. 65a) recorded within the ruins of the chapel a block (0.40 × 0.35 × 0.11m) that I too was able to observe in late 1965 and again in Spring 1968; this block that was no longer visible on my later visits bore a poorly preserved inscription, possibly Hellenistic in date, letter height 6.5cm:

THE SEQUEL TO THE SPARTAN OCCUPATION OF SOUTHERN BOIOTIA

PLATE 44   *Áyios Mámas*, remains of original chapel, as seen in 1965

ἐπὶ
EPME..TI

The letters of the second line were more worn than the three on the top line. I do not find this text in *SEG* but if the implication of ἐπί is that we are dealing with a funerary text, the letters preserved in the second line might suggest a theophoric name, either Ἑρμέας or Ἑρμείας in the dative case, followed by a patronym beginning in TI, the rest being lost. Both forms of the name Hermeas are attested occasionally in Boiotia during the Hellenistic period but always at Thespiai (*LGPN*iiib 143) in whose territory the site at *Áyios Mámas* lies. Names in Τι(μ)- are so many as to prohibit any attempt at restoration of the putative patronym (cf. Bechtel, 1917: 426–431); they are also widespread.

Also found within the chapel remains was a single, quite well preserved Doric capital (Pl. 45). This, together with a possible funerary inscription, may suggest some sort of use other than military (the tower) of the site in Classical or Hellenistic times. The presence of a spring of water at one side of the area cleared around the new church also renders possible uses other than the military, although the water would obviously have been useful for even the smallest garrison manning the circular tower. Since the clearing of the site nothing can be seen today of the scraps of walling that had earlier been observable, including those of the original chapel itself. In 1969 I was able to plan a large circular sheep-pen of fairly recent vintage; construction of this seems to have made reuse of rough building material in advance of the 1973 extensive renovation of

PLATE 45   *Áyios Mámas*, Doric capital

PLATE 46   *Áyios Mámas*, displaced blocks

PLATE 47   *Áyios Mámas*, coping stone

the chapel area but within it were preserved the remains of a small square building (cf. plan, Fig. 31). As far as I could tell none of the large blocks used to build the chapel had the curved nature that would be normal for pieces derived from the adjacent tower although several such blocks lay around (Pl. 46) including one that may have been a coping stone from the top of the tower's wall (Pl. 47).

CHAPTER 11

Further Thoughts on Late Classical and Hellenistic Defence Networks in Boiotia

In the preceding chapter I included in the posited system of the trapezoidal-masonry towers and city enceintes in Southern Boiotia also the two rubble sites at *Palaiothíva* and *Vígla* whose construction may date to the emergency of facing the Spartan invasion of 371 BCE as well as that at *Lykóphio*. Thinking similarly, it may not be going too far to suggest that the same might apply to two other nearby groups of places fortified in rubble masonry, both of which I published separately some years ago.

1   Skroponéri

In my previous publications of this group (latest version, 1992: 117–120) I envisaged it as primarily designed to protect the bay of *Skroponéri*, the single best natural harbour on Boiotia's North coast, and saw it in connection with the creation in the years 365–364 BCE and under the leadership of Epameinondas, of a Boiotian fleet to harry Athenian grain shipments from the North Aigaion; again the rubble construction could reflect a programme of hasty building for an immediate need. In a recent paper Russell (2016) seems to imply that there was more success to Epameinondas' diplomatic moves in the North Aigaion area than in any actual naval campaign but the two scenarios are not mutually exclusive. In any case it can be seen from the maps (Fig. 32–33) to just what extent the inclusion of this group completes the defence of Boiotia in all directions except the East.

The location of some of the sites concerned had been marked on a map of Pierre Guillon (1943: Pl. v) many years ago but without detailed discussion of the individual sites. My previous publications had concentrated on the network aspect also, not treating the details of the sites that compose it. This *lacuna* can here be rectified. All the sites are, of course, on the tops of mountains and hills but, yet again, the network incorporates fortified settlements just as does the Southern network analysed in the preceding chapter. In all, the network includes nine (or ten) fortified settlements, six separate hilltop fortifications and five elevated watch posts.

LATE CLASSICAL AND HELLENISTIC DEFENCE NETWORKS IN BOIOTIA

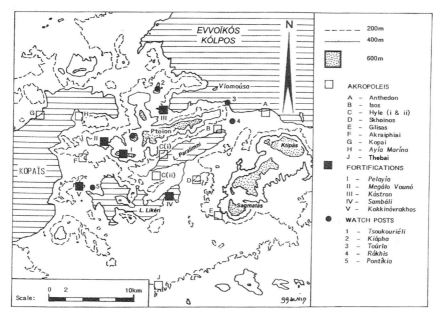

FIGURE 32   The *Skroponéri* area, A: the fortified sites

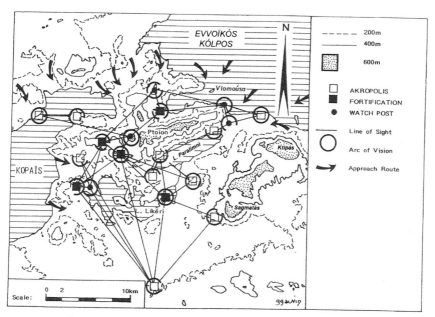

FIGURE 33   The *Skroponéri* area, B: the network

1.1 Settlements

A. ANTHEDON. For description, sketch plan and identification cf. Fossey, 1988: 252–257. The fall of the ground allows the line of the circuit walls to be followed but not much detail can be seen since all is under soil cover. Interval towers have been noticed in the past and the masonry has been described as coursed ashlar but without photographic documentation. The akropolis hill is very low – really nothing more than a hillock – and does not represent any formidable natural defence; it does, however, command a good view over the whole of the coastal plain that constitutes the territory of the city. Its lines of sight give it contact with the watch point at *Toúrlo* and that at *Rákhis*. It is thus tied into the network to provide information about the directions of its visual control, together with *Toúrlo* again (and *Kiápha*?), that is information concerning approaches from the North Euboian Gulf.

B. ISOS. For description, plan and identification cf. Fossey, 1988: 257–261. Apart from the mediaeval tower that gives the name *Pýrgos* to this hill at the North East end of Lake *Paralímni*, there are two walling circuits, of which the inner one appears to be in rubble masonry of small stones but is too poorly preserved to permit certainty; the outer circuit is much more solidly built using quite large blocks in masonry that varies between being nearly rubble and tending towards polygonal (Pl. 48). The outer circuit has an entrance on the South side, coming, that is, from the direction of the main cluster of buildings from the lower town clustered around the foot of this low akropolis hill.

Ci. HYLE i (= *Khelonókastro* the main akropolis at *Oúngra*). For description, plan and identification cf. Fossey, 1988: 235–238. This mountain top site on the North West side of Lake *Paralímni* nestles against the South East flank of Mount Ptoion. Its small, roughly flat top is surrounded by a circuit in solid rubble walling with large blocks (Pl. 49) among the stones of which was found an inscribed fragment of archaic Korinthian pottery; this provides a *terminus post quem* for the construction of the wall. Outside this small (*c.* 60m East-West × *c.* 80m North-South) enclosure lies another, much larger circuit also in rubble masonry but of a less substantial nature (Pl. 50) and less well preserved than the inner one. Again it is fortunate that detailed examination of the wall produced a few sherds of LH IIIB pottery again among the stones and thus providing another *terminus post quem* for the wall's construction. These dates obviously do not have any necessary connection with the function of the akropolis in the context of the proposed signalling network since they relate to the long history of occupation of this site that runs from at least as early

PLATE 48   *Pýrgos Paralímnis*, outer circuit, outer face on South West side

PLATE 49   *Khelonókastro*, South East wall of inner circuit, outer face

as the first stages of the EH period down to the 4th century BCE. They simply underline the fact that rubble walling could be built – even in a hurry – at almost any time; it is this possibility that makes important the odd occasions on which datable material is found on the non-settlement sites that will be considered below. In addition to those indications much of the assessment of such groups of sites must be based on geographic and historical probabilities. Despite its commanding height and the strength of its natural defences, this akropolis has a somewhat reduced range of vision beyond its own territory: to the cities of Isos (*Pýrgos*

PLATE 50   *Khelonókastro*, North West wall of outer circuit, outer face

Paralímnis) and Skhoinos (*Mouríki*) and to the fort on *Sambáli*. This limit in communications would appear to be the *raison d'être* for the second small fortification nearby, discussed in the following entry.

Cii.   HYLE ii (= *Oúngra* South). In addition to the actual akropolis at *Khelonókastro* the site at *Oúngra* has a second hilltop fortification to its South, so far unpublished. A rough circuit wall in rubble masonry runs around the hill's top; not well preserved, it is much obscured by thorn bushes and similar vegetation (Pl. 51). There seem to be no traces of internal buildings and no surface pottery was observed but the thick shrub cover made this almost inevitable. Since it is clear that the real akropolis at Hyle/*Oúngra* was indeed the *Khelonókastro* fortification just described, it is obvious that this small fort extends the range of signalling possible to and from ancient Hyle simply by connecting to the *Pelayía* hub; it has no other obvious function.

D.   SKHOINOS, at modern *Mouríki*. For description, plan and identification cf. Fossey, 1988: 229–232. The akropolis, marked by the chapel of Prophítis Elías, is a steep sided hill to the North East of the modern village. Its flat top measures *c.* 140m NNE-SSW × *c.* 40m NNW-SSE. To the SSE its long side needs no artificial protection being defended by a line of steep cliffs broken only briefly at one point where two short bits of wall define the entrance through which passes the path leading up from the lower town site at the position of the modern village below. Along the NNE side the top is bounded by walling in two different styles: a central portion consists of well-constructed polygonal masonry (Pl. 52) with an irregular,

PLATE 51   *Oúngra* South, North West wall, lower site in background with *Khelonókastro* (arrow) above

jogging trace while the parts to both East and West ends are in the usual rubble masonry (Pl. 53). There is a point where the rubble wall to the West meets the polygonal work and overlies it showing that the rubble wall is later than, and incorporates part of an earlier polygonal structure. This akropolis has lines of sight to Hyle (*Oúngra-Khelonókastro*), to *Likéri-Litharés* and to Thebai.

E.   GLISAS, at modern *Sýrtzi*. For description, plan and identification cf. Fossey, 1988: 217–223. This is the most outlying member of this network and its presence would not have really been a necessity; nevertheless, with its clear lines of sight to *Likéri-Litharés* and to Thebai, it may be seen as reinforcing communication. Its small akropolis ("*Toúrleza*") has no need of fortification on the South and South East sides where the hill falls away in sheer cliffs; to West, North and North East the hill's top is encircled by a wall in good polygonal masonry similar to that seen at the preceding site of Skhoinos/*Mouríki*. The akropolis had two entrances, to South East and South West where paths come up from the modern village and the lower town of antiquity. There are several traces of internal buildings.

F.   AKRAIPHIAI by modern *Kardhítsa*. For description and identification cf. Fossey, 1988: 265–271. The city site was occupied at least from Late

PLATE 52   *Mouríki*, North West wall, detail of outer face (polygonal masonry)

PLATE 53   *Mouríki*, rough masonry in another part of North West wall

Geometric to Roman times but has not been explored in any great deal, unlike the nearby nekropoleis. The history of its walling is far from clear but two phases have been suggested, the earlier one in rough polygonal work reinforced in later times with coursed poros blocks; in places, however, the coursed work is not purely composed of rectangular ashlars but shows tendencies toward trapezoidal (cf. Guillon, 1948: pl. XI). Like other cities such as Kopai and Anthedon it is an outlying part of the network; its function should have been to control approaches from the Eastern Kopaïs and to transmit information and warning via *Sambáli* and even directly to Thebai for those are the only two places with which it has direct lines of sight; at the same time *Sambáli* fed by way of *Pelayía* into the main *réseau*. In her plan of the area Vlakhoyiánni (2003: Abb. 1) indicates the name of the city site as *Vígliza* ("watch point").

G. KOPAI at modern *Topólia*. For description and identification cf. Fossey, 1988: 277–281. Little can be seen of walls and structural remains since the modern town lies right on top of the ancient. The site is on what today appears to be a steep sided hill rising out of the flat Kopaïc plain but what was, in antiquity, an island rising out of the lake's waters. Although it dominates a lot of the North East bay of the Kopaïs its only lines of communication are with *Ayía Marína* across that same bay and with the all-important fort on *Pelayía*. It served, however, to link *Ayía Marína* with the rest of the network and thus, together with *Kiápha*, to control approaches to or across the North East Kopaïs from the very Eastern parts of Opountian Lokris.

H. *Ayía Marína*. For description and plan cf. Fossey, 1988: 283–286. This is the site of a town of antiquity whose identity escapes us completely but which was inhabited from at least the EH period down to Roman times with but a possible break in the early Dark Ages. Its fortification gives the appearance of dating from Mykenaian times and I have argued elsewhere that it, together with the preceding site, was part of a Late Bronze Age network protecting the drainage system of the Kopaïc Lake. It may have continued to play such a part in this later network.

J. THEBAI. There is little need to examine in detail this site. For description and identification cf. Fossey, 1988: 199–208. As the principal city of Eastern and Central Boiotia, and one which was occupied without break (except for the very brief one after its destruction by Alexandros the Great) it seems always to have been a fortified city with extensive lines of sight to many points in the proposed network, especially the crucial *Pelayía* fort, as well as the other forts on *Sambáli* and *Kokkinóvrakhos*, and also to the cities of Glisas and Akraiphiai.

PLATE 54   *Pelayía*, East wall of circuit

1.2   *Fortifications*

I. *Pelayía* is the name of the very high peak of Mount Ptoion. On this peak, incorporating the geodesic post in its North East corner, is a small enclosure in rubble walling (Pl. 54). Its side to the North had no need of fortifications in view of the steep cliffs there that plummet to the upland plain below where is located the *Pelayía* convent. Short walls to East, South and West enclose an area resembling a truncated wedge in plan; the area enclosed measures approximately 15m along the cliff on its North side, about 15–20m across to the South wall which itself is only about 10m long. There are no traces of internal structures and no sherds appear on the surface. The site has excellent views in very many directions: over Lake *Likéri* and the Theban plain; over *Mouríki, Oúngra, Platanáki* and the hills along the South side of Lake *Paralímni*; as far as *Sýrtzi* (ancient Glisas) and Mount *Sagmatás*; over the North East Kopaïs and even beyond towards *Malesína* in Opountian Lokris; generally over the Kopaïs, the hills to its North as well as those to its South East and East (including the mass of Mount *Phagás*). At the Northern foot of the cliffs there occurs a spring that provides water for the convent but which, in antiquity could have furnished the same necessity to anyone occupying the fort above. It is clear that if this postulated signalling network functioned *Pelayía* would be a main hub in it.

II. The Ptoion Fort occupies the top of a spur jutting out in a West-South-West direction from the ridge of Mount Ptoion and looking immediately down onto the sanctuary of Apollon Ptoieus from the East (Pl. 55). The summit of this spur is enclosed by a circuit wall, all except the Eastern

PLATE 55   Ptoion Fort and Ptoion below, from West-South-West

part of the North side where abrupt cliffs obviate any need for artificial defence. A 4m gap at the West end of the cliffs seems to have allowed for a single entrance to the enceinte but otherwise the surrounding wall, c. 1.50m thick, runs around the peak in a series of irregular lines without any further break. The masonry of this wall appears, at first sight, to be the usual rubble but closer examination shows that the lower course in many parts is composed of polygonal blocks with rubble work on top (Pll. 56 & 57); it was solidly constructed and so survives in parts to a height of 1.50m. It thus seems that the fortification knew two periods of construction, an original wall in polygonal providing the base for a later one in the more hurried building work of rubble masonry. Some piles of stones may be what remains of internal structures whose presence is also surely indicated by the many tile fragments, including Classical painted pieces, that litter the ground surface within the walls. There are also many surface sherds of pottery, quite a lot of them being Late Roman ripple ware suggesting a possible reuse of the site in that period and even longer use of the site is suggested by the finding of a piece of a parallel-sided obsidian blade as well as one piece of worked flint. I had omitted this site from previous accounts of this postulated network because of its apparently limited capabilities of control and signalling but it is now included, on the one hand because of the similarity of structural sequence to that seen at *Tsoukouriéli* and at *Megálo Vounó* (see following) and, on the other in light of the realisation that it has in fact good control over movements along the road North from the Apollon sanctuary at *Perdhikóvrisi* towards the North East Kopaïs and also along the road from/to

PLATE 56   Ptoion Fort, mixed masonry in circuit wall

PLATE 57   Ptoion Fort, more mixed masonry in circuit wall

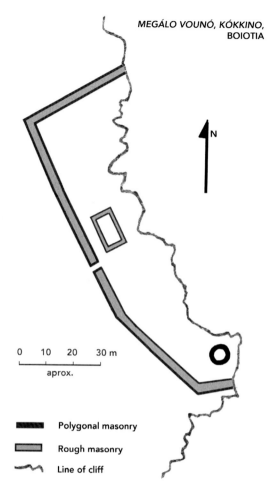

FIGURE 34 *Megálo Vounó, Kókkino*

the site of ancient Akraiphiai (*Kardhítsa*) in addition to the presence of several useful lines of sight: to Akraiphiai, to *Megálo Voúno*, to *Pondíkia*, and to *Kokkinóvrakhos*.

III. *Megálo Vounó* (*Kókkino*) is a mountain that faces that of the Ptoion Fort across the road that leads North from the area of the Apolline sanctuary in the direction of *Kókkinon* and *Lármes* (= ancient Larymna in Opountian Lokris). A small fort runs Northwest-Southeast along the edge of a cliff that overlooks the sanctuary of Apollon Ptoieus (*Perdhikóvrisi*); the steep cliff provides a natural defence on the North East side, while the remainder is enclosed by a circuit wall (Fig. 34) in mostly rubble masonry that also makes use of very large, roughly polygonal facing blocks (Pll. 58–59). In the middle of the South West wall is a narrow gap or

PLATE 58   *Megálo Vounó (Kókkino)*, line of circuit wall on West side

PLATE 59   *Megálo Vounó (Kókkino)*, circuit wall, detail of masonry

PLATE 60   *Megálo Vounó (Kókkino)*, entrance through circuit

PLATE 61   *Megálo Vounó (Kókkino)*, tower in polygonal masonry

entrance (Pl. 60). Just inside this entrance are the remains of a single oblong building; otherwise the only other structural vestiges visible in the interior occur in the South East corner where occur the remains of a well-constructed circular tower in polygonal work (Pl. 61) that may have been the source of the large blocks in the otherwise rubble circuit wall. No surface pottery was recorded. The site has an excellent view over Lake *Likéri* and the Kopaïc plain, especially its North East bay and obviously communicates with both the Ptoion Fort and the *Pelayía* site as well as those at *Kiápha* and *Kokkinóvrakhos* but the view Eastwards is restricted by *Pelayía* and other mountains. It could help control, together with the Ptoion fort, traffic down the road from *Kókkino* but otherwise its function within the postulated network would have been rather limited. Nevertheless it could have played a role within the postulated network like the Ptoion Fort; the similarity of walling sequences at both *Megálo Vounó* and the Ptoion Fort (polygonal followed by and largely incorporated into later rubble fortifications) is exactly that seen also in the *Tsoukouriéli* tower. As all three fortifications appear to reflect the same sequence of events they may also reflect the same historical purpose.

IV. *Kástron* (*Skroponéri*). At the head of the magnificent natural harbour formed by the bay of *Skroponéri* is a hill (Pl. 62) capped by a fortification. This *kástron* (Fig. 35) itself is a roughly circular flat area with a diameter

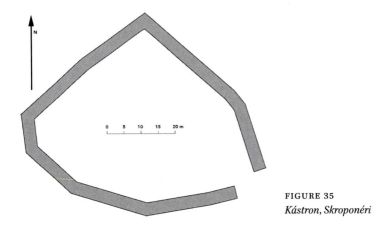

FIGURE 35
Kástron, Skroponéri

PLATE 62   *Skroponéri* bay with *kástro* in foreground, seen from *Máli Dárdha*

PLATE 63   *Skroponéri Kástron*, outer face of West wall by West corner

PLATE 64   *Skroponéri Kástron*, detail of masonry

varying between 52.50m (NE-SW) and 56.50 (NNW-SSE) enclosed by a wall 3.40m thick and; the circuit wall is solidly constructed of quite large blocks (Pll. 63 & 64). A single entrance on the SSE is approximately 0.60m wide (Pl. 65). The site dominates the whole bay and to either side of its foot, where is also located a spring of fresh water, the beaches that extend quite some distance and would be ideal for drawing up vessels,

PLATE 65   *Skroponéri Kástron*, entrance to circuit

especially since a small island (*Vlomoúsa*) in the middle of the entrance to the bay breaks up incoming currents thus ensuring a calm interior to the bay. There are other springs of slightly brackish water at either end of the main beach. Along the beach can be seen a column drum (height 0.50cm × diameter *c.* 0.40) and various aligned blocks largely hidden by the stones and pebbles of the shore as well as a number of potsherds, especially amphora handles.

[Not particularly pertinent to the discussion of fortification networks but still concerning the *kástron* hill, it may be worthwhile to add to my previous, brief account of the hill (Fossey, 1988: 262–263) the fact that high on the South West slopes of the *Kástron* hill but outside the fortification, there is at least a dozen separate buildings each with two and three rooms and with apsidal ends (Pl. 66); one orientated North West to South East measured 7.30m in length and 3.95 in width and had a 1.05 wide entrance a little off-centre in the long Northerly wall. Some of these houses have walls preserved to a meter height; in addition there is at least one substantial terrace wall in the area supporting a group of olive trees. The occasional sherds of Late Roman ripple ware to be found on the site's surface would suggest that this may be a site of late antique date; I previously proposed that this might possibly be a candidate for the essentially unknown settlement of Phokai (Ptolemaios iii. 14, 8).]

LATE CLASSICAL AND HELLENISTIC DEFENCE NETWORKS IN BOIOTIA 189

PLATE 66   *Skroponéri*, building remains on South slopes of *Kástron* hill

V. *Sambáli* is a mountain with two peaks (Pl. 67) against the East side of Lake *Likéri* overlooking, from its own East side, the *Voúliama* discussed in chapter 2. The Northern peak bears the remains of a complicated fortification (Fig. 36). The North end of the peak ends in steep cliffs that continue part way down the West side; these cliffs obviated any need for walls. Running South from the cliffs is a gradually down-sloping elongated oval area with two circuits of badly preserved rubble walling

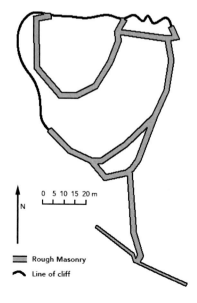

FIGURE 36   The fort on *Sambáli*

PLATE 67   *Sambáli*, general from East

PLATE 68   *Sambáli*, long South wall of circuit, detail of masonry in inner face

(Pl. 68). The smaller inner circuit encloses the very highest part of the peak; beyond it the larger, outer circuit has an inexplicable but smaller extension reaching further outwards and enclosed by an extra wall from which yet a further single wall in the same masonry runs due South for a short distance ending in one more group of walls whose nature and purpose defy comprehension. No traces of internal structures were visible but the ground surface yielded many pieces of coarse red pottery as well as at least one sherd of Classical black glazed ware. The site has good views to Thebai, to the *Pelayía* fort, to the main akropolis at *Oúngra* (*Khelonókastro*), to *Mouríki* (ancient Skhoinos), to *Sírtzi* (ancient Glisas), to the site of *Litharés* on the South side of Lake *Likéri*, and even to the distant site at *Dhrítsa* (ancient Heleon in Tanagrike).

VI. *Kokkinóvrakhos* South is the Southern peak of a large mountain mass lying at the Western side of Lake *Likéri* and overlooking the Kopaïc Plain from the East. Its small, fairly flat top is roughly a half oval in shape and slopes gently towards the South East. It is surrounded to South, East and North East by very steep slopes; to the North West the slope is much gentler and it seems that the easiest line of approach would have been from the West across the saddle that connects to the main mass of *Kokkinóvrakhos*. The top is protected by a circuit wall that follows a very irregular trace with many jogs, some of them quite small (Fig. 37); this wall, in rubble masonry with some quite large blocks (Pll. 69–70), seems to have been *c.* 2m in thickness but is in a very damaged state today. Odd piles of rubble in the interior may betoken the presence originally of internal structures but no plan is now discernable. A few very worn sherds were noticed on the surface including one possibly black-glazed; there was also one piece

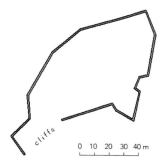

FIGURE 37   The fort at *Kokkinóvrakhos* South

PLATE 69   *Kokkinóvrakhos* South, line of circuit wall from inside

PLATE 70   *Kokkinóvrakhos* South, detail of masonry in circuit wall

of a parallel-sided obsidian blade. The site has excellent lines of sight to Thebai, to the akropolis at *Sorós, Moustaphádhes* (in the Parasopia), to *Klimatariaí* in Lake *Likéri*, to the forts at *Megálo Vounó* (*Kókkino*), above the Ptoion and on the summit of *Pelayía* as well as to the nearby small walled site at *Pondíkia*.

1.3   Watch Posts

1. *Tsoukouriéli*. This tower stands in a remote, isolated position difficult of access. It is circular in plan with diameter varying between 7.20 and 7.40m. The wall, 1.55m in thickness, stands in parts up to two courses high but in other parts is very much ruined; it is constructed basically in a rough masonry that presents occasionally a tendency to polygonal (Pll. 71–72). That mixture raises the question whether there might have stood an earlier tower in that polygonal style whose remnants could have been incorporated into a later tower in the rubble work that is what mostly subsists today. To which of two such possible phases belong the painted tile fragments observed around the building is unclear. Construction of the geodesic pillar in the centre of the tower's remains, moreover, probably did not ensure a better preservation of a structure in what was mostly rough, rubble masonry. The possibility that a (circular?) tower in polygonal masonry may have stood here recalls the existence of the circular tower in polygonal work within the fortification on *Megálo Vounó* (*Kókkino*). The combination of earlier polygonal masonry incorporated into a later rubble walling is obviously reminiscent of the situation just described for the Ptoion Fort. This watch station has easy visual communication with the *Skroponéri* fort, with the *Kiápha* lookout position,

PLATE 71   *Tsoukouriéli*, tower from West

PLATE 72   *Tsoukouriéli*, tower from East

with the forts on *Pelayía* and *Megálo Vounó* (*Kókkino*), as also with *Ayía Marína* and *Topólia* (Kopai) in the North East Kopaïs.

2. *Kiápha* is a mountain peak to the North of the whole complex and is the one site in this whole group that I have never visited personally. It is here included on the basis of information given to me by villagers of *Kardhítsa*/Akraiphiai to the effect that its peak indeed bears the remains of another fortification. Accordingly no dimensions or account of the masonry is available. Its position really dominates a great deal of the surrounding territory and is a very logical place to locate a signal station. There are clear lines of sight to it from the *Skroponéri kástron*, from *Toúrlo*, from *Megálo Vounó* (*Kókkino*), and from both *Ayía Marína* and *Topólia* (ancient Kopai) in the North East Kopaïs.

PLATE 73   *Toúrlo* (arrow) at East end of Ptoion range, seen from plain of Anthedon

[The report of a fortification on this height contrasts with the assurances given by local people that no such remains are to be observed on the top of *Máli Dárdha*, an imposing mountain with extensive views in many directions; this peak lies *about* midway between *Tsoukouriéli* and *Kiápha*. This too would have made a logical inclusion in the network but the report by locals that there are no indications of use in antiquity to be observed was subsequently confirmed by personal examination.]

3. *Toúrlo* is the small conical rocky peak at the very Eastern end of the Ptoion mountain range (Pl. 73); in this position it dominates the whole entrance to the Bay of *Skroponéri*. There is no tower here but remnants of walling appear at the South West foot of the peak (Pl. 74); a 6m length of rough walling runs almost due West-East and at the latter end makes a short 2.10m jog directly South before turning nearly due West-East again for 2.50m. From behind these walls one can easily climb up to the top of the peak; this has been levelled out to produce a flat platform that could have served eminently well for signal fires. Around the walls at the foot of the peak are tile fragments and many potsherds, including LH III and Hellenistic pieces as well as a few bits of Classical black glazed ware. In addition to its visual control over the bay's entrance, this position has clear lines of sight to Anthedon, to *Rákhis*, and to both the *Skroponéri* fort and the lookout post on *Kiápha*.

4. *Rákhis* is a hill at the North East end of Lake *Paralímni*. It has two elevated ends or peaks both bearing traces of ancient structures. On the Northerly peak are the badly preserved remains of a circular building c. 4m in diameter (Pl. 75), obviously originally hollow. Around lie a number of tile fragments and at least one black glazed potsherd (Pl. 76). On the

PLATE 74   *Toúrlo*, walling on shoulder below flat peak

PLATE 75   *Rákhis*, remains of circular building on Northern Peak

Southerly peak, around a geodesic post, are the badly preserved remains of a roughly square structure (Pl. 77); in fact its plan is more of a trapezoid measuring 4m on its North side, 5m on its East, 4.5m on the South and only 3.5 to the West. No surface sherds appeared to be visible here. Both positions have lines of sight to *Toúrlo*; the West one has a clear line to *Pýrgos Paralímnis* but only sees the very Western edge of the harbour area

PLATE 76   *Rákhis*, North Peak, associated surface sherds

PLATE 77   *Rákhis*, South Peak, remains of walling

at Anthedon, while the Eastern one has no communications at all with *Pýrgos Paralímnis* but has a clear line to Anthedon. The two positions must have functioned together to ensure connections between *Pýrgos Paralímnis* and Anthedon.

PLATE 78   *Pondíkia*, wall running South

5. *Pondíkia* is not a tower as such but rather a small peninsula fortification. The end part of a ridge is cut off by a rubble wall *c.* 1.50m thick (Pl. 78) that makes a single slight bend (*c.* 10°) between two stretches, the one to the West being 21.50m long and that to the East a little shorter at 15m. On the other sides the roughly semi-circular area is delimited by slopes

that drop away fairly steeply. While it does have lines of sight to Thebai and Akraiphiai, to the Ptoion Fort and to the forts on *Megálo Vounó* and on *Kokkinóvrakhos* South, this is not what one envisages for a normal signal station and it presumably served more as a subsidiary to the nearby *Kokkinóvrakhos* South. It is not essential to the functioning of the network here postulated and might even have been little more than a livestock pen of almost any date; it is included here purely since Guillon marked it as an ancient fortification on his map of the area and it could just possibly have served to reinforce lines of signalling, though I am far from convinced of this.

1.4 Summary

As the maps (Figs. 32–33) show, many lines of sight in this proposed network could be considered reduplicative but this is not entirely the case and many overlaps would merely give greater surety that information was passed along. The cities already existed and were merely incorporated into the overall scheme; this might have been particularly important for the most outlying of them, Kopai (with *Ayía Marína*) and Anthedon. The role of others such as Glisas and Akraiphiai, even Skhoinos, might appear more peripheral but, again, they could well have served as reinforcement for the sure transmission of information. Obviously understanding of such a network must come from the sites, both fortifications and watch posts that, it is here suggested, were added to constitute a whole system of communications of the type we have postulated for South and West Boiotia.

2 Anaphorítes

Part of the Boiotian East may in fact have been protected if the possible remnants of yet another suggested network of rubble fortlets are included; here fortified settlements play a much less essential role. In a previous publication (Fossey, 1992: 120–122) I attempted to elucidate the sequence in a series of constructions on the *Anaphorítes* ridge that separates from the plains of Central Boiotia the much smaller coastal plain of *Kháleia* lying immediately across the straits of the Euripos from Khalkis; the original study of this was published by the late S.C. "Kees" Bakhuizen (1970) in a detailed report that obviates any need here for lengthy description of the sort given elsewhere in this text for other networks. On the basis of the Bakhuizen volume and my own field investigations in 1965 I suggested in 1992 a sequence of three stages.

Stage 1 saw a set of small rubble fortlets on some of the peaks on the line, in particular those on *Galatsidhéza* and *Tsoúka Madhári*, as also possibly one on *Megálo Vounó* (which would have disappeared under the extensive fort later constructed there), and ending with the akropolis of Aulis (for which cf. Fossey, 1988: 70–71). Appropriately it is one of the clearly earlier rubble fortifications, that on *Galatasídheza*, that provided the line of sight to Thebai and thus tied in this group to the whole; I had not appreciated that fact when writing my 1992 account of this *Anaphorítes* network and the line of sight was not marked on its accompanying map. It is worth observing also that this long line of communication could have been reinforced by the possibility of using an intermediate position on the *Lykovoúni* akropolis of the settlement Harma in the Tanagraian tetrakomion (Fossey, 1988: 85–89).

Stage 2 saw construction in dressed masonry of the large *Megálo Vounó* fort that may have been undertaken for Phillipos II of Makedonia or for one of his Antigonid successors to create the third "fetter of Greece" at Khalkis, pairing with those at Korinthos in the North East Peloponnesos and Demetrias on the Pagasitic Gulf (cf. Polybios xviii. 11, 4–8, especially 5 concerning the expression "πέδας Ἑλληνικάς" as later on apparently used explicitly by Philippos V to describe an already existing situation that he had inherited). Not only does the masonry of the walling circuit contrast with the other rubble constructions, although it is not consistently built in the same style; it is also noticeable that the *Megálo Vounó* fortification includes internal buildings and a cistern (again Bakhuizen, 1970: 42–65 gives a detailed description and plan of the whole fortress with plates showing the variety of walling styles in the circuit) whereas the interior of the rubble fortlets is largely bare. *Megálo Vounó* was obviously intended for long term occupation, as befits its posited role as one of the "fetters".

Stage 3 consisted in a wall, again in rubble masonry, running along the entire ridge from *Klephtoloútsa* to *Megálo Vounó* but not coordinated with, or connecting to the small fortlets and also seemingly turned against the Boiotian plains to the South.

It is the first of the three stages that concerns us here. The sort of detailed description just given for the *Skroponéri* system is hardly necessary in this case, given the full analysis already published by Bakhuizen. The mountainous nature of the terrain gives a series of peaks high enough to dominate the surrounding areas. As just said this postulated first version of a network seems to consist of the posts on *Galatsídeza*, *Mikró Vounó*, probably *Megálo Vounó* and possibly the akropolis of Aulis. We may observe simply that the two fortlets actually connected to the later wall, *Klephtóloutsa* and *Tsoúka Madhári*, would

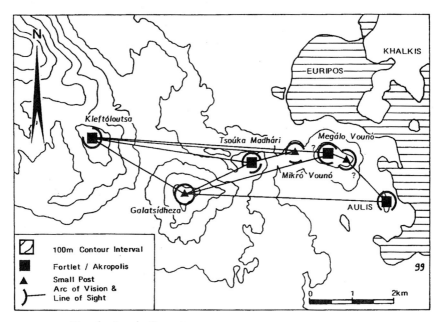

FIGURE 38   Map: the *Anaphorítes* system

have been superfluous; whatever the former of these would have been able to observe would have been clearly visible to observers at the post on *Galatsídheza* and likewise whatever *Tsoúka Madhári* might be supposed to control would have been equally visible to anyone on the combination of *Megálo* and *Mikró Vounó*. As with the other networks we have been considering, the inclusion of the existing akropolis of Aulis (for description, plan and identity cf. Fossey, 1988: 68–74) would be natural, just as would be the use of Harma/*Lykovoúni* (for description, plan and identification cf. Fossey, 1988: 85–89) to strengthen the long line of signalling from *Galatsídheza* to Thebai. The new map (Fig. 38) now shows the results of incorporation into the other two systems and all the lines of approach that the totality could control.

It remains a fact that the Eastern plains of Tanagrike, and perhaps the Eastern parts of the Parasopia, seem to be the only parts of Boiotia's periphery that were not entirely protected by this sort of defence system. At the same time any menacing movements from this area towards Central Boiotia would have been clearly visible again from *Galatsídheza* in particular but also to some extent from *Megálo Vounó* although not in such a concentrated way. What is more there are good lines of sight from *Galatsídheza* to already existing settlement sites in the territory of Tanagra, especially to that city itself and even more so to the formidable, strongly fortified akropolis at *Brátzi* with its solid

PLATE 79   *Brátzi*, South wall from outside

PLATE 80   *Brátzi*, gate in South wall

walls (Pll. 79 & 80) possibly belonging to the mysterious place Stephon (for description, plan and identification cf. Fossey, 1988: 49–52 & 53–56, especially 56). A line of sight also exists between *Galatsídheza* and the ancient town of Heleon by modern *Dhrítza* (for description, plan and identification cf. Fossey, 1988: 89–94), like Harma one of the Tanagraian tetrakomion.

A further line of sight from *Galatsídhezai* would lead to another member of the same tetrakomion, ancient Mykalessos at *Rhitsóna* (for description and

PLATE 81   *Sorós, Moustaphádhes*, general view of mountain from North West

identification cf. Fossey, 1988: 80–85). While Mykalessos, without any real akropolis at all, could not have played any contributory role in the network we may reflect that, had such a warning system on the *Anaphorítis* ridge existed in the late 5th century BCE, the town of Mykalessos could surely not have been taken unawares and without warning of the impending murderous attack across the mountains of that ridge conducted by Diitrephes and his Thrakian mercenaries in 413 BCE (Thoukydides vii. 29, 2–4 "καὶ αἱρεῖ ἀφυλάκτοις τε ἐπιπεσὼν καὶ ἀπροσδοκήτοις μὴ ἄν ποτέ τινας σφίσιν ἀπὸ θαλάσσης τοσοῦτον ἐπαναβάντας ἐπιθέσθαι"; discussion in Fossey, 1988: 84).

It may finally be noted that the Eastern Parasopia was also not isolated from these other potential defence systems. The soaring peak (Pl. 81) of *Sorós, Moustaphádhes* (= ancient Skolos, cf. Fossey, 1988: 119–126) not only has extensive command over the entire upper valley of the Asopos with lines of sight to Plataiai, *Pantanássa* (= ancient Hysiai, cf. Fossey, 1988: 112–115), to *Dharimári* (= ancient Erythrai, cf. Fossey, 1988: 116–119), and to *Khlembotsári* (= ancient Eilesion, cf. Fossey, 1988: 127–131) as well as to the higher parts of Thebai; it also has direct lines of sight to *Galatsidhéza* and *Pelayía* that seem to provide focal points for the two networks we have just discussed. *Sorós* was an important site, as the akropolis of Skolos that knew several periods of fortification in three different styles of walling (Kyklopean and two separate phases in polygonal) and obviously had a long period of use; similarly *Khlembotsári* as the settlement akropolis of Eilesion had two periods of walling (polygonal and ashlar); the walls of Plataiai are well known but no walling can be seen of any akropolis for Hysiai at *Pantanássa* and further East at the site of ancient Erythrai, *Dharimári* the akropolis is surrounded by rough rubble walling of the type we have seen in the *Skroponéri* and *Anaphorítes* systems. If this view is right it is clear that the Parasopia was already protected in effect by its settlement akropoleis with their lines of sight focussing on one of the members.

2.1 Postscript: Defence Networks Elsewhere: Some Elements of Comparison

Josiah Ober (1985: 208) found evidence for a similar network in Attike and argued that it should be dated to the period 385–340 BCE. We may quote a sentence from his conclusions: "The system of forts and watch posts was designed both to stop small-scale raids by freebooters or highwaymen and to delay major invasions until reinforcements, called up by relays of fire signals, could arrive at the frontier". It sounds basically like what has been proposed above and his map of the system (1985: 110) is remarkably similar to what has been demonstrated above for Boiotia but in the Boiotian scheme there is a certain difference and a significant addition to the scheme. In Boiotia the signal towers connected a series not of forts but of fortified settlements that should have had their own military forces (when they were not on campaign in the context of a larger Boiotian force). The more significant addition is represented by the lower site at *Kakósi*/Thisbe. The latter has all the appearance of a veritable fortress built alongside an already fortified city. The site is extensive, built on a flat plateau not on a hill with natural defences to determine the lines of man-built added walls. Where cliffs around the sides of the plateau are convenient they are followed but the main parts of the circuit walls run straight across the flat surface of the plateau. We have no way of knowing whether something similar existed at Thespiai and/or Thebai but the *Kakósi* lower site could house a considerable garrison of men able to deploy quickly across the flat *polje* to its South (to cover the two harbours at *Áyios Ioánnes* and *Vathý*), along the foot slopes of Helikon to the West (to reach *Khóstia* and thus to forestall any incursion by *Saránda* bay from where any hostile force would, in any case, have to struggle up the very steep incline from the beach to the level of the fortified city of Khorseiai) and along the same foot slopes in the opposite direction (to reach a place in the area of *Xeronomí* whence there are two potential routes to meet and repel invaders arriving by *Alikí*/Siphai).

Mark Munn (1993) followed on the work of Ober dealing primarily with the strategy that lay behind the system of fortifications in Attike and the changes in defensive mentality that took place in the earlier 4th century BCE. Both Ober and Munn publish photographs of several of the sites, in particular, of course, the five principal fortified settlements at *Yiphtókastro*/Eleutherai, at *Kavásala*/Panakton, at *Khassiá*/Phyle, at *Kotróni*/Aphidnai and at *Ovriókastro*/Rhamnous, all of them sites where the masonry shows the same style as in our

Boiotian and Phokian networks (the site at *Myoúpolis*/Oinoe does not have much walling well preserved to be sure of its style). When, however, we look at their photographs of the towers the similarity seems to end for those illustrated do not present the same ordered building style seen in the two networks, Boiotian and Phokian: e.g. the *Velatoúri* tower (Ober pl. 7; Munn pll. 39–40) is in trapezoidal work but with much more irregular coursing than seen in our areas; similarly the *Kandíli* tower (Ober pl. 8) is in purely rough masonry, an even rougher form of which appears at the Hymettos tower (Munn pl. 34) and the *Plakotó* tower (Munn pll. 37–38) shows such a variety of building styles within its construction that it is difficult to see how what survives can all have been built at one time.

My former student Phil Smith (2008: 89–02 + Fig. 47) followed up on my ideas and found evidence for a similar system in Megaris during the 4th century. In this he was also building on the work of Symphorien Van de Maele (1993); the system was not, however, the main aim of his work and thus his text does not illustrate the masonry of the signal towers but only that seen at the two principal coastal sites, *Alepokhóri*/Pagai and *Pórto Yermenó*/Aigosthena which shows exactly the same style as seen in the Boiotian, Phokian and Attic systems. In a similar way another former student of mine took up the study of fortifications and networks thereof in the North East Peloponnesos; Ginette Gauvin (1993) demonstrated quite clearly the existence of just such networks in the territories of ancient Kleonai and ancient Phlious in the Southern Korinthia. Unfortunately the monograph she planned on the subject has not yet seen the light of day but if and when it does it will be a major contribution based on intensive fieldwork and personal autopsy over many years.

Elsewhere in the Peloponnesos Yánis Píkoulas (1984 and 1988: 185–186) noted the presence of a scatter of square towers in the parts of Arkadia that belonged to Tegea and Mantineia; in the latter case he believes that they belong "στὸ ἴδιο ἀμυντικὸ σύστημα τῆς Μαντινείας τοῦ 4ου π.C. αἰώνα". He did not appear to take the matter any further and one would have liked to see these towers marked on an analytical map to see how this suggested system might have functioned. He did, however, contrast this with the territory of Megalopolis where his extensive fieldwork over many seasons had not noticed any towers. In fact many years after Píkoulas the defence network of Mantineia was studied in detail by Maher and Moway (2018) who show how a ring of square towers in "coursed polygonal masonry" controls the territory of the city and the routeways leading into it, communicating by lines of sight with the city itself and with each other; on several of these towers there even appears to be the same sort of corner drafting seen in our Boiotian examples. They propose to date this network to the period of the reconstruction of the city in the context of forming the Arkadian League under Theban encouragement after the Boiotians had defeated the Spartans on the lands of the same city in 362 BCE, thus in the same period as we are proposing for the Boiotian network.

Norman Ashton (1991) studied over several years the strikingly high number of 55 ancient towers, all circular in plan, on the island of Siphnos. He proposed to see the first of them as constructed in the later 6th century BCE while building of the latest he places in the 3rd century BCE. The earliest he sees as two-storied places of permanent occupation, often accompanied by a well or cistern; he notes the location of them in relation to the mining sites of the silver that was responsible for the island's early prosperity. He envisages them serving as watch posts communicating with the fortified akropolis and as constructed in the wake of a raid by the Samians on the island c. 525 BCE. He places the second phase of tower building in the 5th century when he says that the "network ... was expanded in order that a complete signalling system should exist around the island, capable of not only sending and receiving messages to and from the acropoleis, but also facilitating the interchange of communications with one another. The principal method of signalling must have been by smoke and fire ..." In support of the nature of the signals he adduces the testimony of Thoukydides, Aineios Taktikos, and Polybios; cf. our remarks in chapter 8 above. The third phase of tower construction Ashton does not date, leaving simply the implication that it occurred somewhere in the 4th century; he regards the towers of this period as refuges for local population in times of attack by marauders. The final phase Ashton places in the 3rd century BCE when the towers were "sited on or very near to fertile terraces, often with no independent strategic view or signalling position, and in some cases no views of the sea at all"; he thus considers them as principal structures at farming settlements. There are possible similarities between the Siphnian towers and the Boiotian ones; the story in both cases perhaps begins with reaction to a hostile invasion and in both cases the resulting network communicates with the cities or larger settlements. But there the similarity seems to end. The towers are so widespread across the island of Siphnos that any network seems to be a blanket cover whereas the Boiotian situation is really a network that has been thought out for a specific purpose without many superfluous lines of communication. The Boiotian towers could not have housed more than three or perhaps four people at the most while the Siphnian ones show much evidence of provision for inhabitants and internal structures to house them. In short while the Siphnian situation consists in many towers that could communicate with each other, their prime function seems to be to provide refuges for local people; the Boiotian towers are always deliberately located for maximum control of routes with minimum investment in their creation and no obvious attention to local inhabitants. Although in some cases they are located in or near a habitation site (e.g. *Pyrgáki*/Askra), in others they are in exposed locations with no indication of an associated habitation (e.g. *Áyios Ioánnes* and *Evangelistria*) and a couple (*Áyios Mámas* and *Mavrovoúni*) are next to ancient sanctuary sites, one of them but a minor shrine, the other a major cult centre with neither showing indication of settlement until the one (*Mavrovoúni*) becomes a military base with buildings and water provisions for an intended long-term use. There appears to be little relationship between these Siphnian towers and the East Central Greek ones.

In a reaction to Ober's work Frederick Cooper (2000) proposed a re-evaluation of Boiotian fortifications with the stimulating title of "The fortifications of Epaminondas and the rise of the monumental Greek city". In it he concludes that "the Boiotians were supreme in fortification construction for nearly sixty years, 395 to 338 BCE." Obviously for anybody writing about such matters from a Boiotian point of view this is a pleasing conclusion but some of the discussion that leads up to it needs re-examining. We have already tried to show that Boiotia, in our view essentially after Leuktra, was the first area to provide itself with a real defence system. What seems to be missing from Cooper's study is the full incorporation of the watchtowers deliberately sited to give maximum cover of the territory and its approaches with minimum spread of resources. He concentrates on walls of the fortified sites. Also it may be felt that he mistreads in regarding the three South coast fortified settlements as showing contemporary walling in their circuits; we have tried, at *Khóstia*/Khorseiai to show that the bulk of the preserved walling should be dated to the reconstruction of the city's walls after their demolition by the Phokians in 347/6 BCE (Diodoros Sikeliotes xvi. 58 & 60). That walling is plain ashlar just as is the masonry in the well preserved akropolis of Boiotian Orkhomenos, a city often destroyed by the Thebans, the last time being in 349 BCE, just over a decade after which it was rebuilt by Philippos and Alexandros following on from their defeat of the Thebans and allies at the battle of Khaironeia in 338 BCE (e.g. Pausanias ix. 37, 8). It thus seems that, using the material from both these sites, we can date plain ashlar masonry to the later 4th century BCE (and after, of course) while the coursed trapezoidal that we see in so many of the sites in our suggested system may be dated approximately to the second quarter of that century. In other words it is unlikely that the bulk of the preserved walls at *Khóstia* are exactly contemporary with the coursed trapezoidal masonry at *Alikí* and *Livadhóstro* (and in the related watchtowers), to say nothing of that seen in the similar work seen in the fortifications of Eastern Phokis and Megaris, all of which we attribute to the time of Epameinondas. It is further interesting to observe the same coursed trapezoidal work in fortifications known to be due to the Thebans of Epameinondas' time: Messene and Mantineia both show the same evenly coursed mixture of trapezoidal and rectangular blocks together with the same corner drafting on the corners of the interval towers – so similar that they could all have been built by masons from the same school as those who built such fortifications as seen at Siphai/*Alikí*, Kreusis/*Livadhóstro* and Thisbe/*Kakósi* as well as the intervening watch towers.

CHAPTER 12

A Valley in the Hills East of *Thívai*

Comparatively few finds of Classical or later date from Boiotian Thebai (modern *Thívai* or *Thíva*) have been published in detail until the recent discovery and excavation of the important sanctuary of Herakles immediately outside the Kadmeia walls to the South East currently being published by Aravantinos (2007, 2009, 2014, 2015, 2017). Bonanno-Aravantinos (2012, 2014), Kalliga (2017) and others. The final publication of that excavation has not yet appeared. The Herakleion thus lay by the road from the Elektra Gates in the Kadmeia enceinte to the sanctuary of Ismenian Apollon; at the latter sanctuary excavation has recently been taken up again, more than a century after the work there of Keramópoullos (1917); again no full reports are available but judging from what appears on the website of Bucknell University that is partnering the local archaeological ephoreia in this project, most material found so far has been Roman and later. In what had been published before the discovery of the Herakleion there had been a concentration on material dating to the Bronze Age, notably in the publications of Keramópoullos (1917) and Symeonoglou (1973). In 1965 and 1966 I had the opportunity to observe a lot of material found adjacent to the city site, found not during excavation but in a rather more individual manner.

If one drives along the dirt road running a little over a kilometre East from the South East corner of the modern city towards the large church of *Moskhopódhi* one passes, to the immediate South of the road, a shrine to the *Zoödhókhos Piyí*; about half way between this shrine and the end of the road by the church at *Moskhopódhi*, one can look down Northwards (Pl. 82) into a winding stream bed (on Symeonoglou, 1985, pl. 1, it is labelled "Moschopodi River") that debouches into the Theban plain by the East side of the suburb of *Áyioi Theódhoroi* (cf. map Fig. 39). During the period (1965–1966) when I lived in modern *Thíva* I came to know a workman who, in good weather, often assisted by his wife, spent every Sunday morning scratching in the sand at the bottom of the dry stream-bed. His main purpose was to discover coins for sale to the museum to supplement his meagre income as a worker for the town administration. He found a considerable range of coins and other small metal objects that he would show me before taking the coins into the museum offices (what subsequently became of the other small objects I was never told). Sometimes I would only have a very little time to record my observations of the artifacts, while on other occasions I had more leisure to record them fully; this

A VALLEY IN THE HILLS EAST OF THÍVAI

PLATE 82   *Thívai*, valley to East of the city, seen from South

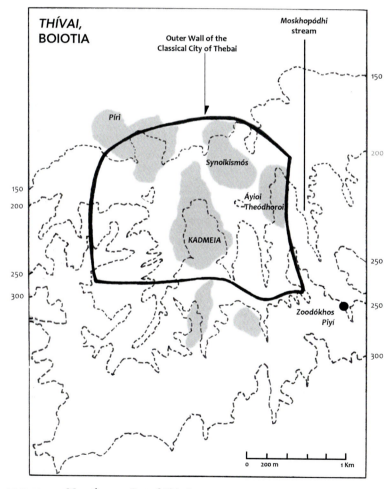

FIGURE 39   Map: the area East of *Thívai*
LINE OF WALL DERIVED FROM SYMEONOGLOU, 1985: FIG. 3.6.

will explain the inconsistencies of detail in the following account. When time allowed I tried to weigh and measure as well as, occasionally, to sketch in addition to identifying them; on other occasions I could only try to achieve their identification. Fortunately identification was, for the most part, easy since many of the coins and the other objects were well preserved; especially was this the case with the silver coins.

In view of the amount and nature of this material together with some historical conclusions which can be tentatively drawn from it all, it seems worthwhile to publish my observations, based on the notes I made a little over half a century ago, notes which I have frequently revisited in the interval. It must be stressed that the scratching in the sand did not constitute in any way an illegal excavation; the stream-bed is/was not an archaeological site and was altogether too narrow to have ever been inhabited; rather it had obviously provided a collection basin for material washed down from the higher ground around.

It will be noticed that the coins are all small, even the silver pieces; that the finder was able to distinguish some of them from other pieces of grit in the stream bed (one he actually described to me as being as large as a lentil), says much for his eyesight and powers of observation. That all the pieces were found close to the site of ancient Thebai means there is no doubt as to their authenticity; indeed, although the bulk of the coins seen here is of local minting, it is clear that those Boiotian coins which have been shown or suspected to be forgeries are of larger silver denominations than those seen here (Demetriadi & Hepworth, 1984).

The rest of the material is also composed of small pieces, mostly of bronze, some of iron, including arrow-heads, small tools of varying nature and a lot of amorphous bits, as well as an interesting group of lead sling-shot, some of them inscribed. We will present the coins first, then the sling-shot, and finally the variety of the remaining metal and other pieces.

1   The Coins

Very little numismatic evidence from Boiotia as a whole has ever been published. We know, of course, of the hoards from Orkhomenos, from "Boeotia, opposite Chalkis", the earlier one from Thebai, one listed as from "Chalkis (or Boeotia)", that from Anthedon as well as that from the Kopaïs and the later ones from Thebai (Thompson *et all.*, 1973: nos. 78, 163, 193, 205, 223, 229 and 233 respectively + *Numismatic Chronicle* 1996: 279 no. 94; more recently Vlakhoyiánni, 2000), but of these only those from Orkhomenos (date *c.* 323

BCE), Thebai (dates *c.* 225–200 BCE, *c.* 168 BCE and 168–146 BCE) and Anthedon (date *c.* 191 BCE) have real proveniences and are essentially Hellenistic; the others are too anonymous and we have left aside completely those simply assigned to "Boiotia" in general or to "Euboia (or Boiotia)" (Thompson *et all.*, 1973: nos. 42, 59, 65; add two listed by Vlakhoyiánni, 2000: 107–108, nn. 39–41). Otherwise there are the small numbers of coins found in the excavations at Haliartos by Austin (1926–1927: 138–139; 1931–1932: 201–202) and in our own excavations at *Khóstia* (Fossey, 1986: 101–105); the few found at Eutresis, apart from a single Roman imperial piece, all dated to Byzantine and Frankish times (Goldman, 1931: 8); more recently Vlakhoyiánni (2009) has published 29 coins found mostly in graves during rescue excavations in the cemetery of Akraiphiai, largely Hellenistic issues by the Boiotian League but including also occasional pieces struck, again during Hellenistic times at other mints (two of Lokris but otherwise singles of Athenai, Korinthos, Histiaia on Euboia, Phlious, Kleonai, Lakonia, Krannon in Thessalia, Amphipolis in Makedonia). The group of coins to be presented here, with its geographical and chronological range, presents similarities in the geographic origins of the pieces with the smaller group found in the cemetery of Akraiphiai but shows a much wider chronological range; it is, therefore, something of an addition to the lacunary picture of coin circulation at the city of Thebai and perhaps in the territory of Boiotia; as just indicated, the published material from hoards is largely restricted to Hellenistic times, especially the earlier 2nd century BCE, in the period preceding the disbandment of the Boiotian Confederation by the Romans (whatever the exact date of that event). This group is plainly not to be considered in the same terms as a hoard.

Among the silver pieces no large denominations are present and the assemblage thus has the appearance of "small change", a context in which the bronze "token" pieces are, of course, completely at home.

1.1 *Boiotia*

Not surprisingly a large percentage of the coins is either Theban or minted by other Boiotian cities so our list may start there. Apart from the parallels cited for individual pieces, the classification of Boiotian coins follows that of Head (1881, more briefly 1910: 343–355). Although old, this classification has in general not been superseded; on occasion one hears that a scholar is proposing a comprehensive study of Boiotian coins but no such study is yet in the public domain. That being said, it is obvious that in what follows I use Head's traditional dating purely for consistency with so many other publications; I do not propose to enter into the debate over the chronology of early Greek coinage which is far from over and, in any case, I am not in a position to contribute much to it from the Boiotian point of view. In this way the dating of coins in what follows for the period before the mid-5th century BCE may be subject to much revision. In general it appears that the early Boiotian coinage has been down-dated to the later 6th century (cf. chapter 4).

1.1.1 Thebai

1. AR *tetartemorion* (?), ⌀ 0.48 — 600–550 BCE
   Obverse: Boiotian Shield
   Reverse: Incuse square of Aiginetan pattern
   Cf. the series *BMC Central Greece* 32–33, nos. 1–14.

2. AR *Obol*, ⌀ 0.89~0.72 — 550–480 BCE
   Obverse: Boiotian Shield
   Reverse: Crossed *theta* in incuse square
   Cf. the series *BMC Central Greece* 68, nos. 11–12 and 17.

3. AR *Hemiobol*, ⌀ 0.62~0.56 — 550–480 BCE
   Obverse: Half Boiotian Shield
   Reverse: Crossed *theta* in incuse square
   Cf. *BMC Central Greece* 68, nos. 13–16.

4. AR *Hemiobol*, ⌀ 0.77~0.62 — 446–426 BCE
   Obverse: Half Boiotian Shield
   Reverse: Kantharos in incuse square
   Cf. *BMC Central Greece* 73, nos. 43–46 (all also inscribed ΘΕΒ).

5. AR *Tetartemorion*, ⌀ 0.59~0.52 — 446–426 BCE
   Obverse: Boiotian Shield
   Reverse: Kantharos, ΘΕ in incuse square (*theta* crossed)
   Cf. *BMC Central Greece* 73, nos. 43–46 (all inscribed ΘΕΒ).

6. AR *Hemidrakhma*, ⌀ 1.26 — 426–395 BCE
   Obverse: Boiotian Shield
   Reverse: Kantharos; above club; to either side of vessel's stem ΘΕΒ (*theta* dotted)
   Cf. *BMC Central Greece* 75, nos. 64–65.

7. AR *Obol* — 426–395 BCE
   Obverse: Boiotian Shield
   Reverse: Club between Θ and ivy-leaf
   Cf. *BMC Central Greece* 74, no. 53.

8. AR *Hemiobol* — 426–395 BCE
   Obverse: Half Boiotian Shield
   Reverse: Bunch of grapes
   Cf. *BMC Central Greece* 77, no. 88.

9. AR *Tetartemorion*, ⌀ 0.66~0.58   426–395 BCE
   Obverse: Boiotian Shield
   Reverse: Club between ivy leaf and dotted *theta*
   Cf. *BMC Central Greece* 74, no. 53.

10. AR *Tetartemorion*, ⌀ 0.72~0.62   426–395 BCE
    Obverse: Boiotian Shield
    Reverse: Club between ivy leaf and dotted *theta*
    Cf. *BMC Central Greece* 74, no. 53.

11. AR *Tetartemorion*?, ⌀ 0.71~0.66   426–387 BCE
    Obverse: Boiotian Shield
    Reverse: Club between vine leaf and dotted *theta*
    Cf. *BMC Central Greece* 74, no. 53.

12. AR *Tetartemorion*?, ⌀ 0.69~0.66   426–387 BCE
    Obverse: Boiotian Shield
    Reverse: Club between vine leaf and dotted *theta*
    Cf. *BMC Central Greece* 74, no. 53.

13. AR *Hemiobol*, ⌀ 0.83   426–387 BCE
    Obverse: Half Boiotian Shield
    Reverse: Club with vine leaf above and underneath ΘEBA (form of *theta* unclear)
    Cf. *BMC Central Greece* 74, no. 53.

14. AR *Hemidrakhma*, ⌀ 1.49~1.29   395–387 BCE
    Obverse: Boiotian Shield
    Reverse: Kantharos with club above and to either side of vessel's stem Θ-E
    Cf. *BMC Central Greece* 80, no. 110.

15. AR *Hemiobol*, ⌀ 0.89~0.79   395–387 BCE
    Obverse: Half Boiotian Shield
    Reverse: Kantharos with Θ-E to either side of stem
    Cf. *BMC Central Greece* 80, no. 110 (with club also, as preceding).

16. AR *Tetartemorion*, ⌀ 0.74~0.67   395–387 BCE
    Obverse: Boiotian Shield (very circular)
    Reverse: Kantharos with Θ-E to either side of stem
    Cf. preceding.

17. AR *Obol*, ⌀ 0.93   387–374 BCE
    Obverse: Boiotian Shield with club across one end
    Reverse: ΘE, head of young Herakles with lion skin r., all in concave surface
    Cf. *BMC Central Greece* 84, nos. 169–170.

18. AE, ⌀ 0.5   379–338 BCE

Obverse: Head of young Herakles
Reverse: Club, above arrow; name of a magistrate(?) ΛAAN above club and, below arrow, letters ΘE (*theta* dotted). If the last two letters stand for the city of Thebai this coin must have been minted before adoption of the Attic/Ionian script and thus should date earlier than that expressed in the standard Head system as indicated above.
Cf. *BMC Central Greece* 85, nos. 176–177.
For name Λαᾱ́νδρος cf. *LGPN*iii.b, 252.

19. AE, ⌀ 0.5   379–338 BCE
Obverse: Head of young Herakles
Reverse: Club beneath bow; above all name ΑΡΙΣ and below, second name: ΦΕΙΔΟ
Cf. *BMC Central Greece* 85, nos. 180–181 (N.B. the name ΑΡΙΣ also occurs, but alone, on nos. 178–179 and on 86, no. 189, while on 84, no. 165 we read ΦΙ-ΔΟ alone; likewise on 87, nos. 195–198 ΦΕΙΔΟ is read alone).
Names in Φειδο- and Φιδο- are not very plentiful in Boiotia (*LGPN*iii.b: 417–418 and 420): attested are only Φειδόλαος, Φειδόμηλος/Φιδόμειλος and the basic Φ[ε]ίδων (the latter a possibility here only if not abbreviated from the nominative) so one of these might be the magistrate named here. On the other hand names in Ἀρισ-, as elsewhere in the Greek world, are numerous (*LGPN*iii.b: 50–64). What is, however, interesting about this combination is that clearly two different names are indicated; this is not always the case in pieces of this category where combinations such as ΘΕΟ and ΤΙ could just as well represent a single name such as Θεότιμος as the beginnings of two separate names. The same applies to the combination ΟΝΑ and ΣΙ [cf. no. 20 below] and might also hold good for ΠΥΡ and ΡΙ except that here the second element would have to call for reconstructing such a rare name as Ῥίνκος or Ῥίνκων, each attested but once in Boiotia, respectively at Orkhomenos and Akraiphiai (*LGPN*iii.b: 371); on balance it seems better to leave this combination as presupposing one name such as Πύρριχος. What is clear is that the names of these magistrates (always assuming that they actually were magistrates) could occur singly or in pairs on the bronze tokens whereas, on the apparently contemporary silver coinage, the indications are that every inscription seems to represent but one name, never a clear pair. One reason for doubting their identity as magistrates' names might be the considerable difference in the lists of inscriptions recorded on these bronze tokens and those attested on silver pieces (cf. the lists drawn up by Head, 1881: 63–66 for the silver and 70–71 for the bronze). Roesch (in Taillardat & Roesch, 1966, especially 85–87) showed that the change from epichoric

script to the Attic-Ionian alphabet took place in Boiotia c. 395 BCE and that accordingly, since some of these "magistrate" names on the coins are in epichoric lettering, this series must have begun its life earlier than the date of 379 BCE proposed by Head: "aussi n'est-il pas impossible qu'à part une brève interruption entre 386 et 378 – époque de la dissolution de la Confédération – ce monnayage fédéral ait débuté vers 400 ou même un peu avant".

20. AE, 0.5   379–338 BCE
    Obverse: Head of young Herakles
    Reverse: Club alone; above ONA and below ΣΙ(?)Ι
    Cf. *BMC Central Greece* 86, nos. 190–192.
    Names in Ὀνασι- are sufficiently common in Boiotia (*LGPN*iii.b: 325–326) to prohibit any attempt to reconstruct some specific name.

21. AE, ⌀ 0.5   379–338 BCE
    Obverse: Head of young Herakles
    Reverse: Club with caduceus below; above [Ο]ΛΥΜ
    Cf. *BMC Central Greece* 87, no. 193.
    Ὀλύμπιχος *vel sim.*? Again names on this root are very common in Boiotia (*LGPN*iii.b: 323–324).

22. AE, ⌀ 0.5   379–338 BCE
    Obverse: Head of young Herakles
    Reverse: Club beneath bow; above all name ΘΕΟ and, below, ΤΙ
    Cf. *BMC Central Greece* 85, nos. 174–175.
    Θεότιμος or Θεοτιμίδας? These seem to be the only possible reconstructions attested in Boiotia (*LGPN*iii.b: 193) and, while neither is remarkably frequent the former, being more common (17 examples, as opposed to 2) is perhaps to be preferred; cf. no. 19 above on the name Θεότιμος.

23. AE, ⌀ 0.5   379–338 BCE
    Obverse: Head of young Herakles
    Reverse: Club, rest too worn to read
    Obviously same series as *BMC Central Greece* 85–88, nos. 172–206.

24. AE, ⌀ 0.5   379–338 BCE
    Obverse: Head of young Herakles
    Reverse: Club, rest too worn to read, possibly a bow above
    As preceding.

25. AE, ⌀ 0.8   Imperial times
    Obverse: Female head (Tykhe?) r., turreted, ΘΗΒΑΙ-ΩΝ
    Reverse: Dionysos (?) standing r., holding kantharos; most of inscription too worn to read but the letters ΜΑΡΚΟΥ are clear enough to suggest restoring [ἐπὶ πολεμ(άρχου) Γ.Κ.] Μάρκου.

Cf. Head, 1881: 96.

We are probably not far wrong if we consider the *kantharoi*, bunches of grapes and vine (sometimes called "ivy") leaves seen on some of the smaller coins, of which several examples are listed above, as referring to the cult of Dionysos, seen here himself on the reverse. With so many instances in this coinage of reference also to the cult of Herakles (his head on nos. 17–24 and the frequent occurrence of his club) it is interesting to recall with Schachter (1981: 185–192 in general on the Dionysiac cult at Thebai, esp. 187 on the common birthplace of the two divine figures; cf. 1986: 14–30 on the cult of Herakles at Thebai) that Dionysos, like Herakles, was considered to have been born at Thebai.

1.1.2   Orkhomenos

26.   AR *Obol*, ⌀ 0.94~0.9   600–480 BCE
       Obverse: Corn grain
       Reverse: Incuse square in five unequal parts, two of them containing the letters E and P (both written retrograde)
       Cf. *BMC Central Greece* 53, no. 13.

27.   AR *Obol*, ⌀ 0.88   600–480 BCE
       Obverse: Corn grain
       Reverse: Incuse square of Aiginetan pattern; no inscription
       Cf. *BMC Central Greece* 53, no. 13 (although no inscription on present piece).

28.   AR *Obol*, ⌀ 0.81   600–480 BCE
       Obverse: Corn grain
       Reverse: Four-part incuse pattern; no inscription
       Cf. *BMC Central Greece* 53, no. 10.

29.   AR *Hemiobol*, ⌀ 0.79   387–374 BCE
       Obverse: Half corn grain
       Reverse: Ear of corn with E and P to each side of stem
       Cf. *BMC Central Greece* 53, no. 13.

30. AR *Obol*   387–374 BCE
       Obverse: Three corn grains; EP
       Reverse: Horse prancing r.
       Cf. *BMC Central Greece*, 55, nos. 30–34.

1.1.3   "(H)aliartos"

31.   AR *Obol*, ⌀ 0.79   before 480 BCE
       Obverse: Boiotian Shield
       Reverse: Incuse square containing H (with double cross-bar)

Cf. *BMC Central Greece* 49, no. 10.

Boiotian issues with archaic *heta* on them have traditionally been attributed to Haliartos cf. *BMC Central Greece* 48–49, Head, 1881: 11 & 14–15; 1886: 345. As we discussed in chapter 4, about 30 years ago Etienne & Knoepfler (1976: 218–226 + list 383–390) argued quite strongly that the attribution should not be maintained since the normal version of the city's name did not have an initial aspirate (its name should, therefore, be written Aliartos/ΑΡΙΑΡΤΟΣ although there is an indication that in the Homeric Catalogue of Ships an initial aspirate is intentional). We have seen reasons to suggest other Boiotian candidates for the role of city minting these "H" issues. Indeed, if my identification of one of these places is correct, Heleon by the modern village of *Dhrítsa*, half way between Thebai and Tanagra, was plainly a much more important and flourishing habitation – from the Early Bronze Age through to Late Roman times (Fossey, 1988: 89–95) – than can ever be claimed for Hyettos at *Dhéndri*, North of the Kopaïs (cf. Fossey, 1988: 293–295). The question of the archaic mints of Boiotia requires much further work.

1.1.4   Tanagra

32.   AR *Obol*, ⌀ 0.97   387–374 BCE
Obverse: Boiotian Shield (well centred)
Reverse: Forepart of horse prancing r. with T in front of legs and A underneath chest; all in concave field
Cf. *BMC Central Greece* 62–63, nos. 29–45.

33.   AR *Obol*, ⌀ 0.97   387–374 BCE
Obverse: Boiotian Shield (off-centre)
Reverse: Forepart of horse prancing r. (also off-centre) with T above very detailed mane and A in front of legs; all in concave field
A variant of the preceding.

34.   AE ⌀ 0.95   387–374 BCE
Obverse: Boiotian Shield (well centred)
Reverse: Forepart of horse prancing r. with TA underneath chest and legs; all in concave field
A variant of the preceding two (*q.v.*) but in bronze. On the possible significance of the horse on Tanagran coinage (seen in all three preceding pieces) cf. Schachter, 1958.

1.1.5   Mykalessos

35.   AR *Obol* ⌀ 1.05   387–374 BCE
Obverse: Boiotian Shield (slightly off-centre)

Reverse: Thunderbolt with M and Y to either side
Cf. *BMC Central Greece* 51, nos. 1–2.
The thunderbolt should perhaps refer to a cult of Zeus but there is no evidence for such a cult at Mykalessos.

1.1.6 Pharai

36. AR *Tetartemorion* ⌀ 0.55–0.45   550–480 BCE
Obverse: Boiotian Shield
Reverse: Φ (?) in incuse square
Cf. *BMC Central Greece* 57, no. 1.
This piece had been nearly half chipped away; even the shield took some identifying and the letter *phi* on the reverse was far from clear. The latter is at least a purely circular letter with no projecting *hasta*.

37. AR *Obol* ⌀ 1.06–0.96   387–374 BCE
Obverse: Boiotian Shield
Reverse: Amphora with letters Φ and A to either side
Cf. *BMC Central Greece* 57, nos. 3–5 (these with extra symbol).

1.1.7 Thespiai

38. AR *Obol* ⌀ 0.11–0.1   387–374 BCE
Obverse: Boiotian Shield (well-centred)
Reverse: Crescent beneath letters ΘΕΣ (dotted *theta*, three-bar *sigma*)
Cf. *BMC Central Greece* 90, nos. 4–8.

39. AR *Obol* ⌀ 0.105–0.1   387–374 BCE
Obverse: Boiotian Shield (well-centred)
Reverse: Two crescents back-to-back; in the four quarters so formed the letters ΘΕΣΠΙ (dotted *theta*, three-bar *sigma*, *pi* with shorter right arm)
Cf. *BMC Central Greece* 90, nos. 1–2.

40. AR *Obol* ⌀ 0/95–0.88   387–374 BCE
Obverse: Boiotian Shield with vertical crescent emblem on it
Reverse: Head of Aphrodite Melainis(?) r.; behind nape of neck Θ (dotted and worn)
Cf. *BMC Central Greece* 91, no. 12.

41. AR *Hemiobol* ⌀ 0.79–0.88   387–374 BCE
Obverse: Half Boiotian Shield with horizontal crescent emblem on it
Reverse: Head of Aphrodite (badly worn and no inscription legible)
Cf. *BMC Central Greece* 9, no. 12.

1.1.8 Boiotian Federal Issues (Uncertain Mints)

42. AR *tetartemorion* ⌀ 0.69   6th–5th cent. BCE

Obverse: Boiotian Shield with segmented rim (off-centre)
Reverse: Horizontal *beta* (with small, flattened curls), above small *epsilon* (with pendant tail from upright stroke)

The letter forms are clearly archaic thus dating at the latest in the early 4th century BCE; absence of any trace of the incuse square on the reverse may suggest a date in the later 5th century. The *beta* makes it clearly a federal issue but does the small *epsilon* indicate a particular place of minting, since it does not form part of the usual general inscription BOI etc.? If so then the only name that can come to mind has to be that of E/Orkhomenos but no parallel is immediately obvious for this combination.

43. AR *hemiobol* ⌀ 0.76–0.85   387–374 BCE?
    Obverse: Half Boiotian Shield
    Reverse: Bunch of grapes; to either side B-O
    Cf. *BMC Central Greece* 36, no. 38–41 (all with full shield), Head, 1881: 58, nos. *f* & *g* (both *tetartemoria*).

44. AE ⌀ 2.07–1.99   288–244 BCE
    Obverse: Head of Athena wearing crested "Korinthian" helmet
    Reverse: Trophy of arms, ΒΟΙΩΤΩΝ
    Cf. *BMC Central Greece* 39, nos. 64–65, pl. VI. 2; Head, 1881: 83.
    This piece was very badly worn. Is it possible that the trophy refers to the Boiotian participation in the Aitolians' ultimate defeat of the Galatian invaders in *c.* 279 BCE (Pausanias x. 23. 11)? The Boiotians had joined the Aitolians in large force in the preceding attempt to block the invaders at Thermopylai (Pausanias x. 20, 3).

45. AE ⌀ 1.76–1.66   244–197 BCE
    Obverse: Head of Herakles r. with lion skin
    Reverse: Poseidon standing l., leaning on a trident (holding dolphin); ΒΟΙΩ[ΤΩΝ]
    Cf. *BMC Central Greece* 41, nos. 81–89, pl. VI. 8.
    Very worn and, like many of the Boiotian bronzes of this type, apparently (Head, 1881: 87) struck over bronze coins of Antigonos (Doson?), as seen here in the combination of the head of Herakles remaining from the original obverse (as opposed to the intended head of Demeter, see the following three pieces) with the new Boiotian reverse. This Boiotian reverse clearly refers to the federal sanctuary of Poseidon at Onkhestos (cf. nos. 46–56 below).

46. AE ⌀ 1.77–1.68   220–197 BCE
    Obverse: Head of Demeter facing three-quarters r.
    Reverse: Poseidon standing l., leaning on a trident (holding dolphin); ΒΟΙΩΤΩΝ

Cf. *BMC Central Greece* 41, nos. 81–89, pl. VI. 8. The appearance the preceding piece (*q.v.*) was perhaps supposed to have before being overstruck.

47. AE ⌀ 1.88–1.69   220–197 BCE
    Obverse: Head of Demeter facing three-quarters r.
    Reverse: Poseidon standing l., leaning on a trident (holding dolphin); ΒΟΙΩΤΩΝ
    Cf. *BMC Central Greece* 41, nos. 81–89, pl. VI. 8. Like the preceding piece, presenting the appearance no. 45 was perhaps supposed to have. Much more worn than no. 46.

48. AE ⌀ 1.76–1.74   220–197 BCE
    Obverse: Head of Demeter facing three-quarters r.
    Reverse: Poseidon standing l., leaning on a trident holding dolphin; ΒΟΙΩΤΩΝ
    Cf. *BMC Central Greece* 41, nos. 81–89, pl. VI. 8. Again the appearance no. 45 was perhaps supposed to have. Although the coin was even more worn in general, the dolphin on the reverse was clearer than on nos. 46–47.

49. AE ⌀ 1.82–1.72   220–197 BCE
    Obverse: Head of Demeter facing three-quarters r.
    Reverse: Poseidon standing l., leaning on a trident (holding dolphin) ΒΟΙΩΤΩΝ
    Cf. *BMC Central Greece* 41, nos. 81–89, pl. VI. 8. See nos. 46–48. Extremely worn on obverse.

50. AE ⌀ 1.79–1.71   220–197 BCE
    Obverse: Head of Demeter facing three-quarters r.
    Reverse: Poseidon standing l., leaning on a trident (holding dolphin) ΒΟΙΩΤΩΝ
    Cf. *BMC Central Greece* 41, nos. 81–89, pl. VI. 8. As nos. 46–49. Also extremely worn on obverse.

51. AE ⌀ 1.89–1.84   220–197 BCE
    Obverse: Head of Demeter facing three-quarters r.
    Reverse: Poseidon standing l., leaning on a trident (holding dolphin) ΒΟΙΩΤΩΝ
    Cf. *BMC Central Greece* 41, nos. 81–89, pl. VI. 8. As nos. 46–50. Barely legible.

52. AE ⌀ 1.76–1.73   220–197 BCE
    Obverse: Head of Demeter facing three-quarters r.
    Reverse: Poseidon standing l., leaning on a trident (holding dolphin) ΒΟΙΩΤΩΝ
    Cf. *BMC Central Greece* 41, nos. 81–89, pl. VI. 8. As nos. 46–50. Barely legible; also chipped on edge above Demeter's head.

53. AE ⌀ 1.66–1.54 220–197 BCE
   [Obverse: Head of Demeter facing three-quarters r.]
   Reverse: Poseidon standing l., leaning on a trident (holding dolphin) BOIΩTΩN
   Cf. *BMC Central Greece* 41, nos. 81–89, pl. VI. 8. See nos. 46–52. Only legible (just) on reverse; obverse worn away completely, it could, therefore, even have been like no. 45.

54. AE ⌀ 1.67–1.60 220–197 BCE
   [Obverse: Head of Demeter facing three-quarters r.]
   Reverse: Poseidon standing l., leaning on a trident (holding dolphin) BOIΩTΩN
   Cf. *BMC Central Greece* 41, nos. 81–89, pl. VI. 8. As nos. 46–53. Obverse completely illegible but reverse fairly clear although worn.

55. AE ⌀ 1.89–1.84 220–197 BCE
   [Obverse: Head of Demeter facing three-quarters r.]
   Reverse: Poseidon standing l., leaning on a trident (holding dolphin) BOIΩTΩN
   Cf. *BMC Central Greece* 41, nos. 81–89, pl. VI. 8. As nos. 46–54. Obverse completely illegible and reverse less clear than proceeding.

56. AE ⌀ 1.72–1.61 220–197 BCE
   [Obverse: Head of Demeter facing three-quarters r.]
   Reverse: Poseidon standing l., leaning on a trident (holding dolphin) BOIΩTΩN
   Cf. *BMC Central Greece* 41, nos. 81–89, pl. VI. 8. As nos. 46–55. Obverse completely illegible but reverse fairly clear although worn.

57–84 (26 examples). AE ⌀ varies c. 1.37 = 1.1 196–146 BCE
   Obverse: Boiotian Shield
   Reverse: BOIΩTΩN, trident, sometimes, to r. a dolphin
   Cf. *BMC Central Greece* 43, nos. 108–111, pl. VI. 12.
   Head (1881: 90–92) argued that these small bronzes might, in fact, have been token *oboloi* minted no longer in silver. The trident may be taken as an abbreviated reference to the federal sanctuary of Poseidon at Onkhestos taking the place of the depiction of the god himself leaning on such a trident (cf. nos. 46–56).

1.2   *Euboia*

1.2.1   Khalkis

85–90 (6 examples). AE ⌀ all c. 1.21 369–336 BCE
   Obverse: Head of Hera facing
   Reverse: Eagle flying r. holding snake in beak (XAΛ mostly illegible)

Cf. *BMC Central Greece* 111–114.

All the pieces are so worn that distinguishing them from the following type is not always easy.

91–92 (2 examples). AE ⌀ 1.3–1.2   196–146 BCE
   Obverse: Head of Hera facing, on Ionic capital
   Reverse: Eagle flying r. holding snake
   Cf. *BMC Central Greece* 115–116, nos. 96–103.
   Again badly worn; only the Ionic capital serves really to distinguish these coins from those of the preceding type.

1.2.2   Eretria

93. AE ⌀ 1.33–1.3   378–338 BCE
   Obverse: Head of nymph (Eretria?) r. with rolled hair
   Reverse: Head and neck of a bull three-quarters r., EYBO to left
   Cf. *BMC Central Greece* 97, no. 33.
   Head (1910: 363) attributes these small bronzes to a mint at Eretria (whence both the obverse and reverse types) issuing small change for the island as a whole. At the same time there seems little to distinguish them from pieces that might have been minted in the period 196–146 BCE.

94. AE ⌀ 1.03   378–338 BCE
   Obverse: Head of nymph (Eretria?) r. with rolled hair
   Reverse: Head and neck of a bull three-quarters r., [EYBO to left]
   See comment on previous piece.

95. AE ⌀ 1.14–1.13   378–338 BCE
   Obverse: Head of nymph (Eretria?) r. with rolled hair
   Reverse: Head and neck of a bull three-quarters r., [EYBO to left]
   A very badly worn and chipped piece of the same sort as the preceding two. See comment on 89.

96. AE ⌀ 1.0   378–338 BCE
   Obverse: Head of nymph (Eretria?) r. with rolled hair
   Reverse: Head and neck of a bull three-quarters r., [EYBO to left]
   Very badly worn on the reverse; piece of the same sort as the preceding three.

97. AE ⌀ 1.33–1.3   378–338 BCE
   Obverse: Bull standing r.
   Reverse: Bunch of grapes, no inscription visible
   This badly worn piece is another of the small bronze types attributed by Head (1910: 363) to a mint at Eretria (whence both the obverse and reverse motifs) issuing small change for the island as a whole. Again, however, it seems possible that it too was minted in 167–146 BCE.

1.2.3 Histiaia

98. AE ⌀ 1.5–1.3   369–336 BCE
   Obverse: Head of Maenad r.
   Reverse: Bull walking r.; ΙΣΤΙ
   Cf. *BMC Central Greece* 126, nos. 21–22.

99. AE ⌀ 1.4–1.3   369–336 BCE
   Obverse: Head of Maenad r.
   Reverse: Bull walking r.; ΙΣΤΙ
   Cf. *BMC Central Greece* 126, nos. 21–22.

100. AE ⌀ 1.4–1.3   369–336 BCE
   Obverse: Head of Maenad r.
   Reverse: Bull walking r.; ΙΣΤΙ
   Cf. *BMC Central Greece* 126, nos. 21–22.
   Much more worn (and unevenly struck?) than the two preceding examples.

101. AE ⌀ 1.5–1.3   369–336 BCE
   Obverse: Head of Maenad r.
   Reverse: Bull walking r.; above club (*vel sim.*); to right, ΙΣΤΙ
   Cf. *BMC Central Greece* 126, nos. 14–15?

1.3 *Opountian Lokris*

102. AR *Obol* ⌀ 1.1–0.97   387–369 (and later?)
   Obverse: Amphora with vine leaf by either shoulder; ΟΠ-ΟΝ to sides of lower belly
   Reverse: 12-ray star (ἠῶος ἀστήρ, the emblem of the Eastern Lokrians, Strabon ix. 416)
   Cf. *BMC Central Greece* 1, nos. 2–3.

103. AE ⌀ 1.25–1.22   387–369 (and later)
   Obverse: Helmeted head of Athena r.
   Reverse: Bunch of grapes ΟΠ(ΟΥ)Ν(ΤΙΩΝ)
   Cf. *BMC Central Greece* 4, no 37.0.

1.4 *Epiknemidian Lokris*

104. AE ⌀ 1.38–1.22   *c.* 338–*c.* 300 BCE
   Obverse: Head of Athena with crested Korinthian helmet
   Reverse: Bunch of grapes; ΛΟΚΡ-ΕΠΙΚΝΑ
   Cf. *BMC Central Greece* 7, nos. 57–60.
   The parallels given only have the inscription ΛΟΚ-ΡΩΝ but Head allows for this variety in his introductory remark on page 5.

105. AE ⌀ 1.38–1.28   c. 338–c. 300 BCE
Obverse: Head of Athena with crested Korinthian helmet
Reverse: Bunch of grapes; ΛΟΚΡ-ΕΠΙΚΝΑ
Cf. *BMC Central Greece* 7, nos. 57–60.
See commentary on previous piece. Very worn.

1.5   *East Lokris (Opountian or Epiknemidian)*

106. AE ⌀ 1.3–1.2   c. 338–300 BCE
Obverse: Head of Athena wearing crested Korinthian helmet r.; above A[N?]
Reverse: Bunch of grapes; ΛΟΚ-ΡΩΝ
Cf. *BMC Central Greece* 8, nos. 61–62.

107. AE ⌀ 1.38–1.22   c. 338–300 BCE
Obverse: Head of Athena wearing crested Korinthian helmet r.
Reverse: Bunch of grapes; ΛΟΚ-ΡΩΝ
Cf. *BMC Central Greece* 7, nos. 57–60.

108. AE ⌀ 1.3–1.2   c. 338–300 BCE
Obverse: Head of Athena wearing crested Korinthian helmet r.; above A[N?]
Reverse: Three bunches of grapes surrounded by border of entwined vine
Cf. *BMC Central Greece* 7, no. 50 but here without visible inscription.

109. AE ⌀ 1.3–1.2   c. 338–300 BCE
Obverse: Head of Athena wearing crested Korinthian helmet r.; above A[N?]
Reverse: Three bunches of grapes surrounded by border of entwined vine
Cf. *BMC Central Greece* 7, no. 50 but here without visible inscription.

1.6   *Phokis*

110. AR *Obol*   480–420 BCE
Obverse: Bull's head facing; ΦΟ
Reverse: Forepart of bear in incuse square
Cf. *BMC Central Greece* 17–18, nos. 34–42.

111–116 (6 examples). AE ⌀ varies c. 1.63–1.23   371–357 BCE
Obverse: Head of Athena turned slightly to l.
Reverse: Wreath around Φ
Cf. *BMC Central Greece* 20, nos. 66–74, pl. III. 17.
Some more worn than others.

117–118 (2 examples). AE ⌀ c. 1.3   371–357 BCE
Obverse: Head of Athena turned slightly to l.
Reverse: Wreath around ΦΩ

Cf. *BMC Central Greece* 20, nos. 76–77.
Both worn on obverse.

1.7   *Athenai*

119. AE ⌀ 1.30–1.24   406–393 BCE
Obverse: Head of Athena helmeted r.
Reverse: Two owls, heads facing, within wreath.
Cf. *BMC Attica, Megaris, Aegina* no. 209.

120. AE ⌀ c. 1.1   393–322 BCE
Obverse: Head of Athena in crested helmet l.
Reverse: Owl facing, within olive wreath; ΑΘ (retrograde)
Similar to *BMC Attica, Megaris, Aegina* no. 240.

1.8   *Eleusis*

121. AE   350–300 BCE
Obverse: Triptolemos mounting winged chariot pulled by serpents
Reverse: Pig r.; ΕΛΕΥ in exergue; all within corn wreath
Cf. *BMC Attica, Megaris, Aegina* no. 10.

1.9   *Korinthos*

122. AR *Obol?*   400–338 BCE
Obverse: Pegasos with pointed wing flying r.
Reverse: Helmeted head of Athena l. with winged caduceus behind; all in incuse square
Cf. *BMC Corinth and Colonies* no. 155.

123–130 (8 examples). AE ⌀ c. 1.2   350–243 BCE
Obverse: Pegasos with pointed wing flying l.
Reverse: Vertical trident on all; some with additional symbol (tripod, unclear circle, twice a club, A)
Cf. *BMC Corinth and Colonies* 55–56, nos. 446–471.

1.10   *Peloponnesos*

1.10.1   Phliasia

131–132. (2 examples, one unrecorded). AE ⌀ 1.25   431–370 BCE
Obverse: Bull butting l.
Reverse: Φ surrounded by four pellets
Cf. *BMC Peloponnesus* 34, nos. 16–17.

1.10.2   Sikyonia

133. AR *hemidrakhma*   400–300 BCE

Obverse: Khimaira l.; ΣΙ
Reverse: Dove flying l.
Cf. *BMC Peloponnesus* 118.

1.10.3 Arkadia
134. AE ⌀ 1.48–1,45   370–c. 280 BCE
Obverse: Horned head of young Pan l.
Reverse: APK monogram with syrinx between legs of *alpha*
Cf. *BMC Peloponnesus* 174–175, nos. 55–72.
Many of these have extra letters but not the present case.

1.10.4 Akhaian League, Aigeira
135. AR *hemidrakhma*   274–146 BCE
Obverse: Laureate head of Zeus
Reverse: AX monogram centre, AP at sides and forepart of goat above; all within laurel wreath
Cf. *BMC Peloponnesus* no. 16.

1.10.5 Elis
136. AE   146–143 BCE
Obverse: Laureate head of Zeus r.
Reverse: FAΛΕΙΩΝ in olive wreath
Cf. *BMC Peloponnesus* no. 149.

1.11 *Northern Greece*
1.11.1 Thessalian Confederacy
137. AE ⌀ 1.88–1.72   196–146–344 BCE
Obverse: Helmeted head of Athena r.; inscription, if any, not visible
Reverse: Horse prancing l.; inscription, if any, not visible
Cf. *BMC Thessaly to Aetolia* 5, nos. 62–63 (with inscriptions).
138. AE size not recorded   196–146 BCE
Obverse: Head of Athena; ΙΠΠΑΤΑΣ (name of magistrate?)
Reverse: Horse trotting; ΘΕΣΣΑΛΩΝ
Cf. *BMC Thessaly to Aetolia* no. 5, no. 62.

1.11.2 Pharsalos
139. AE ⌀ 1.46–1.4   400–344 BCE
Obverse: Head of Athena with crested helmet, l.
Reverse: Prancing horse with rider r. around it ΦΑΡ
Cf. *BMC Thessaly to Aetolia* 44, nos. 19–20.

1.11.3 Maroneia

140. AE ⌀ 1.33–1.29   400–350 BCE
   Obverse: Horse prancing r.; underneath belly M
   Reverse: Vine in square; around it on three sides ΜΑΡΩΝΙΤΩΝ
   Cf. *BMC The Tauric Chersonese, Sarmatia, Dacia, Moesia, Thrace etc.* no. 65.

1.12 *Delos*

141. AE ⌀ 1.37–1.22   308–87 BCE
   Obverse: Head of Apollon r.
   Reverse: Lyre; in field to l. Δ
   Cf. *BMC Crete and Aegean Islands* 99, nos. 4–8.

142–143 (2 examples). AE   200–87 BCE
   Obverse: Laureate head of Apollon l.
   Reverse: Lyre; ΔΗ
   A variant of the preceding (*q.v.*).

1.13 *Lykia?*

1.13.1 Antiphellos?

144. AE ⌀ 1.06   2nd cent. BCE
   Obverse: Head of Apollon
   Reverse: ANT monogram
   Cf. *BMC Lycia, Pamphilia and Pisidia* 41, no. 1? (Extra symbol of dolphin to l. on reverse.)

145. AE ⌀ 1.0   2nd cent. BCE
   Obverse: Dolphin
   Reverse: ANT monogram
   No exact parallels?

1.14 *Troas?*

1.14.1 Gergis

146. AE ⌀ 0.97   *c.* 400–350 BCE
   Obverse: Head of Sibyl laureate facing
   Reverse: Sphinx seated r.; in field r. Δ
   Cf. *BMC Troas, Aeolis and Lesbos* 55, nos. 2–4 although the inscription on no. 2, ΓΕΡ is missing on our piece.

1.15 *Monarchs of Makedonia*

1.15.1 Philippos II

147. AE size not recorded   359–336 BCE

Obverse: Laureate head of Apollon
Reverse: Youth on horseback; ΦΙΛΙΠΠΟΥ
Cf. Head, 1910: 224, *q.v.* also for summary of some suggested meanings for the significance of the horseman reverse types in the coinage of Philippos II.

1.15.2   Alexandros III (the Great)
148.   AE ⌀ 1.36–1.28   336–323 BCE
Obverse: Head of young Herakles in lion skin r.
Reverse: ΑΛΕΞΑΝΔΡΟΥ between club and quiver or bow in case (?)
Cf. Head, 1910: 226.
Coins like this may have been issued for some while after the death of Alexandros and thus fall into the same category as the following piece (Head, 1886: 227).

1.15.3   Kassandros
149–150 (2 examples). AE ⌀ 1.98, 2.07–1.87   316–298 BCE
Obverse: Head of Herakles in lion skin r.
Reverse: ΒΑΣΙΛΕΩΣ ΚΑΣΣΑΝΔΡΟΥ, boy on horseback r.
Cf. Head, 1910: 228.
Inscription only legible in parts on each piece. Apart from the name of the king these coins continue the types established on the coinage of Alexandros seen in no. 148 above. The regal name was only placed on the bronze coins of Kassandros; gold and silver pieces, it seems, were still issued, in effect, under the name of Alexandros.
151–152 (2 examples). AE ⌀ 1.54, 1.67–1.61   316–298 BCE
Obverse: Head of Herakles in lion skin r.
Reverse: [ΒΑΣΙΛΕΩΣ ΚΑΣΣΑΝΔΡΟΥ], boy on horseback r.
Cf. Head, 1910: 228.
No inscription legible on these smaller pieces which, otherwise, repeat the iconography of the preceding two (*q.v.*).

1.15.4   Demetrios Poliorketes
153.   AE ⌀ 1.48   306–283 BCE
Obverse: Helmeted head of Athena r.
Reverse: BA, prow of boat with axe in front of it; beneath Δ & Π (ligature)
Cf. Head, 1910: 230, though the specific inscription is not there listed. Cf. also Newell, 1927: 159 no. 178 who suggested the product of a mint in the Hellespontine Region; the relevant plate is not clear enough to see

whether the inscription below the ship's prow is in fact ΔΙΙ as Newell thought or whether it is ΔΠ as on the present piece.

1.15.5   Antigonos Gonatas (or Doson?)
154. AE ⌀ 1.61–1.55   277–239 BCE
   Obverse: Helmeted head of Athena r.
   Reverse: BA around head of youth (Pan?) erecting a trophy to r.; below ANTI in monogram
   Cf. Head, 1910: 232.

1.16   *Monarchs of Syria*
(all hastily recorded and details perhaps not entirely reliable)

1.16.1   Seleukos I
155. Small AR (exact size not recorded)   312–280 BCE
   Obverse: Head of Herakles r. (Alexandros type)
   Reverse: Zeus seated l. ΣΕΛΕΥΚΟΥ ΒΑΣΙΛΕΩΣ
   Cf. *BMC, Seleucid Kings of Syria* 6 (but a larger denomination).
156. AE   312–280 BCE
   Obverse: Head of Medusa winged
   Reverse: Humped bull butting r.; ΣΕΛΕΥΚΟΥ ΒΑΣΙΛΕΩΣ
   Cf. *BMC, Seleucid Kings of Syria* 62/8.

1.16.2   Antiokhos VIII?
157. AR *drakhma*   121–96 BCE
   Obverse: Head of king diademed r.
   Reverse: Tripod-lebes; ΒΑΣΙΛΕΩΣ ΑΝΤΙΟΧΟΥ rest illegible
   Cf. *BMC, Seleucid Kings of Syria* Antiokhos XI, 6 var.
158. AR size note noted   94–83 BCE
   Obverse: Head of king diademed r.
   Reverse: Zeus standing naked l., holding star and sceptre (?); ΒΑΣΙΛΕΩΣ ΑΝΤΙΟΧΟΥ ΕΥΣΕΒΟΥΣ ΦΙΛΟΠΑΤΟΡΟΣ; all within wreath
   Cf. *BMC, Seleucid Kings of Syria* 1.

1.17   *Roman Province of Makedonia*
159–161 (3 examples). AE ⌀ 1.41~1.22   158–146 BCE
   Obverse: Head of Herakles r.
   Reverse: Club; above and below M and TET (i.e. ΜΑΚΕΔΟΝΩΝ and ΤΕΤΑΡΤΗΣ meaning 4th legion?)

1.18   *Miscellaneous*

162–163 (2 examples). AE ⌀ 1.23–1.16   ?

Obverse: Illegible

Reverse: Anchor, no visible inscription

Little can be said of these two badly corroded and chipped small coins except that the anchor might recall issues of Seleukos I (cf. Head, 1910: 756).

2   **Lead Sling Shot**

1. Shape of olive pit; large example, 4.6 long × 2.5 wide × 2.0 thick. Wt. 94.15gr. Complete and mostly covered with an even patina of white lead carbonate. Not well formed in that the two halves of the mould did not meet flush, causing a rhomboid cross-section and a line of overlap all around. Undecorated.

2. Olive pit shape; medium-sized example. 3.3 long × 1.9 wide × 1.3 thick. Wt. 41.25gr. Complete and with a discontinuous patina of white carbonate; cut obliquely at base to separate from stem in mould. Surface pitted in parts and with a large hollow on one side; all caused by incomplete exclusion of air from the mould?

   Inscriptions: "obverse", B (ht. 1.5) across main axis of shot,

   "reverse", OI (ht. *c.* 1.2) in same direction but badly worn

Commentary:

The inscriptions BOI or simply B (cf. following item) are usually taken to refer to the Boiotians (Vischer, 1878: 256 no. 23 and 260–261 no. 25; Guarducci II, 1969: 518; Empereur, 1981: 557 no. 7 [wt. 55gr]; Foss, 1975: 40 no. 2 [wt. 41.6gr]; Shefton, 1978: 13).

3. Olive pit shape; medium-sized example. 3.5 long × 2.9 wide × 1.3 thick. Wt. 46.15gr. Complete and mostly without patina. Surface slightly pitted and a small "air bubble" on one side but otherwise well-formed and stem neatly severed.

   Inscription: B across main axis of the shot.

Commentary:

Cf. preceding.

4. Olive pit shape; medium-sized example. 3.3 long × 1.5 wide × 1.3 thick. Wt. 41.57gr. Complete and mostly covered by patina on "obverse" but "reverse" largely unpatinated. Surface smooth all over, even where not patinated; stem neatly severed.
Decoration: "obverse" eight-pointed star (∅ c. 1.2)
Inscription: "reverse" ΑΙΣΧΡΙΩΝΔΟ (letter ht. c. 0.2) along object's main axis.

Commentary:

Although the root name Αἰσχρίων may be found in many parts of the Greek world, in the form Αἰσχρ(ι)ώνδας (or Αἰσχριώνδης/Ἠσχρ(ι)ώνδας/Ἠσχρ(ι)ώνδης) appears to be much more rare. Within Boiotia three instances occur at Akraiphiai, one at Thebai (*LGPN*iiib, 19 & 185) and another possibly at *Dhritsa/Heleon* (Roller, 1989: #35 = *IG*vii 550) that is Central and Eastern parts; in Attike there are seven instances in the forms Αἰσχρωνίδης/Αἰσχρώνδης (*LGPN*ii, 16); a single case is found at Khalkis (*LGPN*i, 21); there appear to be none in the rest of Central Greece and the Peloponnesos. This concentration in Eastern and Central Boiotia, with Attike and Khalkis suggests that the name is here local to Thebai, or at least to Boiotia.

For the star emblem on sling shot East Lokrian coinage is cited as a parallel (Vischer, 1878: 250, no. 4 [only six rays, no inscription and unknown provenance; wt. 31.3gr] and 267, no. 46 [eight rays; inscription on other face illegible, provenance again unknown, wt. 35.8gr]; Empereur, 1982: 561, no. 22[?]). We may possibly refer also to a shot of unknown provenance in the Kanellopoulos collection (wt. 77gr) bearing the inscription ΟΠΠΟΥΝ (Empereur, 1981: 561, no. 19) and to two others bearing a monogram interpreted as Ὑπο[κναμιδίων] (Vischer, 1878: 268, no. 48 [wt. 24.6gr] and Hellmann, 1982: 84, no. 40 [wt. 25.75gr]). The implication of the preceding discussion of the name might be that the name on the piece tends to suggest that this shot may not have anything to do with East Lokris at all and that Vischer's interpretation may possibly need revisiting.

5. Medium sized olive pit shape. 3.2 long × 1.6 wide × 1.3 thick. Wt. 34.2gr. Complete and mostly covered with an even patina of carbonate. Surface smooth even where not patinated; no air holes and, overall, well formed with stem neatly severed.
Inscription: ΞΕΝΟΚ.Ε (letter ht. 0,2, *omicron* 0.1, along main axis of object; other face blank).

Commentary:

Ξενοκλέα (see also following item); for the particularly Boiotian nature of such nominatives in–α without final *sigma* cf. Blümel, 1982: 233. Names of this type in normal formation (Ξενοκλέας, Ξενοκλίας, Ξενοκλεῖς, Ξενοκλῆς etc.) occur in small numbers across Boiotia (4 at each of Thebai and Tanagra, 3 at each of Akraiphiai and Orkhomenos, 2 at each of Thespiai and Hyettos, single instances at Lebadeia, Khaironeia and Oropos) as well as three at Megara and two at Aigosthena in neighbouring Megaris, three in Phokis, two in West Lokris and one in Opountia (*LGPN*iiib, 316). There are several instances further North in Thessalia (*LGPN*iiib, 316), a great many in Attike (*LGPN*ii, 345–346) and indeed quite a few in the Aigaian islands, especially on nearby Euboia (*LGPN*i, 343). The name could thus easily be at home in Thebai or surrounding areas and its specifically Boiotian form means that we have no reason to look elsewhere for the origin of our man, even if a number of instances of the name recur on Rhodos – which is interesting in light of the special reputation of Rhodian slingers (Xenophon, *Anabasis* iii. 3, 17). We may also note a slingshot from Korkyra bearing the name Ξενοκλέως and another of uncertain provenience (*IG* ix.1², iv: 1150 a & b).

6. Medium sized olive pit shape. 3.3 long × 1.6 wide × 1.3 thick. Wt. 29.62gr. Complete and covered by a fairly continuous patina. Mould not completely filled on the uninscribed side (hence light weight?) and surface rough, including several large pits; slight projection where stem severed. Inscription: ΞΕ.ΟΚΛΕΑ (letter ht. 0.2, *omicron* 0.1) along main axis of object; other face apparently blank.

Commentary:

Cf. no. 5 – from the same mould. The discrepancy in weight between nos. 5 and 6 is surprising, given the identity of the mould and the logically close similarity of dimensions.

7. Medium sized olive pit shape. 3.0 long × 1.7 wide × 1.3 thick. Wt. 35.2gr. Complete, with discontinuous carbonate patina (more even on one face than on the other). Surface pitted and a few large "air holes" but, in general, evenly produced and with stem neatly severed. Undecorated and uninscribed.

8. Medium sized piece, olive pit shape. 2.85 long × 1.7 wide × 1.3 thick. Wt. 31.8gr. Complete and unpatinated, with rough surface. The two halves of the mould did not meet quite flush thus producing a slight "seam" all around but the mould was completely filled up (no air holes) and the stem neatly severed. Undecorated and uninscribed.

9. Another medium sized olive pit shape. 2.7 long × 1.6 wide × 1.2 thick. Wt. 30.0gr. Complete and unpatinated with rough surface. Slight seam all around marking join of mould halves and a little flat on one side (mould not quite filled, causing thinner size?); cut obliquely at one end in severing the stem (hence short length). Undecorated and uninscribed.

10. Medium sized, olive pit shape. 2.5 long × 1.65 wide × 1.1 thick. Wt. 25.7gr. Complete and mostly unpatinated with rough surface. Slight seam along one side at mould join; again one face a bit flat and again stem cut with an oblique stroke removing a little of one end with the stem. Undecorated and uninscribed.

11. Spherical shot (or weight?). ⌀ 1.7; length of small projecting stem 0.5. Wt. 34.1gr. Complete and unpatinated with mostly rough surface (smoother at stem end). Stem smoothly cut but there are a couple of slanting cuts across the other "end" of the sphere. No trace of any mould join; undecorated and uninscribed.

Commentary:

Despite its variant shape the similarity of its means of production (cf. the stem) and its weight invite comparison with the regular slingshot seen above. It is difficult to see what else it might have been unless a weight of some sort with the bit of stem left to facilitate handling (like the knobs on the upper surface of the weights in an old-fashioned precision balance).

2.1 *General Commentary*

As Jean-Yves Empereur (1981: 556–557) has remarked, it is common to try to identify people named on Greek slingshot with members of the entourages of Philippos II or Alexandros the Great. This fashion obviously stems from the analysis by Robinson (1941: 418–443) of the many examples found during his excavations at Olynthos in the Khalkidike that had indeed been besieged and sacked by Philippos II and where the occurrence of recognisable names is thus not surprising. Given that Thebai received the same treatment at the hands of Alexandros it might be tempting again to search for such identifications but no Αἰσχρ(ι)ώδας and no Ξενοκλῆς is known to have figured in these Makedonian military circles (Berve, 1926) and, moreover, neither appears to be attested as a Makedonian anthroponym in general (*LGPN*iv, 12 & 259–260).

At the same time lead slingshot in the Greek world are generally dated to the 4th–3rd centuries BCE (Michaelidou-Nicolaou, 1972: 359) and the lettering style on our inscribed ones here in no way contradicts such a dating. It goes without saying that the siege of Thebai by Alexandros falls well in this period and provides the most appropriate historical context for military activities around the city such as those possibly implied by the slingshot and indeed by other objects, such as the iron and bronze arrowheads, found in the same streambed (cf. below).

We have seen that the two names present on these pieces are both fully at home in Boiotia and specifically even at Thebai. What is more, both names could possibly be associated with leading families of that city in the 4th and early 3rd centuries BCE. A certain Ἡ/Αἰσχρ(ι)ώνδας Θιομνάστω/ιος is attested both as Theban aphedriateuon and (subsequently?) as federal arkhon in the earlier 3rd century BCE (Koumanoúdhes, 1979: no. 71 cf. *LGPN*iiib, 185). The name Ξενοκλῆς may be connected with the Ξενο- whose name occurs on Theban coinage of the mid-4th century and may thus have been a magistrate responsible for the city's mint (Koumanoúdhes, 1979: no. 1473) and the occurrence of one Ξενοκλεῖς Ἰσμεινίου (*vel sim.*; Koumanoúdhes, 1979: no. 1474 who writes Ξενοκλίδ(α)ς (Ἰ)σμεινι[ῆος]) leads to the possibility that the name is associated with the family which produced several leading Thebans named Ismeinias (Koumanoúdhes, 1979: nos. 1006, 1007, 1009, 1011, 1012; cf. *LGPN*iiib, 212). Naturally there is no certainty in this sort of suggestion, simply an obvious possibility that the two persons mentioned on the slingshot could be seen as members of leading Theban families in the 4th and 3rd centuries.

All this is far from searching to make connections between these slingshot and the sack of Thebai by Alexandros. Three of the pieces bear names that are most probably local Theban ones and two others carry the B for Boiotia. It would, of course, be possible to see in these material used by Thebans to defend their city against Alexandros and the presence of several bronze and iron arrow heads also from the same streambed (listed below) could be seen as leading in the same direction but I think there is a much more likely explanation to which I will return in the conclusions to this chapter. [It will also appear later that the iron arrowheads have parallels rather from the Byzantine period and are thus unlikely to reflect activity anywhere near the time of Alexandros.]

Although our set of slingshot consists of only ten items and thus pales into insignificance alongside a collection such as that of Olynthos, measuring in the several hundreds, it is interesting to notice how representative a sample this group is. If we take all the examples from the Greek world for which dimensions have been published (Robinson, 1941; Fosse, 1975; Empereur, 1981; Hellmann, 1982; also the summary remarks by Williams *et all.*, 1998: 311, n. 35) it becomes clear that the large bulk of such objects presents lengths varying between 2.6 and 3.6cm with widths also varying, between 1.4 and 2.3; outside this core lies a small number of larger pieces whose lengths and widths may reach as much as 4.8 and 2.6 respectively. Nine of our ten objects lie well within the dimensions of the bulk and our group presents just one of the rare large outsiders. If we take those for which weights are recorded (to those with dimensions recorded we can add also those in Vischer, 1878a & b where weights are given) we find again the bulk falling within certain limits (19–47gr) while the larger outliers, with very few exceptions, cluster into one of two groups (66~81gr and 93~101gr); again we see that nine of our ten pieces fall – not surprisingly – into the main class while our one outsize example lies in the group of the heaviest shot.

Rihll (2009) working from a data base of some 1400 examples of slingshot from Roman and Greek contexts finds that most slingshot measure 30–40mm in length and weigh 30–40g. She does not separate out subgroups as I have tried to do despite working with a much smaller sample. Although her discussion is very wide-ranging the reader will probably regret that the article did not include a table of her 1400 examples with provenance (when known) and with dimensions (perhaps the maximum width could be given in addition to the length) and weights.

This recognition of three classes of slingshot may remind one of two texts describing a particularly formidable group of slingers in antiquity, namely the inhabitants of the Balearic islands in the West Mediterranean:

σφενδόνας δὲ περὶ τῇ κεφαλῇ τρεῖς μελαγκρανίνας ἢ τριχίνας ἢ νευρίνας τὴν μὲν μακρόκωλον πρὸς μακροβολίας, τὴν δὲ βραχύκωλον πρὸς τὰς ἐν βραχείβολας τὴν δὲ μέσην πρὸς τὰς μέσας.

They have three slings around the head platted of rushes, one made of hair, one made of sinews. The long sling they use for hitting at far distance, the short one for near marks and the middle one for those between.
STRABON iii. 5, 300

ὁπλισμὸς δ' ἐστὶν αὐτοῖς τρεῖς σφενδόναι, καὶ τούτων μίαν μὲν περὶ τὴν κεφαλὴν ἔχουσιν, ἄλλην δὲ περὶ γαστέρα, τρίτην δ' ἐν ταῖς χερσί.

Their weaponry comprises three slings one of which they keep around their heads, another around their waists and the third they hold in their hands.
DIODOROS SIKELIOTES v. 18, 3

Despite some differences of detail it is plain that both these texts specify three sorts of slings although only Strabon accounts for their different sizes and related uses. This suggests the possibility that the three sizes of slingshot we have discussed above might correspond to the three different sizes of sling and the different conditions under which each was used. A further question would then be whether it is coincidence that all but one of the shot we have been considering from Thebai were ones for short distance use and whether this would not be appropriate for defenders located on the city wall that may have run along the ridge to the immediate West and firing down on adversaries moving through the stream bed below that could well be considered as close targets.

Where our small group has its particular interest is, of course, in the inscribed pieces since fully half of our examples fall into this class whereas elsewhere the majority seems to have been unmarked (Robinson, 1941: 418–419). At the same time a recent article by Amanda Kelly (2012) has catalogued and discussed a series of similar Kretan slingshot. As she points out, the fact that the inscribed shot were cast together with inscription shows that the latter had a preordained purpose; out of her catalogue of 40 pieces 32 are inscribed and six more have symbols (trident or thunderbolt) on them, while only two are unadorned. She is able to suggest, or even to show that several of the inscriptions indicate the city for, or at which they were produced (Knossos, Gortyn, Phalarsa, Aptera) and others, like with some of the Olynthian examples as interpreted by Robinson, may refer to military commanders: Kleandros (possibly son of Polemokrates who provided mercenaries to Alexandros?) and a certain Συλάδα[ς]. These make interesting comparison with our present pieces with B or BOI (Βοιωτῶν?) and the individual masculine names, Αἰσχρ(ι)ώνδας and Ξενοκλέα.

If our pieces are in fact Boiotian the presence on the one of a marking normally taken as a heraldic device referring to Opountian Lokris (cf. Fossey, 1990: 4) may have an interesting connotation. There are indications (cf. Fossey, 1990: 162) of close relations between Boiotia and the Opountians at times during the 4th century and these are even clearer in the 3rd; it may thus not be entirely illogical to see in our no. 4 a testimony to a Lokrian involvement of some sort in military activity at Thebai in precisely that period.

3   Other Lead Objects

1. Disk (weight?). ∅ 3.3~3.1 × max thickness 1.0. Wt. 48.3gr. Complete and covered with continuous patina of white carbonate. Slightly irregular outline to circle; lentoid profile perforated with a central hole (∅ 0.6). Slight lip all around edge, within which, on one face, a series of circular impressions. Other face undecorated.
2. Portion of small flat female figurine apparently stepping r. with arms stretched out towards front and back. Head, feet and extremities of both

FIGURE 40   Sketch of a lead figurine

arms missing. Pleats running the length of the skirt of the garment; upper part less clear. For a rough sketch cf. Fig. 40. Back roughly flat. Maximum preserved dimensions: ht. 2.03 × width 1.73 × thickness 0.42. Probably a small votive piece.

4   Arrowheads

4.1   *Bronze*

1. length 2.0, max. width at barbs, 0.82. Dark, smooth patina under light surface incrustation. Socket connects to small hole (for attaching pin?) a little more than half way along the point.
2. length 1.53, max. width at barbs, 0.88. Dark, smooth patina under heavy surface incrustation. Socket connects to small hole (for attaching pin?) about half way along the point. Two of the barbs very blunted.
3. length 1.65, max. width at barbs, 1.02. Dark, smooth patina under heavy surface incrustation. Socket connects to small hole (for attaching pin?) near the point. Two of the barbs broken off.
4. length 1.54, max. width at barbs, 0.86. Dark, smooth patina under slight surface incrustation. No attachment hole. Two of the barbs very blunted.
5. length 1.53, max. width at barbs, 0.88. Dark, smooth patina under surface incrustation.
6. length 2.51, max. width at barbs, 0.76. Apparently smooth patina under heavy surface incrustation. Socket continues into even (i.e. deliberately so cast) hole emerging between two of the barbs – for purposes of attachment to the shaft?

Commentary:

   The first four of these small points are of the type 3B5, "three edged, barbed with interior socket" in the classification of Snodgrass (1964: 152–153), while the last two are also three-sided and barbed, but with a projecting socket (in the case of no. 5 only projecting very slightly), a cross between types 3B1 and 3B5 of the same typology. Snodgrass has argued for this being an essentially Greek type, possibly not of external origin; he also refers to one with a date as late as Hellenistic times, though most of his examples are inevitably early, given the focus of his study. Nos. 1–5 may be compared to pieces found at Olynthos (Robinson, 1941: 383, nos. 1911 and 1912) dating to the time of Philippos II of Makedonia. No. 6 is like one, also in bronze, from Korinthos (Davidson, 1952: 200, no. 1516) similarly dated to the 4th century BCE.

4.2   *Iron*
1. Thin, flat lozenge-shaped blade surmounting a hemispherical boss and then a long slender shaft, the same length as the blade. Length 5.15, max. width 1.35, max. thickness (at the boss) 0.6. Lightly corroded.
2. Narrow triangular blade, flattened rhomboid in cross-section, surmounting a slightly elongated conical boss, beyond which a tapering shaft (broken at the far end) of similar length to the whole head. Length 4.75, max. width 0.85, max. thickness (conical boss) 0.69. Lightly corroded.
3. Sharp, pyramidal head, length 2.21 × max. width 0.98, tapering slightly before opening out into a round socket, 2.51 long × 1.08 max. diam. Overall length 5.02. Heavily corroded.
4. Sharp, pyramidal head, length 1.93 (point bent over) × max. width 0.82, tapering slightly before opening out into a round socket, 2.98 long × 1.45 max diam. (open end somewhat splayed). Overall length 4.89. Heavily corroded.
5. Sharp, but not offset pyramidal head, length 2.8, whose four sides gradually merge into a round socket, 1.67 deep × 1.11 max. diam. Overall length 4.84. Heavily corroded.

Commentary:

The first two are similar in that they have the boss but without the barbs seen in all the variants of type 1 in Snodgrass (1964: 144–148); similar iron examples from Sardis (Waldbaum, 1983: 37, nos. 57–69) and Korinthos (Davidson, 1952: 200, nos. 1529–1530) are dated to Byzantine and even Late Byzantine times. They are, nonetheless, clearly arrowheads, whereas the nature(s) of the remaining three objects is/are more doubtful.

The latter three are plainly points to be mounted on a shaft but they possess none of the details intended to make the point stick in the flesh of the quarry and they would produce a much heavier point on the arrow than the first two above and than all the bronze points listed in the previous section. Perhaps these points on narrow shafts served some other purpose. Nos. 3–4 are reminiscent in form of catapult bolt-heads (cf. Manning, 1985: 170–176), but much smaller than even the smallest of them. No. 5 is similar to, but smaller than the spear butt from Sardis (Waldbaum, 1983: 32, no. 16); it also looks, in form, like the "conical ferrules" in the classification of Manning (1985: 140–141) who indeed considers that they may have served as spear butts among other functions, but again the present example is much smaller than his pieces.

5 Other Bronze Objects

5.1 *Graving Tools*

1–5 (five examples). Scorpers (or scaupers) all of similar form with slightly different dimensions (lengths vary 2.34~4.37). Short shaft with square cross section (thickness 0.25~3.2), flattened or rounded at one end and shaped to a chisel blade at the other. All covered with an even patina.

6–7 (two examples, one not recorded in detail but of same form as the other). A combined tool, both scorper and enlarged graver point. Length 3.95; shaft with square cross-section (0.32 × 0.29). In one direction at 1.61 from end shaft thickens (0.59) out to form an elongated cone ending in a point. At the other end the shaft is flattened to form a small chisel blade as in the preceding five pieces. Fairly even patina.

8. Enlarged graver point. Similar to the one end of the two preceding pieces except that the enlarged end is not conical but keeps the swelling four sides of the shaft to form an elongated pyramid. The other extremity simply ends abruptly but is not apparently broken. (Since the tool is too short to be manipulated comfortably by hand it may have been set into a wooden handle). Length 2.42; shaft cross-section 0.32 × 0.32; base of pyramidal end 0.45 × length of pyramid 1.5. Even patina.

9. Enlarged graver point on long shaft. End away from point broken off at length 6.56. Square cross-section 0.26 × 0.26. Last 1.3 of shaft thickened out slightly (0.34, less that the two preceding pieces) to form conical point. Uneven patina and some incrustation.

10–11 (two examples). Simple points of different lengths (2.39 and 1.78) with square cross-section to shaft (thickness 0.26~0.16); one end flattened across and the other drawn to a fine point. Even patina.

12. Double point, length 4.43 (slightly bent in middle) with oblong cross-section to shaft (0.24x 0.19). Tapers more to one end to produce a fine point; other end has a blunter point. Even patina.

Commentary:

Fine engraving tools of these sorts are still in use for miniature glyptic and jewellery today. A selection of types available can be seen at www.grobetusa.com. Some of these items, especially no. 8, may have been set into a (wooden?)

handle but certainly not those with two functional ends and most of them were probably operated simply by hand to produce delicate decoration on the soft surface of cold bronze or on wood. They were plainly not punches intended to be struck into molten metal for they are too short to keep the artisan's hand comfortably distant from a hot working surface (for discussion see Manning, 1985: 9–10).

5.2   Needles and Pins

N.B. these are distinguished from the objects in the previous category by the round cross-section of their shafts as opposed to the square cross-section seen in the gravers. On the lack of any diagnostic or dating development of needle-shapes cf. Raubitschek, 1998: 112, n. 26.

1. Needle complete from head to c. 5.3cm along shaft ($\varnothing$ 0.18~0.16); rest broken away and remaining end bent nearly at right-angles. Oval-shaped eye (0.38 × 0.1) at 0.4 from head. Evenly patinated.

2. Head of needle with oval eye (0.45 × c. 0.8) just 0.2 from actual head; only 2.14 of original length preserved; $\varnothing$ of shaft 0.16. Evenly patinated.

3. Needle, complete from eye to point, head broken off; shaft slightly bent. Preserved length 6.8, max. $\varnothing$ 0.17. Oval eye 4.0+ long but width not preserved. Evenly patinated.

4. Needle, portion from break at the eye to break at mid-shaft; preserved length 0.46, $\varnothing$ of shaft 0.14. Only one side of eye preserved; impossible to measure dimensions. Evenly patinated.

5–7 (three examples). Short portions of needles from break at eye to little way down shaft; preserved lengths: 2.4 ($\varnothing$ c. 0.19), 2.0 ($\varnothing$ 0.18), 1.64 ($\varnothing$ 0.15). Evenly patinated.

8–9 (two examples). Point ends of broken pins or needles; heads and eyes missing. Preserved lengths: 5.08 (slightly bent, $\varnothing$ 0.14), 3.25 ($\varnothing$ 0.14). Evenly patinated.

10. Broken part of needle or pin shaft. Preserved length 2.0 but one end turned back nearly 180°, other end wire-thin and bent ($\varnothing$ 0.1). Corroded.

11. Head of hair pin (*vel sim.*). Spherical head ($\varnothing$ 0.66) at end of short preserved bit (length 3.6) of shaft ($\varnothing$ of round cross-section, 0.18), bent almost at right-angles 1.6 from head. Evenly patinated. For type cf. examples from Isthmia (Raubitschek, 1998: 48–49, nos. 191–193, all of uncertain date).

12. Ornamental head of dress (?) pin. Main feature of the head is an inverted cone with five protruding segments around it, surmounted by a single ring and a small sphere; below the cone are two fine rings, a very short piece of shaft, interrupted by another ring bordering a bulb which is bordered below also by (another) ring; the shaft breaks off just below the last mentioned ring.

Preserved length 2.72 × max ⌀ (base of the cone) 0.98; ⌀ of shaft *c.* 0.4. Some patination but also quite corroded.

6 Miscellaneous

1. A bronze "unguent spoon" with shaft about 10cm long and a tiny bowl at one end and a point at the other. Even patina. The identification of this type of object as a spoon for perfumed oil is not convincing. They have also been classed as surgical instruments for probing and removing small objects from patients' ears (Milne, 1907: 63–68; cf. Waldbaum, 1983: 105–107). It is also worth considering whether they could not have served as simple *styloi* with the pointed end for writing and the "spoon" for smoothing the wax to correct errors or to reuse the tablet; indeed there is reason to think that surgical and writing instruments were not always distinguished (Milne, 1907: 772–73). This "spoon" would have been simpler – and cheaper? – to produce than the usual *stylos* with its decorated flat "eraser" end (cf. Raubitschek, 1998: 110) but would have served exactly the same purpose and probably just as well.
2. A bronze *fibula* similar to the "Certosa" type, for which the only parallels I know from a Greek context are those found at Olynthos (Robinson, 1941: 104–106, especially no. 352, pl. XXI) and two unpublished ones from Boiotia *Khóstia* (Fossey, forthcoming). Length 8.6, height of bow 2.5. Pin missing. Patinated but also incrusted. The catch plate is much shorter than on the typical "Certosa" type of *fibula*.
3. Also from the streambed came many more pieces of metal:
a) several long strands of bronze, either wire or parts of the shafts of more pins, a couple of bronze handles for small vessels (one horizontal, one vertical), other parts of unidentifiable but moulded bronze objects, including a couple of very small rings and at least one rivet;
b) one, lightly corroded long (15.3) iron nail with round, flat head and square cross-section tapering to the point, like Type II from Sardis apparently used "for joining smaller timbers and fixing hinges and other fittings" (Waldbaum, 1983: 68, *q.v.* for discussion of parallels);
c) a couple of round flat iron discs, nail-heads (?), heavily corroded;
d) several amorphous points of iron, all quite corroded;
e) many amorphous pieces of lead, looking remarkably like discards of molten metal.

In addition to all this metal work I was also shown part of a bone or ivory seal. Since this is difficult to describe I made a rough drawing, cf. Fig. 41.

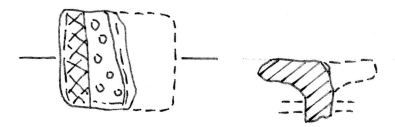

FIGURE 41   Sketch of part of a bone or ivory seal

7   Some Tentative Conclusions

1. As already indicated this streambed can never have been really inhabited and has plainly acted simply as a collecting basin for small objects carried and washed down the steep sides in a never-ending process. If the pieces have come from the surrounding higher ground their presence and nature may have something to tell us about the sort of activities going on in those upper areas. If the Byzantine dating of the iron arrowheads is correct it places them apart from the rest of the material accumulated for the coins are numerous enough to indicate that the general date runs from late archaic times to at least the middle of the Hellenistic period; it is noticeable that the only two coins that may postdate the middle of the 2nd century BCE are two possible bronzes of Antiokhos VIII but their identification is not fully assured and Roman coins of later republican and imperial date appear to be absent.

2. The stream valley runs outside what were the limits of the city of Thebai at its greatest extents. In fact the ridge of hills along its West side carries the line of the Eastern wall of the city in Classical times (Symeonoglou, 1985: fig. 3.6). Thus the material discussed above could have derived from this Eastern extremity of the city except that the coins, as we have just seen, run in date from archaic through Hellenistic times. It is Symeonoglou's belief that the city only extended to this ridge in Classical times and that, in particular after the city's destruction by Alexandros and its subsequent reconstruction under Kassandros, it had shrunk to its earlier size, restricted purely to the Kadmeia. It is indeed true that Thebai had shrunk to that size by early Roman imperial times as we are told first by Strabon (ix. 403), around the turn of the eras, and then a century or so later by Pausanias (ix. 7. 6), We have, however, little hard evidence for the situation in earlier Hellenistic times. Symeonoglou rightly remarks "it is impossible to identify the wall of Kassandros on the basis of the existing archaeological evidence"; he then suggests that the reconstructed wall

would have followed the line of the archaic and earlier fortifications surrounding simply the Kadmeia (Symeonoglou, 1985: 148 + fig. 3.1). The evidence from the streambed, however, suggests rather that, at least for the earlier Hellenistic period there was plenty of activity on this Eastern side of the city. Consequently we may be able to envisage that the reconstruction of Kassandros, on the East side of Thebai at least, may have followed the line of the preceding Classical circuit wall. In the heyday of the Hellenistic confederation Thebai was an important enough member and a sizeable population might be expected. Its reduction to the small size noted for early Roman imperial times could be seen as part of that process of population impoverishment remarked upon precisely around the middle of the 2nd century BCE by the writer Polybios (xxxvi. 17. 5; cf. Fossey, 1988: 441).

3. The objects may also tell us something of the nature of the activity on this Eastern side of the city. I am struck be the presence of small metalworking tools alongside lumps of molten lead and quantities of worked fragments and amorphous pieces of bronze (for melting down and reuse?). Accordingly I posit the idea that this Eastern fringe may have been an area of smiths' workshops producing perhaps even the lead shot and iron and bronze weapons, as well as some finer pieces. Even a tentative suggestion of this sort has its use in a case like that of Thebai where the modern city, lying as it does atop the ancient, prohibits any full investigation and reconstruction of the city's urban organisation.

4. The picture of commercial relations given by the coins is much what we might have expected. Out of the 163 coins recorded, 25 (= 15%) are attributed to Thebai itself and a further 57 (= 35%) are assigned to other Boiotian mints, though even some of them (from "uncertain mints") may in fact also have been produced at Thebai. In short half the total coins are purely local. We may add to this the fact that a further 45 (= 28%) come from immediately neighbouring areas (Euboia, Phokis, Attike, Megaris, Opountian and possibly Epiknemidian Lokris). The total now grows to 127 (= 78%) that come from Eastern Central Greece; within the remaining 22% the numbers are insignificant: five are Peloponnesian, four are Northern Greek, three come from each of Delos and Asia Minor, while 12 date from Hellenistic monarchs (eight minted for Makedonian kings that might be expected to circulate widely in Greece as a whole and possibly four Syrians whose presence might be less obvious) and two belong again to Makedonia but this time under early Roman (republican) rule. There is no way of knowing whether these coins are the product of commerce in the posited area of smiths' workshops or whether they simply represent general circulation and transactions but they surely testify to fair activity during approximately four centuries on the surrounding uplands, perhaps in

particular the ridge to the West of the stream and thus in the Eastern edge of the city.

Unfortunately the numbers are too few to reach any conclusions as to changes in circulation over time but it is interesting to note that in his commentary on two Theban hoards of Hellenistic date Tony Hackens (1969: esp. 728–729) was able to see geographic patterns similar to what we have just outlined on a general basis across time, namely that relations with areas outside Boiotia itself were essentially with Euboia, Eastern Lokris, Phokis and the Northern Peloponnesos.

CHAPTER 13

An Unusual Hero Cult in East Central Greece

ἐπὶ Ἑλένῃ ἡρωίδι[1]

∴

In my book *Epigraphica Boeotica II* I examined certain aspects of a cult of the Horseman-Hero in Boiotia during Roman Imperial Times (Fossey, 2014: chapter 7); this paper continues that study.

1 The Horseman-Hero at Home and Nearby

The cult of the Horseman-Hero is, of course, essentially a Thrakian phenomenon known from more than 2,000 sculpted examples found in Bulgarian Thrake and the surrounding areas. The seminal publication of these relief sculptures was that of Kazarov (1938) who suggested differentiating between three overall types: the simple horseman, the horseman departing for the hunt and the horseman returning from the hunt although it has been pointed out that the second and third of these types were varieties of one sort (e.g. Dimitrova, 2002: 210). Despite this the tripartite typology later served to structure the three-volume study by Gočeva and Oppermann (1979–1984) to which were added other volumes on related material from the Rumanian section of Moesia Inferior and Dacia by Hampartumian (1979) and on that from the former Jugoslavia by Cermanović-Kuzmanović (1997). The sculpted stones representing the Horseman-Hero found in the Balkans are both votive and funerary often invoking the "Hero God". On these stones there is a great and imaginative variety within the iconography of the relief carvings the basic nature of which was briefly summarized, by Vayios Liapis (2011: 103): "the hero is always depicted as a horseman, with further variations including the horseman as a hunter, a cult figure associated with sacrificial ritual or with the chthonic

---

[1] The reference is to my friend and colleague the late Rev'd Dr Ellen Aitken (1961–2014). A presentation of this subject was given at a colloquium held in honour of her memory at McGill University in Spring 2015. That occasion prompted this reworking of the subject.

realm, or as a warrior"; in fact there is a great deal of variety within the many actual Thrakian examples which was described by Toporov (1990: 47–48) as follows. "The centre of the composition ... consists of the figure of the Thracian Horseman (either in motion or standing still), usually oriented left to right. The horseman is most frequently holding a spear, club, whip, etc. in his right hand; sometimes he is holding the horse's reins in both hands. As a rule, the left-hand side of the composition is occupied by an altar, which is quadrangular or round, sometimes with flames (often one of the horse's forelegs is above this altar) and a tree around which a serpent is twisting. Below the horse we can often see a dog, a wild boar or some other (often unidentified) wild animal (occasionally a lion). Sometimes a servant can be seen behind the horse, usually clutching its tail. In some cases the number of figures increases with the appearance of someone resembling an assistant or co-participant: there is also a greater variety of objects (wreath, beaker, vessels, lamp, table, pillar) of animals (a hare in the horse's feet, a deer next to the tree or pillar, eagle, fish), symbolic classifiers (Sun. Moon, stars, eggs), etc." In fact some quite frequent tendencies can be noticed: the altar is often absent in cases where the horseman carries a weapon (especially a spear or lance) and is accompanied by animals suggestive of the hunt; for the most part the simple horseman is accompanied by the altar which may or may not have flames on it and above which one of the horse's forelegs may be raised; quite often there is a tree sometimes looking as if it springs from the altar, sometimes situated behind it; this tree which, in general, often has a snake twined around it, may be seen on scenes of the horseman as hunter, even in the absence of the altar. Overall the range of iconography seen in reliefs of the horseman, as witness the complex classification presented in the article "Hero equitans" of the *Lexicon iconographicum mythologiae classicae*, is seemingly endless, though not in the group with which we are here concerned. Elsewhere even the setting of the relief carvings on the stones that bear them can be very varied too, as will be seen by consulting the illustrations in the volumes of *IGBR* and the studies of the hero listed above.

Dimitrova (2002) quite rightly points out that the image of the horseman has a long history in Greek relief sculpture and that it continues in Roman times as the frequent subject of the reliefs on some carved tombstones, especially perhaps in the imperial provinces of Europe with their military nature. The large variety of such Roman reliefs is conveniently summarized by Schleiermacher (1984: Typentafel I–IV) but, outside Greece and the Balkans the word "hero" is noticeable by its absence and the altar seems to be a rare optional. These stones are, therefore, not evidence of a hero cult that is the subject of our study here and we will leave them on one side.

There is reason to think that the Horseman-Hero may have been some sort of generic male divinity to whom other names could easily be attached. Indeed geographic names do seem to have served to identify his local significance in many places. Dimitrova (2002: 210) lists a goodly number of such local names. In addition the hero has been seen as subject to many syncretic associations of which the most interesting is perhaps that with Asklapios, a connection given perhaps some credence by the presence of the snake-entwined tree so common in the Thrakian reliefs of the horseman (Dontcheva, 2002). Gočeva (1992) also argued for a particular association with Apollon and other syncretic alliances have been proposed; we shall return to this subject briefly later.

It is worth noting that those found in Rumania and the former Jugoslavia were often set up by Roman (or Romanised) soldiers suggesting that there any cult indicated had military associations (Grbić, 2013; for observations on the different details also in depiction of these "Danubian" horsemen stones cf. Dimitrova, 2002: 220). On the other hand in Thrake proper (essentially modern Bulgaria) the anthroponyms involved are usually native Thrakian and not Roman. The same holds true of the examples of rider images of Roman date in Northern Greece (parts of ancient Thrake and Makedonia; cf. Petsas, 1978; on the large number of unpublished relevant pieces in Northern Greece cf. Samsaris, 1993: 325, n. 1; cf. Samsaris, 1984); the iconography may be comparable but, as in Central Europe, the word "hero" is conspicuous by its absence, an observation that applies equally well to the many depictions of horsemen gathered by Berthe Rantz (1983). It is representations of the specific connection hero-horseman with which we are concerned here. There are also many examples of reliefs depicting the "Thrakian Horseman" on tombstones in Thessalia but here too no corpus of them has been drawn up. Some, at least, of these Thessalian examples do include the word "hero" and might thus be compared with the Thrakian examples as well as with those we will re-examine in Boiotia were it not for the fact that these Thessalian examples also include fairly regularly the words χαῖρε and χρήστε sometimes together, sometimes singly and, while these same two words, again either singly or together, are common on a variety of other Boiotian tombstones they are almost never so far seen on the Horseman-Hero grave markers of that area to which we shall shortly turn our attention. The distribution of these horseman tombstones in Thessalia is interesting. In the absence of a corpus specifically devoted to their study we may treat *IG* ix.2, produced in 1908, as a sample all the time realising, naturally, that many additional instances will have been found subsequently. There is an obvious concentration of such texts at Larissa (*IG* ix.2, 649–976 – especially after *IG* ix.2, 777 and then with 1349 and 1350 to be added from the addenda

– there are over 125 funerary inscriptions containing the word ἥρως in various cases, numbers and gender). Outside Larissa the presence is much thinner: one (*IG* ix.2, 486) supposedly from Atrax to the West of Larissa [although my colleagues at Lyon inform me that the *corpus* of Atrax, whose publication is imminent, contains in fact no examples of the horseman-hero on either tombstones or votive stelai], two from Krannon (*IG* ix.2, 469 & 484) to the South West of Larissa, nine from Phalanna (*IG* ix.2, 1257–1263) to the North West of Larissa, three from Azoros and Oloosson (*IG* ix.2, 1309, 1312, 1313 and 1317) in the very North of inland Thessalia [to these may be added three from Pythion also in the Northern reaches (Lucas, 1997 #70 and two others)], one from the village of Salsilar (*IG* ix.2, 1031) just to the East of Larissa, five from the Dotion Pedion a little further to the East of Salisar, two from Pharsala (Decourt, 1995: 105 & 108) to the South of Larissa, one instance from *Vólos* (*IG* ix.2, 1170) and an isolated instance from the village of *Kokotoús* (*IG* ix.2, 101) in Phthiotis [another isolated case in the South comes from Eretria (Decourt, 1995: 129)]. It is abundantly clear that the outstandingly large percentage of these tombstones comes from the Larissan plain and Larissa itself and then, to a much lesser degree, from areas to East, North, West and Southwest of Larissa. The instances to the South are very scarce by contrast.

From Methone in Magnesia, on the Eastern side of the Pagasitic Gulf comes a solitary dedication to the hero: Πυθόδωρος Πρωταγόρου Ἡρῶϊ (*IG* ix.2, 1199), above which is a relief carving of a "hero" leading a deer with a dog jumping underneath it; this contrasts with the depiction of a mounted horseman in relief carvings on many of the tombstones just listed and the association with the horseman-hero is thus not clear. From *Vólos* comes another enigmatic text: on a stone urn are carved in relief three horses heads alternating with three snakes and, between one of the pairs the inscription Ἡρώιων Ἡρωϊσσῶν κτίστων (*IG* ix.2, 1129); here the horses' heads make association with the horseman-hero probable and, in fact, the snakes further confirm this for, in many of the horseman reliefs on the Thessalian tombstones listed previously, the horseman and his mount are accompanied not only by an altar that they face but also, beyond the altar, by a tree with a snake curling around it, like in the actual Thrakian pieces as described above, but apparently without the further extra elements seen in the examples to the North. The snake could, of course, suggest a khthonic aspect but as it curls around the tree in a manner similar to the depiction of the snake wrapped around the staff of Asklapios here in Thessalia it might suggest some sort of syncretism between that deity and the hero as well as in Thrake where, as we have already seen, the snake and tree also occur frequently; the possibility of just such a syncretism was put forward some years ago by Dontcheva (2002). Apart from the possible dedication from Methone there is apparently another votive that was found back in the Thessalian North where it is at home with the bulk of the relevant texts: from Pythion comes this votive stele with the inscription Ἀγαθῶν Ἡρώνι εὐχήν (Lucas, 1992 #70; *AE* 1923, 160: #386e).[2] This dialectal (? Cf. Cermanović-Kuzmanović *et all.*, 1992: 1019) form of the dative resembles the word normal in Latin inscriptions to the Hero (Seure, 1912: 139) giving *Heros, Heronos, Heroni* in Latin, whereas in Greek the dative is usually Ἡρῶϊ. It is interesting to note that a very recently published book concentrating on Religion in Thessalia during the Classical and Hellenistic periods (Mili, 2015; cf. page 1 for chronological limits) has no reference to the horseman-hero and in fact none to any hero cult in that area; this can only reinforce the same sort of dating to the Roman period that we see in Boiotia.

If the horseman-hero is very scarce in Southern Thessalia, further South we encounter a real absence of such reliefs and inscriptions in most of Phthiotis, in both parts of Eastern Lokris, in Phokis and in North West Boiotia; outside a special and restricted zone in Central and South West Boiotia they are, in fact, otherwise unknown in Central Greece (East and West), including Attike and Megaris [just as they appear to be absent from the Peloponnesos, from the Ionian islands and from the islands of the Central and Southern Aigaion]. In this way it is clear that the Boiotian group lies isolated from those regions of Northern Greece and the Balkans where the Horseman-Hero is most at home.

2   The Horseman-Hero in Eastern Central Greece

Given such complete isolation from the Thrakian homeland of this cultic figure and from the areas of its immediate Southwards extension to Makedonia and Thessalia, the occurrence of a small but concentrated group of tombstones with relief carvings of hero-horsemen in Southern and South Western Boiotia (cf. Map, Fig. 42) has always intrigued me. None the less the Thrakian connection of this Boiotian cult is made clear by the consistency of the attestations using the word "Hero"; above the sunken panel within which the relief carving of the rider is presented, is located the funerary text, in most cases consisting simply of three words "to X the hero" – ἐπὶ τίνι ἥρωι *vel sim.*, though there are two instances (*IThesp* 1170–1171) where the word "hero" is omitted but where

---

[2] For a lot of the information concerning this Thessalian material I am much indebted to my friends and colleagues of the Thessalian team in Lyon, Dr Bruno Helly, Dr Jean-Claude Decourt, Dr Gérard Lucas and in particular my old friend and collaborator Dr Laurence Darmezin.

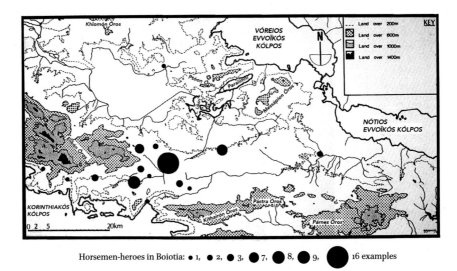

Horsemen-heroes in Boiotia: ● 1, ● 2, ● 3, ● 7, ● 8, ● 9, ● 16 examples

FIGURE 42   Distribution of horseman-hero relief carvings in Boiotia

the relief carving of a horseman makes clear the association with the many other tombstones where this representation similarly occurs; in addition there are two further cases (*IThesp* 1172–1173) where, rather than ἐπί with the dative, the deceased's name is given in the nominative again followed by the word ἥρως. By comparison with the horseman-hero's texts elsewhere, the Boiotian inscriptions are singularly brief.

An important difference in comparison with the Thrakian material is represented by the fact that in Boiotia these inscriptions are – with but one possible exception – exclusively funerary; there do not appear to be any votive cases other than the single exception that we will consider later. While it is worth remembering the evidence that Dimitrova (2002: 224–226) adduced regarding the Thrakian attitude to death and the afterlife that led her to the conclusion that "there is no iconographic distinction between funerary and votive reliefs in the case of the Thracian rider", it remains a fact that with the one possible exception noted, the Boiotian group is purely funerary.

There are several distinctions to be drawn between the Boiotian examples and those from Thrake and surrounding areas: the range of iconography in the horseman representations (Fossey, 2014: 118 Pl. 3) is much more limited than that seen in Thrake, although the stones from the Greek cities of the Thrakian Black Sea coast seem to be more iconographically restrained than those of the interior (Seure, 1912, pt. 4); on the other hand the Thrakian stones generally tend to have texts much longer than the laconic three words of the Boiotian ones and the format of the Boiotian stones themselves is also much less varied

PLATE 83   *Parapoúnyia*, church of Saints Pétros & Pávlos; horseman-hero relief, *IG*vii 2153, *IThesp* 1193A–B

for the riders virtually always occur in a simple rectangular and slightly sunken panel (Pl. 83 [*IThesp* 1193A–B, from *Parapoúnyia* = *EB*ii 37–38]), the only quasi exceptions being an apparently unfinished one where the panel has a upwardly curved top giving it the appearance of a niche (Pl. 84 [*IThesp* 1207 from *Parapoúnyia* = *EB*ii 40]) and one strange piece where the surface of the stone has a large circular shield in high relief and the scene itself is depicted on the surface of that shield (*IThesp* 1224 from near to *Neokhóri*). There are also a few cases where the bottom line of the panel has been indented, e.g. *IThesp* 1204 and another block where no inscription is preserved and which is known to me only from a photograph and description by the late Paul Roesch (1982: 134–135, Pl. VIII, 2 – note that the legends of his nos. 1 and 2 have been

PLATE 84   *Parapoúnyia*, church of Saints Pétros & Pávlos; horseman-hero relief, *IThesp* 1207

reversed); in both instances the extension downwards of the bottom edge of the otherwise rectangular panel has been made in order to accommodate the depiction of the altar.

[The first two stones just mentioned have some other peculiarities The former (*IThesp* 1204) is the only example so far known from Boiotia where **two** horsemen face each other across a large altar above which each horse has an uplifted hoof; this is vaguely reminiscent of a relief slab from Krupac in Eastern Jugoslavia (Dimitrova, 2002: fig. 6) where two horsemen face each other across an altar next to which is a tree and serpent while the inscription below is a dedication to Apollon and Asklapios thus perhaps suggesting syncretic affiliations for each of the two riders. The stone illustrated by Roesch, on the other hand, in addition to being uninscribed, shows a second, much smaller and much shallower rectangular panel below the main one and somewhat off-centre to the left; this contains the frontal depiction of a standing female figure very roughly sculpted and shown holding some sort of jug in her outstretched right hand. The addition of this female figure, an element that finds no parallel in Boiotia (or in Thessalia, to the best of my knowledge) recalls the presence of associated female figures, possibly goddesses, on some of the Thrakian cases (Stoyanov, 1985; cf. Seure, 1912, pt. 2, for associated groups of females, possibly nymphs). Another unusual aspect to this stone is the appearance to either side of this subsidiary panel of further attempts to decorate, but only with simple outline engraving: to the right three animals, possibly dogs, jumping towards the left and to the other side a pruning knife (?) and a two-handled jug. Roesch took these last elements to indicate a connection with viticulture but these simply incised depictions at the bottom of the stone have every appearance of being later than the principal relief which, in itself, is already of a very crude nature and shows the horseman dressed in civilian style by contrast with the shield and helmet normally seen on reliefs of this Boiotian group; at the same time we may note that a syncretism between the Horseman-Hero and Dionysos, the god of wine, has been suggested for Northern Greece and Thrake (Seyrig, 1927: 198–219).]

In my previous account of this cult and its inscriptions I indicated that, while there is an obvious basic, albeit somewhat simplified similarity to the Thrakian pieces, when we turn to the names of the deceased persons commemorated on these tombstones in Boiotia it becomes clear that these do not represent Thrakian immigrants for most of them bear regular Greek names, names that are, moreover, also essentially well attested in other specifically Boiotian texts. While the last point is valid as far as it goes, it now strikes me that I was rather brief in my previous treatment of the names.

3 The Personal Names

The male names so far recorded in this Boiotian group are:

1. Ἀγαθόπους – *IG*vii 2122 (Körte, 1878: 375–376, no. 137), *IThesp* 1170. From *Palaiopanayiá* near to the entrance of the Valley of the Muses, West of Thespiai. The absence here of the word "hero", unusual as it is, may seem relatively unimportant by comparison with the other striking peculiarity of the text in that the deceased, apparently represented as a horseman (the stone appears to have gone missing and verification is thus impossible), has a demotic identifying him as from Khaironeia. The name is rare with only two occurrences at Plataiai and a single one at Thebai; elsewhere in Central Greece it is entirely absent and it is still very infrequent in Thessalia (*LGPN*iiib 6). In neighbouring Attike, on the other hand, it is very frequent with 95 instances (*LGPN*ii 4) and in Euboia next to Boiotia there are four appearances, two at Eretria, two at Karystos, while in the rest of the Aigaion we have the total of five cases on Krete, four on Amorgos, three on each of Kos and Thera but just singletons on Andros, Kalymnos and Paros (*LGPN*i 3–4). In North West Greece the complete absence seen in West Central Greece would continue, were it not for a single instance of imperial date at Nikopolis in Epeiros; this can essentially be disregarded but the very thin representation in the Peloponnesos is more noticeable: after two cases on Aigina near to the Attic frequency, we have just three instances in Lakonia, two in Korinthia and a mere one in Arkadia, all of which contrasts with a certain popularity in Magna Graecia and Sikelia (*LGPN*iiia 4–5). A single case at Pantikapaion is the only attestation in the North Pontos but there are several instances in Northern Greece and the South Balkans: Makedonia has six and Thrake five (*LGPN*iv 3). Similarly the name is absent from the Southern Black Sea but in North West Asia Minor, from Bithynia to Lydia there are 63 fairly well scattered instances (*LGPN*va 3–4); in coastal Asia Minor there are only singletons in Kilikia and Pamphylia but quite many in Karia (25) and Lykia (13), cf. *LGPN*vb 3–4.

2. Ἄγαθος – *IG*vii 4244, *IThesp* 1206. From Thespiai, same stone as Δάμων and Εἰρήνη (*qq.v.*). This reading of the name may be preferred to that given in *IThesp*: Dittenberger in *IG* had given the text as "ἐπ' Ἀγάθῳ ἥρωι" where Roesch or his editors obviously chose to read "Ἐπαγάθῳ ἥρωι" saying that elision of the *iota* is rare, but the other two entries on the stone are consistent in having the preposition ἐπί before the name. The name thus preferred here is indeed rare but it is attested by single cases at Thespiai and Thebai in Boiotia, at Naupaktos in Western Lokris and at Thessalian Atrax (*LGPN*iiib 6); it is equally rare in the large Attic onomastikon with only five cases (*LGPN*ii 5), just as, in the entire Aigaion it is seen only once on Paros (*LGPN*i 4). The

alternative name, Ἐπάγαθος, is but a little more frequent in Boiotia with only three cases at Orkhomenos, one at Thebai and four at Thespiai; indeed apart from five mentions at the international centre of Delphoi, it is absent from the entire remainder of Central Greece and has only five scattered cases in Thessalia (*LGPN*iiib 134). On the other hand, in Attike it is very well represented with 112 appearances (*LGPN*ii 143–144) but in North West Greece there is only one case at Epidamnos and in the Peloponnesos its presence is restricted to two occurrences in Messenia and single ones in Korinthia and Lakonia and its sole appearance further West is an instance in Campania (*LGPN*iiia 5). Apart from a single case in Thrake there are no appearances in Northern Greece, the Southern Balkans and the Northern Pontic area (*LGPN*iv 3) while in the South Black Sea two cases are seen, one in Pontos and one in Bithynia, but there is otherwise an absence in North West Asia Minor (*LGPN*va 4) and the situation in the remainder of coastal Asia Minor continues very thin: just four cases in Karia and one in Kilikia (*LGPN*vb 4).

3. Ἀλέξανδρος – *IG*vii 2123 (Körte, 1878: 362–363, no. 98), *IThesp* 1174. From *Erimókastro* by ancient Thespiai. This name is attested in very small numbers at several places in Boiotia: Anthedon (3 cases), Koroneia (2), Tanagra (2), Khaironeia (1), Lebadeia (1), Orkhomenos (1), Oropos (1), Plataiai (1), Thebai (1); by comparison the 12 cases at Thespiai demonstrate a particular popularity in that city; in the rest of East Central Greece there are several instances in Ozolian Lokris but in Phokis (excluding the 20 at international Delphoi) only one at Daulis next to Boiotia, none in Opountia and Megaris but nearly 100 in Thessalia (*LGPN*iiib 21). Further West there are plentiful cases in Aitolia and Akarnania, followed even by two solitary appearances on Kerkyra and Kephalinia and by yet greater numbers in Epeiros and Illyria; every part of the Peloponnesos provides many examples while Magna Graecia has 61 cases and Sikelia has a further ten (*LGPN*iiia 23–25). In Attike, by contrast, the name is omnipresent with 364 appearances (*LGPN*ii 18–20). Similarly in the Aigaion the name is widespread including a certain representation on Boiotia's neighbour Euboia with seven cases at Eretria, three at Khalkis, another three at Karystos and a lone one at Histiaia; particular concentrations are found on Krete (27 examples) and Rhodos (35 cases) but most islands have at least a few instances (*LGPN*i 24–25). Not surprisingly there is a plethora of examples across Makedonia, Thrake and the Northern Pontic zone (*LGPN*iv 14–17). This frequency continues all around the Black Sea and throughout Asia Minor (*LGPN*va 16–20 & vb 17–19).

Overall the relative paucity of cases in Boiotia is quite striking.

4. Ἀριστίων *IG*vii 2124 (Körte, 1878: no. 119); *IThesp* 1175; *ADelt* 1973 [1977] pl. 236a; *EB*ii 39, pl. 34. From *Parapoúnyia* (church of Áyioi Pétros kai Pávlos). The

text given in *IThesp* is Ἀλεξίων but this is incorrect; cf. my remarks in *EB*ii. On the common existence of this name Ἀριστίων throughout Boiotia, as in some other parts of Greece, cf. Fossey, 2014: 252.

5. Ἀρίστων – *BCH* 1922: 269, no. 106 + 1958: 146, no. 233, *IThesp* 1176. From *Táteza*; stone apparently lost. Another instance of the name Ἀρίστων on an apparently related stone is *IG*vii 2126 (Körte, 1878: 372, no. 126), *IThesp* 1224. From near *Neokhóri*, West of Thespiai. This time the scene in relief shows a man standing and holding the reins of a horse, the whole carved into the surface of a round shield; his cuirass has an apparently military sense and the round shield recalls that seen on several of the mounted Horsemen-Heroes. A particularity of this second text is that the deceased is given his patronymic; this patronymic is Δομεστίχου and the only other appearance of that name occurs in *IG*vii 2443 where we encounter a certain Δομέστιχος Ἀρίστωνος. The two people must be related for otherwise the pairing of the names would be an incredible coincidence; which of the two, however, is the father and which the son? We will need to revisit *IG*vii 2443 but meanwhile we should note that, despite the very real rarity of the patronymic of *IG*vii 2126, the name Ἀρίστων is, by contrast, ultra-common with at least 138 cases scattered across Boiotia and another 160 in other parts of East Central Greece and Thessalia (*LGPN*iiib 62–64), together with 203 cases in Attike (*LGPN*ii 61–63), 23 on neighbouring Euboia and a wide scatter over the Aigaian islands including a particular concentration of 50 on Rhodos and rather smaller numbers elsewhere (Kos with 28, Khios with eight, Krete with seven, Keos – close to Euboia – with seven, the rest with numbers ranging between one and three; cf. *LGPN*i 77–79). In North West and West Central Greece we have nine instances in Aitolia, seven in Akarnania, six in Epeiros, nine in Illyria and a few in the Ionian islands but then there is a very healthy representation in all parts of the Peloponnesos, particularly noticeable in Lakonia with 20 cases; across the Adriatic there are 17 cases in Magna Graecia and 33 in Sikelia (*LGPN*iiia 68–69). The name is quite common across Makedonia, Thrake and especially the Northern Pontic region (*LGPN*iv 46–47), a popularity that continues in the South Black Sea area and in Asia Minor (*LGPN*va 67 & vb 58).

6. *Βιοφέλημος* (on the stone apparently Βιοφίλημος) – *IG*vii 2128 (Körte, 1878: 365, no. 105), *IThesp* 1177. From *Mavromáti*, a little to the North of Thespiai. The name is a *hapax* in Boiotia and the rest of Central Greece (*LGPN*iiib 86); indeed it seems absent from the entire Greek world, as other volumes of *LGPN* show. Paul Roesch was apparently unable to find the stone, like everybody else since Körte, so the text cannot be verified and we may entertain doubts as to the correctness of its reading.

7. Γλαύκων so far unpublished. Observed by our team when excavating at Khóstia, ancient Khorsiai in the extreme South West corner of Boiotia; present location apparently unknown. Γλαύκων is the least common of the names on the root Γλαυκ- all of which are widespread across Boiotia (*LGPN*iiib 91–92); this particular form is attested just once at each of Oropos, Anthedon and Thebai, with two occurrences at Thespiai and, while absent from the rest of Central Greece, apart from a few cases at international Delphoi, and from Thessalia as a whole, next door, in Attike, it is quite present in 51 cases (*LGPN*ii 94 – given the importance in Athenai of the owl as a symbol of the patron goddess Athena, it is not surprising that anthroponyms on the root γλαυκ- are quite common with a total of c. 254 cases, *ibid.* 93–94). In the Aigaion, by contrast, it is most infrequent even on the larger islands: there are only two on Boiotia's neighbour Euboia, none on Rhodos, just three on each of Kythnos, Lesbos and Thasos, two on each of Keos and Teos, with singletons on Astypalaia, Khios, Krete and Naxos (*LGPN*i 108). It is absent from North West Greece, except for a single occurrence at Dodona and, in a similar manner, the entire Peloponnesos is represented by a sole case in Arkadia, just as one example in Sikelia is the lone appearance across the Adriatic (*LGPN*iiia 99). It is also absent from Makedonia, Thrake and the entire Black Sea zone but in North West Asia Minor (*sc.* Ionia and Lydia) there are 27 examples (*LGPN*va 110), whereas in the rest of coastal Asia Minor its presence is limited to four instances in Karia (*LGPN*vb 91).

8. Δάμων – *IG*vii 4244, *IThesp* 1206, same stone as Ἄγαθος and Εἰρήνη (*qq.v.*). From Thespiai. This name is ultra-common across Boiotia and Thessalia and is frequent in much of East Central Greece as a whole (*LGPN*iiib 104–106). In the present spelling the name occurs just 25 times in the large onomastikon of Attike with a further 18 appearances in the form Δήμων (*LGPN*iiib 99 & 114). In the Aigaion there is quite a concentration on Rhodos with 25 cases and, next door to Boiotia, on Euboia five at Khalkis, three at Eretria and another three at Histiaia, while numbers are much smaller on those other islands where cases do occur: Astypalaia (4 instances), Kos (3), Melos (3), Samos (3), Thasos (3), Lesbos (2), Tenos (2), the remainder with singletons on Andros, Ios and Nisyros (*LGPN*i 118–119). In North West and West Central Greece the presence is thinner but there are some cases in all parts of the Peloponnesos (Korinthia has three, Argolis eight, Arkadia four, Lakonia four, Messenia eight and Elis just one at international Olympia); small numbers continue in Magna Graecia with eight and in Sikelia with ten and it is only these last two that have any cases in the spelling Δήμων – the former with a princely two examples and Sikelia with just one (*LGPN*iiia 126). We find just six occurrences of Δάμων in Makedonia, four in Thrake (+ one Δήμων) and three across the Northern Pontic area (*LGPN*ii 87

& 95). *LGPN*va 117–118 and vb 97 give a few instances of Δάμων in the Pontos (2), Ionia (5 cases), Lydia (1), Mysia (8), Karia (9), Lykia (2) and Kilikia (1), to which may be added three instances of Δήμων in Karia and one in Kilikia (*LGPN*vb 106).

9. Διοκλεῖς – *ADelt* 1960 (1963): 148, pl. 126β, *IThesp* 1178. From the site of Thespiai itself. This personal name is well attested across Boiotia in both the regular form Διοκλῆς (which also is noted across much else of Central Greece) and the dialectal one, Διοκλεῖς; related names such as Διοκλείδας/Διοκλίδας, and forms such as Διόκλια, Διουκλεῖς are also attested in Boiotia but only rarely (*LGPN*iiib 118–119 & 123). Very popular in Attike with 238 examples (*LGPN*ii 119–121), our present name is quite frequent in many parts of the Aigaion with 17 cases on Boiotia's neighbour Euboia and one more on nearby Keos, a considerable concentration in the South East (25 on Kos and 28 on Rhodos), smaller groups on some other islands (seven on Krete, three on Thasos, and two on each of Kalymnos, Samos, Tenos, and Thera), while a few other islands show just one case each: Amorgos, Karpathos, Khios, Nisyros, Peparethos, Pholegandros and Skiathos (*LGPN*i 135). North West and West Central Greece have a few instances: five in Aitolia, four in Akarnania, two in Epeiros and three in Illyria; most regions of the Peloponnesos, except Messenia, are represented by small numbers of instances: Korinthia and Elis each have two, Arkadia and Akhaia each three, Argolis five while Lakonia has a comparative plethora of 15; finally Magna Graecia has seven and Sikelia twelve (*LGPN*iiia 127–128). As Διοκλῆς the name occurs eight times in Makedonia, ten times in Thrake but only six times across the entire North Pontic zone (*LGPN*iv 100). Ten cases of Διοκλῆς in Bithynia and four in Pontos make a small presence in the South Black Sea that leads to six in Troas, three in Aiolis and 30 in Mysia followed by 22 in Ionia, 18 in Lydia, 66 in Karia, 14 in Kilikia and two in Lykia (*LGPN*vb 113), thus leaving North West Asia Minor with a healthy number of appearances (*LGPN*va 135).

10. Διονύσιος – The name occurs on two texts: a) *IG*vii 2130 (Körte, 1878: 375, no. 136), *IThesp* 1179 [from Thespiai]; b) *ADelt* 1970, *Khron*. 232, no. 13 + *ADelt* 1971, *Khron* pl. 191α, *IThesp* 1180 [from *Xeronomí*]. The name is particularly common, not only in Boiotia (cf. Fossey, 1991: 56) but also in the whole of East Central Greece and Thessalia (*LGPN*iiib 120–122); in Attike it shows as many as 1103 times (*LGPN*ii 122–127), while, in the Aigaion, it is present in considerable numbers on such a widespread distribution that we need only single out the islands close to Boiotia, Euboia with 25 at Khalkis, 44 at Eretria, four at Histiaia and three at Karystos, and on close-by Keos another six (*LGPN*i 136–139). The very wide spread in numbers continues in North West and West Central Greece, as well as the entire Peloponnesos and Magna Graecia with 55 and

Sikelia with a similar 53; the latter demonstrate the popularity of the name on the other side of the Adriatic (*LGPN*iiia 129–130). This name occurs in 660 cases spread widely across Makedonia, Thrake and the Northern Black Sea (*LGPN*iv 101–105), just as a total of nearly 900 are spread across the Southern Black Sea and North West Asia Minor (*LGPN*va 137–142), followed by a further 844 in the rest of coastal Asia Minor (*LGPN*vb 115–119).

11. Δόσιμος – *IThesp* 1204. From Thespiai, same stone as "Τυγχάνων" (*q.v.*). The name is as much a *hapax* as is Τυγχάνων; Bechtel (1917), moreover, lists nothing at all even vaguely similar. It is only a passing thought but it does occur to me that, particularly in a badly worn inscription, the sloped line and the lower horizontal bar of a *zeta* might be seen as the left-right upsloping side of a *delta* together with its bottom horizontal line. If this happens to be correct then we might read ἐπὶ Ζοσίμῳ (for Ζωσίμῳ) giving a name that is well attested in Boiotia during the earlier imperial period with two cases at Akraiphiai, six at Anthedon, singletons at both Kopai and Koroneia, three at Lebadeia, four at Plataiai, eight at Tanagra, just four again at Thebai and especially nineteen at Thespiai (*LGPN*iiib 178); this is, of course, purely speculation.

12. Εἰσίων – In this spelling the name occurs twice on horseman-hero stones: a) *IG*vii 2135 (Körte, 1878: 366, no. 110), *IThesp* 1182 [from *Xeronomí* in the territory of Thespiai]; b) *IG*vii2143 (Körte, 1878: 367–368, no. 114), *IThesp* 1181 [from *Táteza*]. In its regular orthography Ἰσίων is especially noted in South West Boiotia with ten instances in the area of Thespiai and a singleton at Thisbe, as well as other single instances at Oropos and Lebadeia; in addition there is a single case at Halai in neighbouring Opountian Lokris and further North four cases are noted at Larissa, the only appearances in the whole of Thessalia (*LGPN*iiib 212). In Attike it occurs, in the regular orthography, just 36 times (*LGPN*ii 242) and in the Aigaion a very sparse distribution shows, for Boiotia's neighbour Euboia, only three at Eretria and a single one at Khalkis, three on each of Khios and Paros, two on each of Kos, Peparethos and Samos, followed by singletons on Amorgos, Rhodos, Samothrake and Thasos (*LGPN*i 239). Absent completely from North West and West Central Greece, its presence in the Peloponnesos is limited to five cases in Argolis and one in Lakonia while, across the Adriatic, it is restricted to two cases in Magna Graecia and a solitary one in Sikelia (*LGPN*iiia 224). The name Ἰσίων is only found rarely in the Northern parts of the Greek world with just two cases in Makedonia, six in Thrake and a lonely one in the Northern Black Sea (*LGPN*iv 178) while there are none observed in the Southern Black Sea and in the whole of North West Asia Minor there is a total of just three or four cases in Ionia (*LGPN*va 232) followed by 15 examples in Karia and nothing elsewhere in coastal Asia Minor (*LGPN*vb 219). A theophoric name related to the cult of the Egyptian gods.

13. Εἴρανος – *IG*vii 2131 (Körte, 1878: 364, no. 101), *IThesp* 1171. From *Palaiopanagía* in the territory of Thespiai. Although a variety of names based on the word εἰρήνη does occur this one is virtually a *hapax*, completely absent from North West and Central Greece as a whole, including Attike and Megaris, from Thessalia, the Aigaion, the Peloponnesos, South Italy-Sikelia, Makedonia, Thrake and from the entire Black Sea area and the whole of Asia Minor. The editors of *LGPN*iiib (211) consider that it stands (by a form of iotacism?) for Ἴρανος both here and in just a single other Boiotian instance at Tanagra (*IG*vii 416, 542 & 543) but this hardly solves the problem since Ἴρανος is nowhere else to be found in Boiotia although there are three cases of Ἰράνα, two at Tanagra and one at Thebai, respectively *IG*vii 1114, 1115 & 2421: both are completely absent from Megaris, all of Central Greece, Thessalia, Attike, the Peloponnesos (except for a single Ἰράνα at Argos, *LGPN*iiia 223), North West Greece (including the Ionian islands), Makedonia, Thrake, the entire Aigaion, Kyrenaike, Magna Graecia and Sikelia, Cyprus, the entire Black Sea area and North Western Anatolia. In short both versions of the name are equally rare in the extreme. Although represented so rarely it is clear that, if the name can be said to be "at home" anywhere it is in Boiotia. Whatever the name, this text is also another example of the rare omission of the word "hero".

14. Ἐπαφρίων – *IG*vii 2628 (Körte, 1878: 361, no. 94); *EB* ii 35, fig. 25. Found at *Thívai*. This theophoric name, related to the cult of Aphrodite, is uncommon in Boiotia but is attested thrice at Thebai and four times at Thespiai, in the centre of the hero cult attestations as well as once at Megara; otherwise it is absent from East Central Greece and Thessalia (*LGPN*iiib 135). In other parts of the Greek world it is – at the most – very rare and often completely absent; for a discussion of its distribution cf. Fossey, 2014: 236–238 [to that account should be added just three appearances in Karia (*LGPN*vb 137)].

15. [Ἐπίμ]αχ[ος] would seem to me to be the most tempting reconstruction of the name in *IG*vii 2690 (Körte, 1878: 360, no. 93) from *Thívai*. Dittenberger already had suggested a name ending in -μάχος. If my tentative suggestion to reconstruct the whole name should prove correct we may note that the name recurs just once in Boiotia, at Thespiai, and at Kytenion in Doris; in the rest of East Central Greece and the whole of Thessalia it is absent (*LGPN*iiib 138); its infrequence continues with a mere nine cases in Attike (*LGPN*ii 151), with just two in the entire Aigaion, one on each of Euboia (Karystos) and Samothrake (*LGPN*i 158), with just two more in South Italy and another two in the entire Peloponnesos, one of them in Korinthia across the Gulf from Southern Boiotia (*LGPN*iiia 148). Apart from a solitary Makedonian case (*LGPN*iv 121) the name is absent from that area, as from Thrake and the entire Black Sea area. Similarly in the whole of Asia Minor there are only single isolated cases at Kyme in Aiolis

(*LGPN*va 160) and two in Lykia (*LGPN*vb 141). All this discussion arises, however, from a speculation, though not entirely "idle speculation".

16. Εὐάμερος in an inscription classed as if from Phokis but, in fact, from Záltza, ancient Boulis, basically an independent small coastal city between South West Boiotia and South East Phokis, adjacent to *Khóstia*/Khorsiai (cf. Γλαύκων above). *ADelt* 1994 [1999] 316; *ADelt* 2001–2004 [2012] *Khron.* 413 + fig. 10 (*ed. pr.*); Rousset, 2012, 1665–1668 + fig. 2 (detailed account). The name in this dialectal form recurs once actually at neighbouring Khorsiai (*IG*vii 2400 of imperial date), thrice at Koroneia in Hellenistic times (*IG*vii 2952 and 2953 plus *AEph* 1936, *Khron.* 30 no. 197 II, line 17); it is also attested thrice within Thespike, each time with a Horseman-Hero relief: a) at *Palaiopanayiá*, Körte. 1878: 364, no. 103, *IThesp* 1183; b) from *Táteza*, *BCH* 1922: 269–270, no. 107 + 1958: 147, no. 236, *IThesp* 1184; c) *IThesp* 1231 [first published account] from an unspecified location within Thespike. The last example has certain traits that distinguish it somewhat from the bulk of the stones in that, despite the masculine name, it is a woman who is presented with a horse in the relief carving; there is also a second line of text bearing another masculine name, Ἀπολλωνίδας, without the usual preposition or the word hero; the relevance of this second name is unclear and I thus eschew further comment.

Although infrequent elsewhere in Eastern Central Greece, the main name is quite common in Boiotia in the normal spelling, Εὐήμερος, with single attestations at Akraiphiai, Khaironeia and Thisbe, two more at each of Plataiai and Thebai, a surprising three at the lesser city of Anthedon but then a grand total of 12 at Thespiai and in its area (*LGPN*iiib 154); to these should be added the very few instances in the dialectal form Εὐάμερος mentioned above: the one at Khorsiai, three more at Koroneia and another three at Thespiai (*LGPN*iiib 147). The name, always in the non-dialectal spelling, is not very common in Attike (*LGPN*ii 168 gives only 36 examples); in the present dialectal spelling it occurs just three times in the Aigaion with single cases at Lyttos on Krete, at Khalkis on Euboia and on Thera but the regular Εὐήμερος is a little more frequent, seen twice on each of Kos, Thasos and Thera and then in singles on Khios, on Krete, at Eretria on Euboia, on Naxos, Paros and Tenos (*LGPN*i 174). Its appearances in North West and West Central Greece are limited to one in each area; a singleton at Kamarina represents the whole of Magna Graecia and Sikelia while in the Peloponnesos there are but single examples in Akhaia and Argolis, as well as nearby Aigina, none in Korinthia or Elis but then the two Southern areas produce small concentrations, Lakonia with nine cases and Messenia with another four (*LGPN*iiia 158). It is completely absent from Makedonia, Thrake and the North Black Sea. In the South Black Sea Εὐήμερος occurs only twice in Bithynia but then there is a small scatter in Asia Minor with two instances in Troas, eight in Ionia, four in Mysia and one in Lydia (*LGPN*va 176), together with ten occurrences in Karia (*LGPN*vb 161). Once more we have a name that is at home in Boiotia and absent from Thrake and surrounding areas thus negating any possibility of a movement of people from the latter bringing the cult with them to East Central Greece.

17. Εὔπορος – *IG*vii 2137 (Körte, 1878: 365, no. 107), *IThesp* 1185. From *Xeronomí* in the area of Thespiai. Of the 18 attestations of this name in Boiotia 16 occur at Thespiai; the other two cases are singletons at Thebai and Oropos while in the rest of Eastern Central Greece it appears only as singletons at Megara and at Khaleion in Ozolian Lokris and in Thessalia its presence is restricted to four instances at Larissa, three at Demetrias and singletons in Magnesia, at Hypata and at Oloosson (*LGPN*iiib 164). By contrast, in Attike 161 cases are recorded (*LGPN*ii 181–182), while across the Aigaion there is a small scatter of instances without any particular concentration: three cases on Boiotia's neighbour Euboia give two to Eretria and one to Khalkis with another singleton on nearby Keos: there are three again on each of Krete, Rhodos and Thasos, then two on Andros, Kos and Tenos followed by singletons on Amorgos, Astypalaia and Paros (*LGPN*i 183). Completely absent from West Central Greece, in the North West it picks up a bit with four cases in Epeiros and five in Illyria; in the Peloponnesos its spread is uneven with a single instance in Akhaia, another in Elis, together with yet another on neighbouring Zakynthos, four in Korinthia, seven in Argolis, six in Lakonia but none in Messenia and Arkadia; finally there are just three cases in South Italy and none in Sikelia (*LGPN*iiia 173). When we look at the Northern parts of the Greek world we find 18 instances of the name in Makedonia but noticeably none at all in Thrake and only one in the Northern Black Sea area (*LGPN*iv 135). On the South side of the Black Sea there are three instances in Pontos and two in Bithynia, then 12 in Ionia and two in each of Mysia and Lydia (*LGPN*va 181); then come 29 cases in Karia, one in Kilikia and three in Lykia (*LGPN*vb 166).

It is clear that the name is particularly "at home" in Thespike, the area where the cult is most present. The absence in Thrake again seems significant.

18. Ζώπυρος – *IG*vii 2139 (Körte, 1878: 362, no. 96), *IThesp* 1186. From *Palaiopanayiá* a short distance to the West of Thespiai. There is another instance of this name on a tombstone from the area of Thespiai: *IThesp* 1172 (previously unpublished and with no indication of its exact provenience within Thespike). Ζώπυρος is a common name across Boiotia and even several surrounding areas of Eastern Central Greece (Phokis, both Lokrides, Megaris, Euboia and Attike) as well as nearby Euboia; for a full account of the distribution of the name cf. Fossey, 2005: 124–125, summarized in 2014: 180; to these should be added for Asia Minor the 45 cases in Karia with two in Kilikia and single ones in each of Lykia and Pamphylia (*LGPN*vb 179).

19. [Ἡρα]κλᾶς is the suggested reconstruction of the name on *IG*vii 2173 (Körte, 1878: 367, no. 113), *IThesp* 1187. While that name is indeed attested in Boiotia, it is not common at all apart from six cases at or near Thespiai, otherwise merely singletons at Tanagra and Plataiai; it is even absent in the rest of East Central Greece apart from just one case at Halai of Opountian Lokris, and the singleton at Larissa is the only Thessalian appearance (*LGPN*iiib 181). With only 11 cases in Attike (*LGPN*ii 204) and only a total of six scattered across the Aigaian islands including one at Karystos on Euboia (*LGPN*i 202), its rarity continues, as it does in the Peloponnesos where there are merely two cases in Lakonia and a single one in Arkadia, while it is completely absent from North West and West Central Greece and the 13 in Magna Graecia contrast with the absence entirely from Sikelia (*LGPN*iiia 193). In Makedonia six cases lead to five in Thrake and then four in the Northern Pontic area (*LGPN*iv 153). In the South Black Sea there is only one case, in Bithynia at the Western end of the Sea and two in neighbouring Troas that lead to a small cluster in Ionia which, in its turn, tails off to a mere two in Lydia (*LGPN*va 200) which continue with three in Karia and singletons in Kilikia, Lykia and Pamphylia (*LGPN*vb 185). If this reconstruction is correct then we are dealing with a theophoric name connected with the cult of Herakles but since the reconstruction actually seems, at the very least, unconvincing perhaps further discussion is pointless.

20 & 21. *Θεόγιτος* and *Θεόγειτος* – respectively a) *IG*vii 2140 (Körte, 1878: 366, no. 108), *IThesp* 1189 and b) *IG*vii 2141, *IThesp* 1188. The second from *Xeronomí* in the Western territory of Thespiai, the former without specific indication as to provenience within Thespike. In the first form this name occurs on this occasion alone in Boiotia but, as Θεόγειτος, it is seen twice more at Thespiai itself and, while the potential form Θιόγ(ε)ιτος does not occur at all there is at least one instance of the feminine Θιογίτα and a few of the cognates Θιογείτων and, in particular Θιογίτων (11 cases at Orkhomenos, five at Tanagra, four at Akraiphiai, two at Anthedon and singletons at Khaironeia, Kopai and Lebadeia, a distribution plainly centred on the Kopaïs, especially its West side); outside Boiotia Θεόγειτος appears just once in Thessalia but nowhere else in East Central Greece (*LGPN*iiib 188) and is completely absent from the Aigaian islands. The name is a very uncommon one although the two elements that form it are frequently combined into other compound names and other versions of this combination with different endings are also attested (e.g. Θεογίτων, the only form attested – merely 13 times – in Attike, cf. *LGPN*ii 213). The form Θεογίτων is all that appears in the Peloponnesos and then only twice in Arkadia and the same can be said for West Central Greece where this form alone appears just once in Akarnania; not even this, or indeed any other related name, is to be

found in North West Greece and in South Italy and Sikelia (*LGPN*iiia 201) and it is equally absent from Makedonia, Thrake, the whole Black Sea region and from entire Asia Minor. Obviously generically theophoric name not associated necessarily with any specific cult and with no Thrakian connections.

22. *Καλλι - - -* SEG ii 229 + SEG xix 370, *IThesp* 1190. From *Episkopí* at the site normally identified with Askra. One reconstruction of the name that has been suggested is Κάλλι[ππος] but Καλλί[γιτος] is also given as a possibility; neither reconstruction can be clearly preferred and, generally speaking, names in Καλλι- are numerous enough to deter any expression of preference. The name thus calls for no further comment.

23. *Λυσίμαχος* – *IG*vii 2145 (Körte, 1878: 370, no. 122), *IThesp* 1203A. From *Karandás* in the Western part of the Thespike. Same stone as that bearing Παράμονος (*q.v.*). Not a particularly common name in Central Greece generally, with the exception of Attike (131 cases in *LGPN*ii 292–293), but attested twice at Thespiai and by singletons at several other places in Boiotia (Oropos, Tanagra, Thebai and Khaironeia) and rarely elsewhere (Fossey, 2005: 148–149); in Thessalia, by contrast, it is really quite frequent (*LGPN*iiib 266–267) as it is in the Aigaian islands where 66 cases, including ten on Euboia, are noted (*LGPN*i 293). Where in West Central Greece its presence is limited to one instance in Akarnania, in the North West it is rather more present with nine cases in Epeiros, five in Illyria and even two in Dalmatia and there are just a few instances in the Ionian islands, one on each of Leukas, Kephalenia and Kerkyra (*LGPN*iiia 283–284); in the Peloponnesos we have again an uneven distribution: absence in Korinthia and Elis, just one case in Akhaia, one more in Arkadia, ten in Lakonia but only three in Messenia and across the Adriatic there are three examples in Campania and another three in Sikelia (*LGPN*iiia 283–284). The presence in North West Greece is more than surpassed by the representations in the North and North East parts of the Greek world with 67 cases in Makedonia but only five in Thrake and then 24 in the North Black Sea (*LGPN*iv 215–216). It is infrequent in the Southern Black Sea with only one instance in Pontos and three in Bithynia but Asia Minor picks up with nine cases in Mysia, a noticeable 24 in Ionia and seven in Lydia (*LGPN*va 275), followed by 43 in Karia, 28 in Lykia, as well as single instances in both Kilikia and Pamphylia (*LGPN*vb 266–267).

24. *Λυσί[στρατος?]* – *IG*vii 2163 (Körte 1878: 363, no. 100) *IThesp* 1192A. From Thespiai (same stone as Ὁμολώϊχος and Σώσανδρος below). A puzzling text; Körte seems only to have read an initial ἐπὶ which Lolling apparently did not see since Dittenberger brackets the word; it would also seem that the first four letters of the name (and perhaps its reconstruction?), together with the logical word ἥρωϊ are due to Lolling for Körte reads nothing after the preposition.

The reconstruction does not inspire confidence: generally speaking names in Λυσι- are much more common in other parts of East Central Greece and particularly Thessalia than in Boiotia (cf. *LGPN*iiib 266–267); the name proposed only recurs once in the area with a sculptor at Thebai. One must note that another name, on the same initial root, such as Λύσιππος with three instances at Thespiai, three at Thebai and one at Plataiai might be more convincing but without a fresh reading of the stone itself nothing should be restored and the proposition of Lolling and Dittenberger should be left aside, despite its unquestioning acceptance by the editors of Paul Roesch's posthumous Thespian *corpus*.

25. *Μικ[ιάδ]ης IG*vii 2629 from Thebai. I mistrust the reconstruction of this name for which I know of no parallel in Boiotia or in the rest of East Central Greece, including Attike, and Thessalia; nor do we find it in the Aigaion except for a single case at Eretria on neighbouring Euboia; a single isolated example of Μικιάδας on Kerkyra offers but little encouragement given that it is the only related name of any shape in the whole of North West and West Central Greece (*LGPN*i 313) and neither the name itself nor any possible relative is observed anywhere across the Adriatic, as is the case in Makedonia, Thrake and the entire Black Sea area as well as the whole of Asia Minor. This is an ultra rare name though a few names in Μικ- do exist but fewer with any termination in -ης (cf. *LGPN*iiib 284–286 where the single Μικρυλίδας might appear the most promising Boiotian example – from Thebai – although perhaps too long).

26. *Μουσᾶς* – *IG*vii 1715 (Körte 1878: 374, no. 130). Found in a chapel of the Taxiárkhes at an unnamed location in or near the Western Parasopia. The relief carving on the stone shows a standing woman holding the reins of a horse before an altar. Despite the female nature of the figure the deceased was clearly a man given the masculine form of ἥρωϊ; otherwise it would be tempting to see here the feminine name Μοῦσα which would better correspond with the figure of the standing woman. Μουσᾶς is obviously a theophoric appellation related to the cult of the Muses on Mount Helikon in South West Boiotia although this is the only occurrence of the name in the whole of Boiotia (Fossey, 2014: 126); on the other hand there is a small number of other names on the root Μουσ- scattered sparsely across Boiotia, Megaris and Thessalia (*LGPN*iiib 294). In Attike we have two instances of the related feminine Μοῦσα and many other names on the same root but not this name itself (*LGPN*ii 321–322). The latter name, Μοῦσα, occurs a few times on various Aigaian islands as does the masculine Μουσαῖος; other related names are infrequent (*LGPN*i 321). The name Μουσᾶς itself is again absent from West Central and North West Greece but there is a range of cognates in most parts as well as in Sikelia and Magna Graecia

(*LGPN*iiia 306). In Makedonia and Thrake, as in Asia Minor, we find quite a few examples of Μοῦσα and even more of Μουσαῖος (*LGPN*iv 243, *LGPN*va 325 & *LGPN*vb 305); all are rare around the Pontos but in Ionia a single case occurs of the name proposed here but not elsewhere in coastal Asia Minor despite the presence of cognate names (*LGPN*vb 305). On the related name Μούσων and other cognates both in Boiotia and beyond cf. Fossey, 2014: 277.

27. Νεικίας – *IG*vii 2153 (cf. *ADelt* 1973 [1977] 284; *SEG* xxvii 58); *IThesp* 1193A; Piterós, 2008: 605–606, no. 9: *EB*ii 37. On the same stone as Σωταίρος (*q.v.*). From *Parapoúnyia* near the area usually identified with the battlefield of Leuktra, South of Thespiai. For a discussion of the wide distribution of the name Νεικίας (Νικίας, Νικέας) throughout Greece cf. Fossey, 2014: 185–186 [to which should now be added the 59 cases in areas of coastal Asia Minor (*LGPN*vb 317–318)]. The form Νικίας occurs on another Horseman relief: *IG*vii 2152 (Körte, 1878: 371, no. 124), *IThesp* 1225 from *Livadhóstro* (ancient Kreusis, the port of Thespiai); here is an instance of a standing man holding the reins of a horse rather than riding it. We may also note the presence at Plataiai of a funerary text reading simply ἐπὶ Νεικίᾳ ἥρωι (*IG*vii 1716); unfortunately the *lemma* in *IG*vii gives no description of the stone so we have no way of telling whether a horseman is involved.

28. Νικάνωρ – *ADelt* 1970: *Khron. I*: 232, no. 1, *IThesp* 1194. There is some confusion in the *IThesp* entry: this is said to be the same stone as that bearing Körte, 1878: 368, no. 116 but the dimensions of the stone differ greatly and Körte's description – that barely anything of the inscription was legible – was given by Dittenberger as *IG*vii 2175 which then appears as *IThesp* 1199, in the *lemma* of which there is no reference to Körte. A photo of *IG*vii 2175 was published by Spyrópoulos in *ADelt* 1970: pl. 193γ; this allows a reading of the second inscription which Körte had not been able to decipher, cf. Φίλιππος below. The name Νικάνωρ is not frequent in Boiotia with just single examples at Akraiphiai, Hyettos and Plataiai, two at Thebai, three at Khaironeia and four at Thespiai, while it is frequent in Thessalia to the North and occurs often at Delphoi but otherwise in Eastern Central Greece there is only a solitary example at Naupaktos (*LGPN*iiib 299); at the same time in Aitolia there are seven cases but none in neighbouring Akarnania and only two in the Ionian islands, one on Kerkyra and the other on Leukas, but then the picture picks up for the North West with 75 instances in Epeiros and another nine in Illyria; when, however, we turn to the Peloponnesos we find only three in Korinthia and one in Argolis, four in Akhaia, three in Arkadia, none in Elis, only one in Lakonia and just three in Messenia, while across the Adriatic we have just six in Magna Graecia and a lonely two in Sikelia (*LGPN*iiia 3167–318). In Attike, on the other hand, we find 54 instances (*LGPN*ii 330–331) and, in the Aigaion, 60 cases scattered across the

islands attest to some popularity (*LGPN*i 329–330). Abundantly represented by 105 instances in Makedonia, it appears only 11 times in Thrake and a mere four times in the whole North Black Sea zone (*LGPN*iv 250–251). In the South Black Sea it is only represented by single instances in Pontos and Bithynia followed by another isolated case in Aiolis but then we have 24 in Mysia, 19 in Ionia and 12 in Lydia (*LGPN*va 332) as well as 25 in Karia, 16 in Kilikia, nine in Lykia and two in Pamphylia (*LGPN*vb 315).

29. [Νί]κων – *IG*vii 2172, *IThesp* 1195. Not sufficient of the text survives to make any restoration of the name convincing; it is, therefore, not considered further here.

30. Ὁμολώϊχος – *IG*vii 2165 (Körte, 1878: 363, no. 100), *IThesp* 1192C. From Thespiai (same stone as "Λυσί[στρατος?]" and Σώσανδρος *qq.v.*). All anthroponyms in Ὁμολώϊ- are peculiar to Boiotia and widely spread across its territory with a notable preponderance in Thespike; it is based on the name of a specifically Boiotian month, and is thus absent entirely from the rest of East Central Greece and Thessalia (*LGPN*iiib 324–325), as it is essentially from the entire Greek world. So peculiarly Boiotian is this and related names that we must suppose that the two isolated instances of Ὁμολώϊχος in Attike, and the single Ὁμολωῖς also found there, are the result of migration from Boiotia or intermarriage with a Boiotian, *vel sim.* (*LGPN*ii 351). Once again a name completely without Thrakian connection and so much "at home" in Boiotia.

31. Ὀνησᾶς – *IThesp* 1196. No indication of exact provenance; there is even no clear indication that it is from Thespike since it is simply located in the museum at *Thívai* not that at *Erimókastro*. At the same time the name, while very rare, does recur twice in Boiotia, precisely at Thespiai, while in the remainder of Eastern Central Greece and Thessalia it only occurs in three cases at international Delphoi and once in Phthiotis (*LGPN*iiib 326). In Attike, alongside 13 cases of Ὀνησᾶς, there are several other names on the same root (*LGPN*ii 352–353) but the presence of Ὀνησᾶς in the Aigaion is limited to two instances, one on Paros and the other on Tenos, while Cyprus actually produces three instances together with a further 11 examples of the closely related Ὀνάσας and Ὀνασᾶς (*LGPN*i 349–351; I am puzzled by the varying accentuation since the instances come essentially from unaccented epigraphic texts!). In North West and West Central Greece it is completely absent and in the Peloponnesos, with the exception of a cluster of seven in Arkadia, it is only present twice in Lakonia and once in each of Argolis, Elis and Messenia, with another singleton on Aigina and another outlying singleton in Sikelia (*LGPN*iiia 343). There is a single case in each of Makedonia and Thrake (*LGPN*iv 263) but nothing at all in the entire Black Sea area and even North West Asia Minor has only a total of four instances, two in Ionia and one in each of Lydia and Mysia (*LGPN*va 345);

in the rest of coastal Asia Minor there are no examples although there are a few isolated cases of related names, especially ones that use' Ονη/ασι- as the first part of a compound name but none of these is at all numerous (*LGPN*vb 327328).

32. *Παράμονος* – *IG*vii 2146 & 2147 (Körte, 1878: 370, no. 122), *IThesp* 1203B and 1203C. From *Karandás* in Western Thespike. Yet another instance of the name Παράμονος in a text associated with a relief showing a standing man and a horse occurs on a stone from Thespiai: *BCH* 1922: 269, no. 105 & 1958: 147, no. 238, *IThesp* 1226. For the frequency of this name particularly in Boiotia but also in fact, in East Central Greece as a whole, i.e. including Attike and Euboia cf. Fossey, 1991: 224 & 2005: 172–173 where the thinner representations in most other parts of Greece are discussed. The significance of the name in inscription *IThesp* 1203B is unclear but in 1203C it is of the type usual to the Horseman-Hero stones; is it possible that inscription B should be read as Π(α)ρ(α)μόνου thus possibly giving a patronymic to Λυσίμαχος of inscription A? We may compare with Εὔταξις Χαρέου of *BCH* 1922: 270–271, no. 108 & 1958: 142–143, no. 216 *bis*.

33. *Παρθενοκλῆς* – *ADelt* 1970, *Khron*: 232, no. 4 + 1971, *Khron*: pl. 191β, *IThesp* 1197. From *Xeronomí*. The name is a rare one attested merely thrice at each of Thebai (but cf. below) and Thespiai and nowhere else in Eastern Central Greece and with only a single appearance in Thessalia (*LGPN*iiib 335), only three cases in Attike (*LGPN*ii 361), none in any of the Aigaian islands, the Peloponnesos, North West and West Central Greece and none in Magna Graecia or Sikelia. By contrast, while the name is absent from both Makedonia and Thrake, in the North side of the Black Sea it occurs 20 times, this being the largest concentration of the name in the entire Greek world (*LGPN*iv 272–273). On the other hand in the South Black Sea it is absent and this continues into the whole of Asia Minor with just a solitary example of this name in Karia (*LGPN*vb 344). For all its comparative frequency in the North Pontos, this name represents no Thrakian connection.

34. *Σάτυρ[ος]* – *IG*vii 2161 (Körte, 1878: 375, no. 133), *IThesp* 1232. No indication of exact find spot in Thespike. The relief shows a standing woman (taken to be a priestess because of the key she holds in her left hand) with a horse whose reins she holds with her right hand. Although they do not restore the ending of the name the editors of Paul Roesch's *corpus* indicate in the *lemma* to this text that they considered it a masculine name; presumably they had Σάτυρος in mind. Since, however, there is no clear indication of gender in the inscription with the word for "hero" being lost (if it was ever there) perhaps we should also entertain the possibility, in the light of the depiction of a woman standing with the horse, that we might logically restore it rather as Σατυρ[ίνα]

(cf. Bechtel, 1917: 567; seen at Oropos, Thebai and nearby Eretria, respectively Petrákos, 1997: 323; *BCH* 1898: 271, no. 2; *LGPN*i 402) or, perhaps more likely, Σατύρ[α] (seen at Tanagra, *IG*vii 1382), present in 13 instances in Attike (*LGPN*ii 394) as well as twice on Rhodos and once on Tenos, (*LGPN*i 402) or once in Makedonia (*LGPN*iv 305) and again once in each of Mysia (*LGPN*va 399) and Karia (*LGPN*vb 379)? In light of this Σατύρα is tentatively included in the short list of feminine names given below but perhaps the candidacy of Σατυρίνα should not be forgotten. For the much broader distribution of the masculine name, including a certain spread around Boiotia, cf. Fossey, 2005: 181–183; to this for coastal Asia Minor should be added the 17 examples from Karia, the two from Kilikia and the five in Lykia given in *LGPN*vb 379–380.

35. Σώσανδρος – *IG*vii 2164 (Körte, 1878: 363, no. 100), *IThesp* 1192B. From Thespiai (same stone as "Λυσί[στρατος?]" and Ὁμολώϊχος above). Although common enough in other parts of Eastern Central Greece this name is not so frequent in Boiotia; it is, nonetheless, attested in an interesting distribution: apart from single cases at Koroneia and Orkhomenos and two at Thebai, there are six instances precisely at Thespiai; beyond Boiotia we find it once at Stephane (?) in Phokis outside of international Delphoi (Fossey, 2014: 39–40), once again at Megara, seven times in Ozolian Lokris and three in the small prosopography of Doris but then a host of 31 instances in Thessalia (*LGPN*iiib 391–392). In Attike there are also 31 instances (*LGPN*ii 414); in the Aigaion a few cases occur on a small number of islands (*LGPN*i 420 lists two instances on each of Krete, Peparethos and Rhodos, as well as singletons on Kasos, Lesbos, Naxos, Telos and Thasos) but then in North West Greece there is a host of 28 occurrences in Epeiros and three more in Dalmatia, while in West Central Greece we find five instances in Aitolia, six in Akarnania, two on Kerkyra and three on Leukas but the distribution thins out again in the Peloponnesos with merely one in Korinthia, two in each of Argolis, Lakonia and Arkadia, just one in Akhaia, and just one again in Messenia and two on nearby Aigina; across the Adriatic we find only four cases in Southern Italy and seven in Sikelia (*LGPN*iiia 411–412). Four cases in Makedonia, three in Thrake and one in the Northern Pontic zone constitute the very thin presence in the Northern Greek world (*LGPN*iv 323). In the Southern Black Sea region we find nothing, while in Asia Minor we find ten cases in Ionia, five in Mysia, three in Lydia but only one in Bithynia (*LGPN*va 418) followed by 15 cases in Karia, two in Kilikia and one in Lydia (*LGPN*vb 396).

36. Σ[ωσ]ικράτης – *IG*vii 2364. From Thisbe. The reading does not inspire complete confidence; the representation given in *IG* (presumably provided by Lolling since Körte did not record this example) is such as to suggest that it was not just two letters that were missing, more likely five or even six. In addition

the initial *sigma* is uncertain; what is recorded in the diagram could indeed be what remained of a square *sigma* but equally possibly part of an *epsilon* or even of a *beta*. I do not, however, find any convincing alternative. If we tentatively accept, therefore, the published version we can see that Σωσικράτης occurs rather infrequently in Boiotia: six instances at Thespiai, three at Lebadeia and then singletons at Khaironeia, Lebadeia and Tanagra; it is equally infrequent in the rest of East Central Greece with just three instances in Opountia (one at each of Halai, Larymna and Opous), four in Ozolian Lokris, two at Naupaktos and one at each of Oiantheia and Phlygonion, another four at Megara and in Phokis (leaving aside the 11 at international Delphoi) two cases at Elateia and singletons at Antikyra, Daulis, Hyampolis and Tithorea; even in Thessalia the name is rarely seen with mere singletons at Homolion, Lamia, Krannon and Gonnoi (*LGPN*iiib 393–394). In the rich onomastikon of Attike there are only 48 cases (*LGPN*ii 416–417); in the Aigaion, of 57 instances 39 are found on Rhodos alone, the remainder being pairs on Amorgos, Krete, Euboia (one at each of Eretria and Karystos) and Samos or singletons on Astypalaia, Imbros, Melos, Nisyros, Syros, Tenos and Thera (*LGPN*i 422). In North West and West Central Greece its presence is ultra-rare with just four cases in Illyria but only one in each of Aitolia and Akarnania and another off the coast on Kephalenia; when, however, we turn to the Peloponnesos the picture changes with six in Akhaia, another six in Korinthia, four in Argolis, nine in Arkadia, six in Messenia and then a grand total of 24 in Lakonia, while across the Adriatic in South Italy we have a total of nine and on Sikelia a mere four (*LGPN*iiia 413). There are only seven cases of the name in Makedonia as a whole and then four in Thrake and finally just two in the Northern Black Sea area (*LGPN*iv 324); while there are only instances in the South Black sea at its Western end – Bithynia with six examples – while Ionia has 16 cases and Lydia just one (*LGPN*va 419), Karia a further six and Lykia just one (*LGPN*vb 396).

37. Σωταίρος *IG*vii 2154 (cf. *ADelt* 1973 [1977] 284; *SEG* xxvii 58); *IThesp* 1193B; Piterós, 2008: 605–606, no. 9: *EB*ii 37. From *Parapoúnyia* in Southern Thespike, same stone as Νεικίας above. On the predominance at Thespiai of Boiotian examples of this name in both the forms Σωταίρος and Σωτήρος, cf. Fossey, 2014: 250–251 & the 38 examples given in *LGPN*iiib 397–398; otherwise it is seen in scattered examples at Thebai, Thisbe, and at a few other locations mostly around the Kopaïs, specifically Akraiphiai with four instances, Kopai and Khaironeia with two each and then single cases at each of Koroneia, Lebadeia and Thisbe; it is also attested just twice in Phokis and once in Thessalia (*LGPN*iiib 397–399). Very rare in Attike (*LGPN*ii 420 lists only three cases). For the very thin – sometimes even non-existent – distribution outside East Central Greece cf. Fossey, 2014: 250–251 [to which add the single example of Σωτήρος in Karia (*LGPN*vb

398)]; as indicated then there is an absence of examples in Thrake and North Pontos, thus denying any Thrakian connection.

38. Σωτηρίδας – IGvii 2807 (Körte, 1878: 369, no. 120), EBii pl. 1. From *Topólia* (ancient Kopai) built into the church of the κοίμησις τῆς Θεοτόκου. In Boiotia, the rest of East Central Greece and Thessalia (in either of the forms Σωτηρίδας or Σωτηρίδης) this name is very infrequent: four cases at each of Thespiai and Thebai, singletons at Anthedon, Kopai, Oropos and Tanagra for Boiotia; one example at Halai in Opountia, another singleton at Physkeis in Ozolian Lokris and single instances again at the two Thessalian cities of Kallithero and Pherai (*LGPN*iiib 397–398). Not a common name in Attike (*LGPN*ii 421 lists only 18 examples) and very uncommon in the Aigaion (*LGPN*i 426–427 gives only four instances on Krete, two on Rhodos and then merely single cases on Kos and Lesbos). The thinness of distribution continues with single cases only in each of Aitolia, Akarnania and Epeiros, another singleton on Aigina is followed by a few in the North Peloponnesos – four in Akhaia, another four in Argolis, only two in Korinthia and just one in each of Arkadia and Elis and a mere two in Messenia, against all of which the total of 16 in Lakonia is quite striking; across the Adriatic we find just a solitary case in Sikelia (*LGPN*iiia 418). Σωτηρίδας occurs just once in Makedonia while Σωτηρίδης adds a second case in Makedonia balanced by another pair in Thrake, beyond which both are absent in the North Black Sea area (*LGPN*iv 326). There are single instances of Σωτηρίδης in each of Bithynia, Mysia and Troas (*LGPN*va 421) followed by two in Karia and single ones in Kilikia and Lykia (*LGPN*vb 398). My previous comments on this name were overly brief (Fossey, 1991: 223), an oversight now remedied!

39. Σωτίω[ν] – IGvii 2297 (first recorded by Lolling). From *Kakósi* on the site of ancient Thisbe. Not a common name in Boiotia (or in most of Eastern Central Greece), it is seen in single examples at only a few places: Anthedon, Koroneia(?), Oropos, Thebai, Thespiai and Thisbe, the last three lying within the concentrated area of the cult; not very frequent in Attike (*LGPN*ii 422 lists only 21 instances) or the Aigaion (*LGPN*i 427–428 gives a single instance on Boiotia's neighbour Euboia, six cases on Thera, four on Krete, three on Samos, two on Kos and single instances on Andros and Thasos). It is comparatively better represented in North West and West Central Greece with five examples in Epeiros and seven in Illyria, then only two cases in Aitolia but a striking 22 in Akarnania, and in the Ionian islands a mere one on Korkyra but two on the small island of Ithaka, another two on Leukas and four on Kephalenia; turning to the Peloponnesos, after four cases seen in Akhaia, in the North West and thus close to Akarnania and the Ionian islands, and another three in Elis to the immediate South, we find another very thin distribution of cases: one in each of Argolis, Arkadia and Lakonia, echoed in a sense by a solitary case

in Southern Italy (*LGPN*iiia 419–420). There are no occurrences in Makedonia, Thrake and the Northern Black Sea but there is a single case in Bithynia at the South West part of the Black Sea and then in Ionia there are three cases (*LGPN*va 422) with a further four in Karia and a singleton in Lykia (*LGPN*vb 398–399). This name was previously treated by me (Fossey, 1991: 222) but too briefly; an improved discussion followed a few years later (Fossey, 2003: 77–78) and absence of any Thrakian connection is clear. The relevance of the other name (Λαμπρίς) inscribed in a second line above the relief is not clear but is obviously not in a form seen in the inscriptions; like Σωτᾶς (see below under Φιλλῆος) it should probably be left aside in the present context. We also note the absence of the word "hero" but the relief of a horseman permits the inclusion here of the first inscription.

40. *Τυγχάνων* – *IThesp* 1204. From Thespiai; same stone as Δόσιμος (*q.v.*). This name appears to be a *hapax*; Bechtel (1917) lists nothing at all like it and nothing even vaguely similar occurs in the enormous Attic onomastikon but the editors of Paul Roesch's *corpus* seem sure of the reading. It is, however, surprising that they appear not to have considered – or, at least, they make no note of doing so – the possibility that the first line, in fact, should be read as simply the name Ἐπιτυγχάνων or, in the dative case, Ἐπιτυγχάνοντι; this is a Greek anthroponym already attested at Thespiai (*LGPN*iiib 140). It is clear that we should expect the preposition ἐπί just as occurs with Δόσιμος in the second line, especially since the plural of ἥρωσι at the end of that same second line of the inscription implies that the text concerning the two was written at one time, as does the unique relief carving showing two facing horsemen each with his horse raising a foreleg over a common altar. The unity of the whole text is clearly shown by comparison with the case of the two inscriptions of *IThesp* 1203 [*IG*vii 2145 & 2147] plainly inscribed separately and each accompanying a separate relief carving, the two placed one above the other, each of a horseman but on the same stone and with the word ἥρωι *vel sim.* in the singular for each of Λυσίμαχος and Παράμονος. Dr Laurence Darmezin examined for me the squeeze of the inscription in the Roesch archive in Lyon and observed that there is in fact space for a second ἐπί between the elements as given in the publication (her email to me reads "Tu verras sur l'estampage qu'entre le premier 'ἐπί' et la séquence 'Τυγχ' il y a un espace assez grand [où on ne voit pas grand-chose malheureusement] pour un autre 'ἐπί', ce qui ferait 'ἐπὶ Ἐπιτυγχάνοντι' ...? Mais ce n'est vraiment qu'une remarque en passant"). Dr Darmezin is rightly cautious in expressing her passing though but we really should consider the possibility that her thought might well be correct; remembering that inscriptions were often painted on the stone first before final incision, we might envisage

the possibility that the text may have been originally painted onto the stone as "ἐπὶ Ἐπιτυγχάνοντι" and that, when the inscription was subsequently carved, the mason committed a haplography, perhaps thinking that the repeated ἐπί was a mistake in the painted version confronting him. A mason might be led to this conclusion especially since he would be thinking letter-by-letter and not concentrating on the whole text in the way that a painter of the original text might do so much more easily; after all chiselling a letter into the stone takes much longer than simply painting one. The second line of this text is still puzzling with its *hapax* unless our suggestion that "Δόσιμος" might be a misreading of Ζόσιμος (for Ζώσιμος) should ultimately prove to be correct (cf. above).

41. *Φιλλῆος* – *IG*vii 2167 (Körte 1878: 366, no. 109), *IThesp* 1198A. Exact provenience within Thespike not clear in *IG* but Körte specified *Xeronomí* and Paul Roesch reminds us that it was moved thence by the Archaeological Service to *Thívai* in 1968. In this spelling the personal name recurs but once in Boiotia, at Thebai (*LGPN*iiib 425; N.B. the present occurrence is missing therefrom, having been listed under Φιλλέας). In the form Φιλλέας, however, it is well attested in the area where the hero-horseman is at home: apart from a single instance at Tanagra, there are five cases at Thebai and seven in the Thespike with no others anywhere else in Boiotia (*LGPN*iiib 425). In Attike it occurs much more often with a single *lambda* (54 examples in *LGPN*ii 446–447, while *ibid*. 452 gives only two instances with double *lambda*); in the Aigaion single instances of Φιλλέας occur on Khios and at Khalkis on Euboia while Φιλέας is also found on Euboia, with nine examples at Eretria and single ones at Khalkis and Histiaia, being elsewhere limited to two instances on Kos and singletons on Oliaros and Rhodos (*LGPN*i 459). With the double *lambda* it is seen just twice in Aitolia, once in Akarnania and once again in Illyria (*LGPN*iiia 454–455), with the single *lambda* there are two isolated cases in Dalmatia but nothing else in North West and West Central Greece contrasting with a small distribution in the Peloponnesos: only one in Akhaia but seven in Argolis, four in Lakonia, three in Messenia and a princely 11 in Arkadia, with numbers dropping off again across the Adriatic where we find three at Taras alone in Southern Italy and just two at Tauromenion on Sikelia (*LGPN*iiia 448). There is just a solitary case of Φιλέας in the Northern Black Sea and another single instance of Φιλλέας in Makedonia but nothing in Thrake (*LGPN*iv 343 & 347); this version of the name occurs just once in the South Black Sea, in Pontos, and there is a single example also in Troas and another in Mysia but then in Ionia there are six (*LGPN*va 447) but in the rest of coastal Asia Minor only 10 examples in Karia and just one in Lykia (*LGPN*vb 425). The relevance of the second inscription on this stone (Σωτᾶ χρηστέ) is not clear and is hardly appropriate for what

we know about the inscriptions – a later reuse of the stone? My discussion (Fossey, 2014: 126) of the name Φίλλης was altogether too brief, hence the need for this fuller account.

42. *Φίλιππος* – *IG*vii 2175, *ADelt* 1971: pl. 193γ, *IThesp* 1199B. From *Xironomí*. The name is widely attested across Boiotia: of the 42 instances eight occur at Thebai and as many as thirteen at Thespiai; elsewhere in Eastern Central Greece it is much less common but Thessalia again sports 83 cases (*LGPN*iiib 423). In Attike also it is very well represented (*LGPN*ii 450–451 gives 157 cases); in the Aigaion 151 cases are spread across many islands, especially on Euboia, with five occurrences at Khalkis, 25 at Eretria, two at Histiaia and one at Karystos, 37 on Kos, 21 on Rhodos, 19 on Thasos, five on both Amorgos and Krete, three on each of Tenos, Imbros and Samos, followed by pairs on Kos, Lesbos and Naxos with finally single cases on Anaphe, Paros, Peparethos, Thasos and Thera (*LGPN*i 462–463). The name is particularly popular in North West Greece with 67 cases in Epeiros and a further 21 in Illyria; by contrast the totals of four for Akarnania, just a solitary one in Aitolia, another singleton on Kephalinia and a pair on Kerkyra are followed by a very uneven Peloponnesian representation with just four in each of Akhaia and Korinthia, seven in Argolis, a mere two in Elis but nine in Arkadia and then a somewhat surprising 24 in Lakonia and eight in Messenia; in South Italy there is another large total of 32 instances but in Sikelia the representation drops to a mere eight (*LGPN*iiia 451–452). It is hardly surprising that there should be a plethora of 208 cases in Makedonia but the name is also quite well represented with 31 instances in neighbouring Thrake and even the North Pontic area presents a further 22 examples of it (*LGPN*iv 344–346). 136 instances are spread along the South Black Sea area and North West Asia Minor: two cases in Pontos, 20 in Bithynia, one in Troas, five in Aiolis, 27 in Mysia, 40 in Ionia and another 40 in Lydia (*LGPN*va 449–450) with 60 in Karia, ten in Kilikia 27 in Lykia and four in Pamphylia (*LGPN*vb 426–427). Much too Panhellenic a name to suggest any specifically Thrakian connection.

The female names are far fewer:

43. *Ἀθηναΐς* – Μ(αρκία) Ἀθηναΐς *IG*vii 2658 (Körte, 1878: 373, no. 129). From Thebai. The relief depicts a woman standing by a horse in front of an altar. A second inscription is read below the relief carving (*IG*vii 2659) for Εὔχιος ἥρως, cf. above. Ἀθηναΐς is not a very common name in Boiotia being attested, in addition to a second occurrence at Thebai, also in single instances at both Oropos and Khaironeia as well as at Thespiai (*LGPN*iiib). Not surprisingly, given that it is a theophoric name based on the name of their patron goddess the people of Attike used it at least 48 times (*LGPN*ii 11), whereas in the Aigaion it is found in small numbers on several islands, including three at Eretria and two

at Khalkis on Boiotia's neighbour Euboia, four on Khios, four on Rhodos, two on Kos and single cases on Amorgos, Krete, Karpathos, Lesbos, Samos, Syros, Telos and Thasos (*LGPN*i 16). Apart from an isolated case in Illyria the name is absent from North West and West Central Greece and, in just the same way, a solitary occurrence in Argolis underlines the otherwise complete absence in the Peloponnesos; eight cases in South Italy and just two in Sikelia finish off the picture of the uneven but largely very thin distribution of this name in the Westerly direction (*LGPN*iiia 16). In a Northerly and Northeasterly direction we note seven cases in Makedonia, six in Thrake and five in the North Black Sea (*LGPN*iv 9). On the opposite side of the Black Sea there are four cases of this name in Pontos and another four in Bithynia, then one in each of Troas and Aiolis, followed by 12 in Ionia, nine in Mysia and seven in Lydia (*LGPN*va 9–10). Another case where I cannot understand variant accentuation of names drawn from unaccentuated epigraphic texts so I have combined the cases of Ἀθηναΐς and Ἀθήναις listed in *LGPN*vb10–11: 13 in Karia, six in Kilkia, four in Lykia and a single one in Pamphylia.

44. Ἀθηνώ – *IThesp* 1233A. From *Xeronomí*. The relief carving shows a woman standing with a horse and an altar. The stone had earlier been used as a simple tombstone with the name Σώτιμος *vel sim.*; in its second, quite different use for the horsewoman its was inverted and the relief and inscription then carved. The name Ἀθηνώ is very rare in Boiotia but, in addition to this Thespian incidence, it does reappear once at each of Tanagra and Thebai (*LGPN*iiib 16); it is absent from the rest of West and East Central Greece, from North West Greece, from Thessalia, from the entire Peloponnesos, as also from South Italy and Sikelia. Despite its theophoric connection to the patron goddess of Athenai, in Attike its presence is limited to just three known examples (*LGPN*ii 13) and, in the Aigaion, apart from one at each of Eretria, Histiaia and Khalkis (adjacent to East Boiotia and near to Attike, of course), there are merely singletons on Khios, Rhodos and Samos (*LGPN*i 17). There are only four instances of the name in Makedonia but none in Thrake and only a solitary one in the North Black Sea (*LGPN*iv 10). Absent in the South Black Sea, there is also only one instance in the whole of North West Asia Minor, in Ionia (*LGPN*va 11) but further South we find two in Karia and four in Kilikia (*LGPN*vb 12).

45. Εἰρήνη – *IThesp* 1206. From Thespiai, on same stone as Ἄγαθος and Δάμων *qqv.* The name is far from common in Boiotia but is attested twice at Thebai and once at each of Oropos, Plataiai, Thespiai and Lebadeia (the latter in the form Εἰράνα) and, while in Phokis there are five cases of Εἰράνα, in each of Ozolian Lokris and Megaris there is but a single instance of Εἰρήνη; in Thessalia, on the other hand, there are nine cases (*LGPN*iiib 130). The 35 examples in Attike (*LGPN*ii 139) are a significant presence for a feminine name, given the

predominance throughout the Greek world of recorded masculine identities. The picture is thin in the Aigaion apart from four at Eretria on neighbouring Euboia; otherwise we have three on Kos, a pair on Paros and mere singletons on Khios, Rhodos, Samos and Tenos (*LGPN*i 147). Absent in North West and West Central Greece (except for a single Εἰράνα in Illyria), its rarity continues in the Peloponnesos with but one example of Εἰρήνη in each of Korinthia and Argolis and two more in Lakonia, while Εἰράνα appears just once in each of Akhaia and Arkadia; across the Adriatic representation improves a little with eight cases of Εἰρήνη in South Italy followed by three cases of Εἰράνα and eight of Εἰρήνη in Sikelia (*LGPN*iiia 138). In the North and North East we find nine cases of the name Εἰρήνη in Makedonia, six in Thrake and three in the North Pontic area while Εἰράνα is found once in Thrake and twice in the North Black Sea (*LGPN*iv 115). On the South side of the Black Sea there are two instances of the name Εἰρήνη in each of Pontos and Bithynia and then in North West Asia Minor, one in each of Troas and Aiolis, two in Mysia and finally eight in each of Ionia and Lydia (*LGPN*va 151); in the rest of coastal Asia Minor we find 14 cases in Karia, seven in Kilikia and seven in Lykia (*LGPN*vb 129).

46. *Εὔταξις* – *BCH* 1922: 270–271, no. 108 & 1958: 142–143, no. 216*bis*, *IThesp* 1205. From Thespiai. The earlier editions only read an initial " ἐπί" and nothing else; the name was restored by Paul Roesch but is puzzling since no such name is attested in the Greek world. Bechtel (1917: 175) gives what should be a related masculine, Εὐταξίδας, from Lindos on Rhodos, the only case in the entire Aigaion, unless we count a single example of Εὐταξία on Kos (cf. *LGPN*i 185) and even this is completely absent from Eastern Central Greece and Thessalia, from Northern Greece and the entire Black Sea area, while a single case of Εὐταξία in Ionia is the only instance of anything on the same root in North West Asia Minor (*LGPN*va 183) but further South there are five in Karia (*LGPN*vb 167); similarly in Attike there are but three cases of Εὐταξία and nothing else related (*LGPN*ii 184): the same can be said of North West Greece with just three instances again of Εὐταξία alone in Illyria and a single one in Apulia for the whole area across the Adriatic, while no related name at all occurs in the whole of West Central Greece including the Ionian islands, or in the entire Peloponnesos (*LGPN*iiia 177). [One may wonder whether behind the reading Εὐταξίδει may lay the dative of the name Εὐπράξις?]

47. *Καφισία* – *IG*vii 2144 (Körte, 1878: 363, no. 99), *IThesp* 1191. From *Palaiópyrgos* in the entrance of the Valley of the Muses to the West of Thespiai. Names on the root Καφισ- are amongst the most common in Boiotia because of the presence of the river Kephissos and the Kephissian (= Kopaïc) Lake/Plain (Fossey, 1991: 63, 143 & 224; 2005: 141–142). The presence in neighbouring Attike of a homonymous river gives rise there also to a number of anthroponyms on

the root Κα/ηφισ- (*LGPN*ii 257–261) but only two are given as Κηφισία (*ibid.* 258). A few other names on the root occur at Eretria and Khalkis on Euboia and on Kalymnos (all three singletons), then a surprising six on Kos (*LGPN*i 254). This picture is completed with scattered cases: six in Korinthia, obviously near to both Attike and Boiotia, but representation within the Peloponnesos then drops off to single instances in Akhaia, Argolis, Arkadia, Lakonia and Messenia, while in North West Greece there is a complete gap and in West Central Greece we find only an isolated one in Aitolia, just as there is only one in South Italy and none in Sikelia (*LGPN*iiia 239). Although the current feminine is absent there we find a perhaps surprising presence of two instances of Κηφισόδοτος and one of Κηφισός in the Northern Pontic area while Makedonia furnishes four examples of Κηφισόδωρος – rather surprising so far from the bulk of the names on this root (*LGPN*iv 191); the Pontic examples could perhaps be seen as reflecting Boiotian interests in the area (cf. chapter 7 above). On the East side of the Aigaion there are a few isolated cases of related masculine anthroponyms: two of Καφισίας and one of each of Κηφίσιος, Κηφισίων, Κηφισόδοτος and Κηφισοφῶν in Ionia, two instances of Κηφισόδωρος in Mysia (*LGPN*va 245) and three more of the same in Karia (*LGPN*vb 230), all of them far from either Kephissos river. [N.B. In my previous listing of the Horseman-Hero names (Fossey, 2014: 126) I wrongly doubled the *sigma* in this entry.]

48. Λυκίσκα – *BCH* 1922: 268, no. 101 & 1958: 126, note 1. *IThesp* 1234. Apparently from a place called "*Misorákhi*" in the Thespike. The relief shows a standing woman with a horse. The name is extremely rare: in Central Greece the only other instance is at Triteia in Ozolian Lokris; the cognate masculine Λ(ιο)-υκίσκος also is not frequent but is encountered more often than this feminine for, within Boiotia, it is seen once at each of Khaironeia, Orkhomenos, Thebai, and Thisbe and twice at Thespiai (for all references cf. *LGPN*iiib 260–263). In Attike 36 examples of the masculine highlight the complete absence of the feminine seen here (*LGPN*ii 287) and the same holds good for the Aigaion but on an even smaller scale (*LGPN*i 290 lists, for Euboia, single cases of Λυκίσκος at Eretria, Karystos and Khalkis and merely three more single instances, one on each of Khios, Rhodos and Thasos). In North West Greece both masculine and feminine show much greater representation than anywhere else; in Epeiros 40 instances of the masculine are found alongside 14 cases of the feminine but otherwise in the rest of North West and West Central Greece, as in most parts of the Peloponnesos, while there are examples they are very infrequent; this means for the feminine just four cases in Aitolia and then only single examples in Illyria, Kephalinia, Kerkyra and Akarnania followed by none at all in the Peloponnesos unlike the male seen in small numbers at various parts in addition to the Epeirotic cluster: Illyria (8 cases), Dalmatia (1), Aitolia (9),

Akarnania (10), Kerkyra (2), Kephalinia (2), Ithaka (1), Leukas (1), Akhaia (3), Korinthia (1), Argolis (1), Arkadia (2), Elis (3), Lakonia (1) and Messenia (2) – clearly the masculine presence diminishes considerably in the areas where the feminine is absent; across the Adriatic the feminine is only present once on Sikelia and the masculine is seen 11 times on the same island but only four times in South Italy (*LGPN*iiia 278–279). To the North and North East, while there are no cases of the feminine, the masculine appears twice in Makedonia and four times in the Northern Pontic zone (*LGPN*iv 214). Similarly there are no cases of the feminine in either the South Black Sea or North West Asia Minor but there is a single occurrence of the masculine, Λυκίσκος in Bithynia, six in Ionia (*LGPN*va 273) with four in Karia, one in Kilikia and nine in Lykia (*LGPN*vb 265). The numbers given above make clear that the name in its masculine form particularly has a comparatively strong representation in Northwestern areas of Greece i.e. Aitolia, Illyria as well as Epeiros but this frequency does not extend to the North East and Thrake.

49. Νίκη – I would propose to restore *IG*vii 2152 (Körte, 1878: 371, no. 124), *IThesp* 1225 to read [Ἐ]πὶ Νίκη ἡρ[ωίδος]. Since the relief carving shows a man holding a horse by the reins this may be comparable to the tombstone of Ἀθηναΐς above, in that another woman's grave marker shows the horse being held not ridden. The name is rare in Boiotia, attested once at each of Thebai and Thisbe but not elsewhere in Eastern Central Greece although there are 12 instances in Thessalia (*LGPN*iiib 302); other names on the root Νικ- are, however, frequent enough in Boiotia (Fossey, 2005: 160–167). For the cognate Νεικίας see above. In Attike the name Νίκη is rather frequent for a feminine one (*LGPN*ii 331–332 lists 16 cases) and a certain number of cases of this same feminine name are attested across the Aigaion where – in a distribution largely of single cases, as on Anaphe, Andros, on Euboia (Eretria), Ios, Kalymnos, Kos, Lesbos, Naxos, Rhodos, Samos, and Syros – there is a surprising cluster of eight on Amorgos for otherwise the only places with more than one instance are Paros and Thasos with three each and Khios with two (*LGPN*i 332). In North West Greece there are two cases in each of Epeiros and Illyria and single cases are also seen on both Kerkyra and Kephalinia but there is a complete absence in West Central Greece as there is for most of the Peloponnesos, the only examples being one in Akhaia and three in Argolis; otherwise we may note a single occurrence on Aigina before passing across the Adriatic to find 33 instances in South Italy and eight in Sikelia (*LGPN*iiia 320). In Makedonia the name is quite popular with 40 cases whereas in Thrake there are only four instances and in the North Pontic zone the name recurs but twice (*LGPN*iv 251–252). Across the Black Sea there is just a single case of Νίκη in Pontos but then five in Bithynia followed by one in Troas, two in Mysia and 12 in Ionia, followed by a particularly large presence

of 18 13 in Lydia (*LGPN*va 333); the presence continues with 14 in Karia, eight in Kilikia thirteen in Lykia and two in Pamphylia (*LGPN*vb 316).

50. *Παραμόνα* – *IG*vii 2159, *IThesp* 12351, Church of Áyios Vlássios near village of *Palaiopanayiá* West of Thespiai. The relief shows a standing woman and horse. The inscription is longer than usual stating both the patronymic ([Νί]κωνος) and giving the name of her husband (not restorable) and *his* patronymic (Παραμό[νου]). For the distribution of this very common name, especially in the cognate masculine, cf. Παραμόνος above and Fossey, 2004: 172–173; for the feminine Παραμόνη cf. also two cases in Karia and one in Kilikia (*LGPN*vb 343).

51. *Σατύρ[α]/Σατυρ[ίνα]?* – cf. Σάτυρος above among the male names for the possibility of restoring rather a feminine name to accord with the depiction of a woman (taken to be a priestess) with a horse in the relief carving. Though absent from Thessalia and West Central Greece, in Boiotia both names are attested: Σατύρα once at Tanagra and Σατυρίνα once at each of Oropos and Thebai (*LGPN*iiib 374). Σατύρα occurs 13 times in Attike but Σατυρίνα never – although the masculine Σατυρίνος is there but only in two instances (*LGPN*iii 394); in the Aigaion we find one Σατυρίνα at Khalkis on Euboia close to Boiotia, two instances of Σατύρα on Rhodos and one on Tenos while there is a single Σατύρη on Samos all in contrast with the plentiful occurrence of the masculine (*LGPN*i 402–403). Σατύρα occurs just once in Makedonia but not in Thrake or the North Black Sea while in the last named area the masculine Σατυρίνος occurs just once but not the cognate feminine (*LGPN*iv 305). Also absent in the South Black Sea, the feminine Σατύρα and the masculine Σατυρίνος each occur just once in Mysia but the masculine Σάτυρος is seen 13 times in Pontos and twice in Bithynia, as well as five times in Aiolis and six in Troas with Ionia providing 16 cases and Mysia another seven (*LGPN*va 399) followed by an isolated case of each of Σατύρα and Σατυρῖνος in Karia (*LGPN*vb 379) but no instance of Σατυρίνα in coastal Asia Minor.

52. *Σεκοῦνδα* – *IThesp* 1236 (with no indication of exact find spot within Thespike, but if indeed it is the same stone as published by de Ridder, *BCH* 1922: 267 no. 99, according to a suggestion in the Roesch *corpus*, then it may derive from *Episkopí* at the foot of ancient Askra). Apparently the relief shows a woman and a horse but the description in *IThesp* is painfully laconic; this may be improved by reference to *BCH* 1922, 267 no. 99. The name (= Latin Secunda, of course) is most rare: without the *upsilon* it recurs once in Boiotia, at Oropos; it is absent in the rest of East Central Greece but, in the present spelling, it recurs twice in Thessalia where there are also a few attestations of the cognate masculine (*LGPN*iiib 375–376). In Attike, alongside of 39 examples of the masculine there is just one of the present feminine (*LGPN*ii 395) whereas, in the Aigaion, there is cluster of five feminine cases on Thasos and single ones

on Krete, Lesbos and Paros in a near absence of the masculine (*LGPN*i 403). In Illyria and Lakonia there are just two isolated instances of the name while the masculine, after a solitary case in Epeiros and a complete absence in West Central Greece, occurs just once in Korinthia and four times in Arkadia and nowhere else in the Peloponnesos; across the Adriatic there is only a single instance of the masculine in Sikelia but accompanied by a cluster of five cases of the present feminine, while in South Italy the masculine is seen twice and the feminine just once (*LGPN*iiia 391). After all this thinness of distribution it is a surprise to turn North and to find in Makedonia 13 instances of the feminine and 28 of the masculine, while in Thrake there are 18 instances of the feminine and only two of the masculine and in the North Pontic zone there are two masculine cases and one feminine (*LGPN*iv 306–307); the Makedonian concentration is striking. The incidence of 19 cases of the feminine in Lydia – accompanied by 21 of the cognate masculine – is also quite striking; there are similarly 11 cases of the feminine in Ionia, accompanied by 22 examples of the masculine; in the North West corner of Asia Minor we have one instance of the feminine and none of the masculine in Aiolis, two of the feminine and six of the masculine in Troas, three of the feminine and 21 of the masculine in Bithynia; in Pontos only the masculine is present, in two examples (*LGPN*va 399–400)l. In Karia we have eight cases of Σεκοῦνδος and four of Σεκοῦνδα, while, in Kilikia there are four of the masculine and three of the feminine (*LGPN*vb 380). One of the rare instances in this list of names where there is strong representation in Thrake (and neighbouring Makedonia, of course) though the name is clearly Greek/Latin, not native Thrakian.

53. [Σ]οφία – *IG*vii 2171, *IThesp* 1237. There is no indication of the exact find spot within Thespike. The relief indeed shows a standing woman with a horse but the editors of the text have read after her name the word "ἱερέα" (priestess) where one might usually expect the mention of "heroine". I am not sure, therefore, if this text belongs to the group. At the same time it appears that one of the other few women in this group may have been a priestess (cf. Σατύρα? above). The name Σοφία is very rare in Boiotia with just one example at Tanagra (in addition to this case at Thespiai) and in Thessalia with just one instance at Thebai while it is completely absent from the remainder of East Central Greece (*LGPN*iiib 382). The large onomastikon of Attike has only five cases listed (*LGPN*ii 402); the islands provide a mere one at Gortyn on Krete (*LGPN*i 410). Absent in North West and West Central Greece, the name occurs but once in the Peloponnesos, in Akhaia; there are two cases in South Italy and three in Sikelia (*LGPN*iiia 399). The infrequence continues in the North with just three cases in Makedonia and two in Thrake and none in the North Black Sea (*LGPN*iv 315). There are also none in the South Black Sea and only

one isolated case in the whole of Asia Minor, at Ephesos (*LGPN*va 408) with two in Karia and one in Kilikia (*LGPN*vb 387).

Roman names:
The conjunction of Π. Αἴλιος with the normal Greek name Σώσανδρος (*q.v.* above) and of Μαρκία with the equally Greek Ἀθηναῖς (cf. α above), just like Σεκοῦνδα have nothing to surprise us; they merely remind us of the Roman date of all these texts, as does the single Ῥοῦφος (above).

At the end of this onomastic analysis we see that it is often possible to discern names on the Horseman-hero inscriptions of Boiotia that have absolutely no Thrakian connection. On the other hand so many of the names are well attested in Boiotia and one particular case is eloquent in itself, that is Ὁμολωΐχος, a name that is so specifically Boiotian as to leave no doubt that there is here no Thrakian connection. The cult has to be taken as definitely Boiotian with purely local adherents – this despite the simple, reduced similarity to some Thrakian iconographic representations.

4 The Nature of the Cult in Boiotia

This group of tombstones has plainly a particular religious meaning and yet the Horseman-Hero himself remains anonymous while the deceased commemorated by the tombstones are, by contrast, so clearly named, as we have just seen. In his extensive listing of Boiotian cults Schachter (1981–1994) omits this cult, probably because of this anonymity and perhaps also because there are no recognizable sanctuaries of the cult (hence the apparent absence of votive texts?) by contrast with Thrake where many actual sanctuaries of the hero have been discovered (Samsaris, 1993: 326). So it is to this question of the nature of the cult that we must now address ourselves.

We should start off with an additional comment on that point in my previous account where I cited another relief carving on a slab from Thespiai that shows a horse with the left foreleg raised facing two standing figures, a veiled woman and a child; the inscription – first copied by Lolling and thus not in the list of Körte – was originally restored (*IG* vii 1813) to read:

[Ἱκ]έσιος εἵρωϊ ἀνέ[θεικε].

This dedication would obviously reinforce the idea of an anonymous hero; Paul Roesch, however, read the text a little differently (*IThesp* 283 bis):

Ἱκέσιος Ἑρμ(ῆ)
ἀνέθειχε

If this revised version of the text were correct it would raise the problem of the relationship between a horseman and Hermes. Examination of the photos in the Roesch archive in Lyon makes clear, *pace* the editors of Paul Roesch's posthumous *corpus* of Thespian inscriptions, that the horse in this relief did have a mount since, in addition to the muzzle and the lower part of the horse's body the left foot and lower leg of the horseman are preserved and it thus becomes obvious that this relief is to be compared with the relief carvings of horsemen-heroes; the position of the animal most resembles those of my type II, except for the absence of an altar beneath its upraised foreleg and it is to be noted that the altar only starts to appear in examples of type I/II. Overall the detail in the garments of woman and child are of a quality that would associate them rather with the sculpting on types I and II, thus perhaps early in the sequence of the reliefs. The inscription is difficult to read but on the photos I can see an obvious *omega* following the *rho* in the first line, thus confirming the original reading ἥρῶϊ rather than a reference to Hermes. What the relationship is between the Horseman-Hero and the other two figures in this relief is not clear; such extra figures only seem to appear in my types III/IV and IV. If it is now correctly read this stone gives us the one example in Boiotia of a votive to the Horseman-Hero. We might fairly assume that a votive would have been found near to a relevant sanctuary; if this is so then the find spot of this stone at Thespiai itself reinforces the overall impression that the attestations of the Horseman-Hero in Boiotia cluster around that city.

What then is the connection behind this strange separation of the cult in Boiotia from its homeland rather far away in the North? For the Thrakian examples of the Horseman-Hero, as we have earlier seen, there have been attempts to see syncretisms with various divinities of whom Asklapios is the clearest (Dontcheva, 2002; *pace* Dimitrova, 2002), where the presence of the serpent, very often on a tree, is seen as the most explicit symbol of the syncretism. In the Thessalian reliefs, in addition to horseman and altar as elsewhere, there is again a frequent presence of a tree with a snake wound around it suggesting a continued association with Asklapios this far South of Thrake itself. In Boiotia, however, the cult of Asklapios is not particularly widespread; there appear to be cult centres of this divinity at Orkhomenos, Khaironeia, Hyettos and possibly Lebadeia, all far outside the area of the horseman-hero attestations; otherwise a sanctuary seems to be attested at Thespiai and just possibly another at Thisbe (for all cases cf. Schachter, 1981: 107–110), both obviously in the area of the cult of the Horseman-hero. In any case there are no instances of tree and serpent in the Boiotian reliefs so any possible syncretism *here* with

Asklapios is rather to be discounted. At the same time it is interesting to recall that there was an isolated cult of Herakles in North West Boiotia where the hero was attributed with healing powers, like those of Asklapios; this probably means little in the present context but should not be omitted.

Other syncretisms have been suggested for the Horseman-hero. Recently Vayios Liapis (2011) presented the circumstantial evidence suggesting that there may be an identity with the Thrakian hero of Homeric times, Rhesus (cf. Samsaris, 1984: 285). Rhesus and his cult were, however, unknown in Greece proper. There is possibly a particularly close association with Dionysos (Samsaris, 1993: 329), whose cult is present in many parts of Boiotia (cf. Schachter, 1981: 172–195) but there is nothing of Dionysiac import in the iconography of the Boiotian reliefs of the Horseman-hero; similarly in Thrake evidence of syncretism with Apollon, specifically in the Roman period, was examined some years ago by Gočeva (1992) but in Boiotia we find no explicit associations of the two cults, although Apollon is also a commonly attested cultic presence there. In light of all this it seems that we should probably rather ask, in the first instance at least, whether there is not some other candidate for syncretism with the Boiotian cult of the Hero-Horseman – if it is felt really necessary to posit any sort of syncretism.

In my earlier account of the cult in Boiotia, I pointed to the fact that Boiotia – much like Thrake indeed – has one particular hero cult very much in evidence, precisely that of Herakles (for Herakles' cult in Thrake cf. some material discussed by Rabadžiev, 1986). What is more, as I showed in that earlier account, the distribution of Herakles cults in Boiotia corresponds closely to that of the Horseman-Hero attestations. The latter distribution is repeated on the map (Fig. 10). The possible association of the (originally Thrakian?) Hero-Horseman with the important Hero figure of Boiotian legend can profit from fuller examination here.

From our earlier discussion of the Herakles cults (chapter 4) it is obvious that a goodly number of the South-Centre-East group of Herakles cults can be seen to have an early date in at least Archaic times (Tanagra, Thebai, Thespiai and Khorsiai) or in times relating to the traditions of an even earlier situation (the two sites toward the Teneric plain and the Kabeirion). It is these last two with the traditional association to early times that should retain our attention for a minute. We note first of all that, in the one case, the epithet supplies a connection between Herakles and horses – "Hippodetes", binder of horses. The context is the hero acting in his traditional role as defender of his Theban birthplace against the Orkhomenians who did in fact establish control over North Western Boiotia in early times. Τοὺς ... Ὀρχομενίους φασὶν ἐς τοῦτο ἀφῖχθαι στρατιᾷ καὶ τὸν Ἡρακλέα νύκτωρ τοὺς ἵππους λαβόντα συνδῆσαί σφισιν τοὺς ὑπὸ τοῖς ἅρμασι – "They say that the Orkhomenians with their army came here and that Herakles overnight took their horses and bound them with their chariots." (Pausanias ix. 26, 1).

[There is another account of Theban-Orkhomenian conflict that refers to the second of the mythical cases listed earlier. Again Herakles is the defender of Thebai against Orkhomenian heralds sent by their king Erginos to demand tribute from the Thebans (Pausanias ix. 37, 1–3). Herakles treated the heralds in a graphically hostile way and brought to an end the question of tribute (Pausanias ix. 25, 4). There is no connection to horses here and the supposed sequence of these two mythical events is not clear.]

There is yet another conflict between the same two Boiotian cities, one in which, according to myth, Herakles again played the role of *prostates* of Thebai. The hero was credited with blocking the swallow holes in the Kopaïc plain causing its flooding and thus destroying the Orkhomenian economy (cf. brief discussion at Fossey, 1990: 86–87). Again, despite the common role of the hero there is no connection with horses. When, however, we turn to the story of Pyraikhmes, king of Euboia, who was at war with the Boiotians, we find horses again connected with Herakles: Πυραίχμης βασιλεὺς Εὐβοέων ἐπολέμει Βοιωτοῖς, ὃν Ἡρακλῆς ἔτι νέος ὢν ἐνίκησε· πώλοις δὲ προσδήσας καὶ εἰς δύο μέρη διελὼν τὸν Πυραίχμην ἄταφον ἔρριψεν – "when Pyraikhmes, king of the Euboians, was at war with the Boiotians Herakles, although still young, defeated him; he tied him to colts and thus had him torn into two parts which he threw away leaving Pyraikhmes thus unburied" (Pseudo-Ploutarkhos, *Synagoge Historion Parallelon Hellenikon kai Romaikon* 7).

These stories of Herakles concern his earlier life, that part associated with his birthplace and first homeland, Thebai (and Boiotia by association), but what of the second part of the hero's life, that involving his famous labours at the orders of Eurystheus of Tiryns? Among those 12 labours the eighth seems to bring various elements together. After Herakles had captured the Kretan bull in the seventh labour Eurystheus ordered him to get the man-eating mares of Diomedes. This Diomedes was not the homonymous hero known in the Homeric *Ilias*, later to become king of Argos in succession to his maternal grandfather Adrastos, another well-known figure from Greek mythology as king of Sikyon during his exile from Argos and thus from the stories of the *Seven against Thebai* and the *Epigonoi*. The Diomedes in question was rather king of a Thrakian tribe called the Bistones who lived South of the Rhodope Mountains near to Abdera (Plinius, *naturalis historia* iv. 11, 18) and he had accustomed his mares to eat human flesh. According to Apollodoros Herakles set off with a team of volunteers and sailed across the Aigaion to Bistonia where he and his companions overcame the people guarding the mares which they started to drive towards the sea. In the meanwhile the Bistones realized what was happening and sent soldiers to retake the animals. Since a fight was brewing Herakles freed himself to take part in it by entrusting the mares to his young friend Abderos. That youth was devoured by the same mares and, after defeating Diomedes, Herakles fed him to his own mares that were apparently tamed after feeding on the flesh of their very master. In commemoration of the unfortunate youth Herakles founded the city of Abdera and named it after him; he then sailed for Argolis with the mares on board but Eurystheus subsequently freed them. There are variations on the story but these are the main common elements. In short this story connects Herakles with horses and Thrake – a situation that could explain why the Horseman-Hero in Boiotia could logically be associated with Herakles.

There is, however, more to it than just that. Herakles' own connections with Thrake, and specifically with horses there, may very well be the key to this association but the mechanism by which the cult was introduced in Roman imperial times into such a restricted area, so isolated from the original is still puzzling. There is, however, a possible parallel for a postulated cultic introduction from the North while the restricted distribution of this hero cult, obviously largely connected with funerary matters, may find yet another parallel with funerary sodalities in a different part of Boiotia.

An inscription from the Serapeion of Thessalonike (*IG*x.2, 255) purports to provide the *aition* for the implantation from Thessalonike to Opous of a branch of the cult of the Egyptian deities Serapis and Isis in later Hellenistic times. Opous was, of course, the capital of Opountian Lokris, the country lying to the immediate North of Western Boiotia and thus a really close neighbour. This sort of *aition* must always be of suspect historicity but has to be taken with a larger grain of sand than usual in this case since there is a spread of related Egyptian cults in the areas immediately surrounding Opous (Fossey, 1990: 156). If nothing else, however, the *aition* does suggest that inhabitants of East Central Greece in Late Hellenistic-Early Imperial times would not find anything strange about the idea of a cultic importation into their area from the North end of the Aigaion.

More interesting is the presence in another part of Boiotia in Hellenistic and Roman times of a particular type of funerary text (Fossey, 1991: 190–195). The area of Tanagra in the Eastern part of Boiotia has produced a series of rather plain tombstones set up apparently by funerary associations (the words used are σύνοδος for the group and, in Boiotian dialect, for its members σουνθούτη) some of which carry compound appellations consisting of the name of a deity followed by the termination–ιασταί, such as Ἀφροδισιασταί. In a previous account of these texts I was able to show (Fossey, 1991: chapter 15) that such sodality names – though elsewhere without the funerary nature – occur in other parts of the Greek world with a particular distribution: the largest number of such names occurs on Rhodos but there are instances scattered across the Aigaion between that island and Eastern Boiotia, including particularly Delos. Of especial interest are the example at Pagai in neighbouring Megaris of the σύνοδος τῶν Ἡρακλεϊστῶν, and that of a σύνοδος τῶν Ἀμφιεραϊστῶν in the immediately neighbouring Northern part of Attike at Rhamnous showing that these names can be associated with heroes as well as deities proper and, in this connection most interesting of all, back in Boiotia itself, at Akraiphiai, is the existence of a σύνοδος τῶν ἡρῳαστῶν. The existence of the latter may prompt the thought that our Horseman-Hero tombstones in general might be the work of some sorts of funerary σύνοδοι although without necessarily the same type of -(ι)ασταί names. It is perhaps worth noting that only one of the earliest hero grave markers occurs in the area of Tanagra if the text is correctly restored which Dittenberger seems to doubt (*IG* vii 4238); otherwise there is no overlap in the distributions of these two groups of tombstones, the horsemen-heroes and the συνθύται, just as there is no chronological overlap. In fact, Samsaris (1993: 330–331) discusses briefly the existence of Thrakian "brotherhoods" of worshippers of the Hero and, interestingly enough, one of them, attested at Philippoi in Greek Makedonia, goes by the name "ποσιασταὶ Ἡρ(ωνος)" (*BCH* 1923: 64–67, no. 24).

5 Postscript

Many years ago Charles Picard (1956: 4) eloquently pleaded for a fuller accounting of the representations of the Horseman-Hero, especially outside Thrake: "Cela donnerait occasion de préciser divers elements essentiels à l'étude: extension dans l'espace du culte du Héros Cavalier; surtout, date et durée de sa prise au pouvoir; longevité, survivance". It is hoped that this account of the incidence in Eastern Central Greece may have contributed somewhat to a fuller eventual understanding of the cult.

It has also perhaps added to the ensemble of other cults with which that of the hero may have been subjected to syncretism. To Asklapios, Rhesos and Dionysos we have been tempted to add the suggestion of an association with Herakles.

We may add a Boiotian note to Picard (1956: 11) who says "On s'en apperçoit par la repetition des symbols spéciaux, don't le dispositive ne varie guère, et notamment pour cet element très important, parfois central, du décor traditionnel, que forment, l'arbre et l'autel, le serpent, le sanglier vu à mi-corps". We have seen that in Central Greece the only one of these elements that appears at all, and that appears regularly, is the altar. The Boiotian version of the cult was, from all points of view, iconographic and epigraphic, much simpler than elsewhere.

In an appendix to my previous paper on the Boiotian cult of the Horseman-hero (Fossey, 2014: chapter 7) I referred briefly to a discussion of some of the Boiotian relief tombstones depicting the hero published some years ago by Vasiliki Makhaira (2000), a discussion that was incomplete by nature having only dealt with the cases housed then in the Theban museum and taking no account of the examples still built into the walls of churches or gathered round them. Nevertheless, reflecting on the nature of her treatment that I then found far too complicated I now realise why she felt it necessary to create such a detailed typology; it was surely the result of her participation in producing that of the horseman-hero reliefs in general that appears in *LIMC*. There she and her co-authors were dealing with well over 2000 cases; that number inevitably allowed for an enormous variety of representations, as we mentioned above. To introduce such a typological approach with only just over 50 Boiotian cases must, as I pointed out, result in categories that sometimes contain but one example. We have seen that the small group of the Boiotian examples is notable for the simplicity seen in the reliefs, a simplicity that is better encompassed in an equally simple typology. The very isolation of the Boiotian group from their Northern cousins that we have been at pains to demonstrate implies that customers for hero relief carvings in Boiotia must have been little – if at all – conscious of the variety of representations to be found in Thrake and surrounding areas. The limited range of representations seen in Boiotia is surely a matter of personal requirements and, as I earlier grouped them, a matter of chronology.

Appendix 1: Synoptic List of Many of the Boiotian Horseman-Hero Reliefs

In the following list occur all the reliefs of Boiotian Horseman-hero for which I have details. This list allows demonstration of certain commonalities as well as rarities. For example we can see in the list that there are only four instances of the name in the nominative case. On the other hand 30 examples show the horse facing the viewer's left while on 21 it faces the opposite direction. Nine reliefs show the horse galloping, 20 show it prancing and 19 show it stationary.

Place	Körte #	*IGvii* #	Stand Gallop Prance	Right or Left?	Rider?	Leader?	Altar?	Name	"Hero"?	Nom./Dat.?
Tanagra	143		Gallop	Left	x			–	–	–
	145		Gallop	Right	x			–	–	–
Kaparélli	130	1715	Stand	Left		x	x	Μουσᾶς	x	Dat.
Thebai	93	2690	Prance	Left	x		x	..μάχος	x	Dat.
	94	2628	Prance	Left	x		x	Ἐπαφρίων	x	Nom.
	121		Stand?	Right	x			–		
	129	2658 &	Stand	Right		x		Μαρχία Ἀθηναῖς	x	Dat.
		2659						Εὔχιος	x	Dat.
	138		Stand	Left		x				
	142		Stand	Left		x				
	145		Gallop	Left	x					
		2629	?	?	x					
Kopai	120	2807	Gallop	Left	x			Μιχιάδης	x	Nom.
Hyettos	146		Prance	Left	x		x	Σωτηρίδης	x	Dat.
Thespiai	97	2178	Prance	Left	x		x	?	x	Dat.
	98	2123	Prance	Right	x		x	Ἀλέξανδρος	x	Dat.
	99	2144	Prance	Left	x		x	Καφισία θυτηςχ	x	Dat.
	100	2163	Prance	Left	x		x	Λυσι........	x	Dat.

(App. 1 cont.)

Place	Körte #	IGvii #	Stand Gallop Prance	Right or Left?	Rider?	Leader?	Altar?	Name	"Hero"?	Nom./Dat.?
		2164						Π. Αἴλιος Σώσανδρος	x	Dat.
		2165						Ὁμολόϊχος	x	Dat.
	123		Gallop	Left	2					
	125		Stand	Right		x				
	126	2126	Stand	Right		x		Ἀρίστων Δομέστικος	x	Dat.
	132		Stand	Left		x				
	133	2161	Stand	Left		x		Σάτυρος?	?	Dat.
	136	2130	Prance	Right?	x		x	Διόνυσος	x	Dat.
	144		Gallop	Left						
		1813			x			Ἱκέσιος	x	Nom.
		2141			x		x	Φίλλης	x	Dat.
		2167			x		x	Θεόγειτος	x	Dat.
		2172			x					
(Roesch, 1982: Pl. VIII.2)			Stand	Left	x		x	- - - ων	x?	Dat.?

(App. 1 cont.)

Place	Körte #	IGvii #	Stand Gallop Prance	Right or Left?	Rider?	Leader?	Altar?	Name	"Hero"?	Nom./Dat.?
		4244			x			Εἰρήνη	x	Dat.
								Ἄγαθος	x	Dat.
								Δάμων	x	Dat.
Mavromáti	104		Prance	Left	x		x			
	105	2128	Prance	Left	x		x	Βιοφίλημος	?	Dat.
Palaiopanayiá	96	2139	Prance	Left	x		x	Ζώπυρος	x	Dat.
	101	2131	Prance	Left	x		x	Εὔφανος	?	Dat.
	102		Prance	Right	x		x			
	103		Prance	Right	x		x			
	106		?	Left	x		x			
	127	2177	Stand	Left		x	?		x	Dat.
Livadhóstro	124	2152	Stand	Right		x	x		x	Dat.
Parapoúnyia	95		Prance	Right	x		x			
	118	2153 & 2154	Gallop	Right	x			Νεικαρίας	x	Dat.
								Σώταιρος	x	Dat.
	119	2124	Prance	Left	x			Ἀλεξίων	x	Dat.
Táteza	113	2173–4	?	Left	x		x		x	Dat.
	114	2143	Gallop	Left	x		x	Εἰστίων	x	Dat.
	117		Prance	Left	x		x		x	Dat.

AN UNUSUAL HERO CULT IN EAST CENTRAL GREECE 291

(App. 1 cont.)

Place	Körte #	IGvii #	Stand Gallop Prance	Right or Left?	Rider?	Leader?	Altar?	Name	"Hero"?	Nom./Dat.?
Karandás	122	2145	Stand	Right	x		x	Λυσίμαχος	x	Dat.
	"	2147	Prance	Right	x		x	Παράμονος	x	Dat.
Xeronomí	107	2137	Prance	Right	x		x	Εὔπορος	x	Dat.
	108	2140	Stand	Left	x		x	Θεόγιτος	x	Dat.
	109	2167–8	Stand	Left	x		x	Φίλλγος	x	Dat.
	110	2135	Prance	Right	x		x	Εἰσίων	x	Dat.
	111		Stand	Right	x		x			
	112		Stand	Left	x		x			
	116		Gallop	Right	x		x	?	x	?
	128		Stand	Right		x	x			
	131		Stand	Right		x	x			
Thisbe	134	2343			x		?	Κάλλιππος	x	
135	2362				x		?	Ῥοῦφος	x	Dat.
	2364				x		?	Σωστράτης	x	Dat.
Khóstia	unpublished				x		?	Γλαύκων	x	Dat.
Záltza	Rousset, 2012		Stand	Right	x		x	Εὐάμερος	x	Nom.

Appendix 2: Some Epigraphic Considerations

A. *IG* vii 2443

The stone is simply described as a large white marble piece in the museum of *Thívai* with apparently an inventory number of 21. It was copied by Lolling without any comment on its place of origin or any further details of the stone and its dimensions. The fragmentary text, as preserved, is simply a list in two columns of masculine names each with its patronymic.

Column a:

........ν [Δ]ήμωνος
[Δ]ομέστιχος Ἀρίστωνος
Σάων Εὐξένου
Παράμ[ο]νος Παραμόνου
[Δ]ι[ο]φάνης Ἀ[σ]κληπιάδου   5
[Π]αρθενο[κλ]ῆς Σιμίου
Ὁμολώϊχος Καφισίου
Ἀθηνόδωρος
Ἀθηνοδώρου
Εὔπλ[η]στος   10
Τραϊανοῦ
Σωτᾶς Σωτᾶ   [10]
Σωτᾶς Διονυσίου
Ἀφροδίσιος
Φιλίππου   15
Μίδιος Ζωΐλου
Παράμονος Ἀφροδισίου   [15]
Ἀφροδίσιος Παραμόνου
Μητρᾶς Δάμων[ος]
Κλεῖτος Ἑρμίου   20
[Ἀ]ρίστων Ἐπαφρο[δίτου]
[Ε]ὐφρόσυνο[ς] ......   [20]
[Ε]ὐφρόσυ[νος] ......
[Ζ]ωΐλο[ς]

Column b:

Παρθενοκλῆς Σιμα[λίωνος]
Δάμων Λυσάνδ[ρου]

Ἀλέξανδ[ρος] . . . .
Νικίας Μενά[νδρου]
Σωτήριχος Σ 5
Παράμονος Δημ . . . .
Διοκλῆς Διο . . . . . .
Παράμο[νος] . . . .
Πα . . . .
Ὀνήσιμος 10
-κας Ὀνη[σίμου]
Ποπ . . . . . .
Ἀρμ . . . . . .
Μα . . . .

Note: In the original text of *IG*vii the apparent line numbering in column a) was rather a numbering of the entries on the list. Thus Ἀθηνόδωρος Ἀθηνοδώρου, Εὔπλ(η)στος Τραϊανοῦ and Ἀφροδίσιος Φιλίππου are numbered as though both name and patronym occurred on the same line whereas, in reality, they are split with each on a separate line. It seems to be more appropriate, and more in accord with normal epigraphic practice, to number lines as they actually are on the stone. The "line numbers" of *IG*vii are given in square brackets.

Dittenberger draws attention to the presence of Roman names as indication of the imperial date of the text, more specifically the entry Τραϊανός indicates that it was not inscribed before the early second century CE; without this he would rather have been inclined to date the inscription to the preceding century. He groups this list with some other lists of names + patronyms, *IG*vii 2441, 2442, 2444 and 2445 of which the first two are ephebic lists, a nature that cannot necessarily be assigned to the current text. For those first two texts, carved on two sides of the same stone broken into three pieces (inventory numbers 116 & 60), we are given no details of colour, size or provenience but we do notice the complete absence of Roman names a detail that led Dittenberger to date them around the turn of the eras; we also note that the wholly Greek names in both present no peculiarities.

*IG*vii 2443 does, on the other hand, present some onomastic peculiarities. We have already commented on the relationship between the Ἀρίστων Δομεστίχου of a Horseman-Hero stone and Δομέστιχος Ἀρίστωνος here but let us remember that 2443 also contains one of the only occurrences of the very rare name Παρθενοκλῆς other than its appearance again on one of the horseman reliefs. It is, therefore, legitimate to consider the possibility that this stone may derive from Thespiai. We must remember that all we know of this stone is that it was already in the Theban museum when Lolling copied it and we are given no idea of its provenience.

B. *IG* vii 2444 and 2445

The other two lists grouped together in *IG* vii (2444 & 2445) were, like the one just examined here (2443), both dated by Dittenberger to the 2nd century CE and they contain all the nine cases of the name Σωτᾶς attributed to Thebai whereas the bulk (14 cases) of Boiotian occurrences of that name are found in Thespian territory with pairs of instances at both Oropos and Plataiai and single outliers at Khaironeia and Thisbe (*LGPN* iiib 397). It is perhaps interesting that the example from Thisbe (*IG* vii 2363) is a tombstone for two men both described as heroes. The text reads as follows:

Ἐπὶ ἥρωϊ
Συμφόρῳ.
χαῖρε
Σωτᾶ
ἥρως.

There is no record of the stone except that it is grey, and certainly no indication that it bore any relief carving of a horseman or anything else. It is clear, however, that the forms of the letters indicated in *IG* vii imply that the first two lines are a later (3rd century CE?) re-use of the stone for a second burial. Lines 3–5 should represent the original use (1st or early 2nd century CE?) of the stone combining the frequent formulation of χαῖρε with the deceased's name to which has been added the word ἥρως standing where the patronym might otherwise occur. It is noticeable that in the Horseman-Hero tombstones the patronym of the deceased is normally not given: his status as a hero is obviously what is important. It is the presence of the name Σωτᾶς in connection with hero status that is of interest here and may reinforce a little the idea that *IG* vii 2444 and 2445 may have some relevance not just to Thespiai but perhaps also to the cult there. [How distinction is made in *LGPN* between Σωτᾶς and Σώτας I am not sure since all cases come, of course, from unaccented texts; I have, therefore grouped them together for the preceding statistics.]

While one of the Oropian occurrences of the name is not especially remarkable, a simple 2nd–1st century stele giving the name of the deceased as Ἀρίστων Σωτᾶ (*EΩ* 555), the other case is particularly interesting. *EΩ* 565 dating to 3rd–2nd century BCE reads:

Βενδιδώρα
Σώτου.

A clear case that one Σώτας or Σώτος has given his daughter a name with definitely Thrakian connections. This does not imply anything clear for Boiotia since the cult of the Thrakian goddess Bendis had been introduced to Athenai in the later 5th century (Platon, *Politeia* 327a & Strabon, *Geographia* x. 3, 16 & 18) and, given Oropos' position of ambivalence, belonging at times to Attike, the origin of the name may well lie at Athenai, where there is indeed a single instance of the name (*IG*ii² 4866) in Bendidora daughter of Zenon and a certain foreigner (we may perhaps assume Thrakian) Βε(ν) διφάνης being honoured with Athenian citizenship in 401–400 BCE because of his participation in the defeat under Thrasyboulos at Phyle and Peiraieus of respectively a Spartan garrison and then the Athenian oligarchic forces (Osborne, 1981–1982: D6, B III); otherwise names on this root do not occur in Attike (*LGPN*ii 87). There is a variety of names on the root Βενδι- in Thrake and neighbouring Makedonia (cf. *LGPN*iv 67–68) but, despite the Thrakian origin of the cult of Bendis, these theophoric names are remarkably infrequent. Elsewhere in the Greek world, with the exception of a few cases on Thasos close to Thrake (Βενδις – accent unclear – and Βενδοῦς) and, a surprising single instance on Euboia (*LGPN*i 100), perhaps, like the Oropian instance, an introduction from Attike, such names are absent from the Aigaion, as they are from the Peloponnesos, West Central and North West Greece and from Sikelia and Magna Graecia with the exception of a solitary occurrence of Βενδίς in Loukania (*LGPN*iiia 90). Despite the appropriateness of the Thrakian association thus suggested we must recall that it is some 300–400 years earlier than the Horseman-Hero tombstones in Boiotia with which we are here concerned.

In a similar manner *IG*vii 2444 contains the only occurrence of the name Ἐπιτυγχάνων attributed to Thebai whereas this name occurs at least three times at Thespiai (*LGPN*iiib 140), to which may well be added a fourth case if our suggestion concerning the inscription on one of the Horseman-Hero reliefs (no. 40 in the onomastic list above) is correct. The only other apparent occurrence of the name in Boiotia is at Akraiphiai. It there occurs in a list of 38 φίλοι who, in the first third of the 2nd century CE, set up a marble statue, more than life-size, of a certain *agonothetes* Paramonos Aphrodeisiou who had been a Panhellenic representative (*BCH* 1898: 246–249 nos. 2, 3 & 4). Among these "friends" is named one Δημήτριος Ἐπιτυνχάνοντος. Although the dedication was officially approved ψηφίσματι βουλῆς καὶ δήμου at Akraiphiai, particularly given the honorand's panhellenic status, there is no especially compelling reason to regard **all** the friends as necessarily citizens of Akraiphiai and we might envisage a friend – or even several friends – from elsewhere taking part in honouring Paramonos and thus question whether this is indeed an Akraiphian occurrence of the name Ἐπιτυγχάνων. Roesch (1982: 184) underlines the difficulty of deducing any details concerning the nature of this group of friends so the question remains open but we must notice that it is precisely in this same list at Akraiphiai alone that occur all two of the Boiotian instances of the closely related and generally rare name Ἐπιτύγχανος (*LGPN*iiib 140). Were all three persons citizens of Akraiphiai or did they perhaps all come from elsewhere in the context of Panhellenic athletics? At least it must be clear that there is no reason not to entertain the idea that they might possibly have come from Thespiai thus putting there all the cases of these very rare and related names.

In just the same way *IG*vii 2445 contains the remaining two Boiotian instances of the name Παρθενοκλῆς. It is also perhaps worth noting that *IG*vii 2445 contains one of the very few Boiotian instances of the name Ἀγαθόπους, but this may mean little since the deceased with this name is specifically identified as a citizen of Khaironeia and we have already seen that the name, although very rare in Boiotia is common enough in some other parts of Greece.

Given this discussion of the names Ἐπιτυγχάνων and Ἐπιτύγχανος together with the statistics around the name Σώτας as well as the case of Παρθενοκλῆς and, to a lesser extent that of Ἀγαθόπους we may further ask whether these two lists, *IG*vii 2444 and 2445, although they are now located in the Theban museum, may not have come from Thespiai. Again we are given no details of the origin of these two stones but are simply told that they are "Thebis in museo".

In short we may legitimately consider the possibility that all three of these inscribed lists may have been taken from Thespiai or its immediate area to the museum at *Thívai* during the 19th century since they were all seen there by Lolling who seems to have provided Dittenberger with far less details concerning these particular stones themselves than was his wont. If they were so moved it is unlikely to have been at the same time since their inventory numbers (a rare detail apparently noted by Lolling) are quite different but this in no way denies the possibility that they were all so moved and ended up being presented side by side in *IG*vii because of the close similarity that they presented as lists of names, this being obviously the cause of their being grouped also with *IG*vii 2441 and 2442, although the actual nature of those two lists there as ephebic records is clear and such clarity is denied us for 2443–2445. It would be nothing more than pure speculation, of course, to do more than wonder whether these lists might have something, more than onomastic coincidence, to do with the cult of the Horseman-Hero and his adherents.

Appendix 3

After my first presentation of this subject at the Pontic Conference (Varna, Bulgaria, in 1997) my friend Prof Sergei Saprykin thought I should have taken into account the horseman reliefs of the North Pontic area and referred me to the then recent publication of those existing at the Hermitage in Saint Petersburg by Dr Lyudmila Davidova (1990). Dr Davidova kindly provided me with a copy of her catalogue and I was able to see that there is very little in common between these North Pontic reliefs and those found in Boiotia, not even very much in common with the material from the Balkans, let alone that from Thessalia, which we have discussed above. In the inscriptions that accompany the North Pontic reliefs the word ἥρως never seems to occur; we never see an altar, nor a tree nor the snake. Among the 58 funerary reliefs published by Dr Davidova only nine show a horseman (in one case two confronted horsemen).

CHAPTER 14

Another Boiotian Folktale

During the years of travelling around Boiotia and the surrounding areas I came across several interesting folk stories, two of which have received comment earlier in this volume (chapters 2 and 9). A further one may merit some discussion here.

In the very North West corner of Boiotia, in the hills that separate the North West bay of the Kopaïs from the Easternmost Phokian part of the Kephissós valley, is an isolated 11th century Byzantine church of Áyios Nikólaos ("Άγιος Νικόλαος στά καμπιά" = *Saint Nikólaos in the Fields*) to which the story refers. Its position is more exactly defined as lying in a saddle that separates two mountain masses. To the North West is Mt. *Palaiovoúni* on the Northern side of which is the fortified site of *Mavrókastro* (on the British Army Staff maps called *Makrókastro*) that Photis Dassios (1995) has argued was intended as a Phokian fort to block the otherwise concealed advance of Boiotian forces from the Kopaïs into the North East corner of Phokis in 347 BCE. To the South and South East is the long West-East ridge of Mt. *Doudouvána*, the ancient Akóntion, on the Eastern end of which is situated the akropolis of Boiotian Orkhomenos (Fossey, 1988: 351–356). The church is most easily and frequently approached from the village of *Tsamáli*; despite the rough terrain over which the road then ascends, the top of the saddle is surprisingly fertile with trees and bushes surrounding the church and cultivable flat ground around, green with vegetation. The church, and the monastery that once accompanied it (now only preserved in scattered remains) is dedicated to the Holy Martyr Saint Nikolaos the Younger ("ὁ Νέος"), not to the more usual Saint Nikólaos the "wonderworker", Bishop of Mira in Lykia, whose generosity, especially towards children, made him the archetype of Santa Claus.

The village of *Tsamáli* was renamed *Dhiónysos* on remarkably slender evidence – like so many results of the attempts by the Polítis committee (1909–1920) to purify the toponymia of modern Greece as part of a process of building national identity; some place names had already been changed on a piecemeal manner and others were to be so treated in the wave of anti-Turkish feelings after the Asia Minor catastrophe of 1921–1922 (Mackridge, 2009: 21–23). This particular renaming of *Tsamáli* gained some encouragement in the finding, by the Bavarian archaeologists previously working at Orkhomenos, of the remains of a small sanctuary of Classical date (5th and 4th century material only) by the village. The Bavarians suggested that this sanctuary might have been dedicated to Dionysos (Bulle, 1907: 116); there was no direct evidence to support this suggestion.

In addition to the fact that the pottery found there contained many fragments of drinking vessels not inappropriate in a Dionysiac shrine, the possibility of a dedication to Dionysos was obviously suggested by a passage in the 38th "Greek Question" of Ploutarkhos concerning the Minyades who, in insanity, tore apart and ate the son of one of them:

> καὶ μέχρι νῦν Ὀρχομένιοι τὰς ἀπὸ τοῦ γένους οὕτω καλοῦσι (sc. Ὀλείας = ὀλοάς). καὶ γίγνεται παρ' ἐνιαυτὸν ἐν τοῖς Ἀγριωνίοις φυγὴ καὶ δίωξις αὐτῶν ὑπὸ τοῦ ἱερέως τοῦ Διονύσου ξίφος ἔχοντος. ἔξεστι δὲ τὴν καταληφθεῖσαν ἀνέλει, καὶ ἀνεῖλεν ἐφ' ἡμῶν Ζωίλος ὁ ἱερεύς.
>
> *Even today the Orkhomenians call the women of this family "Oleias" ("muderers"). Every other year during the festival of the Agrionia it happens that they take flight and are chased by the priest of Dionysos with sword in hand; he is allowed to kill any that he catches, as the priest Zoilos in our time killed (one).*
>
> PLOUTARKHOS *Ethika* 299E–300A

There is no indication in the text of Ploutarkhos concerning the direction of the flight from Orkhomenos (or even that the women actually left the city) so the assumption that they ran in Westerly direction bringing them towards modern *Tsamáli* and the association of the Classical sanctuary with the cult of Dionysos may seem to have little, if any, justification. On the other hand, Schachter (1981: 180) has drawn attention to a line in Hesykhios (s.v. Ἀγριανέαιον· ἀκόντιον) suggesting that the flight may have taken place on (or along?) Mt. Akontion and thus, in fact, towards the West. The Agrionia were the main festival in honour of Dionysos at Orkhomenos. [It will be noted that I follow Schachter and others in understanding the words παρ' ἐνιαυτόν to mean "every second year".]

In the end, however, even if the women did flee in a Westerly direction there is just no indication as such that they came anywhere near to the site of the later Byzantine church of Áyios Nikólaos stá kambiá but the possibility remains and it is interesting to see what, if any, association there may be between this bizarre Orkhomenian rite and an equally strange story that concerns the church.

First, however, it will be useful to consider the story of this Saint Nikólaos the Younger. This is conveniently provided on the webpage of the Holy

(Greek Orthodox) Diocese of *Thívai* (www.ecclesia.gr/greek/dioceses/Thebes/photos_nik_neos.html visited on 8th August 2015) within whose ambit the church lies.

Nikólaos, who lived probably in the 7th–8th centuries CE, came from the East (exactly where is unspecified); there, despite his religious nature from an early age, he had had a distinguished military career as a young officer rising to high rank. At one point his king sent him to Thessalia where he went to Mt. *Vounéni* and there encountered a group of (in one version 12, in another 10) monks and hermits who welcomed him into their midst whereupon he abandoned his former life and his ranks and privileges. Sometime afterwards pagan Avars invaded Greece laying waste and killing [The Avars occupied the Peloponnesos from 587–805 CE according to the *Chronicle of Monemvasia* (cf. convenient summary by Davidson and Horvaith, 1937) in addition to their control of North Greece, Thessalia, Central Greece including Attike, possibly established before that of the Peloponnesos]. Despite being warned of their danger Nikólaos and his fellow monks awaited their fate and when the Avars arrived they beheaded the other monks but when they saw that Nikólaos was an attractive man they tried to persuade him to join in worship of their pagan idols. The saint refused despite the use of much torture in an effort to persuade him; they lashed him so hard that his body turned red and in the end, tying him to a tree, they pierced him with arrows and spears, finally beheading him too. At the place of his torment, at *Vounéni* near Larissa it is said that blood flows from the trunks of some trees, being those where Nikólaos' fellows were killed; this blood floods the roots of a cut tree which is said to be that to which the saint himself was tied when tortured and executed.

The website of St. John the Baptist Russian Orthodox Cathedral in Washington DC (www.stjohndc.org/Russian/saints/SaintsE/e_9905c.htm consulted 6th September 2015) gives an alternative version. This version says that it was the Emperor Leo VI (The Wise) who sent Nikolaos to Larissa in Thessalia with 1000 soldiers and that it was Arabs who invaded Thessalia in 601 slaughtering the populace. Nikolaos apparently realised that he and his troops could not defend the city that he ordered to be evacuated followed by a military retreat. Nikólaos himself, with a small troop of his soldiers joined a community of 12 monks on a mountain top *c.* 12km away from Larissa. When the enemy arrived Nikólaos and his soldiers resisted them but were taken, imprisoned and tortured; most of them were killed. Nikolaos himself fled and hid in cave in a forest near to the settlement of *Vounénissa*; near to the cave was an enormous oak tree. Finally discovered by the Arabs he was imprisoned; he steadfastly refused to renounce his Christian faith and so the Arabs killed him by stabbing him with his own spear. Later when the bishop was able to return to Larissa he had the relics of these martyrs transferred to the city; the remains of Nikolaos were miraculously found in a hollow in the trunk of the oak. The oak is said to exist still and every year on the feast of Nikolaos' martyrdom (9th May) services are held next to it and from it flows forth a blood-like liquid with healing qualities.

Despite the differences between these two versions there are principal points in common: the Eastern origin of the saint; his being sent as a military commander to Thessalia; the foreign invasion of Thessalia; the connection with *Vounéni*; the joining with a small monastic community; the torture and subsequent execution of his companions; finally his own capture, torture, refusal to abandon his faith and his execution with a spear and the role of a tree that subsequently produced/produces a blood red liquid.

The website of the Theban diocese also records a bizarre story concerning the church itself, the Boiotian Folktale of the title of this chapter. Stones were being brought by boat from *Aidipsós* on Euboia to *Atalándi* thence to be hauled across land for the building of the famous church in the monastery of Ósios Loukás by the site of the ancient city of Steiris in Eastern Phokis (cf. Fossey, 1986b: 32–34). Saint Nikólaos demanded that every convoy of stones leave one here at *kambiá* for the building of his church; I suspect that this detail in the story may have been caused by the fact that the church is built with many worked marble and other blocks with drafted corners and anathyrosis that have, in fact, all the appearance of *spolia* from some ancient site, especially the upper part and capital of an unfluted Ionic column standing near the church. We may note that the obvious route for the transport of the stones to Ósios Loukás would have passed by yet another church of the same Saint Nikolaos the Younger at the hamlet of *Paróri* some 13–14km West-by-North of the church here being discussed; *Paróri* lies close to the pass between the last basin of the river Kephissos before the Kopaïs and the preceding one containing Elateia and Amphikleia; the church is dated to the later (?) 12th century and has been described and discussed at length by Mamaloúkos (1988).

When the story continues we learn that an architect and his assistant were responsible for building the church *stá kambiá* and that, when the master architect saw there that the side that had been constructed by his assistant was finer than what he had built himself he was jealous and pointed to a "defect" in its walling to which the assistant climbed up with a ladder whereupon the master pushed the ladder so that the assistant fell to his death. On the spot grew up a fig tree the sap of which, when branches were cut, ran red (blood). [The website points out that the fig tree is no longer there.]

A slight variation of this story was recounted to me by local shepherds in March 1967. In this version the church was actually built only by the former pupil of the master architect who built the church at Ósios Loukás and that the master came to inspect the work of his ex-pupil; his jealous reaction and its result are the same as in the official story except that the pupil is said to have died as his head hit the ground and that from his head flowed blood from which sprang a tree that had blood-red fruit.

It is interesting to look now at the story of Adonis since it may appear that there are similarities with the two stories already outlined.

The myths of Adonis are complex and we need only summarise the relevant points here since a full account has been given by Jutta Weisser in her article in the *New Pauly* (Suppl. 1–4, *The Reception of Myth and Mythology* on "Adonis"). The growth of a tree with red fruit in the case of Áyios Nikólaos is paralleled by the growth of either the pomegranate tree with its red fruit or other plants with red flowers springing from the blood of Adonis (Graves, 1992: 95). In fact a tree enters the story of Adonis earlier when his mother was said to have been turned into a myrtle tree by the gods to save her from the murderous intent of her father whom she had deceived into an unknowing incestuous relationship with her; the result of the illicit union, Adonis, was born either when the father's sword split the tree or when it was gashed by a boar; stories of his origin connect him to both Syria and Cyprus. The boar introduces another aspect of jealousy; it was either Ares (the husband of Aphrodite jealous of his wife's love for Adonis) who took on the shape of another boar in order to kill Adonis, or it was Apollon who played the same role and whose connection may relate to Adonis' love of hunting or to the variant in the story where his sister Artemis (also a deity of the hunt) was on occasion said to be involved in the jealousy network that surrounded the young Adonis. The complexity is furthered by the connection of the pomegranate to Persephone, one of the jealous contenders for the control of Adonis. Persephone's alternating sojourns on earth and in Hades are like those of Adonis who, it was decided (by Zeus or a delegate), was to spend time shared between Persephone (in Hades) and Aphrodite (in the world), the contending goddesses. Both these figures thus "explain" the rotation of the seasons and are agricultural spirits of a sort.

When we compare the three accounts we see several points in common to all three and others that are common to at least two of them. In the Boiotian folk story the jealousy of the master architect towards his former pupil recalls the jealous rivalry between Aphrodite and Persephone for possession of the beautiful young Adonis. Just as the beauty of the new church was the cause of the jealousy so was the beauty of the baby Adonis the cause of the rivalry between the two goddesses. Furthermore we may suppose that the Avars (or Arabs), noted for their implacable nature as fearsome warriors, may be considered to have been envious of the saint's fortitude in the face of torture. In all accounts we see that jealousy leads to the death of a young man who is either beautiful himself (Adonis was, of course, famous for his beauty and the saint is specifically described as being beautiful) or has produced something of beauty (the church). The death of the youth produces blood (in connection with the head in the case of the saint and the architect) which gives rise to a tree with red sap and/or red fruit (in the case of Adonis sometimes it is plants with red flowers). In the case of the saint and Adonis the young man comes from the East; exactly where is not specified in the case of Nikólaos, whereas Adonis derives either from the Levant (supposedly from Theias, king of Syria as his father) or from Cyprus (by way of another supposed father, Kinyras, the founder of Paphos). It is clear that trees play a significant part in several aspects of the stories: the saint and his fellows are tied to trees to be executed; the bloods of both Adonis and the builder give rise to trees and Adonis himself was born from a tree. Trees are plainly appropriate elements in the story of an agricultural figure like Adonis.

We may finally return to the myth of the Minyades that we cited early on in this account. The priest of Dionysos pursued certain women of Orkhomenos, perhaps in a Westerly direction, wielding a sword, in much the same way as Adonis' mother Smyrna was chased by her sword-bearing father; both swordsmen had murderous intent. An alternative account of the end of Adonis was that he was carried off by Dionysos and the fact that it was only women who were pursued by the priest may remind us that the rites of Adonis were celebrated by women alone, at least if we judge from Athenai. [Perhaps we should recall that there was another story of female insanity associated with the cult of Dionysos located in Boiotia; it is that of the *Bakkhantes* in Euripides' play where women of Thebai in a wild frenzy on Mount Kithairon (cf. Akontion?), carried out the murder of the son of one of them (the king Pentheus) much as one of the original Minyades had provided her son to be killed and devoured.]

The question of the continuity of religious ideas and associations from pagan through to Christian times in the Greek and wider Mediterranean world may raise doubts; it is clear, nevertheless, that there are too many examples of continuity of religious nature at ancient places of worship overlain by Christian churches. Here at Áyios Nikólaos we have seen reason to suspect that there are sufficient elements in common between the story of the saint and that of Adonis. We have also seen that between the stories of both the saint and Adonis on the one hand and the account of the fate of the builder of the church of Áyios Nikólaos on the other there is so much in common when the overall recitals are broken down into their constituent elements that this is most unlikely to be coincidence. Our conclusion must be that there is every reason to suspect that the place occupied in later times by this Byzantine church may well have had a role in rites of Adonis practiced in antiquity by the women of Orkhomenos. It must be repeated that this does not imply the existence of a physical sanctuary of Adonis, a concept apparently otherwise unknown in Greece. Nonetheless perhaps the cult of Adonis should be tentatively added to the list of Boiotian cults.

CHAPTER 15

The Leuktra Epigram (*IG*vii 2462)

S.M.L. Stringer

One of the somewhat unusual features of the Leuktra epigram is its choice of the plural τροπαῖα for what is generally assumed to commemorate a single battle. Translators and commentators vary in their treatment, but the general consensus seems to be that at least one of the two instances of the plural should in fact be interpreted as a singular. Thus Frazer (1898, iii: 435–6) translates "trophies" at line 2, but "trophy" in line 5, while Egger (1878: 25) in French gives "trophée" in both instances, but his Latin version, like Frazer's, renders "tropaea" in line 2, and "tropaeum" in line 5. Egger further argues that the two lines refer to two different objects, one constructed before the battle, involving the shield of Aristomenes, and the other the "trophée definitive" erected after the victory, but he does not discuss the issue of number in either line (*ibid.* 26–27). Buecheler (1877: 479–481) interprets the τροπαῖα as referring the first time specifically to an enemy spear that Xenokrates won in battle, and the second time to a "Siegesdenkmal" which incorporated that spear. Presumably, the authors have assumed that the plural is simply used *metri causa* by a poet who does not appear particularly skilled with the elegiac metre he has chosen. It is true that the adjective νικαφόρον that modifies τροπαῖα is probably easier to handle in the plural, since the singular νῑκᾰφὄρὄν could be only placed before a word beginning with the vowel to avoid a cretic. At the same time, it is certainly *possible* to employ the singular, e.g. ἔγχει καρύσσει νικαφόρον ὧδε τροπαῖον. It would be desirable, therefore, before one concludes that the plural τροπαῖα is simply referring to a single trophy, to be able to demonstrate that the plural was indeed, at least sometimes, used interchangeably with the singular. Otherwise, the alternative possibilities, namely that two or more trophies were erected to commemorate a single battle, or else that two or more trophies were erected to commemorate two or more distinct battles, would appear to deserve serious consideration. [A dual form of τροπαῖον is only attested twice in the *Thesaurus Linguae Graecae*, both times in the writings of Nikephoros Basilaka, a twelfth century orator.]

Only Tuplin (1987: 96–97) explicitly addresses the question of whether one or several trophies is, in fact, intended in the epigram, and whether, more generally, the interpretation of τροπαῖα as a singular can be defended. After noting that it is "possible to find a number of passages in which τρόπαια may be assumed actually to refer to a single trophy" (*ibid.* 97), he gives, as examples of such passages, Thoukydides iii. 112, 8; Euripides *Andromakhe*, 694; *Herakleidai* 786; (?) *Hiketides* 647; *Phoinissai* 572; *Orestes* 712; *Antiope* frag. 9. He then concludes that "it is certainly preferable to follow earlier interpreters in assuming that the same is true here" (97). He does not, however, offer any reasons why such an interpretation is preferable. Each of the examples brought forward in support of a singular meaning for τρόπαια will be discussed in greater detail below. None are without difficulty. Tuplin is, of course, only addressing the issue in passing, as an adjunct to more general historical problems, but the question deserves more detailed consideration in its own right. We shall, therefore, examine the use of the word τροπαῖον, particularly in the plural, in order to determine whether or not there are precedents for the use of a plural form referring to a singular object. [*A priori*, such a use would not be particularly strange. Given that the trophy was composed of a number of pieces of armour, one might well designate it by a plural form, just as ὅπλα can refer collectively to a single suit of armour.] Examples were collected by searching the *Thesaurus Linguae Graecae* for all plural forms of the lemma τροπαῖον from the earliest occurrences to the end of the third century (up to but not including Polybios, as it turned out). A less exhaustive examination was also made of the singular forms.

The word τροπαῖον is not Homeric; nor does it occur in any of the archaic poets. The word itself, and presumably the custom it reflects, appear to belong to the Classical period of the city-state and hoplite warfare. More puzzling is the absence of τροπαῖον in the writings of Herodotos, given that trophies erected during or after the Persian Wars (at Marathon, Salamis and elsewhere) are frequently mentioned by later writers, sometimes even in terms that seem clearly to refer to an actual physical, and still visible, monument. These references to Persian Wars trophies are most frequent in 4th century writers (Xenophon, *Anabasis* iii. 2, 13; Lysias, *Epitaphios* 20, 4; Isokrates *Arkhidamos* 54 & *Plataikos* 59; Georgias *frag.* 5b; Demosthenes *peri tes parapresbeias* 311 & *Olynthiakos* 3, 24; Aiskhines *peri tes parapresbeias* 74). In any case, the word τροπαῖον, like the adjective τροπαῖος, seems to be first attested in the poetry of Aiskhylos (*hepta epi Thebas* 277) and occurs quite frequently in both poetry and prose from then on.

In the majority of cases, a plural form clearly refers to two or more trophies. The most straightforward instances of the plural are those where the number of trophies is specified, either by a numeral, or else by an adjective such as πολλά, or τοσαῦτα (Thoukydides v. 3, 4; vii. 24, 1; vii. 45, 1; Euripides *Troiades* 1222; Andokides, *peri ton mysterion*, 147, 2; Xenophon *Agesilaos*, 6, 3; *Anabasis*, vii. 6, 36; Lysias, *peri tes demeuseos tou Nikiou adelphou epilogos*,

3; *peri tou me katalusai ten patrion politeian Athenesi*, 10; Demosthenes, *pros Leptinen*, 76; 78; 80; *peri syntaxeos*, 26; *kata Meidiou*, 170; Platon, *Menexenos*, 243a; Aristodemos, *FGH* 2a,104, F frag. 1, line 225). The plural is also unambiguously plural in meaning when the number is not specified, but the trophies in question commemorate more than one battle (Platon, *Menexenos*, 245a; Lysias, *peri tes demeuseos tou Nikiou adelphou epilogos*, 3, 5; Aristophanes, *hippeis* 521 [of comic victories]; Isokrates, *epistle* 9, *Arkhidamoi* 3.6). Thoukydides (iv. 134, 1 & vii. 41, 4) describes two battles in which both sides claim victory and set up a trophy; once again, the plural clearly refers to two distinct monuments.

Plural forms can also safely be interpreted as having a plural meaning in passages where the author is referring collectively to all the τρόπαια raised by an individual in the course of his career (e.g. Demosthenes *pros Leptinen* 83), or by a city in the course of its history. Those passages referring to the trophies raised during the Persian Wars have already been listed. One also finds more general references to the trophies of a city's historic victories (Demosthenes, *peri tes Rhodion eleutherias* 35; *kata stephanon* 209 & *peri tes parapresbeias* 16; 307). Unsurprisingly, such references are found chiefly among the orators.

There are a few examples where it is not strictly *necessary* to interpret τρόπαια as plural but, even leaving aside the fact that it is a plural form, this seems the best interpretation. When Xenophon reminds the soldiers that to them, though few in number, the gods "τρόπαια ἵστασθαι διδόασι" (*Hellenika* ii. 4, 15) the present tense seems to imply a general statement, proven by repeated victories. Similarly, Xenophon's description of the eagerness a young man would feel at the possibility of winning glory not only for himself and his family: "ἀλλ' ἱκανὸς γενήσεσθαι δι' ἀνδραγαθίαν καὶ φίλους εὖ ποιεῖν καὶ τὴν πατρίδα αὔξειν τρόπαια τῶν πολεμίων ἱστάμενος" (Xenophon *Symposion* 8. 38) seems stronger if one assumes that the possibility of raising many trophies in a series of campaigns is envisaged, and not only one single exploit. In recounting Aristeides' voluntary poverty, Theophrastos, cited by Ploutarkhos, explains:

καὶ τὴν ἀπὸ τοῦ πένης εἶναι δόξαν
οὐδὲν ἧττον ἀγαπῶν τῆς ἀπὸ τῶν τροπαίων διετέλεσε

THEOPHRASTOS, Fragment 136, section 1, line 10

As Aristeides was a commander in numerous successful battles, including both Marathon and Salamis, there seems no good reason to interpret the plural form as a singular, and so limit him to a single trophy.

Less clear-cut are the cases in which τρόπαια is used primarily figuratively, by a sort of metonymy for the victory itself. Such examples occur primarily in tragedy, and Euripides in particular seems to be quite fond of such imagery. Most of these examples require some individual comment. The situation is simplest when both the "trophy" and the "victory" are metaphorical. For example the chorus of *Elektra* (1172–1174) remarks:

ἀλλ' οἵδε μητρὸς νεοφόνοις ἐν αἵμασιν
πεφυρμένοι βαίνουσιν ἐξ οἴκων πόδα
τροπαῖα, δείγματ' ἀθλίων προσφαγμάτων.

In this case, it makes no sense at all to inquire whether one or more trophies are meant, as the chorus is referring to the bloodstains that show Elektra and Orestes have been successful in their murder. Similarly, when Menelaus cautions Orestes that

οὐ γὰρ ῥάιδιον λόγχηι μιᾶι
στῆσαι τροπαῖα τῶν κακῶν ἅ σοι πάρα
Orestes 712–713

the triumph envisioned is not a military victory, and neither the spear-point nor the trophies can be taken literally.

In other cases, the victory is indeed a military one; however, the action of erecting trophies appears to be more or less metonymous for conquering, and the actual physical object or objects, if they exist at all, are of secondary importance. Euripides appears particularly fond of this expression. In many cases, the trophies, and the victories they would commemorate, are still in the future, which makes the question of their number still further beside the point. A fragment of Euripides (Fragment 10 line 9), as restored by Page, proclaims: ὡς ἢ] θανεῖν δεῖ τῶιδ' ἐν ἡμέρας φάει,/ ἤ τοι] τροπαῖα πολεμίων στῆσαι χερί. Presumably, if the speaker is victorious, he will indeed raise a trophy or, less likely, trophies, but the issue is that he must either conquer or die in the coming battle. It would seem pedantic as well as risky to attempt to use such a passage to support the use of the plural to designate a single τροπαῖον. Five of the seven examples adduced by Tuplin to support a singular interpretation of τροπαῖα seem to fall precisely into this category. Similarly, when the chorus of suppliants enquire: πῶς γὰρ τροπαῖα Ζηνὸς Αἰγέως τόκος / ἔστησεν οἵ τε συμμετασχόντες δορός (*Hiketides* 647), they are in fact inquiring about how Aigeus obtained the victory, not his method of constructing trophies, as the messenger's reply makes clear. In Euripides' *Helene* (1380–1381), Menelaos arms himself, "ὡς βαρβάρων τροπαῖα μυρίων χερὶ / θήσων". The thousand barbarians in the ship with him are certainly an exaggeration, and the battle with the sailors is clearly not an occasion for setting up an actual trophy. Despite the very fragmentary context, "μη.[... Ἐρεχθ]εὺς ὡς τροπαῖα [/ _ἔστη[σε χώρ]αι τῆιδε βαρβά[ρ" (Fragment 65, 12–13), also appears to fall into this category.

In cases where the metaphorical trophy/trophies do not exist even metaphorically, the distinction between singular and plural is still less salient. When the dying Herakles vaunts that "κ' οὐδεὶς τροπαῖ' ἔστησε τῶν ἐμῶν χερῶν," (Sophokles, *Trakhiniai*, 1102), he is, of course, principally saying that no man has ever defeated him. Even if one considers, however, the literal sense of his words, substituting the singular for the plural would make little difference. "No one has set up trophies" and "no one has set up a trophy" come to very much the same thing.

In other cases, τροπαῖα stands for something more specific than the act of conquering. When Herakles

> εἷρπε κλεινὴν Εὐρύτου πέρσας πόλιν,
> νίκης ἄγων τροπαῖα κἀκροθίνια,
> SOPHOKLES, *Trakhiniai* 750–751

he is clearly removing physical objects. He is not, however, likely taking away actual trophies he has erected, which would be both cumbrous and impious, but rather carrying off the arms he has stripped from his enemies; this is the explanation given by Jebb: "τροπαῖα, the arms taken from the enemy" and "ἀκροθίνια, the booty" (1921). τροπαῖα is therefore used in the plural, as σκῦλα is, to refer to a collection of individual items.

When Iokaste asks Polyneikes:

> ... τροπαῖα πῶς ἄρα στήσεις Διί,
> πῶς δ' αὖ κατάρξηι θυμάτων, ἑλὼν πάτραν,
> καὶ σκῦλα γράψεις πῶς ἐπ' Ἰνάχου ῥοαῖς
> EURIPIDES *Phoinissai* 573–5

she is not inquiring how he will obtain victory. Nor, however, is she interested in how he will physically set up trophies, or make sacrifices afterwards. Rather, she wishes to know how, morally, he will celebrate or consecrate a victory obtained fighting against his brother and his native city. The plural in this context seems likely influenced by its proximity to σκῦλα, regularly plural, and θύματα, plural since any generous sacrifice would include more than one victim. Also, since there would be battles between champions at each of the seven Theban gates and not all victorious combatants would necessarily belong to the same side, allowance should be made for a plurality of victors and thus of commemorative markers.

A similar passage occurs in Aiskhylos, also in the context of the brothers' combat before Thebai. Eteokles vows, if he is victorious, "θήσειν τροπαῖα πολεμίων δ' ἐσθήμασι / λάφυρα δαΐων δουρίπληχθ' ἁγνοῖς δόμοις / στέψω πρὸ ναῶν πολεμίων δ' ἐσθήματα" (Aiskhylos, *hepta epi Thebas*, 277–9). The two passages are sufficiently similar that Aiskhylos' lines may well have influenced those of Euripides. In the *Phoinissai*, Iokaste is questioning Polyneikes' ability to fulfil any vows of the sort, without considerable impiety and heartlessness. Eteokles, in Aiskhylos, has made the vow, "πόλεως σεσωμένης" (274). Euripides inquires, via Iokaste, whether Eteokles, in making war against his brother, truly wishes "τυραννεῖν ἢ πόλιν σῶσαι" (560). If the text of these lines were less suspect, it would appear that we might have a case in which τροπαῖα is best, if not absolutely necessarily, interpreted as designating a single trophy. Since it was very unusual to set up more than one trophy to commemorate a single victory, and since his vow is in fact concerned with the physical actions to be undertaken in the case of victory, we might assume that Eteokles is vowing only a single trophy, and presumably confident that he has expressed his vow in terms clear enough that he will not be faulted for erecting only one. The text is, however, almost certainly corrupt; Page (1972: 55) crucifies lines 275–278a of the *hepta*, with the note "locus graviter corruptus".

At *Andromakhe* 694, Peleus complains:

ὅταν τροπαῖα πολεμίων στήσηι στρατός,
οὐ τῶν πονούντων τοὔργον ἡγοῦνται τόδε,
ἀλλ' ὁ στρατηγὸς τὴν δόκησιν ἄρνυται.

Tuplin (1987: 97) considers this a passage in which the plural "may be assumed actually to refer to a single trophy". The reasons one would make this assumption in this particular case are, however, unclear. Certainly, τροπαῖα *could* refer to a single trophy, but both the construction and the idea are, as Tuplin notes, "generalising," and there seems nothing wrong with translating "whenever a general sets up trophies over the enemy ...". True, it is unlikely that, in normal conditions, the general will find himself erecting more than one trophy on any given occasion, but with any luck, he will have more than one occasion to do so, and *whenever* he is so fortunate, it will be he, and not his soldiers, who gains the credit. But furthermore, the actual physical setting up of a trophy or trophies is of secondary importance: one could translate, "whenever a general is victorious over his enemies" and lose little of the sense.

Another passage of Euripides does, at first sight at least, seem to be describing literal, physical τροπαῖα. When the messenger in the *Herakleidai* (786–787) announces to Alkmene that "νικῶμεν ἐχθροὺς καὶ τροπαῖ᾽ ἱδρύεται / παντευχίαν ἔχοντα πολεμίων σέθεν" the present tense and the description of the armour being put upon the trophy/trophies do strongly suggest that the messenger is speaking of a physical object or objects, not merely describing the fact of their victory. But the only physical monument later described is not a regular trophy at all, but rather a "βρέτας / Διὸς τροπαίου" (934–935). It is of course possible that the βρέτας here is something different from the τροπαῖα referred to earlier. Euripides does, however, refer elsewhere to βρέτας Διὸς τροπαῖον: in the *Phoinissai* before the single combat Polyneikes' friends encourage him saying Πολύνεικες, ἐν σοὶ Ζηνὸς ὀρθῶσαι βρέτας / τροπαῖον Ἄργει τ᾽ εὐκλεᾶ δοῦναι λόγον (1250–51) and, afterwards, they say οἱ μὲν Διὸς τροπαῖον ἵστασαν βρέτας, (1473). This conflation of βρέτας and τροπαῖον seems to be unique to Euripides. A search of the *Thesaurus Linguae Graecae* for the two lemmata within one line of each other yields only the three examples cited, and the comments of scholiasts upon them and, since the image so described is indeed decked with the armour of the enemy, it seems preferable to assume that the two are in fact one and the same, in which case, one could consider this passage an example of a plural τροπαῖα referring to a single physical object. However, the fact that the name of the object also changes from τροπαῖον to βρέτας suggests that perhaps the plural of the messenger's first announcement is not to be taken as strictly, literally accurate. The fact that the full armour of πολεμίων, plural, can be set upon the τροπαῖα further suggests that the plural is indeed a plural, and that the messenger, in his excitement, is exaggerating somewhat. The important aspect of his message is that they have triumphed, and the exact means by which they commemorate the victory are of secondary importance, and liable to some embellishment. All the same, one can certainly argue that a single physical object, whether βρέτας or τροπαῖον, may very well be here being designated with the plural form τροπαῖα, and this passage is the closest parallel among the examples so far discussed for such a usage.

It seems, therefore, that in verse, or at least in tragedy (which, with the exception of one fragment of Timotheus on the battle of Salamis, and the passage of Aristophanes cited above, accounts for all of the attested occurrences in verse during the relevant period) plural forms of τροπαῖον may be employed without any particular emphasis on the plural meaning. They are not used, however, to refer to single, concrete objects, but only when the meaning is largely figurative, and the actual literal referent is neither of primary importance, nor, usually, in existence.

By contrast, the singular τροπαῖον is used when it is necessary to designate a single, actual object. However, such a literal use is very rare in verse. Aiskhylos uses the word τροπαῖον only twice, both times in *Hepta epi Thebas*. The context in which the plural occurs has already been discussed. The singular is used by the chorus after the battle: "ἔστακε δ' Ἄτας τροπαῖον ἐν πύλαις / ἐν αἷς ἐθείνοντο, καὶ δυοῖν κρατήσας ἔληξε δαίμων" (955–960). Although this is clearly a very unusual "trophy," the implication does appear to be that there is a physical object erected on the spot where the two brothers killed each other.

The singular of the noun τροπαῖον never occurs in Sophokles, though Ζεὺς Τροπαῖος is mentioned twice.

In Euripides, singular forms occur twice. One is the "Ζηνὸς ... βρέτας / τροπαῖον" (*Phoinissai* 1250–51), which has been already been discussed. In the second case, τροπαῖον ἱστῆναι is clearly equivalent to κρατεῖν; Peleus assures Andromakhe that if they should encounter an enemy, "τροπαῖον αὐτοῦ στήσομαι, πρέσβυς περ ὤν" (*Andromakhe* 763–4). Here the singular is as metaphorical as many of the instances of the plural.

There remains a small number of plural forms that do not fall neatly into one of the categories discussed. Thoukydides once (iii. 12, 8) describes τροπαῖα being set up, apparently by a single army to commemorate a single victory. Of the six times Thoukydides uses the plural, this is the only one where the reasons that more than one trophy was set up are not explained, nor is the number given. But when the singular is intended, it is used. He uses τροπαῖον 51 times. (No cases besides the nominative and accusative occur.) Therefore, although it is unclear why more than one trophy should be erected in this case, one must conclude that that is what is being done. Smith (1894: 253) suggests that the plural is "to be accounted for probably by the divisions of the army mentioned in c. 110 § 2; 112 § 2". Presumably each division would have raised its own trophy.

In the *Menexenos*, Sokrates praises those who fought at Marathon, "πρῶτοι στήσαντες τρόπαια τῶν βαρβάρων" (243a). This is either a use of the plural for singular, an instance of more than one trophy being raised for a single battle, or else simple hyperbole. Given the context, and the oration's numerous other departures from strict fact, hyperbole seems the most likely explanation.

Timotheus' description of the setting up of trophies after the battle of Salamis is puzzling, in so far as it is not evident how the τροπαῖα become or become equated to the Διὸς / ἁγνότατον τέμενος, but the number is unproblematic, since there is in fact reason to believe two separate trophies were erected (Wallace, 1969), one on Salamis (Pausanias i. 36, 1) and the other on Psyttaleia (Ploutarkhos *Aristides*, 9).

What conclusions is it possible to draw from the preceding discussion? In prose, the situation appears quite clear: τροπαῖον refers to a single object, and τροπαῖα to two or more. With very few exceptions, occasioned by unusual circumstances, only one τροπαῖον appears to have been erected per battle. Following this usage, the τροπαῖα of Leuktra would indicate two or more objects, probably raised as a result of two or more battles.

However, the epigram is, of course, written in verse. It is therefore unclear whether prose usage is a fair comparison. And in verse, a plural form is frequently employed in contexts where a singular would seem equally appropriate. However, in none of these cases, is a plural form used to designate a single existing physical object. The strength of this conclusion, that the plural forms are never used to designate a single physical τροπαῖον, is undermined somewhat by the fact that such a single existing physical τροπαῖον, or indeed several physical τροπαῖα, are only very rarely discussed in verse at all. Aiskhylos has one reference to a τροπαῖον, Euripides one, and Sophokles none. The conclusion must therefore remain negative. There are no clear examples of a plural used to designate a single τροπαῖον.

Nothing in the preceding discussion can preclude the *possibility* that in the Leuktra epigram τροπαῖα should in lines 5 and/or 8 be interpreted as a singular. We have seen that there are passages where a singular meaning is, if not necessary, at least possible. And it is further possible that an examination of other inscriptions (as opposed to the literary sources which have been considered here) would yield parallels for such a use. Moreover, in six lines of verse, the poet of the epigram has introduced one *hapax legomenon*, (τηνάκις), one more or less unparalleled construction (ἔιλεν ... κλάρῳ ... φέρειν) and a variety of other unusual turns of phrase. Therefore, although there are no other instances in which τροπαῖα must *necessarily* be construed as referring to a singular, literal, trophy, it might be admitted as a possibility in this particular case, assuming there were strong reasons to do so. However, surely the burden of proof would rest with the side arguing against the straightforward, literal interpretation of the plural noun as having a plural meaning.

Bibliography

Adcock, F.E., 1957: *The Greek and Macedonian Art of War* (Berkeley & Los Angeles).

Ameling, W., 1985: *Die Inschriften von Prusias ad Hypium* (= *Inschriften griechischer Städte aus Kleinasien* 27; Bonn).

Andhreioménou, Angelikí, 1974: "Νεκροταφεῖα παρὰ τὸ ἀρχαῖον Ἀκραίφνιον", *AAA* vii.1: 325–335.

Andhreioménou, Angelikí K., 2007: *Τάναγρα, ἡ ἀνασκαφὴ τοῦ νεκροταφείου (1976–1977, 1989)* (= *BAAE* 252; Athenai).

Aravantinos, Vasileios, 2006: "A New Inscribed 'Kioniskos' from Thebes", *BSA* 101: 369–377.

Aravantinós, Vasíleios, 2009: "Τεκμήρια λατρείας του Ηρακλή και των τέκνων του στη Θήβα. Όταν οι ανασκαφές φωτίζουν τα αρχαία κείμενα", *Philoloyikí Protokhroniá* 66: 297–301.

Aravantinos, Vasileios, 2014: "The Inscriptions from the Sanctuary of Herakles at Thebes: an Overview" in N. Papazarkadas (ed.), 2014: 149–210.

Aravantinós, Vasíleios, 2015: "Το τέμενος του Ηρακλέους στη Θήβα" in Oikonomou (ed.), 2015: 85–103.

Aravantinos, Vasilis, 2017: "The sanctuaries of Herakles and Apollo Ismenios at Thebes: new evidence" in Charalambidou & Morgan (edd.), 2017: 221–230.

Asheri, David, 1963: "Laws of Inheritance, Distribution of Land and Political Constitutions in Ancient Greece", *Historia* 12: 1–21.

Asheri, David, *et all.*, 1972: *Forschungen an der Nordküste Kleinasiens* i (Wien).

Ashton, Norman G. & Pantázoglou, Evángelos Th., 1991: *Siphnos, Ancient Towers B.C. / Σίφνος, Αρχαίοι Πύργοι π.X.* (Athens).

Austin, R.P., 1925/26: "Excavations at Haliartos, 1926", *BSA* 27: 81–91.

Austin, R.P., 1926–1927: "Excavations at Haliartos, 1926, Part II", *BSA* 28: 128–140.

Bakhuizen, S.C. ("Kees"), 1970: *Salganeus and the Fortifications on its Mountains* (= *Chalcidian Studies* ii; Groningen).

Bechtel, Friedrich, 1917: *Die historischen Personennamen des Griechischen bis zur Kaiserzeit* (Halle).

Beck, Hans, 2014: "Ethnic Identity and Integration in Boeotia; the Evidence of the Inscriptions (6th and 5th centuries BC)", in Papazarkadas (ed.), 2014: 19–44.

Beister, Hartmut, 1970: *Untersuchungen zu der Zeit der thebanischen Hegemonie* (München).

Beister, Hartmut, 1973: "Ein thebanisches Tropaion bereits vor Beginn der Schlacht bei Leuktra: zur Interpretation von *IG* VII 2462 und Paus. 4, 32, 5f.", *Chiron* 3: 65–84.

Beister, Hartmut & Buckler, John (edd.), 1989: *Boiotika, Vorträge vom 5. Internationalen Böotien-Kolloquium zu Ehren von Professor Dr. Siegfried Lauffer* (= *Münchner Arbeiten zu alten Geschichte* 2; München).

Bergquist, Birgitta, 1967: *The Archaic Greek Temenos, a study of structure and function* (= *Acta Instituti Atheniensis Regni Sueciae* 4, XIII; Lund).

Berve, Helmut, 1926: *Das Alexanderreich auf prosopographischer Grundlage* (Munich).

Bintliff, John, 2016: "Leiden Ancient Cities of Boeotia Project: the April and August 2016 Seasons" *Teiresias* 46.2: 1–10.

Bilabel, F., 1920: *Die ionische Kolonisation: Untersuchungen über die Gründungen der Ionier, deren stadtliche und kultliche Organisation und Beziehungen zu den Mutterstädten* (= *Philologus* suppl. 14.1; Leipzig).

Blinkenberg, Chr., 1926: *Fibules grecques et orientales* (= *Det Kgl. Danske Videnskabernes Selskab., Hitsorisk-filologiske Meddelelser* xiii,1: Copenhagen).

Blümel, Wolfgang, 1982: *Die aiolischen Dialekte: Phonologie und Morphologie der inschriftlichen Texte aus generativer Sicht* (Göttingen).

BMC = *British Museum Catalogue of Greek Coins*, volumes cited:
  BMC The Tauric Chersonese, Sarmatia, Dacia, Moesia, Thrace etc. (Barclay V. Head & Percy Gardner, 1877);
  BMC, Seleucid Kings of Syria (Percy Gardner, 1878);
  BMC Thessaly to Aetolia (Percy Gardner, 1883);
  BMC Central Greece (Barclay V. Head, 1884);
  BMC Peloponnesus (Percy Gardner, 1887);
  BMC Attica, Megaris, Aegina (Barclay V. Head, 1888);
  BMC Crete and Aegean Islands (Warwick Wroth, 1889);
  BMC Corinth and Colonies (Barclay V. Head, 1889);
  BMC Troas, Aeolis and Lesbos (Warwick Wroth, 1894);
  BMC Lycia, Pamphilia and Pisidia (George F. Hill, 1897).

Bonanno-Aravantinos, Margherita, 2012: "Sculture arcaiche dal santuario di Eracle a Tebe" in Kokkorou-Alevras & Niemeier (edd.), 2012: 33–50.

Bonanno-Aravantinos, Margherita, 2014: "New Inscribed Funerary Monuments from Thebes" in Papazarkadas (ed.), 2014: 252–310.

Boteva, D., 2005: "Soldiers and Veterans Dedicating Votive Monuments with a Representation of the Thracian Horseman within the Provinces of Lower Moesia and Thrace", in Mirković M. (ed). *Römische Städte und Festungen an der Donau, Akten der Regionalen Konferenz* (*Belgrade 16–19 October 2003*; Belgrade).

Bowra, C.M., 1938: "The Daughters of Asopos", *Hermes* 73: 213–221.

Buck, Robert J., 1972: "The Formation of the Boeotian League", *Classical Philology* lxviii.2: 94–101.

Buck, Robert J., 1979: *A History of Boeotia* (Edmonton).

Buck, Robert J., 1985: "Boeotian Oligarchies and Greek Oligarchic Theory", in John M. Fossey & Hubert Giroux (edd.) *Proceedings of the Third International Conference on Boiotian Antiquities* (= *MUMCAH* 2; Amsterdam): 25–31.

Buckler, John, 1980: *The Theban Hegemony, 371–362 BC* (Cambridge, Mass.).

Buckler, John, 1995: "The Battle of Tegyra, 375 BC", in John M. Fossey (ed.), 1995: *Boeotia Antiqua V: Studies on Boiotian Topography, Cults and Terracottas* (= *MUMCAH* 17; Amsterdam).

Buecheler, F., 1877: "Wahrheit und Dichtung über die Schlacht bei Leuktra", *Rheinisches Museum für Philologie* 32: 479–481.

Bulle, Heinrich, 1907: *Orchomenos I: Die älteren Ansiedelungsschichten* (München).

Burr, Victor, 1944: Νεῶν Κατάλογος, *Untersuchungen zum homerischen Schiffskatalog* (= *Klio* beiheft 49).

Burstein, Stanley Mayer, 1976: *Outpost of Hellenism: the emergence of Heraclea on the Black Sea* (Berkeley).

Camp, John McKesson II, 1991: "Notes on the Towers and Borders of Classical Boiotia", *AJA* 95: 193–202.

Camp, John, Ierardi, Michael, McInerney Jeremy, Morgan, Kathryn & Umholtz, Gretchen, 1992: "A Trophy from the Battle of Chaironeia of 86 B.C.", *AJA* 96. w3: 443–455.

Caskey, J.L., 1960: "The Early Helladic Period in the Argolid", *Hesperia* 29: 285–303.

Cermanović-Kusmanović, Aleksandrina, 1982: *Corpus Cultus Equitis Tracii, Études préliminaires aux religions orientales dans l'Empire romain V: Monumenta Intra Fines Iugoslaviae Reperta* (Leiden).

Charalambidou, Xenia & Morgan, Catherine (edd.), 2017: *Interpreting the Seventh Century BC, Tradition and Innovation* (Oxford).

Cloché, P., 1952: *Thèbes de Béotie* (Namur).

Cooper, Frederick A., 2000: "The fortifications of Epaminondas and the rise of the monumental Greek city", in Tracy, James D., (ed.), 2000: *City Walls, the urban enceinte in global perspective* (Cambridge): 155–191 (= chapter 6).

Darmezin, Laurence, 1999: *Les affranchissements par consécration en Béotie et dans le monde grec hellénistique* (Nancy).

Dassios, Photis, 1995: "Diodoros Sikeliotes (XVI.58,4) and the Fortress at Mavrókastro", *Boeotia Antiqua* v: 35–41, pll. 12–19 + endplate.

Davidson, Gladys R., 1952: *Corinth XII: The Minor Objects* (Princeton, NJ).

Davidson, Gladys R. & Horvaith, Tibor, 1937: "The Avar Invasion of Corinth", *Hesperia* vi.2: 227–39.

Davidova, L.I., 1990: Боспорские Надгробные Рельефы V б. до н.э.–III б.н.эю (Leningrad).

De Angelis, Franco, 1991: *Boiotia in the Geometric and Archaic Periods: Population, Settlement and Colonisation* (MA thesis, McGill University, Montréal).

Decourt, Jean-Claude, 1995: *Inscriptions de Thessalie 1. Les cités de la vallée de l'Enipeus* (Paris and Athens).

De Ridder, A., 1895: "Fouilles d'Orchomene" *BCH* 19: 137–224.

De Ridder, A., 1922: "Fouilles de Thespies et de l'hiéron des Muses de l'Hélicon: monuments figurés", BCH **46**: 217–306.

De Vries, Keith, 1970: *A Study of Boeotian Incised Fibulae and their Antecedents* (diss. University of Pennsylvania; photo reprint, Ann Arbor, 1971).

De Vries, Keith, 1971: A brief report on "work in progress", *Teiresias* **1.1**: 10 (= *Teiresias* 71.1.6).

Demetriadi, Vassili & Hepworth, R.G., 1984: "Forgeries of Boeotian Autonomous Staters", *Numismatic Chronicle* **144**: 186–191.

Desborough, V.R., 1964: *The Last Mycenaeans and their Successors* (Oxford).

Dimitrova, Nora, 2002: "Inscriptions and Iconography of the Thracian Rider" *Hesperia* **71.2**: 209–229.

Dittenberger, W., 1892: *Inscriptiones Graecae VII: Inscriptiones Megaridis, Oropiae, Boeotiae* (Berlin).

Donaldson, G.H., 1988: "Signalling Communications and the Roman Imperial Army", *Britannia* **xix**: 349–355.

Dontcheva, Ivanka, 2002: "Le syncrétisme d'Asclépios avec le cavalier thrace", *Kernos* **15**: 317–324.

Ducat, Jean, 1971: *Les kouroi du Ptoion. Le sanctuaire d'Apollon Ptoieus à l'époque archaïque* (= *Bibliothèque des écoles françaises d'Athènes et de Rome* **219**; Paris).

Ducat, Jean, 1973: "La confédération béotienne et l'expansion thébaine à l'époque archaïque", BCH **97.1**: 59–73.

Egger, Rudolf, 1878: "Note sur une inscription métrique commémorative de la bataille de Leuctres." BCH **2** (1878): 22–27.

Empereur, Jean-Yves, 1981: "Collection Paul Canellopoulos (XVII), petits objets inscrits", BCH **105**: 537–568.

Engels, Donald W., 1978: *Alexander the Great and the Logistics of the Macedonian Army* (Berkeley & Los Angeles).

Etienne, Roland & Knoepfler, Denis, 1976: *Hyettos de Béotie et la chronologie des archontes fédéraux entre 250 et 171 avant J.-C.* (= BCH suppl. iii; Athènes).

Farinetti, Emeri, 2011: *Boeotian Landscapes, a GIS-based study for the reconstruction and interpretation of the archaeological datasets of ancient Boeotia* (= BAR International Series **2195**; Oxford).

Farnell, Lewis Richard, 1921: *Greek Hero Cults and Ideas of Immortality* (Oxford).

Foss, Clive, 1975: "Greek Sling Bullets in Oxford" *Archaeological Reports* **21**: 40–44.

Fossey, John M., 1970: "The Identification of Graia", *Euphrosyne* **n.s. iv** 3–22 (= Fossey, 1990: 27–52).

Fossey, John M., 1973/4: "The End of the Bronze Age in the South West Kopaïs", *Euphrosyne* **n.s. vi**: 7–21 (= Fossey, 1990: 53–71).

Fossey, John M., 1980a: "Mycenaean Fortifications of the North East Kopaïs". *OpAth* **xiii.10**: 155–162 (= Fossey, 1990: 72–89).

Fossey, John M., 1980b: "La liste des rois argiens: première partie", *Mélanges en études anciennes offertes à Maurice Lebel* (Québec): 57–75.

Fossey, John M. (ed.), 1981: *Khóstia 1980 A: Preliminary Report on the First Season of Canadian Excavations at Khóstia, Boiotia, Central Greece / Rapport préliminaire sur la première champagne de fouilles canadiennes à Khóstia en Béotie, Grèce Centrale* (Montréal).

Fossey, 1986a: "Aspects de la vie économique et réligieuse" in Fossey (ed.) 1986: 117–131.

Fossey, John M. (ed.), 1986a: *Khóstia I: études diverses* (= *MUMCAH* 5: Amsterdam).

Fossey, John M., 1986b: *The Ancient Topography of Eastern Phokis* (Amsterdam).

Fossey, John M., 1987: "The Cults of Artemis in Argolis", *Euphrosyne* n.s. XV: 71–87.

Fossey, John M., 1988: *Topography and Population of Ancient Boiotia* (Chicago).

Fossey, John M., 1990a: *Papers in Boiotian Topography and History* (Amsterdam).

Fossey, John M., 1990b: *The Ancient Topography of Opountian Lokris* (Amsterdam).

Fossey, John M., 1991: *Epigraphica Boeotica I, Studies in Boiotian Inscriptions* (Amsterdam).

Fossey, John M., 1992: "Two Notes from Thisbe" in Fossey (ed.), 1992: 47–51.

Fossey, John M., (ed.), 1992: *Boeotia Antiqua II, Papers on Recent Work in Boiotian Archaeology and Epigraphy*.

Fossey, John M., 1993: "The Development of Some Defensive Networks in Eastern Central Greece During the Classical Period", in Van de Maele & Fossey (edd.): 109–132.

Fossey, John M. (ed.), 1993: *Boeotia Antiqua III: Papers in Boiotian History, Institutions and Epigraphy in Memory of Paul Roesch* (Amsterdam).

Fossey, John M., 1996: "Some parameters of archaic Greek emigration" in Lordkipanidze & Lévêque (edd.), *Sur les traces des Argonautes* (= *Actes du 6e symposium de Vani [Colchide] 22–29 septembre 1990*) 119–128.

Fossey, John M., 1999: "Boiotia and the Pontic Cities in the Archaic to Hellenistic Periods", in Otar Lordkipanidzé & Pierre Lévêque (edd.), 1990, *La Mer Noire zone de contacts* (= *Actes du VIIe symposium de Vani [Colchide] 26–30 IX 1994*; Paris): 35–40.

Fossey, John M., 2005: *Prosopographiae Graecae Minores II: The Prosopography and Onomastics of Anthedon in Antiquity* (Chicago).

Fossey, John M., 2014: *Epigraphica Boeotica II, Further Studies on Boiotian Inscriptions* (Leiden).

Fossey, John M. & Morin, Jacques, 1986: *Khóstia 1983, rapport préliminaire sur la seconde champagne de fouilles canadiennes à Khóstia en Béotie, Grèce central* (Amsterdam).

Frazer, J.G., 1898: *Pausanias's Description of Greece, translated with commentary* (London).

Gauvin, Ginette, 1993: "Les systèmes de fortifications de Kléonai et Phlionte" in Van de Maele & Fossey (edd.): 133–146.

Gauvin, Ginette & Fossey, John M., 1985: "Livadhóstro: un relevé topographique des fortifications de l'ancienne Kreusis" in Roesch & Argoud (edd.), 1985: 77–86.

Gauvin, Ginette & Morin, Jacques, 1992: "Le site d'Askra et ses carrières" in Fossey (ed.), 1992: 7–15, pll. 1–10.

Giovannini, A., 1969: *Étude historique sur les origines du catalogue des vaisseaux* (= *travaux publiés sous les auspices de la Société Suisse des sciences humaines* 9; Berne).

Gočeva, Zlatozara, 1992: "Le culte d'Apollon", *Dialogues d'histoire ancienne* 18.2: 163–171.

Gočeva, Zlatozara & Oppermann, Manfred, 1979–1984: *Corpus Cultus Equitis Thracii* vols. 1–2.2 (Leiden).

Goldman, Hetty, 1931: *Excavations at Eutresis in Boeotia* (Cambridge, Mass.).

Graves, Robert, 1992: *The Greek Myths* (Harmondsworth).

Grbić, Dragana, 2013: "The Thracian Hero on the Danube, New Interpretation of an Inscription from Diana", *Balcanica* xliv: 7–20.

Gregory, Timothy E., 1992: "Archaeological Explorations in the Thisbe Basin", in Fossey (ed.), 1992: 17–34, pll. 11–19.

Guarducci, Margherita, 1969: *Epigrafia Greca* II, *epigrafi di carattere pubblico* (Rome).

Guillon, Pierre, 1943: *Les Trépieds du Ptoion, deuxième partie: dispositive materiel, signification historique et religieuse* (Paris).

Guillon, Pierre, 1948: *La Béotie antique* (Paris).

Hackens, Tony, 1969: "La circulation monétaire dans la Béotie hellénistique: trésors de Thèbes 1935 et 1965", BCH xciii.2: 701–729.

Hampartumian, Nubar, 1979: *Corpus Cultus Equitis Thracii, Études préliminaires aux religions orientales dans l'Empire romain IV: Moesia Inferior (Romanian Section) and Dacia* (Leiden).

Hampe, Roland, 1936: *Frühe griechische Sagenbilder in Böotien* (Athens).

Hanell, Krister, 1934: *Megarische Studien* (Diss. Lund).

Hanson, Victor Davis, 1989: *The Western Way of War, infantry battle in classical Greece* (New York).

Head, Barclay V., 1881: *On the Chronological Sequence of the Coins of Boeotia*, (originally printed in *Numismatic Chronicle* 1981, 177–275, but most available in the reprinted edition under the title *The Coinage of Boeotia*, Chicago, 1974; the work is sometimes referred to as *History of the Coinage of Boeotia*, or as *The Coins of Ancient Boeotia, a Chronological Sequence*, or simply as *The Coins of Ancient Boeotia*).

Head, Barclay V., 1884: *A Catalogue of the Greek Coins in the British Museum. Central Greece* (London).

Head, Barclay V., 1910: *Historia Numorum, a Manual of Greek Numismatics*[2] (Oxford).

Hellmann, Marie-Christine, 1982: "Collection Froehner: balles de fronde grecques" BCH cvi: 75–87.

Hemberg, B., 1950: *Die Kabiren* (Diss, Uppsala).

Heurtley, W.A., 1923–25: "Notes on the Harbours of S. Boeotia, and sea-trade between Boeotia and Corinth in Prehistoric Times", *BSA* **26**: 38–45.

Hollinshead, Mary S., 1999: "'Adyton' and 'Opisthodomos' and the Inner Room of the Greek Temple", *Hesperia* **68.2**: 189–218.

Hope Simpson, R. & Lazenby, J.F., 1970: *The Catalogue of Ships in Homer's Iliad* (Oxford).

How, W.W. and Wells, J., 1928: *A Commentary on Herodotus with Introduction and Appendices, in two volumes* (Oxford).

Jebb, Sir Richard C., 1921: *The Trachiniae of Sophocles* (Cambridge; abridged from the original larger edition by Gilbert A. Davies).

Jeffery, L.H., 1961: *The Local Scripts of Archaic Greece, a study of the origin of the Greek alphabet and its development from the eighth to the fifth centuries B.C.* (Oxford).

Jöchle, Wolfgang, 1971: "Biology and Pathology of Reproduction in Greek Mythology", *Conception* **4.1**; 1–13.

Johansen, K. Friis, 1923: *Les vases sicyoniens* (Copenhagen).

Kalcyk, Hansjörg & Heinrich, Bert, 1989: "The Munich Kopaïs Project" in John M. Fossey (ed.), *Boeotia Antiqua* I (Amsterdam) 55–71.

Kallet-Marx, Robert M., 1989: "The Evangelistria Watchtower and the Defense of the Zagara Pass" in Beister & Buckler (edd.), 1989: 301–311.

Kalliga, Kyriaki, 2017: "A Group of Small Vases with Subgeometric–early Archaic decoration from the Sanctuary of Herakles at Thebes" in Charalambidou & Morgan (edd.), 2017: 231–144.

Kalliontzis, Yiannis, 2014: "Digging in Storerooms for Inscriptions: An Unpublished Casualty List from Plataia in the Museum of Thebes and the Memory of War in Boeotia" in Papazarkadas (ed.), 2014: 332–372.

Kazarow, G., 1938: *Die Denkmaler des Thrakischen Reitergottes in Bulgarien* (*Dissertationes Pannonicae* II/14; Budapest).

Kelly, Amanda, 2012: "The Cretan slinger at war – a weighty exchange", *BSA* **107**: 273–311.

Keramópoullos, Antónios, 1917: Θηβαϊκά (=Ἀρχαιολογικὸν Δελτίον 3).

Keuls, Eva, 1993: *The Reign of the Phallus: Sexual Politics in Ancient Athens* (Berkeley & Los Angeles).

Kirk, G.S., 1965: *Homer and the Epic* (Cambridge).

Knauss, Jost, 1992: "Purpose and Function of the Ancient Hydraulic Structures at Thisbe", in Fossey (ed.), 1992: 35–46, pll. 20–25.

Kokkorou-Alevras, G. & Niemeier, W.D., 2012: *Neue Funde archaischer Plastik aus Griechischen Heiligtümern und Nekropolen* (München).

Konecny, Andreas, Aravantinos, Vassilis & Marchese, Ron, 2013: *Plataiai, Archäologie und Geschichte einer boiotischen Polis* (= Österreichisches Archäologisches Institut, *Sonderschriften Band* **48**; Wien).

Körte G., 1878: "Die antiken Skulpturen aus Boeotien", *AM* **iii**: 301–422.

Koumanoúdhis, Stéphanos N., 1961: "Une ville béotienne dans Strabon", *RPhil* xxxv: 99–105.

Koumanoúdhes, Stéphanos, 1979: *Θηβαϊκὴ Προσωπογραφία* (Athens).

Larsen, Stephanie, 2007: *Tales of Epic Ancestry, Boiotian Collective Identity in the Late Archaic and Early Classical Periods* (Stuttgart).

Lattimore, Steven, 1998: *Thucydides, The Peloponnesian War, translated with introduction and notes* (Indianapolis).

Lawrence, A.W., 1979: *Greek Aims in Fortification* (Oxford).

Leaf, Walter, 1886: *The Iliad edited with English notes and introduction*, vol. 1, books I–XII (London).

Leake, William Martin, 1830: *Travels in the Morea* (London).

Leake, William Martin, 1835: *Travels in Northern Greece* vol. ii *Attica, Boeotia, Locris and Euboea* (London).

LGPN = *Lexicon of Greek Personal Names*, volumes cited:

i = *The Aegean Islands, Cyprus, Cyrenaica* (P.M. Fraser & E. Matthews, Oxford, 1987);

ii = *Attica* (M.J. Osborne & S.G. Byrne, Oxford, 1994);

iiia = *The Peloponnese, Western Greece, Sicily and Magna Graecia*, edd. P.M. Frazer & Elaine Matthews (Oxford, 1987);

iiib = *Central Greece: from the Megarid to Thessaly* (P.M. Fraser & E. Matthews, Oxford, 2000);

iv = *Macedonia, Thrace, Northern Regions of the Black Sea* (P.M. Fraser & E. Matthews, Oxford, 2005);

va = *Coastal Asia Minor: Pontos to Ionia*, ed. T. Corsten (Oxford, 2010).

vb = *Coastal Asia Minor: Caria to Cilicia*, edd. T.-S. Balzat, R.W.V. Catling, E. Chiricat & F. Marchand (Oxford, 2013).

Liapis, Vayios, 2011: "The Thracian Cult of Rhesus and the *Heros Equitans*", *Kernos* 24: 95–104.

Lolling, Habbo Gerhard, n.d.: *Reisenotizen aus Griechenland 1876 und 1877* (often known as the *Urbädekker*) manuscript eventually brought into print by Bert Heinrich and published 1989 (Berlin).

Lordkipanidze, Otar & Lévêque, Pierre (edd.), 1999: *La Mer Noire, zone de contacts* (Paris).

Lucas, Gérard, 1997: *Les cités antiques de la haute vallée du Titarèse. Étude de topographie et de géographie historique antique* (Thesis, Lyon II; subsequently published, but without the corpus of inscriptions, in 1997, Lyon).

Mackil, Emily, 2014: "Creating a Common Polity in Boeotia", in Papazarkadas (ed.), 2014: 45–67.

Mackil, Emily & van Alfen, Peter G., 2006: "Cooperative Coinage", in van Alfen, Peter G. (ed., 2006), *Agoranomia: Studies in Money and Exchange Presented to John H. Kroll* (New York): 201–246.

Mackridge, Peter, 2009: *Language and National Identity in Greece, 1766–1976* (Oxford).

Maher, Matthew P. & Mowat, Alister, 2018: "The Defense Network in the Chora of Mantineia", *Hesperia* 87.3: 451–495.

Maier, F.G., 1958: "Die Stadtmauer von Thisbe", *AM* 3: 17–25.

Makhairá, Vasilikí, 2000: "Τό Θέμα τοῦ ῞Ηροα Ἱπέα στούς Ἐπιτυμβίους Βωμούς τοῦ Μουσείου Θηβῶν", in Vasíleios Aravantinós (ed.), 2000: Ἐπετηρίς τῆς Ἑταιρείας Βοιωτικῶν Μελετῶν Gα, 848–892.

Mamaloúkos, Stávros B., 1988: "Ὁ Ναὸς τοῦ Ἁγ. Νικολάου τοῦ Νέου κοντὰ στὸ Παρόρι τῆς Βοιωτίας", Ἐπετηρίς τῆς Ἑταιρείας Βοιωτικῶν Μελετῶν Α.α: 492–542.

Manning, W.H., 1985: *Catalogue of the Romano-British Iron Tools, Fittings and Weapons in the British Museum* (London).

McCredie, J.R. & Steinberg, A., 1960: "Two Boeotian Dedications". *Hesperia* xxix: 123–125.

Meidani, Katerina, 2008: "Les relations entre les cités béotiennes à l'époque archaïque", *Kentron* 24: 151–164.

Merkelbach, Reinhold, 1980: *Die Inschriften von Kalchedon* (= *Inschriften griechischer Städte aus Kleinasien* 20; Bonn).

Michailidou-Nikolaou, Ino, 1972: "Ghiande missili di Cipro", *Annuario della scuola archeologica di Atene 1969–1970* xlvii–xlviii: 359–369.

Mili, Maria, 2015: *Religion and Society in Ancient Thessaly* (Oxford).

Milne, John S., 1907: *Surgical Instruments in Greek and Roman Times* (Oxford; reprinted Chicago, 1976).

Moretti, Luigi, 1957: "Olympionikai. I vincitori negle antichi agoni olimpiei", *Memorie Lincei* 8th series 8.2: 53–198.

Moretti, Luigi, 1962: *Ricerche sulle leghe greche* (Roma).

Munn, Mark H., 1993: *The Defense of Attica: the Dema Wall and the Boiotian War of 378–375 B.C.* (Berkeley).

Nachtergael, G., 1975: "Le Catalogue des Vaisseaux et la liste de théorodoques de Delphes", *Le monde grec: pensée, littérature, histoire, documents: Hommages à Claire Préaux*, edd. J. Bingen, G. Cambier & G. Nachtergael (Bruxelles): 45–55.

Newell, Edward T., 1927: *The Coinage of Demetrius Poliorcetes* (London).

Noack, F., 1894: "Arne", *AM* xix: 405–485.

Ober, Josiah, 1985: *Fortress Attica: Defense of the Athenian Land Frontier 404–322 B.C.* (Leiden).

Oikonómou, Stavroúla (ed.), 2015: Ἀρχαιολογικές Συμβολές, τόμος Γ: Βοιωτία & Εὔβοια (Athina).

Oppermann, Manfred & Gočeva, Zlatozara, 1979: *Corpus Cultus Equitis Tracii, Études préliminaires aux religions orientales dans l'Empire romain I: Monumenta Orae Ponti Euxini Bulgariae* (Leiden).

Oppermann, Manfred & Gočeva, Zlatozara, 1981–1984: *Corpus Cultus Equitis Tracii, Études préliminaires aux religions orientales dans l'Empire romain II: Monumenta inter Danubium et Haemum Reperta* (Leiden).

Orlándos, Anastásios, 1915: "Ὁ Ναὸς τοῦ Ἀπόλλωνος Πτώου", *ADelt* 1: 94–110.

Osborne, M.J., 1981–1982: *Naturalization in Athens* vols. I & II (Brussel).
Page, Denys, 1955: *The Homeric Odyssey* (Oxford).
Page, Denys, 1963: *History and the Homeric Iliad* (Berkeley).
Page, Denys (ed.), 1972: *Aeschylus, Septem quae supersunt tragoedias*. (Oxford).
Papakhristodhoúlou, I., 1968: "Ἐρευναὶ εἰς Καλὰ Νησιὰ Περαχώρας", *AAA* i.2: 116–117 [English summary entitled "Antiquities on the Kala Nisia (Alkyonides) of Perachora"].
Papalexandrou, Nassos, 2005: *The Visual Poetics of Power: Warriors, Youths and Tripods in Early Greece* (Lanham).
Papalexandrou, Nassos, 2008: "Boiotian Tripods: the Tenacity of a Panhellenic Symbol in a Regional Context", *Hesperia* 77: 251–282.
Papazarkadas, Nikolaos (ed.), 2014: *The Epigraphy and History of Boeotia: New Finds, New Prospects* (Leiden).
Parker, Holt N., 2008: "The Linguistic Case for the Aiolian Migration Reconsidered", *Hesperia* 77.3: 431–464.
Pečirka, J., 1963: "Land Tenure and the Development of the Athenian Polis", *Geras G. Thompson* (Prague) 183–201.
Petrákos, Vasíleios Khr., 1997: *Οἱ Ἐπιγραφὲς τοῦ Ὠρωποῦ* (= *BAAE* 170; Athínai).
Petsas, Photios, 1978: "Some Pictures of Macedonian Riders as Prototypes of the Thracian Rider", *Pulpudeva, semaines Philippopolitaines de l'histoire et de la culture Thrace* 2: 192–204.
Picard, Charles, 1956: "Nouvelles observations sur diverses représentations du Héros Cavalier des Balkans", *Revue de l'histoire des religions* 150: 1–26.
Píkoulas, Yánis, 1984: "Μαντινειακά", *Horos* 2: 205–207.
Píkoulas, Yánis, 1988: *Ἡ Νότια Μεγαλοπολιτικὴ Χώρα* (Athena).
Piterós, Khrístos I., 2008: "Ἀρχαιότητες και μνημεία των περιοχών Εὔτρησης, Λεύκτρων και Λιβαδόστρας", *Ἐπέτηρις τῆς Ἑταιρείας Βοιωτικῶν Μελετῶν* 4A.1: 581–646.
Platon, Nikolaos & Feyel, Michel, 1938: "L'inventaire sacré de Chostia", *BCH* 62: 149–166, pl. xxviii.
Platon, N. & Touloupa, E., 1964a: "Oriental seals from the palace of Cadmus: unique discoveries in Boeotian Thebes", *Illustrated London News* (Nov. 28): 859–861.
Platon, N. & Touloupa, E., 1964b: "Ivories and Linear B from Thebes", *Illustrated London News* (Dec. 5): 896–897.
Poralla, Paul, 1985: *Prosopographie der Lakedaimonier bis auf die Zeit Alexanders des Großen*[2] (Chicago; ed. from original 1913 version by Alfred S. Bradford).
Price, Susan-Marie, Gourley, Ben & Hagerman, Chris, 1998: "Excavations at Ancient Stymphalos, 1997" *Echos du monde classique* xlii.2: 261–319.
Pritchett, W. Kendrick, 1957: "New Light on Plataea", *AJA* lxi: 9–28.
Pritchett, W. Kendrick, 1965: *Studies in Ancient Greek Topography*. Part I (Berkeley & Los Angeles).

Pritchett, W. Kendrick, 1971: *Ancient Greek Military Practices* Part I (Berkeley & Los Angeles; subsequently reprinted as volume I of *The Greek State at War*).
Pritchett, W. Kendrick, 1974: *The Greek State at War,* Part II (Berkeley & Los Angeles).
Pritchett, W. Kendrick, 1985: *The Greek State at War* Part IV (Berkeley & Los Angeles).
Rabadžiev, Kostadin, 1986: "Images of Heracles in the art of pre-Roman Thrace", *Pulpudeva, semaines Philippopolitaines de l'histoire et de la culture Thrace* 5 (Sofia): 254–257.
Rantz, Berthe, 1983: "Le cavalier thrace – thème iconographique", *Pulpudeva, semaines Philippopolitaines de l'histoire et de la culture Thrace* 4 (Sofia): 200–219.
Raubitschek, Isabelle Kelly, 1998: *Isthmia VII: The Metal Objects (1952–1989)* (Princeton).
Rihll, Tracey, 2009: "Lead 'slingshot' (*glandes*)", *Journal of Roman Archaeology* 22: 146–169.
Robinson, David M., 1941: *Excavations at Olynthus X: Metal and Minor Miscellaneous Finds, an Original Contribution to Greek Life* (Baltimore).
Robinson, R.A., 1938: in Harold North Fowler & Richard Stillwell (edd.), *Corinth, Results of the Excavations Conducted by the American School of Classical Studies at Athens I.1, Introduction, Topography, Architecture* (Cambridge, Mass.): 43–45.
Roesch, Paul, 1972: "Les lois fédérales béotiennes" in John M. Fossey & Albert Schachter (edd.), *Proceedings of the First International Conference on Boiotian Antiquities* (= *Teiresias* suppl. i; Montreal) 61–70.
Roesch, Paul, 1982: *Études béotiennes* (Paris).
Roesch, Paul, 1984: "Un décret inédit de la ligue thébaine", REG 97: 45–60.
Roesch, Paul & Argoud, Gilbert (edd.), 1985: *La Béotie antique, Lyon – Saint-Étienne, 16–20 mai 1983* (Paris).
Roesch, Paul & Fossey, John M., 1978: "Un acte d'affranchissement de Coronée", ZPE 29: 138–141, reprinted as chapter 11 of Fossey, 1991.
Roller, Duane W., 1989: *Tanagran Studies II: The Prosopography of Tanagra in Boiotia* (Amsterdam).
Roller, Duane W., n.d.: "Boiotians in South Italy: Some Thoughts", paper presented at the VIIIth International Conference on Boiotian Antiquities held in Montréal in 1993; the proceedings of the conference remain unpublished.
Rose, C. Brian, 2008: "Separating Fact from Fiction in the Aiolian Migration", *Hesperia* 77.3: 399–430.
Rousset, Denis, 2012: "Les inscription antiques de Phocide et de Doride", *Comptes rendus de l'Académie des inscriptions et belles-lettres, novembre–décembre 2012*: 1659–1689.
Roux, Georges, 1954: "Le Val des Muses et les Muses chez les auteurs anciens", BCH lxxviii: 22–48.
Salmon, J.B., 1984: *Wealthy Corinth. A History of the City to 338 B.C.* (Oxford).
Samsaris, Dimitrios, 1984: "Le culte du cavalier thrace dans la vallée du Bas-Strymon à l'époque romaine (Recherches sur la localisation de ses sanctuaires)", *Dritter*

internationaler thrakologischer Kongress zu Ehren W. Tomascheks, 2–6 Juni 1980, Wieni, 2: 284–289 (Sofia).

Samsaris, Dimitrios Const., 1993: *Les Thraces dans l'empire romaine d'orient (le territoire de la Grèce actuelle) – étude ethno-démographique, sociale, prosopographique et anthroponymique* (Jannina).

Saprykin, Serge I., 1986: *Гераклеа Понтийскя и Херсонес Таврицесций: взаимоотиощения метрополии й колонии в. VI–I вв до и. э.* (Moscow).

Schachter, Albert, 1958: "Horse Coins from Tanagra", *Numismatic Chronicle* series 6, vol. xviii: 43–46.

Schachter, Albert, 1981: *Cults of Boiotia 1. Acheloos to Hera* (= *Bulletin of the Institute of Classical Studies* suppl. 38.1; London).

Schachter, Albert, 1986: *Cults of Boiotia 2. Herakles to Poseidon* (= *Bulletin of the Institute of Classical Studies* suppl. 38.2; London).

Schachter, Albert, 1989 (revised in 2016: 36–50): "Boiotia in the sixth century BC", in H. Beister & J. Buckler (edd.) *Boiotika: Vorträge vom 5. Internationalen Böotien-Kolloquium zu Ehren von Professor Dr. Siegfried Lauffer* (München, 1989): 73–86.

Schachter, Albert, 2014: "Tlepolemos in Boeotia" in Papazarkadas, N. (ed.), 2014: 313–331.

Schachter, Albert, 2016: *Boiotia in Antiquity, Selected Papers* (Cambridge).

Schleiermacher, Mathilde, 1984: *Römische Reitergrabsteine, die kaizerzeitlichen Reliefs des triumphierenden Reiters* (Bonn).

Schwantner, Ernst-Ludwig, 1977a: "Die böotische Hafenstadt Siphai", *AA* 513–551.

Schwantner, Ernst-Ludwig, 1977b: "Wohnen in der klassischen Polis", *Mitteilungen des Deutschen Archäologen-Verbandes e.V* 8.2: 8 + internal reports from Deutsches Archäologisches Institute, Berlin – Architectur-Referat "Survey in Attika, Böotien, Akarnanien und Epirus 1975" and Wohnen in der klassischen Polis "Bericht über 1976 in Böotien, Akarnanien und Epirus ausgeführte Forschungen".

Seure, Georges, 1912, pt. 2: "Étude sur quelques types curieux du Cavalier Thrace", *Revue des Études Anciennes* 14, 2: 137–166.

Seure, Georges, 1912, pt. 4: "Étude sur quelques types curieux du Cavalier Thrace (*Suite et fin*)", *Revue des Études Anciennes* 14, 4: 382–390.

Seyrig, Henri, 1927: "Quatre cultes de Thasos", *BCH* 51: 178–233.

Shefton, Brian, 1978: *Greek Arms & Armour in the Greek Museum, the University of Newcastle upon Tyne* (Newcastle).

Smith, Philip J., 2008: *The Archaeology and Epigraphy of Hellenistic and Roman Megaris, Greece* (Oxford).

Snodgrass, Anthony, 1964: *Early Greek Armour and Weapons* (Hawthorne, NY).

Snodgrass, Anthony, 1980: *Archaic Greece, the age of experiment* (Berkeley & Los Angeles).

Snodgrass, A.M., 1985: "The Site of Askra" in P. Roesch & G. Argoud (edd.), 1985: 87–95.

Sordi, Marta, 1958: *La lega tessalia fino ad Alessandro Magno* (Roma).

Sordi, Marta, 1993: "La battaglia di Ceresso e la secession di Tespie", in Fossey, John M. (ed.), 1993: 25–31.

Spyrópoulos, Theódhoros G., 1971: "Ἀρχαῖαι Βοιωτικαὶ Πόλεις ῎Ερχονται εἰς Φῶς", *AAA* **iv.3**: 319–328.

Stoyanov, Totko, 1985: "Le Cavalier et la Déesse: Observations sur une série de reliefs thraces", *Ktema* **10**: 273–285.

Symeonoglou, Sarantis, 1973: *Kadmeia I: Mycenaean Finds from Thebes, Greece: Excavations at 14 Oedipus St.* (Göteborg).

Symeonoglou, Sarantis, 1985: *The Topography of Thebes from the Bronze Age to Modern Times* (Princeton, NJ).

Taillardat, J. & Roesch, Paul, 1966: "L'inventaire sacré de Thespies; l'alphabet attique en Béotie", *RPhil* **xl.1**: 70–87.

Thompson, George, 1946: *Aeschylus and Athens*² (London).

Thompson, George, 1954: *Studies in Ancient Greek Society, vol. I: The Prehistoric Aegean*² (London).

Thompson *et all.*, 1973 = Thompson, Margaret, Mørkholm, Otto & Kraay, Colin (edd.), 1973: *An Inventory of Greek Coin Hoards* (New York).

Tod, Marcus N., *Greek Historical Inscriptions* vol. II (Oxford).

Tomlinson, R.A., 1969: "Perachora; the Remains Outside the Two Sanctuaries", *BSA* **64**: 155–258, Pll. 45–59.

Tomlinson, R.A., 1977: "The Upper Terraces at Perachora", *BSA* **72**: 197–202.

Tomlinson, R.A. & Fossey, J.M., 1970: "Ancient remains on Mount Mavrovouni, South Boeotia", *BSA* **65**: 243–263, Pll. 66–68.

Toporov, V.N., 1990: "The Thracian Horseman in an Indo-European Perspective", *Orpheus* **"0"**: 46–63.

Tuplin, Christopher J., 1987: "The Leuctra Campaign: Some Outstanding Problems", *Klio* **69**: 72–107.

Ure, P.E., 1922: *Origin of Tyranny* (Cambridge).

Ure, P.N., 1934: *Aryballoi and Figurines from Rhitsona in Boeotia* (= Reading University Studies, Cambridge).

Van de Maele, Symphorien, 1993: "Le réseau mégarien de défense territorial contre l'Attique à l'époque classique" in Van de Maele & Fossey (edd.), 1993: 93–107.

Van de Maele, Symphorien & Fossey, John M. (edd.), 1993: *Fortificationes Antiquae* (= *MUMCAH* **12**; Amsterdam).

Vian, Francis, 1963: *Les origines de Thèbes; Cadmos et les Spartes* (Paris).

Vischer, Wilhelm, 1878: "I. Antike Schleudergeschosse" in his *Kleine Schriften II: Archäologische und epigraphische Schriften* (ed. Achilles Burckhardt, Leipzig).

Vlakhoyiánni, Élena, 2000: "Θησαυρός νομισμάτων από τη Θήβα – A Hoard of Coins from Thebes", *Nomismatiká Khroniká* **17**: 55–113.

Vlakhoyiánni, Élena, 2009: "Τα νομίσματα του νεκροταφείου της Ακραιφίας (σωστική ανασκαφική έρευνα: 1994–1998)", *Αρχαιολογικό έργο Θεσσαλίας και Στερεάς Ελλάδας 3, II. Στέρεα Ελλάδα*: 1007–1027.

Walbank, F. W., 1967: *A Historical Commentary on Polybius, Vol. II, Commentary on Books VII–XVIII* (Oxford).

Waldbaum, Jane C., 1983: *Metalwork from Sardis: the finds through 1974* (Cambridge, Mass.).

Waldstein, Charles & Washington, Henry S., 1891: "Excavations by the American School at Plataia in 1891: Discovery of a Temple of Archaic Plan", *AJA* 7.4: 390–405.

Wallace, P.W., 1969: "Psyttaleia and the Trophies of the Battle of Salamis", *AJA* **73**.3: 293–303.

Will, Edouard, 1955: *Korinthiaka: recherches sur l'histoire et la civilisation de Corinthe des origines aux guerres médiques* (Paris).

Willcock, M.M.,1970: *A Commentary on Homer's Iliad I–VI* (London).

Willetts, R.F., 1967: *The Law Code of Gortyn* (Berlin).

Williams *et all.*, 1998 = Williams, Hector, Schauss, Gerald, Cronkite-Price, Susan-Marie, Gourley, Ben & Hagerman, Chris, 1998: "Excavations at Ancient Stymphalos, 1997", *Echos du monde classique* **xlii**.2: 261–319.

Wiseman, James, 1978: *The Land of the Ancient Corinthians* (= *Studies in Mediterranean Archaeology* L; Göteborg).

1A Epigraphic Sources Quoted or Cited

AA
  1940: 188   132

ADelt
  1917, 421–423, 6   132
  1960 (1963): 148, pl. 126b   258
  1970, *Khron.* 232, no. 4   268
  1970, *Khron.* 232, no. 13   258
  1970: *Khron. I*: 232, no. 1   266
  1971, *Khron* pl. 191α   258
  1971, *Khron*: pl. 191β   268
  1971: pl. 193γ   274
  1973 [1977] 284   266, 270
  1973 [1977] pl. 236a   255
  1994 [1999] 316   261
  2001–2004 [2012]
    Khron. 413 + fig. 10   261

AEph
  2, 1916: 233   134
  1936, *Khron.* 30
    no. 197 II, line 17   261

AJA
  7, 1891: 405–421   133

BCH
  1922: 268, no. 101   277
  1922: 269, no. 105   268
  1922: 269, no. 106   256
  1922: 269–270, no. 107   261
  1922: 270–271, no. 108   263, 268, 276
  1923: 64–67, no. 24   286
  1926: 409, 24   132
  1949: 291, no. 2   134
  1958: 126, note 1   277
  1958: 142–143, no. 216*bis*   276
  1958: 146, no. 233   256
  1958: 147, no. 236   261
  1958: 147, no. 238   268

Chiron
  1976: 18–19, no. 11   132

Darmezin
  1999: nos. 122–135   48

Decourt
  1995: 105 & 108   248
  1995: 129   248

*EB*ii
  35, fig. 25   260
  37   266, 270
  39, pl. 34   255
  pl. 1   271

Gortyn Law Code
  (*IC* iv 72) iv, 1–6   80

IG vii
  281   92
  416   260
  436   48
  542–543   260
  548   90
  1114   260
  1115   260
  1715   265
  1716   266
  1813   281
  2045   136
  2052   136
  2122   254
  2123   255
  2124   255
  2126   256
  2128   256
  2130   258
  2131   260
  2135   259
  2137   262
  2139   262
  2140   263
  2141   263
  2143   259, 290
  2144   276
  2145   264, 272
  2146   268
  2147   268, 272, 291
  2152   266, 278
  2153   266
  2154   270

1A EPIGRAPHIC SOURCES QUOTED OR CITED

IG vii (cont.)

2159	279
2161	268
2163	264
2164	269
2165	267
2167	273
2171	280
2172	267
2173	263
2175	266, 274
2225	117
2232	134
2235	49
2297	271
2359	49
2364	269
2400	261
2421	260
2443	256, 293
2462	143, 144
2628	260
2629	265
2658	274
2690	260
2736	48
2807	271
2952 & 2953	261
3100	111, 131
3101	134
3416	48
3430	134
3564	111, 131
4238	286
4244	254, 257

IG ix.

1^2, iv: 1150 a & b	232
2, 101	248
2, 469	248
2, 484	248
2, 486	248
2, 649–976 plus 1349 & 1350	247
2, 1031	248
2, 1129	248
2, 1170	248
2, 1199	248
2, 1257–1263	248
2, 1309	248
2, 1312	248
2, 1313	248
2, 1317	248

IG x.

2, 225	285

IKalkhedon

7, line 16	90

IPrusias

1–8; 10–12; 14	91

IThesp

38	67
283 bis	281
1170	249, 254
1170–1171	249
1171	260
1172	262
1172–1173	250
1174	255
1175	255
1176	256
1177	256
1178	258
1179	258
1180	258
1181	259
1182	259
1183	261
1184	261
1185	262
1186	262
1187	263
1188	263
1189	263
1190	264
1191	276
1192A	264
1192B	269
1192C	267
1193A	251, 266
1193A–B	251
1193B	270
1194	266

1A EPIGRAPHIC SOURCES QUOTED OR CITED

1195	267	*Olympia-Bericht* viii	
1196	267	[1967] 99, fig. 34.2	58
1197	268		
1198A	273	Piterós	
1199	266	2008: 605–606, no. 9	266, 270
1199B	274		
1203	264, 272	Rousset	
1203A	264	2012: 1665–1668 + fig. 2	261
1203B	268		
1204	251, 253, 259, 272	*SEG* ii	
		229	264
1205	276		
1206	254, 257, 275	*SEG* xviii	
1207	251	166–167	109, 131
1224	251, 256		
1225	266, 278	*SEG* xix	
1226	268	370	263
1231	261		
1232	268	*SEG* xxvi	
1233A	275	524	47
1234	277		
1236	279	*SEG* xxvii	
1237	280	58	266, 270

Lucas
   1992 #70; *AE* 1923, 160:
      #386e   249
   1997 #70   248

1B Ancient Literary Sources Quoted or Cited

Ailianos
poikele historia
   ii. 7 — 82

Aiskhines
peri tes parapresbeias
   74 — 305

Aiskhylos
Agamemnon
   280–314 — 129
Eumenides
   658–659 — 81
Hepta epi Thebas
   277 — 305
   277–279 — 309
   785–787 — 19
   955–960 — 311

Andokides
peri ton mysterion
   147, 2 — 305

Apollodoros
   iii. 10, 8 — 10

Apollonios of Rhodos
   ii. 854 — 89

Aristodemos
FGH 2a. 104, F frag. 1,
   line 225 — 306

Aristophanes
Hippeis
   521 — 306
   660–661 — 131

Aristoteles
Politika
   ii. 1265a–b — 78
   ii 1266b — 84
   ii. 1274a — 77
   ii. 1274b — 77
   ii 1321a, 26–29 — 84

Aspis (Hesiodic *corpus*)
   139–317, esp. 270–272 — 50

Demosthenes
kata Meidiou
   170 — 306
kata stephanon
   209 — 306
Olynthiakos
   3, 24 — 305
peri syntaxeos
   26 — 306
peri tes parapresbeias
   16; 307; 63, 7 — 306
   311 — 305
peri tes Rhodion eleutherias
   35 — 306
pros Leptinen
   76; 78; 80; 83 — 306

Diodoros Sikeliotes
   iv. 64–67, 2 — 18
   xiii. 24, 5–6 — 151
   xiv. 12, 3 — 90
   xv. 52–53 — 147
   xv. 52, 1 — 147
   xv. 54, 2–3 — 140
   xvi. 58 & 60 — 157, 206
   xix. 57, 5 — 130

Euripides
Andromakhe
   694–696 — 305, 309
   763–764 — 311
Antiope
   frag. 9 — 305
Elektra
   1172–1174 — 307
Fragment 10
   line 9 — 307
Fragment 65
   12–13 — 308
Hekabe
   171–172 — 79
Helene
   1380–1381 — 307

1B ANCIENT LITERARY SOURCES QUOTED OR CITED

Herakleidai
786	305
786–787	310
934–935	310

Hiketides
647	305, 307
925–927	19

Iphigeneia en Aulidi
896	79

Iphigeneia en Taurois
238	79

Orestes
712–713	307

Phoinissai
274	309
560	309
572	305
573–575	308
1250–1251	310–311
1473	310

Troiades
1222	305

Georgias
frag. 5b	305

Herodotos
1. 59, 8	80
v. 40, 7	80
vi. 68, 11	80
vii. 183, 1	130
ix. 3, 1	130
ix. 80, 2	130

Hesiodos
erga kai hemerai
376–378	87

Hesykhios
gloss	298

Ilias
ii, 494–516	1, 2, 5, 7, 91
ii, 610–611	3
ii, 619	3
ii, 620–624	3
ii, 719–720	3
vi, 35	9
xiii, 91	9
xiv, 450	10
xiv, 489	9
xv, 329	10
xv, 340	10
xvii, 601 & 605	9

Isokrates
Arkhidamoi
3.6	306

Arkhidamos
54	305

epistle
9	306

Plataikos
59	305

Lysias
Epitaphios
20, 4	305

peri tes demeuseos tou Nikiou adelphou epilogos
3, 5	306

peri tou me katalusai ten patrion politeian Athenesi
10	306

Memnon
(*FGrHist* 434f 12. 2–3)	89

Nonnos
Dionysiaka
xiii, 53–121	7

Pausanias
i. 34, 2	15
i. 34, 3	48
i. 36, 1	311
ii. 23, 2	15
iii. 14, 6	132
iv. 22, 5–6	152
iv. 26, 7	91
iv. 32, 4–6	144
ix. 4, 3	9
ix. 5, 15	9
ix. 7, 6	242
ix. 8, 6–7	16
ix. 9, 1–5	17
ix. 13, 3	131, 147
ix. 13, 4	131

Pausanias (cont.)

ix. 13, 8	151
ix. 18, 1–19, 2	15
ix. 19, 4	20
ix. 19, 5	48
ix. 24, 3	47
ix. 25, 4	48, 284
ix. 26, 1	49, 284
ix. 27, 8	48
ix. 32, 2	49
ix. 32, 4	89
ix. 34, 5	47
ix. 37, 1–3	284
ix. 37, 7	9
ix. 38, 6	48
ix. 39, 3	9
x. 20, 3	219
x. 23, 11	219

Pindaros
Isthmian

iv. 61	48

Nemean

ix, 18–27	18
x, 8–9	19

Olympian

vi, 12–14	19

Pythian

viii, 68, old scholiast	16

Platon
Menexenos

243a	306
245a	306
Nomoi v. 740b–c	85

Plinius
naturalis historia

iv. 11, 42	284
v. 112	90

Ploutarkhos
Aristeides

9	311
xx	133
xx. 6	90

Demosthenes

854d–e	48

Ethika

273c–d	152
299c	43
299e–300a	298
483d	86
515c	7
773c–774d	138
856f	140
866e	30

Kamillos

19	30

Lykourgos

xxii. 4	131

Pelopidas

xx. 3–xxii. 2	139
xx. 4	138

Polybios

x. 43–47	130
xviii. 11, 4–8	199
xxxvi. 17, 5	243

Pseudo-Ploutarkhos
Synagoge Historion Parallelon Hellenikon kai Romaikon

6	20
7	284

Ptolemaios

iii. 14, 8	188
tetrabiblos iv 2[174]	83

Sophokles
Oidipous epi Kolono

1354–1396	19

Philoktetes

26	79

Trakhiniai

61	79
750	308
1102	308

Stephanos of Byzantion

s.v. Ἰτωνία	89
s.v. Πάνελος	91

Strabon

ix. 399	20

1B ANCIENT LITERARY SOURCES QUOTED OR CITED

ix. 401	89		v. 3, 4	305
ix. 402	89		vii. 24, 1	305
ix. 403	242		vii. 29, 2–4	201
ix. 404	20		vii. 41, 4	306
ix. 405	37		vii. 45, 1	305
ix. 407	62		vii. 57, 3	89
ix. 416	223			

Suda

Xenophon
Agesilaos

| H451 | 91 | | 6, 3 | 305 |

Anabasis

Theophrastos

			iii, 2, 13	305
Fragment 136, section 1, line 10	306		iii, 3, 17	232
			vii, 6, 36	305

Hellenika

Thoukydides

			iv. 2, 20	208
ii. 10, 6	3		vi. 4, 3–4	146
ii. 94, 1	130		vi. 4, 7	139
iii. 2, 3	89		*Lakedaimonion Politeia*	
iii. 12, 8	311		xii. 1–2	114
iii. 80, 2	130		xiii	131
iii. 112, 8	305		xiii. 8	131
iv. 98, 2	134		*Symposion*	
iv. 111, 2	130		8. 38	306
iv. 134, 1	306			

2 Ancient and Modern Placenames

Abdera 284–285
Agoriani 5, 7
Aidipsós 300
Aigaion 89–90, 93, 172, 249, 254–255, 257–262, 265–267, 269–271, 273–280, 284–286, 295
Aigeira 226
Aigina 254, 261, 267, 269, 271, 278
Aigosthena 204, 232
Aiolis 89, 258, 260, 267, 274–276, 279–280
Akhtopol 93
Akontion 298, 302
Akraiphiai 26, 37, 39, 41, 44–46, 48–49, 58–59, 61, 109, 177, 179, 183, 193, 198, 211, 214, 231–232, 259, 261, 263, 266, 270, 286, 295
Akrokorinthos 128
Alepokhóri 204
Alikí 98, 116, 148, 158, 203, 206–207
Ambrossos 147–149
Amorgos 254, 258–259, 262, 270, 274–275, 278
Amphiaraion 21–22, 48, 134
Amphikleia 300
Anaphe 274, 278
Anaphorítes 198–199, 202
Anatolia 89, 260
"Ano Siphai" 98
Anthedon 7, 24, 40, 45, 134, 174, 179, 194, 196, 198, 210–211, 255, 257, 259, 261, 263, 271
Antikyra 270
Aphidnai 203
ArgoloKorinthia 10–11
Argos 10, 12, 114, 260, 284
Arkadia 3, 204, 254, 257–258, 262–264, 266–267, 269–271, 273–274, 277–278, 280
Arne 3–4, 7
Askre 7, 87, 89
Áskris 136
Asopis 90
Asopos 51, 53–55, 90–91, 201
Aspledon 7, 9
Astakos 89–90
Astypalaia 257, 262, 270

Atalándi 300
Athenai 43, 51, 58, 83, 92, 95–96, 211, 257, 275, 294–295, 302
Atrax 248, 254
Aulis 7–8, 39, 70, 76, 89, 92, 199–200
Ayía Marína 8, 179, 193, 198
Ayía Triádha 136
Áyioi Theódhoroi 208
Áyios Ioánnes 8, 117, 120, 123, 127, 130–131, 161, 165, 203, 206
Áyios Mámas 149, 161, 166–168, 170, 206
Áyios Nikólaos 5, 123, 125, 128, 135, 297–298, 301–303
Áyios Pandeleḯmon 44
Azoros 248

Bithynia 254–255, 258, 261–264, 267, 269–272, 274–276, 278–280
Black Sea 88–89, 250, 254–265, 267–276, 278–281
Bosporos 89–90, 92–93
Boulis 8, 148, 261
Brátzi 201
Britain 34

Crimea 92
Cyprus 260, 267, 301–302

Dacia 227, 245
Dalmatia 264, 269, 273, 277
Daulis 255, 270
Delos 244, 286
Delphoi 12, 52, 138, 144, 255, 257, 266–267, 269–270
Demetrias 199, 262
Dharimári 5, 202
Dhaskaleió 121–122
Dhéndra 141
Dhiónysos 297
Dhístomon 148
Dhómvraina 116–117, 136
Dhrámesi 4–5
Dhrítza 44, 201
Dodona 54, 257
Donakon 136, 153

2 ANCIENT AND MODERN PLACENAMES

Doris   260, 269
Dotion Pedion   248
Doudouvána   297

East Lokris   28, 231
Eilesion   7, 202
Elateia   270, 300
Elektra Gate   165, 208
Eleusis   24, 51
Eleusis (Boiotian)   4–7
Eleutherai   96–97, 203
Elis   3, 9, 257–258, 261–262, 264, 266–267, 271, 274, 278
Epeiros   54, 254–256, 258, 262, 264, 266, 269, 271, 274, 277–278, 280
Epidamnos   255
Epiknemidian Lokris   243
Episkopí   161, 264, 279
Eretria   28, 222, 248, 254–255, 257–259, 261–262, 265, 269–270, 273–278
Erimókastro   5, 136, 159, 255, 267
Erkhomenos (=Ἐρχομενός)   36
Erythrai   7, 43, 51, 56, 202
Eteonos   7–8, 51
Euboia   28, 52, 211, 232, 243–244, 254–265, 268, 270–271, 273–279, 284, 295, 300
Euripos   198
Eurystheus   284–285
Eutresis   4, 6, 8, 211
Euxine   90, 92–93
Euxinos   89–93
Evangelístria   4, 161

Galatsidhéza   199–202
Glaronísi   121
Glisas   8, 14, 16–17, 20, 22–23, 177, 179–180, 190, 198
Gonnoi   270
Graia   3–4, 7
Graïmádha   5, 7

Halai   40, 259, 263, 270–271
Haliartos/[H]aliartos   7, 9, 26, 37, 39, 41–42, 59, 75, 160, 211, 216–7
Halkyonides   121
Harma   7–8, 15, 20, 22, 42–44, 199–201
Heleon   7, 42–44, 190, 201, 217, 231
Helikon   24, 149, 203, 265

Heraion   67–68, 108, 110, 123, 125
Herakleia   86, 91–92
Herakleia Pontike   91
Histiaia   211, 255, 257–258, 273–275
Hyampolis   270
Hyettos   37, 39–42, 44, 47, 58–59, 217, 232, 266, 282, 288
Hyle   7, 26, 42, 44–45, 62, 174, 176–177
Hymettos   204
Hypata   262
Hyria   7–8, 42
Hysiai   7, 42–43, 51, 97, 202

Illyria   255–256, 258, 262, 264, 266, 270–271, 273–278, 280
Imbros   270, 274
Ionia   257–259, 261–264, 266–267, 269–270, 272–280
Ismenion   17, 26, 52–55, 57, 75–76, 144
Isos   174–175
Istros   86

Kabeira   91
Kabeirian sanctuary   75
Kadmeia   6, 96, 208, 243
Kakkósi   117, 148
Kalá Nisiá   123, 127–128, 134–135
Kalapódhi   75
Kalkhedon   90, 92
Kalymnos   254, 258, 277–278
Kamíni   133
Kanavári   136
Kandíli   204
Kápraina   5, 7
Karandás   136, 138, 264, 268
Kardhítsa   177, 183, 193
Karpathos   258, 275
Karystos   254–255, 258, 260, 263, 270, 274, 277
Kaskavéli   136
Kasos   269
Kastrí Mazíou   5, 160
Kavásala   203
Keos   256–258, 262
Kephalinia   255, 274, 277–278
Kephisian Lake   147
Kephissos   148, 276–277, 300
Keressos   11, 30–35, 57–58

Kerkyra   130, 255, 264–266, 269, 274, 277–278
Khaironeia   3, 5, 7, 27, 29, 48, 134, 138, 145,
   147, 152, 166, 206, 232, 254–255, 261,
   263–264, 266, 270, 274, 277, 282, 294,
   296
Kháleia   7, 198
Khaleion   262
Khalkis   15, 20, 198–199, 231, 255, 257–259,
   261–262, 273–275, 277, 279
Khalybes   93
Khássia   203
Khelonókastro   62, 174, 176–177, 190
Khersonnesos Taurike   92
Khios   256–259, 261, 273, 275–278
Khorsiai   8, 24, 46, 49, 60, 65, 67–68, 148, 157,
   166, 257, 261, 283
Khóstia   4, 8, 60–61, 64, 67–68, 74, 76, 109,
   148, 157, 160, 166, 203, 206, 211, 241, 257,
   261, 291
Kiápha   174, 179, 186, 192–194
Kieros   91
Kithairon   52, 56, 96–97, 151, 302
Kleonai   204, 211
Klephtoloútsa   199
Klimatariaí   62, 192
Kókkino   183, 186, 192–193
Kokkinóvrakhos   179, 183, 186, 191, 198
Kokotoús   248
Koláka   133
Kolkhis   89, 91–92
Kopai   7–8, 44–45, 58, 179, 193, 198, 259, 263,
   270–271, 288
Kopaïc Plain   24, 50, 179, 185, 189, 284
Kopaïs   4, 7–9, 24–27, 29–31, 33–37, 44–47,
   50, 57–59, 62, 69, 152, 179–181, 193, 210,
   217, 263, 270, 297, 300
Korinthia   204, 254–255, 257–258, 260–262,
   264, 266, 269–271, 274, 276–278, 280
Korinthian(s)   27, 77–78, 82, 121, 138–139
Korinthian Gulf   97, 116, 121, 123
Korinthos   40, 77–78, 80, 82, 95, 97, 128, 199,
   211, 238
Korombíli   97–98
Koroneia   7, 37, 39–41, 44, 46–47, 59, 132, 134,
   146–147, 149, 151, 161, 255, 259, 261,
   269–271
Kos   254, 256–259, 261–262, 271, 273–278
Kotróni   203

Krannon   211, 248, 270
Krenides   91
Krete   254–258, 261–262, 269–271, 274–275,
   280
Kreusis   8, 24, 46, 67–68, 146, 149–150,
   154–156, 158, 207, 266
Kriekoúki   7, 43
Kyme   51, 89, 260
Kynoskephalai   96
Kytenion   260
Kythnos   257

Lamia   270
Larissa   247–248, 259, 262–263, 299–300
Lármes   183
Larymna   39–40, 183, 270
Lebadeia   9–10, 47, 111, 131–132, 134, 144–145,
   232, 255, 259, 263, 270, 275, 282
Lesbos   89, 227, 257, 269, 271, 274–275, 278,
   280
Leukas   130, 264, 266, 269, 271, 278
Leuktra   30–32, 35, 97, 131, 138–139, 141,
   143–156, 206, 266, 304, 312
Levádheia   27
Lévktra   141
Likéri   13, 50, 177, 180, 185, 189–192
Lindos   276
Litharés   177, 190
Livadhóstro   8, 155, 158, 206–207, 266, 290
Lokris   28, 84, 133, 183, 211, 231–232, 243–244,
   249, 254–255, 262, 269–271, 275, 277
Lydia   254, 257–258, 261–264, 267, 269–270,
   274–276, 279–280
Lykia   254, 258, 261–264, 267, 269–276,
   278–279, 297
Lykóphio   165, 172
Lykovoúni   5, 199–200

Magnesia   248, 262
Makedonian   233–234, 244, 260, 280
Makrókastro   297
Malesína   180
Máli   165
Máli Dárdha   194
Mantineia   166, 204, 207
Marathon   21, 305–306, 311
Mariandynoi   91
Maroneia   227

2 ANCIENT AND MODERN PLACENAMES

Massalia 86
Mavrókastro 297
Mavrovoúni 25–26, 31, 68–69, 76, 95, 97–98, 100, 109–111, 114–116, 118–120, 123, 127–128, 130–131, 134, 150, 156, 161, 206
Medeon 7
Megálo Vounó 181, 183, 186, 192–193, 198–200
Megarian 89, 91
Megaris 88, 90–91, 96, 204, 207, 225, 232, 243, 249, 255, 260, 262, 265, 275, 286
Messembria 92
Methone 248
Metókhion Platanáki 4
Mideia 3–4, 7, 9
Mikró Vounó 199–200
Miletia 139
Miletos 82, 90
Moesia Inferior 245
Moskhopódhi 208
Mouríki 4, 13, 23, 37, 176–177, 180, 190
Mykalessos 7, 20, 37, 39–41, 43, 48, 59, 201–202, 218
Myoúpolis 204
Mysia 258, 261–262, 264, 267, 269, 271, 273–279

Naupaktos 254, 266, 270
Naxos 257, 261, 269, 274, 278
Nisa 3, 7
Nisyros 257–258, 270

Oëroe 150, 155
Oiantheia 270
Oinoe 204
Okalea 161
Okalee 4, 7
Oloosson 248, 262
Olynthos 233–234, 238, 241
Onkhestos 7, 219, 221
Opountian Lokris 84, 90, 133, 179–180, 183, 236, 259, 263, 285
Opous 270, 285
Orkhomenos 7, 9, 11, 25–26, 35–37, 39–40, 45, 48, 50, 57–58, 97, 134, 156, 206, 210, 214, 219, 232, 255, 263, 269, 277, 282, 297–298, 302–303
Oropia 7, 22, 56

Oropos 7–8, 15, 24, 48, 92, 232, 255, 257, 259, 262, 264, 269, 271, 274–275, 279, 294–295
Ósios Loukás 300–301
Oúngra 5, 26, 28, 45, 61–62, 65–66, 68–69, 74, 76, 174, 176–177, 180, 190
Ovriókastro 203
Ozolian Lokris 255, 262, 269–271, 275, 277

Pagai 204, 286
Pagasitic Gulf 199, 248
Palaiothíva 147–148, 164, 172
Panakton 203
Pantanássa 97, 202
Paphos 302
Paralímni 45, 50, 61–62, 174, 180, 194
Parapoúnyia 141, 143, 145, 149, 153, 251, 255, 266, 270, 290
Parasopia 7, 26, 37, 42–43, 46, 51, 54, 56–57, 90, 97, 134, 166, 192, 200, 202–203, 265
Paróri 300
Paros 254, 259, 261–262, 267, 274, 276, 278, 280
Pastra 43
Peloponnesos 28, 40, 96–97, 128, 155, 199, 204, 231, 244, 249, 254–264, 266–271, 273, 275–278, 280, 295, 299
Peparethos 258–259, 269, 274
Perakhóra 110–111, 123, 128, 134–135
Perdhikóvrisi 181, 183
Peteon 4, 7
Phagás 25, 180
Phalanna 248
Pharai 37, 39–41, 43–44, 59
Pharsala 248
Pharsalos 226
Pherai 271
Phliasia 225
Phlious 204, 211
Phlygonion 270
Phokai 188
Phokis 8, 28, 97, 131–132, 147–148, 153, 155, 166, 207, 232, 243–244, 249, 255, 261–262, 269–270, 275, 297, 300
Pholegandros 258
Phthiotis 248–249, 267
Phyle 203, 295
Physkeis 271

Plakotó 204
Plataiai 7, 9, 11, 24, 26, 28, 42–43, 46, 49, 51, 57–58, 67–68, 74–75, 96–97, 133, 166, 202, 254–255, 259, 261, 263, 265–266, 275, 294
Platanáki 4, 180
Poimandria 43
Pondíkia 183, 192, 197
Pontic 88–89, 93, 255–258, 263, 269, 274, 276–278, 280, 296
Pontos 89–92, 94, 254–255, 258, 262, 264, 266–268, 271, 273–276, 278–280
Prousias 91
Psyttaleia 311
Ptoian 26, 72, 109
Ptoon 24
Pyrgáki 160–161, 206
Pýrgos 8, 174
Pýrgos Paralímnis 175–176, 195–196
Pythion 248–249

Rákhis 174, 194
Rhamnous 21, 203, 286
Rhitsóna 5, 26, 28, 201
Rhodos 89, 232, 255–259, 262, 269–271, 273–279, 286
Rumanian 245

Sagmatás 14, 22, 180
Salamis 10, 305–306, 310–311
Sambáli 13–14, 176, 179, 189
Samos 108, 257–259, 270–271, 274–276, 278–279
Samothrake 259–260
Siákhani 141
Sikelia 88, 254–271, 273–278, 280, 295
Sikyonia 225
Sinope 90–91
Siphai 8, 24, 37, 46, 49, 67–68, 89, 91, 98, 100, 116, 148–150, 154, 158, 166, 203, 207
Siphnos 205
Skaphlai 37, 43
Skhoinos 4, 7, 13, 37, 176–177, 190, 198
Skiathos 258
Skolos 7, 202
Skroponéri 172, 186, 192–194, 199, 202
Skythians 93
Sorós Moustaphádhes 192, 202
Sparta 95–96, 121, 130–132, 138, 144, 152

Steiris 149, 300
Stephon 43, 201
Strovíki 8
Syria 229, 301–302
Syros 270, 275, 278
Sýrtzi 14, 177, 180

Tanagra 3, 5, 7, 9, 24, 26–28, 31, 37, 39–41, 43–45, 48–49, 57, 59, 90–91, 134, 200, 217, 232, 255, 259–260, 263–264, 269–271, 273, 275, 279–280, 283, 285–286, 288
Tanagraia 22
Tanagrike 43, 190, 200
Táteza 136–138, 140–141, 143, 145, 153, 256, 259, 261, 290
Tegyra 97, 156
Telos 269, 275
Tenos 257–258, 261–262, 267, 269–270, 274, 276, 279
Teos 257
Tetrakomia 37, 43–45
Teumessos 16, 20
Thasos 257–259, 261–262, 269, 271, 274–275, 277–279, 295
Thebai 4, 6–7, 9, 15–20, 22, 24, 26–28, 36–37, 39, 41–43, 45, 48–50, 52–55, 57–59, 61, 75, 77–78, 80–87, 89, 91, 95–97, 133–134, 144, 165–166, 177, 179, 190, 192, 198–200, 202–203, 208, 210–211, 214, 216–217, 231–234, 236, 242–243, 254–255, 257, 259–262, 264–266, 268–271, 273–275, 277–280, 283–284, 288, 294–295, 302, 309
Thera 254, 258, 261, 270–271, 274
Thermodon 91
Thermos 75
Thespiai 7, 9, 24, 28, 30, 41–42, 46, 49, 57–58, 67–68, 87, 91, 96–97, 132, 134, 136, 149, 156, 159, 165, 170, 203, 232, 254–272, 274–277, 279–283, 288, 293–296
Thespike 35, 46, 146, 261–264, 267–268, 270, 273, 277, 279–280
Thisbe 7, 24, 28, 41–42, 46, 49, 67, 111, 116–117, 130–131, 134, 136, 146, 148–149, 157, 203, 207, 259, 261, 269–271, 277–278, 282, 291, 294
Thíva 5, 29, 60, 208

2 ANCIENT AND MODERN PLACENAMES

Thívai 6, 14, 137, 208, 260, 267, 273, 292, 296, 299
Thrakians 93
Tipha 49, 89
Tiphys 89, 91
Tithorea 270
Topólia 5, 8, 179, 193, 271
Toúrleza 177
Toúrlo 174, 193–195
Triteia 277
Troas 227, 258, 261, 263, 271, 273–276, 278–280
Troia 89, 130
Tsamáli 297–298
Tsouka Madhári 199–200
Tsoukouriéli 181, 186, 192, 194
Tymbanókambos 13–14
Tziakhanáni 141

Ukraine 93

Valley of the Muses 26, 30, 136, 254, 276
Vathý 116–117, 203
Velatoúri 204
Vígla 147–148, 164, 172
Vlomoúsa 188
Vólos 248
Voúliagma 14, 23
Vouliagméni 110
Vounéni 299–300
Vounénissa 299

Western Lokris 254

Xeronomí 98, 136–138, 203, 258–259, 262–263, 268, 273, 275, 291

Yiphtókastro 96–97, 203

Záltza 8, 148, 261, 291
Zoödókhos Piyí 121, 208

3 Ancient Personal Names, Human and Divine

Adonis 301–303
Adrastos 15–17, 19, 284
Agamemnon 2, 129
Agesilaos 96–97, 305
Agroteira 68, 109, 111, 130–131
Agrotis 111, 131
Aigeus 307
Ailianos 131
Aiskhines 325
Aiskhylos 19, 81, 129, 309, 311–312
Akhilleus 50
Alexandros III 228
Alexandros the Great 62, 179, 233
Alkmene 310
Amarynkeïdes 3
Amphiaraos 14–15, 17–23, 90
Amphimakhos 3
Andokides 305
Andromakhe 311
Antigonos Doson 219, 229
Antigonos Gonatas 229
Antigonos Monophthalmos 130
Antiokhos VIII 242
Antiphellos 227
Aphrodite 218, 260, 301
Apollon 52, 54, 72, 75, 81, 109, 111, 180–181, 183, 208, 227–228, 247, 253, 283, 301
Apollonios of Rhodos 89
Arabs 299, 302
Ares 301
Argives 15–18
Aristeides 306
Aristodemos 306
Aristomenes 144–145, 152, 304
Aristophanes 306, 310
Aristoteles 77, 81–87
Arkhesilaos 9–10, 3
Artemis 68, 70, 89–90, 109–111, 130–135, 167, 301
Asklapios 247–248, 253, 282–283, 286
Athena 75, 219, 223–226, 228–229, 257
Avars 299, 302

Bakkhiads 80
Bakkhilidas 151
Baton 17

Cicero 82, 152

Damis 91
Deineira 79
Demetrios Poliorketes 228
Demokleitos 130
Demosthenes 48
Diitrephes 201
Diodoros Sikeliotes 18, 157
Dionysos 7, 215–216, 253, 283, 286, 298, 302

Eileithyia 134
Elektra 165, 208, 307
Epameinondas 96, 139–140, 144–147, 150–151, 166, 172, 207
Eusebios 90
Euxippe 139

Galen 82
Gergis 227

Habrondas 90
Hades 301
Hegemone 132–133
Hekabe 79
Hera 67–68, 74, 109–110, 126, 222
Herakleides Pontikos 91
Herakles 41, 47–50, 52, 57, 61, 91, 109, 133, 208, 213–216, 219, 228–230, 263, 283–286, 308
Hermeas 170
Herodotos 31, 46, 51, 68, 79–80, 305
Hesiodos 77, 87, 90
Hesykhios 84, 298
Hippo 139
Homolion 270
Hyllos 79

Iokaste 308–309
Iphigeneia 79, 89, 92
Ismenos 18, 90
Isokrates 305

Kadmos 52–53, 89
Kallithero 271
Kassandros 228, 243

3 ANCIENT PERSONAL NAMES, HUMAN AND DIVINE

Khaireas   147–148, 151
Kinyras   302
Kithaironeian Hera   74
Kleombrotos   96–97, 145–150, 155
Kleoxenos   130
Klonios   3, 9–10
Konstantinos Porphyrogenitos   90
Kyknos   50

Leitos   3
Leuktridai   138–140
Lokhia   134
Lykourgos   115
Lysias   82
Lyttos   261

Memnon   89
Menelaos   2
Menoitos   133
Minyades   298, 302
Mnasilaos   144
Molpia   139
Myrto   133

Neoptolemos   79
Nikephoros Basilaka   304
Nonnos   7–8

Oidipous   19
Orestes   78, 307
Orthia   131–132
Orthosia   132–133

Pan   226, 229
Panelos   91
Parthenios   139
Patroklos   133
Pausanias   9, 15–16, 139, 144, 147–148, 152, 219, 243, 284
Pegasos   225
Peleus   309, 311
Pelopidas   96, 138–139, 144
Peneleos   3, 9–10
Pentheus   302
Perikles   93
Persephone   301
Pheidon   78, 80

Philippos II   166, 228, 233, 238
Philippos V   199
Philoktetes   3, 79
Philolaos   77–78, 80, 82–84, 86–87
Phoibidas   96
Phrourarkhidas   139
Pindaros   16, 18–19, 22, 52–54
Platon   6, 67, 81, 85–86
Plinius   90, 284
Ploutarkhos   7, 20, 30, 32–33, 43, 48, 86, 133, 138–140, 150, 152, 298, 306
Polybios   130, 205, 305
Polyneikes   16, 308–310
Polyxeinos   3
Polyxene   79
Poseidon   219–221
Praiai   134
Prothoenor   3, 9–10
Pseudo-Ploutarkhos   20
Ptolemaios   188

Rhesos   286

Seleukos I   230
Skedasos   138–140, 143, 145
Sokrates   311
Soodina   134
Sophokles   19–21, 311–312
Soteira   134
Stephanos of Byzantion   89
Strabon   20, 22, 236

Theano   139
Theias   302
Theophrastos   306
Theopompos   144
Tholpios   3
Thoukydides   3, 89, 130, 205, 311
Timotheus   310–311
Trophonios   145

Xenokrates   144–145, 304
Xenophon   115, 131, 139, 147, 153–155, 306

Zeus   14, 18–19, 22–23, 90, 144, 218, 226, 229, 301
Zoilos   298

4 Selected General Subjects

abortion   82, 87
adoption   83–84
adyton   52–53, 61, 62, 64, 65, 68, 69, 70, 74, 109
agonothetes   295
agora   133
Agrionia   298
Aiginetan standard   35, 40
Aiolian Migration   83, 88, 89
altar   108, 111, chapter 13 *passim*
Amphiktyonic Council   152
amphora   41, 223
anta   65, 69, 70
Argives vs. Thebans   6, 15–23, 284
arrow head   234, 237–239
Arvanitic   xvii–xviii, 138
ashlar   157, 160, 166, 174, 206

boar   246, 301
Boiotian Confederation (cf. Boiotian League)
Boiotian League   10–11, 24, 25, 31–32, chapter 4 *passim*, 83, 91, 93, 95, 97, 156, 166, 211
Boiotian Shield   35, 36, 40, 41, 44, 47, 50, 57, 212–221
bull   222–225
bunch(es) of grapes   212, 216, 219, 222–224

Catalogue of Ships   1–12, 217
cella   62, 64, 68, 69, 70, 74, 76
cistern(s)   105, 106, 120, 121, 123, 125–127, 199, 205
club   212–216, 228–229
coinage   33–46, 50, 58–60, 91, 211
coins   59–60, chapter 12 *passim*
colonization   84, chapter 7 *passim*
corn grain   35–36, 216
crescent   218

dolphin   219–221, 227
distyle   64, 68, 69, 73, 76, 107

eagle   221–222, 246
ephebic lists   292–293, 296
epichoric letter forms   36–45
Epigonoi (cf. Argives vs. Thebans)

Euro   34, 59–60
European Union   34, 59–60

"fetters of Greece"   199
fibula(e)   25, 28–30, 33, 47, 50, 64, 241
fort   116, 203
fortifications   64, 123, 126, 127, 154–155, 165, chapters 10–11 *passim*
fortlet(s)   105–106, 197, 199, 200
fortress   117, 203

garrison   96, 133, 155, 170, 203, 295
goat sacrifice   131
Gortyn Law Code   80
graver   239–240

hero   chapter 13 *passim*
Hekatompedon   75
"helots"   53
hemi-prostyle   93
heroon   61, 109
heta   42–44
hexastyle   76
Hippodromios   150 n. 2
hoards   210–211
horse   139, 216, 217, 226–227, 228, chapter 12 *passim*
horseman   136–137
horseman-hero   94, chapter 13 *passim*
hunter   245–246

ikonostásion   98, 117, 118, 120, 165, 168
in antis   64, 68, 69, 70, 74, 76, 107, 110
incuse square   36, 37, 40, 219, 225
inner room (cf. adyton)
Ionian Migration   88

Kadmeia (the)   6, 96, 208, 209, 242–243
kantharos   212–213, 216
kástro   128, 135, 186
katavóthres   50
khimaira   226
King's Peace   95, 97
Korinthian order   49
Korinthian Pottery (cf. Protokorinthian Pottery)

4   SELECTED GENERAL SUBJECTS   343

Korinthian War   95
Kyklopean (masonry)   160, 202

legislation   77–78, 82, 86, 87
lighthouse   123–125
line(s) of sight   128, 156, 167, chapters 10–11 *passim*
lion skin   213, 219, 228
lookout post   194
lyre   227

matrilineal   80–81
metals   93
metope and triglyph   140–142
mill-sail motif   36
Mithridatic Wars   148
moira   147, 151

needle   240
network   121, 127, chapters 10–11 *passim*

oikoi   11
oligarchic   85–87, 295
opisthodomos   74
owl   225, 257

patrilineal   80–81, 83, 87
Peloponnesian War   75, 95, 96, 130, 151
"perioeci"   53
Persian Wars/Invasion   30–31, 42, 46, 58, 75, 130, 305, 306
phialai   64
pin   240–241
pinakia   64
polygonal masonry   101–105, 107, 108, 109, 110, 112, 113–114, 118, 121, 123, 125, 156, 161, 165–166, chapter 11 *passim*
Poseidonians   56–57
pournária   99
pronaos   62, 64, 68–70, 74–75
Protokorinthian Pottery   25–27, 29, 30, 33, 47, 50, 58, 64, 69
proxenos/proxenoi   92, 93

quarries   105, 107, 161

rough/rubble masonry   101–105, 108, 110, 113–114, 118, 121, 123, 125, 156, 161, 164

165–166, 172, 174, 176, 177, 178, 181, 183, 190–192, 199, 204

scorper   239
serpent   346–348, chapter 13 *passim*
Seven against Thebai (cf. Argives vs. Thebans)
signal fires   128–130, 167, 194, 203, 205
signalling   128–130, 165, chapter 11 *passim*
sling-shot   230–236
snake (cf. serpent)
Spartan(s)   18, 68, 96–97, 110, 114, 120, 132, 134–135, 145, 147, 149, 150–155, 172, 205
Spartan garrison   36
spear butt   238
sphinx   227
star   246
surgical instrument   241
syncretism   247–248, 253, 282–283
syrinx   126

temenos   108, 111
temple   48, chapter 5 *passim*, 99, 107, 109–111, 134
theorodokoi   12
Thessalian Confederacy (cf. Thessalian hegemony)
Thessalian domination (cf. Thessalian hegemony)
Thessalian hegemony   30–31, 33, 46, 50, 150
thunderbolt   18, 218
tower(s)   96, 97, 100, 104, 115, 116, 117, 118, 124, chapter 10 *passim*, 172, 174, 185, 186, 192, 194, 197, 203, 204, 205, 206, 207
trapezoidal masonry   100, 117, chapters 10–11 *passsim*
tree   chapter 14 *passim*
trident   219–221, 225
Troian War/Expedition   133
tropaion/tropaia/trophy   141–153, 219, 229, chapter 15 *passim*

unguent spoon   241

watchposts/watch towers   122, 192, 198, 203, 206
well   105, 107, 121, 205